THE **IMPOSSIBLE** BORDER

Cornell University Press
Ithaca and London

THE
IMPOSSIBLE
BORDER

GERMANY AND THE EAST,
1914–1922

ANNEMARIE H. SAMMARTINO

Frontispiece. The image depicts the 1915 German-Russian border in what is now Lithuania. The fence that is gradually sinking into the swampy earth gives physical form to the impossible frontier that is the subject of this book. Yet, even as the barbed wire sinks into the mire, it is dangerous to try to cross it. Reproduced wih permission Ullstein Bild—Haekel, The Granger Collection, New York.

First published 2010 by Cornell University Press

Printed in the United States of America

Library of Congress Cataloging-in-Publication Data

Sammartino, Annemarie.
  The impossible border : Germany and the east, 1914–1922 / Annemarie H. Sammartino.
    p. cm.
  Includes bibliographical references and index.
  ISBN 978-0-8014-4863-8 (cloth : alk. paper)
  1. Germany—Boundaries. 2. Germany—Emigration and immigration—History—20th century. 3. Citizenship—Germany—History—20th century. 4. World War, 1914–1918—Territorial questions—Germany. 5. Germany—History—1871–1918. 6. Germany—History—1918–1933. I. Title.

  DD117.S26 2010
  940.3′1—dc22

                                            2010021889

Cornell University Press strives to use environmentally responsible suppliers and materials to the fullest extent possible in the publishing of its books. Such materials include vegetable-based, low-VOC inks and acid-free papers that are recycled, totally chlorine-free, or partly composed of nonwood fibers. For further information, visit our website at www.cornellpress.cornell.edu.

Cloth printing   10 9 8 7 6 5 4 3 2 1

For Ryan

Contents

Acknowledgments

I t is a pleasure to begin this book by thanking the people and institutions who made it possible. Research and writing for this book was funded by grants from the International Institute at the University of Michigan, the Council for European Studies, the Quadrille Ball Committee of the Germanistic Society of America, the Fulbright Commission, the Berlin Program for Advanced German and European Studies, the Rackham School of Graduate Studies at the University of Michigan, the Deutscher Akademischer Austauschdienst, and Oberlin College. I am, quite literally, indebted to all of these institutions. Archival research for this book was conducted at the Bundesarchiv in both Koblenz and Lichterfelde, the Geheimes Staatsarchiv Preußischer Kulturbesitz, the Landesarchiv—Berlin, the Sächsisches Hauptstaatsarchiv, the Friedrich Ebert Stiftung, and the Politisches Archiv des Auswärtigen Amts. In each location, archivists provided guidance and answered my flummoxed queries. I am grateful for their generosity, patience, and assistance. Chapter 7 was adapted from my chapter in *Citizenship and National Identity in Twentieth-Century Germany,* ed. Jan Palmowski and Geoff Eley, 57–72 (Stanford, CA: Stanford University Press, 2008), and is used here with the permission of the publishers.

Kathleen Canning, Geoff Eley, and Scott Spector at the University of Michigan taught me how to think like a historian. I have learned much from their examples, advice, and friendship, and I hope that this book lives up to the promise they saw in the project and pushed me to fulfill. At different stages, the Berlin Program at the Freie Universität, Hagen Schulze, Alf Lüdtke, and Stefan-Ludwig Hoffmann gave me the opportunity to present drafts of various chapters to colloquia, which helped me immeasurably. I thank Christof Mauch and Dirk Schumann for giving me the opportunity to spend a year at the German Historical Institute, where the intellectual climate proved crucial to the conceptualization of this project. I am also grateful to John Ackerman, Karen Laun, Julie Nemer, the anonymous reviewers, and the rest of the staff at Cornell University Press for their guidance and assistance. Thanks also to Jessica Csoma for editing the German-language texts.

The writing of a book, especially a first book, provides an opportunity to thank those whose contributions are less visible but nonetheless crucial to its conception and fulfillment. My colleagues at Oberlin College, in general, and in the history department, in particular, have been wonderful, but I need to single out my fellow East Siders, Leonard Smith and Heather Hogan, who have both gone above and beyond the call of duty as mentors, colleagues, and friends. I am extraordinarily grateful and can only offer my friendship and occasional dinners in repayment. My students at Oberlin inspire me with their generosity of spirit, thirst for knowledge, and refusal to compromise. In the current academic climate, I was extraordinarily lucky to find a job at all, so to land one I love is a privilege.

Friends such as Casey McKittrick, Alice Ritscherle, Jessica Cook-Mack, Kayla Friedman, Nate Jezzi, Manuela Achilles, Ulf Lippitz, Nina Ingenkamp, David Tompkins, Eliza Ablovatski, Jennie Hirsh, Tara Zahra, Alexandra Schwartz, Kenneth Mayer, Kristin Kopp, Todd Ettelson, Meredith Raimondo, Clara Oberle, and, last but certainly not least, Brian Hemphill all generously shared their time, wisdom, and humor through this long process. This list is already too long, so for all of you I have left out, please know how grateful I am for your friendship as well. Each of you has, at some time, offered a meal, a kind word, a place to crash, a joke, or even just a well-timed shrug. Thank you for your generosity and for not making me have to ask. Kayleigh DeCapite will always be my "little sister," and I hope that she realizes how much I have learned from her, too.

There are few people who would understand the desire to get a book-related tattoo. There are even fewer who would go with you to get it. And there are yet fewer who would help design it. For being part of this vanishingly small demographic and for being a great editor and a partner in all the things that do not really belong on acknowledgment pages even if I had the words to express them adequately, I offer Eli Rubin my thanks and my heart.

I am profoundly lucky and grateful to have a family that will be proud of this book but would have supported and loved me whatever I did. My parents, Anthony and Pearl Sherman Sammartino, continue to teach me through their examples of integrity and intellectual curiosity. Their stories of their families' struggles as immigrants remind me of the very real emotions behind the processes that I describe in this book. The "Sammartino sisters," Tory and Gabry, have been sounding boards, companions, and distractions (in the best sense of the word) almost since I can remember; for late-night conversations, for inside jokes, and for being there for me when you did not even know I needed you, I am thankful. Finally, although my grandfather, Isaac Sherman, did not live long enough to see this book to its completion, his graduation from college at the age of seventy-one inspired me to write it. Thanks, grandpa.

Abbreviations

AA	Auswärtiges Amt
PAAA	Politisches Archiv des Auswärtiges Amts
BArch	Bundesarchiv
BayHStA	Bayerisches Hauptstaatsarchiv
BMI	Bayerisches Ministerium des Innern
DDP	Deutsche Demokratische Partei
DKP	Deutsches Konsulat Posen
DNVP	Deutschnationale Volkspartei
DRK	Deutsches Rotes Kreuz
DS	Deutscher Schutzbund
DVP	Deutsche Vaterlandspartei
FdR	Fürsorgeverein für deutsche Rückwanderer
FVP	Fortschrittliche Volkspartei
GStA PK	Geheimes Staatsarchiv Preußischer Kulturbesitz
KAPD	Kommunistische Arbeiter-Partei Deutschlands
KM	Kriegsministerium
KPD	Kommunistische Partei Deutschlands
LAB	Landesarchiv Berlin
MA	Ministerium des Äusseren
MInnern	Ministerium des Innern
OKN	Armee Oberkommando Grenzschütz Nord
PMdI	Preussische Ministerium des Innern
PMI	Preußisches Ministerium des Innern

POWs	prisoners of war
RAI	Reichsamt des Innern
RAM	Reichsarbeitsministerium
RFM	Reichsfinanzministerium
RK	Reichskanzlei
RKZF	Reichskommissariat für Zivilgefangene und Flüchtlinge
RMI	Reichsministerium des Innern
RWA	Reichswanderungsamt
RWS	Reichswanderungsstelle
SächsHStA	Sächsisches Hauptstaatsarchiv
SMI	Sächsisches Ministerium des Innern
SPD	Sozialdemokratische Partei Deutschlands
USPD	Unabhängige Sozialdemokratische Partei Deutschlands
VDA	Verein für das Deutschtum im Ausland

THE **IMPOSSIBLE** BORDER

Introduction

The Crisis of Sovereignty

Migration and the Crisis of Sovereignty

Under attack at the end of 1922 for his supposed leniency toward foreigners in Germany, Carl Severing, the Social Democratic Prussian minister of the interior, sought to explain why his border-control policies had failed:

> It seems to me that, from a world-historical perspective, we are confronting a migratory movement that comes from the East, set in motion in part through the construction of the border states [Poland and the Baltics] and oriented toward the West. In this migration, Germany serves as the bridge from East to West. The Eastern Jews are the primary group—not in terms of numbers but as the most visible and most controversial. This cannot be denied, but it should not mean that we treat the problem from a racial perspective, or that we miss the fact that we are dealing with a much larger problem, namely that Germany, in its weakness and poverty, cannot avoid serving as a bridge and also as a cauldron (*Kessel*), from which foreigners can move neither forwards nor backwards.[1]

Faced with the irresistible thrust of "world history," he argued, border control and police actions could only do so much. And, indeed, the migratory movements to which Severing bore witness were of a world historical nature. Within

1. Severing to the Reichsminister des Äusseren, Friedrich von Rosenberg, December 27, 1922. Geheimes Staatsarchiv Preussischer Kulturbesitz [hereafter GStA PK], 1 HA, Rep. 77, Tit. 1814, Nr. 5, 18.

the period 1914–1922, millions of Europeans left their homes as a result of war, postwar settlements, and revolution. Germany was at the center of these migratory movements. Over 1 million former German citizens from France and Poland, tens of thousands of ethnic Germans and *Ostjuden* ("Eastern European Jews"), and hundreds of thousands of Russians found their way to German soil. Meanwhile, tens of thousands of Germans dreamed of leaving what they viewed as the morally and financially bankrupt German state for new settlements in the Baltics and the heart of Soviet Russia. Severing's description of Germany as simultaneously a cauldron and a bridge reflects the highly charged German ambivalence toward these migrants and the borders they crossed. On the one hand, this movement challenged the integrity of the German state and the well-being of its people. Migrants were a problem because they were mobile—Germany was a bridge. On the other hand, migrants were a problem because they did not move farther. The failure of these migrants to leave German soil, either because they could not return to their homelands or because of new U.S. restrictions on immigration, left Germany a seething cauldron.

Hannah Arendt shares Severing's evaluation of the postwar migrations as "world historical," claiming that the failure of postwar states to legally protect these migrants was a fateful step on the way to totalitarianism. Their invisibility to the states that housed them foreshadowed the dictatorial regimes that would shortly strip many Europeans of the state protections they took for granted.[2] She contends that "the higher the ratio of potentially stateless and stateless to the population at large . . . the greater the danger of a gradual transformation into a police state."[3] Arendt makes a serious charge here, one that is exceedingly difficult to prove (what exactly is the "danger of a gradual transformation into a police state," and how would we measure it?) but suggestive nonetheless. Does the totalitarianism of the 1930s have its origin in the migration crisis of the war and postwar decade?

Severing appears to contradict or, at the very least, complicate Arendt's characterization of the interwar period. In the statement quoted previously, he described Germany as a cauldron in an effort to counter attacks by anti-Semites, who charged that he was insufficiently harsh toward Eastern European Jewish immigrants. Much like Severing, Germans, encountering the flood of refugees from Eastern Europe or themselves considering migrating eastward, reevaluated inherited assumptions about the meanings of territory and identity in ways that did not fit easily into a teleology of emergent fascism. German Freikorps soldiers believed that attaining Latvian citizenship was a means toward escaping the treacherous German state and establishing a "pure" national community. *Völkisch* nationalists sought to protect Germany against the incursion of Eastern

2. Hannah Arendt, *The Origins of Totalitarianism* (New York: Harcourt Brace, 1973), 287–88.
3. Ibid.

European Jews while also holding the doors of Germany open to ethnic Germans from Russia. Socialists argued that Germany must provide asylum to these Eastern European Jews even while seeking to reinforce Germany's frontiers against them. Germans from across the political spectrum tolerated the presence of hundreds of thousands of Russian refugees in their capital city with a remarkable lack of resentment.

Although her teleology may be questioned, Arendt is right that the refugees in interwar Europe were the harbingers of something important. The imagined unity of nation, state, and territory that had been the foundation of the European political imaginary was shattered during 1914–1922. Thinking about this period as a "crisis of sovereignty" highlights that Europeans did not experience or understand war, defeat, revolution, and population mobility in isolation; rather, these factors operated in tandem to undermine the relationship among territory, nation, and state. This crisis was particularly acute in the fractured landscape of Central and Eastern Europe, which witnessed a prolonged instability of both state forms and frontiers.[4] Germany's wartime advance into Russian territory and the deterioration of multinational empires during the war began the process of destabilization in the region. After the war ended, the principle of the nation-state appeared to triumph at Versailles; however, it was immediately challenged on the ground by revolutions that demanded loyalties different from those of national belonging and by the existence of national minorities and stateless people who did not fit within new national borders. The crisis of sovereignty was simultaneously material, psychological, and ideological as the volatility of frontiers, ideologies, and populations forced men and women of all political persuasions to ask fundamental questions about the nature of sovereignty: Where was political authority located? What people belonged to a nation? Who belonged to a state? How were boundaries determined? And what was the relationship of a state to those of a different ideological persuasion or national identification within its frontiers?

Across the region, borders became the symbols and spaces of crisis as states fought over their location and sought to control the people who traversed them. In Germany, the border presented two issues, emblematic of the dangers and opportunities created by the crisis of sovereignty and the difficult position the state found itself in as a result. At the outset of the war, Germans had feared a Russian invasion, but German military success instead inspired fantasies, especially on the right, about the annexation and repopulation of captured Russian territory to serve German national imperatives. After the defeat, Germans were

4. On the argument that Russia experienced an extended crisis between 1914 and 1921 in which revolutionary and military factors cannot be separated, see Lars Lih, *Bread and Authority in Russia, 1914–1921* (Berkeley: University of California Press, 1990); Peter Holquist, *Making War, Forging Revolution: Russia's Continuum of Crisis, 1914–1921* (Cambridge, Mass.: Harvard University Press, 2002).

nearly unanimous in their opposition to the new borders imposed at Versailles. A minority sought to escape the shrunken country through emigration, but many others focused their frustration on the porousness of the border and the inability of the state to seal it against the large-scale migrations spawned by the postwar convulsions. These were two fundamentally opposing problems, the one necessitating an offensive solution (expansion) and the other a defensive one (fortification). The combination of the two and the inability of the German state to resolve either one meant that the border was an impossible project—a symbol of futility that offered no easy practical or ideological solution.

The European Crisis of Sovereignty

In the later decades of the nineteenth century, European states sought to strengthen control over their borders and the populations that lived within them.[5] This consolidation of state power was often grounded in nationalism, which also placed a great deal of importance on territory, claiming "the nation's unique history is embodied in the nation's unique piece of territory."[6] The ideology of the nation-state relied on the imagined coincidence of state, nation, and territory.[7] States and nations were mutually dependent; legitimate states were those that represented national communities, whereas legitimate nations were those with a state to call their own.[8] Meanwhile, territory was supposed to provide the setting for both the projection of state power and national belonging. Nation-states derived their authority from the ability of the state to control the territory that a given nation claimed. Russia and Austria-Hungary were the exceptions that proved the rule, as the centrifugal force of nationalism pulled at imperial bonds in both multinational empires. Yet, even for self-defined nation-states, this was a fraught association. The ideology of the nation-state allowed states to mobilize powerful nationalist emotions, but state and nation were never entirely coincident. Frontiers were simultaneously graphic representations of

5. Charles Maier, "Consigning the Twentieth Century to History: Alternative Narratives for the Modern Era," *American Historical Review* 105, no. 3 (2000): 807–31; James Sheehan, "The Problem of Sovereignty in European History," *American Historical Review* 111, no. 1 (2006): 8–9. For Maier, the era of territoriality begins in the 1860s. Sheehan does not see a sharp break during this decade.

6. James Anderson, "Nationalist Ideology and Territory," in *Nationalism, Self-Determination and Political Geography*, ed. Ron J. Johnston, David B. Knight, and Eleonore Kofman (London: Croom Helm, 1988), 24. See also, Anthony D. Smith and Colin Williams, "The National Construction of Social Space," *Progress in Human Geography* 7, no. 4 (1983): 502–18; Jean Gottmann, *The Significance of Territory* (Charlottesville: University of Virginia Press, 1973).

7. On the problem of sovereignty, see Sheehan, "Problem of Sovereignty"; Frances Harry Hinsley, *Sovereignty*, 2nd ed. (New York: Cambridge University Press, 1986); Jens Bartelson, *A Genealogy of Sovereignty* (New York: Cambridge University Press, 1995).

8. Sheehan, "Problem of Sovereignty," 9.

the projection of state power and, for many nationalists, symbols of the incompleteness of the national project. Furthermore, the fiction of unified and autonomous state authority repeatedly collided with the realities of state powers, which were subject to constant negotiation and limits. National borders were never entirely impermeable, and in fact, both nationalist ideology and state power in the late nineteenth century developed under the pressure of and in response to the movement of peoples, goods, and ideas across them.[9]

The history of Germany offers particularly strong evidence for the conflicted and unstable relationship among nation, state, and territory. The boundaries of the German state were redrawn repeatedly during the nineteenth and early twentieth centuries, from the changing territorial borders of the preunification period to the boundaries of 1871, the bloated empire of spring and summer 1918, and finally the reduced territory of the Weimar Republic. To put it differently, in 1920 a fifty-year-old German had lived through at least four German states with five different borders. Not one of these states perfectly expressed the unity of ethnic, linguistic, and cultural homogeneity that lay at the basis of the nationalist imaginary. Moreover, each one of these states reflected a different form of government and a different ideal of the relationship between the state and the governed. In Germany and elsewhere, the postulated unity of nation, state, and territory could function only by overlooking its very impossibility. Germany stood at a crossroads on the eve of World War I. The increasingly popular and strident *völkisch* right challenged the legitimacy of the Reich because of its failure to include all those who belonged to the German nation. Nevertheless, the ambiguities inherent to the nation-state were also often ignored or tolerated, if not necessarily celebrated. That tolerance came to an end in the years that followed.

According to Arendt, "the explosion of 1914 and its severe consequences of instability . . . shattered the façade of Europe's political system to lay bare its hidden frame."[10] In the West, World War I was a grinding war of attrition, fought by huge and immobile armies trapped in vast networks of trenches in the fields of Flanders. The Eastern Front was, by contrast, one of great mobility for both soldiers and civilians.[11] The tangible consequences of a war of movement and

9. Sebastian Conrad, *Globalisierung und Nation im Deutschen Kaiserreich* (Munich: Beck, 2006); Sebastian Conrad and Jürgen Osterhammel, eds., *Das Kaiserreich transnational: Deutschland in der Welt, 1871–1914* (Göttingen: Vandenhoeck und Ruprecht, 2004); Jürgen Osterhammel and Niels P. Petersson, *Globalization: A Short History*, trans. Donna Geyer (Princeton: Princeton University Press, 2003); Jan Scholte, *Globalization: A Critical Introduction* (New York: Palgrave, 2000); Thomas Bender, ed., *Rethinking America in a Global Age* (Berkeley: University of California Press, 2002).

10. Arendt, *Origins of Totalitarianism*, 266.

11. Vejas Liulevicius, *War Land on the Eastern Front: Culture, National Identity and German Occupation in World War I* (New York: Cambridge University Press, 2000); Peter Gatrell, *A Whole Empire Walking: Refugees in Russia during World War I* (Bloomington: Indiana University Press, 1999); Joshua Sanborn, "Unsettling the Empire: Violent Migrations and Social Disaster during World War I," *Journal of Modern History* 77, no. 2 (2005): 290–325.

fantasies of reordering occupied territory unsettled assumptions about the permanence of state authority and frontiers. Meanwhile, the privation and chaos of war sparked a wave of political turmoil that left no European state untouched, leading to full-scale revolutions in Central and Eastern Europe.[12] By the end of 1918, multinational empires held together by dynastic bonds had disappeared from the European continent. With the fall of the Romanov, Habsburg, and Hohenzollern dynasties, class and nation competed for the allegiance of the people of Europe. Both concepts privileged the notion of self-determination, thereby validating "the people" as a political force that trumped the inherited authority of monarchs.[13] The Bolshevik Revolution in Russia convinced both supporters and opponents that revolutionary socialism had the power to alter the frontiers and constitution of states. In 1917–1919, revolutionaries from Moscow to Budapest to Munich drew inspiration from one another as revolutionary upheaval spilled beyond the confines of the former Russian Empire to ignite a regional crisis.[14] Yet the international scope of revolution could also act to constrain radicalism. From the reactionary right to the socialist left, many Germans, conscious of the chaos and violence occurring around them, resisted the anarchic pull of revolution, and the German Revolution never radicalized to the degree that the Russian Revolution did.[15]

12. For this argument made in a Russian context, see Lih, *Bread and Authority in Russia, 1914–1921;* Holquist, *Making War, Forging Revolution.*

13. Arno J. Mayer, *Wilson vs. Lenin: Political Origins of the New Diplomacy, 1918–1918* (New Haven: Yale University Press, 1959). Mayer discusses how the Bolshevik emphasis on self-determination during the negotiations leading up to the Treaty of Brest-Litovsk forced the Allies to go further than they might otherwise have in pushing this doctrine in their own peace negotiations one year later. See also Geoff Eley, "Remapping the Nation: War, Revolutionary Upheaval and State Formation in Eastern Europe, 1914–1923," in *Ukrainian-Jewish Relations in Historical Perspective,* ed. Howard Aster and Peter J. Potichnyi (Edmonton: Canadian Institute of Ukrainian Studies Press, 1983), 213. Both Eley and Mayer recognize the continued importance of "old diplomacy" at the negotiations at Versailles. Nonetheless, the very fact that old-fashioned power politics (particularly that practiced by the Italians) had to be cloaked in the language of self-determination is testament to the latter's power.

14. Francis L. Carsten, *Revolution in Central Europe, 1918–1919* (Aldershot, UK: Wildwood House, 1988); Tibor Hajdu, "Socialist Revolution in Central Europe, 1917–1921," in *Revolution in History,* ed. Roy Porter and Mikulas Teich (New York: Cambridge University Press, 1986), 101–20; Eliza Ablovatski, "Cleansing the Read Nest: Counter-Revolution in Budapest and Munich," PhD diss., Columbia University, 2004. On the revolution in Hungary specifically, see Peter Pastor, *Hungary between Wilson and Lenin: The Hungarian Revolution of 1918–1919 and the Big Three* (New York: Columbia University Press, 1976); Ivan Völgyes, *Hungary in Revolution, 1918–1919: Nine Essays* (Lincoln: University of Nebraska Press, 1971); Oszkár Jászi, *Revolution and Counter-Revolution in Hungary* (New York: H. Fertig, 1969); György Péteri, *Effects of World War I: War Communism in Hungary* (New York: Columbia University Press, 1984). On the Munich revolution, see Karl Bosl, *Bayern im Umbruch: Die Revolution von 1918, ihre Voraussetzungen, ihr Verlauf und ihre Folgen* (Munich: Oldenbourg, 1969); Franz Schade, *Kurt Eisner und die bayerische Sozialdemokratie* (Hannover: Verlag für Literatur und Zeitgeschehen, 1961); Allan Mitchell, *Revolution in Bavaria, 1918–1919: The Eisner Regime and the Soviet Republic* (Princeton: Princeton University Press, 1965).

15. On the failure of the German Revolution to be a "great" revolution, see Heinrich August Winkler, "Revolution by Consensus?: Germany 1918–1919," in *The Problem of Revolution in Ger-*

The treaties of Versailles, Trianon, and St. Germain in 1919 did not resolve the chaos created by war and revolution but, rather, added a new dimension to the crisis of sovereignty. These treaties represented the apotheosis of the ideology of national self-determination, even as they provided dramatic evidence of the impossibility of implementing it in practice. For new nation-states such as Yugoslavia, Poland, and Czechoslovakia, the years after World War I were at once a time of great optimism for nationalists who celebrated the achievement of national sovereignty and of great anxiety about the final placement of frontiers and the uncertain role for the minorities that remained within what were in fact multinational nation-states.[16] For the rump states of Austria, Hungary, and Germany, the specter of defeat and territorial loss further complicated the process of nation-building. At Versailles, Germany had been forced to cede territory to France, Poland, and Denmark, as well as to give up its expected gains in the former tsarist territories. Austria and Hungary were forced to make even more dramatic territorial concessions in the treaties of Trianon and St. Germain. The new boundaries were intended to respect the integrity of national groups, but none of these new countries demonstrated anything like the ideal congruence of nation and state. Indeed, the ethnographic realities of Central and Eastern Europe meant that each state had a highly ambivalent relationship to national borders, and a series of overlapping territorial claims destabilized these settlements as soon as they were drawn up.[17] Many of these states were forced to sign treaties promising to provide basic rights to minorities within their borders. Although Germany did not sign a minority treaty per se, similar clauses did appear

many, 1789–1989, ed. Reinhard Rürup (New York: Berg, 2000), 93. The prevalence of the word *failure* in accounts of Weimar democracy is noteworthy: Sebastian Haffner, *Failure of a Revolution: Germany 1918–1919* (Chicago: Banner Press 1986); Rudolf Cooper, *The Failure of a Revolution: Germany in 1918–1919* (New York: Cambridge University Press, 1955); Ian Kershaw, *Weimar: Why Did German Democracy Fail?* (New York: St. Martin's Press, 1990).

16. On minorities, border issues, and hybridity in Czechoslovakia, see Jeremy King, *Budweisers into Czechs and Germans: A Local History of Bohemian Politics, 1848–1948* (Princeton: Princeton University Press, 2002), chap. 5; Tara Zahra, *Kidnapped Souls: National Indifference and the Battle for Children in the Bohemian Lands, 1900–1948* (Ithaca: Cornell University Press, 2008), chaps. 3–4.

17. On the paroxysms of this nation-making moment in general, see Mayer, *Wilson vs. Lenin;* Alfred Cobban, *The Nation State and National Self-Determination* (New York: Thomas Chrowell, 1969); Hugh Seton-Watson, *Nations and States* (London: Methuen, 1982). The question of national minorities is addressed by Carlile A. Macartney, *National States and National Minorities* (New York: Russell and Russell, 1968); Raymond Pearson, *National Minorities in Eastern Europe, 1848–1945* (London: Macmillan, 1983); Carole Fink, *Defending the Rights of Others* (New York: Cambridge University Press, 2004); Margaret Macmillan, *Paris 1919: Six Months That Changed the World* (New York: Random House, 2003). See also Aviel Roshwald, *Ethnic Nationalism and the Fall of Empires: Central Europe, Russia and the Middle East, 1914–1923* (London: Routledge, 2001). Roshwald pays attention not only to the rise of state systems but to the role of popular nationalism in driving political developments. The literature on revolution and nation-state formation in each of these countries is too extensive to enumerate here.

in the 1922 treaty between Germany and Poland, which regulated the status of Upper Silesia. The League of Nations was supposed to enforce the minority treaties and was also responsible for providing protection to stateless people after the appointment of a High Commissioner for Russian Refugees in 1921. The impotence of the League, however, meant that these theoretical challenges to the sovereign power of the postwar nation-states rarely set practical limits on state action.[18]

Uncertainty about territorial frontiers lingered for years after the British, French, Americans, and Italians concluded their negotiations in the suburbs of Paris. Some of these were later resolved by plebiscites, as in the disputed territories of Allenstein and Marienwerder on the Polish-German border and in the Danish-German border province of Schleswig. In other areas, the negotiators could not reach a resolution and deferred border questions to later conferences. Fighting over the province of Teschen on the Czechoslovak-Polish border continued until 1920, and the border was not resolved fully until the Locarno conference in 1925. The eastern Polish border with Ukraine and Russia was ignored entirely by the diplomats at Versailles. In 1919, Poland invaded and took over the short-lived West Ukrainian People's Republic. In April 1920, Poland invaded Soviet Russia. The Russo-Polish War ended in a stalemate six months later, confirmed by the 1921 Treaty of Riga, which divided the disputed territories between the two states. In the most dramatic case of postwar instability, the territory of current-day Ukraine was occupied by no fewer than six different states between 1917 and 1921 before being incorporated into Poland and the Soviet Union.[19]

By 1922, the immediate postwar situation had largely stabilized in Central and Eastern Europe. In that year, the German-Polish Treaty on Upper Silesia was signed, enabling the final settlement of the Polish-German border; the Nansen Passport was established to regulate Russian refugee movement; and the last Russian prisoners of war (POWs) departed German soil. Also in that year, Germany and Soviet Russia signed the Treaty of Rapallo, which reestablished diplomatic relations, enhanced trade connections, and (secretly) included provisions to forge a military relationship between the two states. Rapallo was in part a creation of men such as Baron Ago von Maltzahn, the head of the Russian section of the Foreign Office Eastern Department, and General Hans von Seeckt, who dreamt of using a German-Russian alliance as a means for escaping

18. On the minorities treaties, see Fink, *Defending the Rights of Others*. On the Nansen Passport, see Claudena Skran, *Refugees in Inter-war Europe: The Emergence of a Regime* (Oxford: Oxford University Press, 1995).

19. Timothy Snyder, *The Reconstruction of Nations: Poland, Ukraine, Lithuania, Belarus, 19569–1999* (New Haven: Yale University Press, 2003), chaps. 3, 7.

the strictures imposed by the Versailles Treaty and the political and military domination of the French, British, and their Central European allies.[20] Rapallo projected the geopolitical ambitions of Seeckt and others into the future, when a revitalized Germany and Russia could dismember Poland and exact revenge on the Western victors in World War I. At the same time, Rapallo represented a kind of equilibrium in the present, in which the two largest powers in Central and Eastern Europe agreed to avoid open conflict. Although Rapallo did not directly cause the end of this era of instability, it left those who hoped for an immediate revision of the status quo (such as anti-Bolshevik Russian émigrés) disappointed. In both material and psychological terms, Rapallo marked a tentative conclusion to the regional crisis of sovereignty that had begun eight years earlier.

The war and postwar crisis initiated a new and qualitatively different chapter in the history of European migration. Prior to 1914, migration was primarily labor migration; there had been very few of the forced population movements that would characterize the rest of the twentieth century.[21] The war sparked a great deal of population mobility, including soldiers moving to the front and refugees displaced by the fighting. It was also during the war that many officials across the continent concluded that the migration of people was a significant threat to the livelihood of a state. A state engaged in total war could not afford citizens who left to escape military service, spies who entered to report to the enemy, or workers who emigrated and took their valuable abilities elsewhere. As a result, identity documents such as visas and passports, designed to track and restrict the movement of people across national borders, came into common use.[22] After the war, this new system of border control was kept in place due to fears about the mobility of both people and ideas. European states feared the consequences of migration as well as the worldwide communist revolution that the Bolsheviks explicitly promoted. Although liberals attempted to rescind wartime restrictions at a Paris conference in 1920, these anxieties meant that modern border controls were there to stay.[23]

20. On the negotiations that resulted in Rapallo, see Horst Linke, *Deutsch-sowjetische Beziehungen bis Rapallo* (Cologne: Wissenschaft und Politik, 1970); Vasily Vourkoutiotis, *Making Common Cause: German-Soviet Relations, 1919–1922* (New York: Palgrave Macmillan, 2007).

21. Arguably the migration of Eastern European Jews that began in the 1880s can be seen as a kind of precursor to twentieth-century refugees. For a discussion of this migration in this context, see Michael Marrus, *The Unwanted: European Refugees in the Twentieth Century* (New York: Oxford University Press, 1986), 9.

22. John Torpey, *The Invention of the Passport: Surveillance, Citizenship and the State* (Cambridge, UK: Cambridge University Press, 2000), chaps. 4–5.

23. Marrus, *Unwanted*, 93.

One historian counts nearly 10 million refugees on the European continent as late as the mid-1920s.[24] These refugees were part of what Michael Marrus terms the world's "first modern refugee crisis."[25] Some refugees fled nation-states in which they found themselves now living as national minorities. Others fled the arrival of regimes whose political leanings they opposed. Both types of refugees were the consequences of the imperfect application of the principles of Bolshevism and nationalism to a region with a hodgepodge of national and political leanings. The sheer number of refugees and the speed of their displacement after World War I made this crisis different from previous refugee movements. The refugees were a symptom of crisis, but they also contributed to that crisis, forcing nation-states to deal with people who belonged neither to the nation nor the state and taxing the capacities of the governments of individual states and the new international refugee regime. The European refugee crisis was one of the factors that led the United States to pass quota laws restricting immigration in 1921 and 1924. These laws, in turn, increased the pressure on European countries, which were left to fend with the refugee problem without the traditional escape valve of migration to the United States.[26] The League of Nations attempted to regulate the refugee situation through the establishment of a High Commission on Refugees in 1921 under the auspices of Fridtjof Nansen, the former polar explorer (see chap. 8). But these efforts did little to dampen the impact of migration in the first years after the war. Every European state and society responded differently to migrants. In the 1920s, France became the world's leading recipient of immigrants, including refugees, an experience that led to a massive expansion of both its police and welfare systems.[27] After years of fighting that produced millions of refugees, Turkey and Greece agreed to a population exchange in 1923 that sent a half million Greek Muslims to Turkey and a million Orthodox Turks to Greece. This effort to purge themselves of potentially restive minorities resulted in a humanitarian catastrophe for the migrants, but calmed relations between the two states.[28] In the closest parallel to Germany, Hungary contended with up to a half million refugees displaced by the breakup of the Austro-Hungarian Empire, who contributed to economic instability, anti-Semitism, and nationalist irredentism.[29]

24. John Hope Simpson, *The Refugee Problem: Report of a Survey* (New York: Oxford University Press, 1939), 62.

25. Marrus, *Unwanted*, 3.

26. Aristide Zolberg, *A Nation by Design: Immigration Policy in the Fashioning of America* (Cambridge, Mass.: Harvard University Press, 2006).

27. Clifford Rosenberg, *Policing Paris: The Origins of Modern Immigration Control between the Wars* (Ithaca: Cornell University Press, 2006).

28. Bruce Clark, *Twice a Stranger: The Mass Expulsions That Forged Modern Greece and Turkey* (Cambridge, Mass.: Harvard University Press, 2006).

29. István Mócsy, *The Effects of World War I: The Uprooted, Hungarian Refugees and Their Impact on Hungary's Domestic Politics, 1918–1921* (New York: Brooklyn College Press, 1984).

The Crisis of Sovereignty in Germany

German historians often view the postwar period as one that gave birth to a new, more dangerous nationalism, radicalized by defeat.[30] A sense of heightened danger also pervades the historiography of Eastern European Jewish immigration after the war.[31] The only full-length study of immigration in the Weimar Republic, Jochen Oltmer's *Migration und Politik in der Weimarer Republik*, stresses the national, economic, and social protectionism of German interactions with immigrants.[32] Undeniably, protectionism played an important role in immigration policy. The radicalization of prewar nationalism both shaped and was in turn fostered by the postwar migration crisis. Nevertheless, plans for radical territorial expansion, new citizenship policies, new schemes for border control, a nascent asylum policy, and wild plans for emigration to the Baltics and the Soviet heartland fully conform neither to the diagnosis of protectionism nor to that of nationalism resurgent.

The combination of hesitation and audacity in the history of migration during the Weimar Republic reflects the place of migration within both the crisis of sovereignty in Eastern and Central European and the narrative of crisis in Weimar Germany. In his classic study of the Weimar Republic, Detlev Peukert describes how it was shaped by a "crisis of classical modernity." According to Peukert, the Weimar Republic was a laboratory where social and cultural ideas of modernity, from the expansion of the welfare state to the new status of women, were tested in a climate of limited political and economic resources.[33] This interpretation emphasizes the productive nature of crisis, in which the loss of old verities allowed new ideas to come to the fore, while also stressing that these experiments faced practical limits that would prove fatal. Taking their cue from

30. On nationalism among the practitioners of the new field of *Ostforschung*, see Michael Burleigh, *Germany Turns Eastward: A Study of Ostforschung in the Third Reich* (Cambridge, UK: Cambridge University Press, 1988); Guntram Herb, *Under the Map of Germany: Nationalism and Propaganda 1918–1945* (London: Routledge, 1997); David Thomas Murphy, *The Heroic Earth: Geopolitical Thought in Weimar Germany, 1918–1933* (Kent, Ohio: Kent State University Press, 1997).

31. Trude Maurer, *Ostjuden in Deutschland, 1918–1933* (Hamburg: Hans Christian, 1986); Steven Aschheim, *Brothers and Strangers: Eastern European Jews in German and German Jewish Consciousness, 1800–1923* (Madison: University of Wisconsin Press, 1982).

32. Jochen Oltmer, *Migration und Politik in der Weimarer Republik* (Göttingen: Vandenhoeck & Ruprecht, 2005), esp. 86–88. Migration in the Weimar Republic is examined briefly by Leslie Page Moch, *Moving Europeans: Migration in Western Europe since 1650* (Bloomington: Indiana University Press, 1992), 161–70; Saskia Sassen, *Migranten, Siedler, Flüchtlinge: Von der Massenwanderung zur Festung Europa* (Frankfurt am Main: Fischer, 2000), 99–114. In his study of European migration, Klaus Bade also gives brief attention to Weimar Germany; Klaus Bade, *Europa in Bewegung: Migration vom späten 18. Jahrhundert bis zur Gegenwart* (Munich: C. H. Beck, 2000), 259–63, 268–70, 278–80.

33. Detlev Peukert, *The Weimar Republic: The Crisis of Classical Modernity* (New York: Hill and Wang, 1993).

Peukert, historians have explored the ambitions of Weimar culture and politics, from the broadening of the welfare state to a revolution in gender relations, a rewriting of citizenship policy, new artistic movements, and even a new openness to cultural influences from abroad.[34] These wide-ranging experiments created their own problems. The German Revolution gave Germans the ability to dream about changing state and society without the resources to realize these ambitions—a fateful combination. Advocates of change were disappointed by the absence of resources, whereas those who feared further upheaval were terrified by the sheer existence of these new ideas. Wolfgang Hardtwig, Moritz Föllmer, and Rüdiger Graf further claim that the omnipresence of a rhetoric of crisis during the Weimar Republic reflected a sense that society had lost its moorings and that new ideas, social formations, or technologies were capable of bringing about either a utopian arcadia or complete catastrophe (or both).[35] In this sense, the rhetoric of crisis was itself a component of crisis because it ratcheted up the stakes of political debate. Every argument could be viewed as a referendum on the fate of Germany itself.[36]

The image of Germany's impossible border—both too strong and too weak, a symbol of threat and of possibility—links this sense of crisis in Germany to the broader European crisis of sovereignty.[37] The German crisis of sovereignty stretched across the political caesuras of defeat and revolution, beginning with German wartime success during World War I, which encouraged fantasies of territorial expansion. The revolution of 1918–1919 did not change the issues on the table, either with regard to the composition of the nation or its territorial extent, but it did radicalize and extend the array of potential solutions, enable new

34. Elizabeth Domańsky, "Militarization and Reproduction in World War I Germany," in *Society, Culture and the State in Germany, 1870–1930*, ed. Geoff Eley (Ann Arbor: University of Michigan Press, 1996), 427–64; Kathleen Canning, "Class vs. Citizenship: Keywords in German Gender History," *Central European History* 37, no. 2 (2004): 225–44; Michael Geyer, "Insurrectionary Warfare: The German Debate about a Levée en Masse in October 1918," *Journal of Modern History* 73 (September 2001): 459–527; Mary Nolan, *Visions of Modernity: American Business and the Modernization of Germany* (New York: Oxford University Press, 1994). See also Peter Fritzsche, "Did Weimar Fail?" *Journal of Modern History* 68, no. 3 (1996): 629–56, for more on the ways that the Weimar Republic allowed for experimentation in a wide variety of fields.

35. Moritz Föllmer and Rüdiger Graf, eds., *Die "Krise" der Weimarer Republik: Zur Kritik eines Deutungsmusters* (Frankfurt: Campus, 2005); Wolfgang Hardtwig, ed., *Ordnung in der Krise: Zur politischen Kulturgeschichte Deutschlands, 1900–1933* (Munich: Oldenbourg, 2007). Föllmer and Graf note that the word *crisis* appears in the titles of over 370 different publications on politics, economics, and society that appeared between 1918 and 1933 (10).

36. See Moritz Föllmer, "The Problem of National Solidarity in Interwar Germany," *German History* 23, no. 2 (2005): 202–31.

37. On the importance of the border as a symbol of loss in Weimar Germany and the role that it played in foreign policy and *völkisch* thought, see Vanessa Conze, "'Unverheilte Brandwunden in der Außenhaut des Volkskörpers': Der deutsche Grenz-Diskurs der Zwischenkriegszeit (1919–1939)," in *Ordnung in der Krise: Zur politischen Kulturgeschichte Deutschlands 1900–1933*, ed. Wolfgang Hardtwig, 21–48 (Munich: Oldenbourg, 2007).

actors, and make all concerned aware of the limits of German capabilities to enact the plans they conceptualized. The German crisis of sovereignty had several dimensions: (1) an unstable relationship between the state and the territory it controlled; (2) a more general instability of borders in the region; (3) bitter political divisions that erupted in 1918 in revolution and persisted for years thereafter; (4) an increasing emphasis, for those on both sides of the political spectrum, on the people (*Volk*) as a source of legitimacy for and against the state; and (5) migration, which was both a cause and symptom of crisis.

Migration lay at the intersection of domestic and foreign policy and, as such, was a stage for working through the political, ideological, and moral consequences of the crisis of sovereignty. Old ideological frameworks did not provide clear guidelines on how to deal with new situations. The Weimar Constitution was similarly unhelpful. Article 113 stated merely that "Reich communities speaking a foreign language may not be deprived of their national identity, especially in the use of their mother language in education, in local administration and jurisdiction."[38] The rights of individuals who did not live in majority-minority communities were not mentioned in the constitution, nor did it address the issue of migrants. Germany faced thousands of starving people who needed emergency care, it had a housing crisis made worse by the presence of hundreds of thousands of immigrants, and it had difficulty maintaining effective border control. The symbolic and ideological importance of migration during and after the war exacerbated the difficulty of handling these practical challenges. From the first years of the war, when ethnic German suffering became a justification for the demographic reorganization of the occupied territories, migration was a potent political symbol. The symbolic role of migrants increased after the war ended, when Germans denied the magnitude of their revolution and the stab-in-the-back myth enabled the denial of defeat, instead assigning responsibility for the trauma of Germany to the Treaty of Versailles and the postwar migrations.[39]

In each case, the factors were different. Border guards adjudicating the claims of the flood of people at the Polish-German border demanding entry into Germany and support from the German state had to choose whether to value ethnicity, current citizenship status, former citizenship status, or culture. Germans who emigrated to Soviet Russia had to decide what, if any, connection they would retain to Germany or would forge with the Russians they worked alongside. Interior Ministry officials had to decide how to allocate scarce resources and balance humanitarian concerns with fears about the impact of migration on the German people. What followed was neither ambiguity nor openness but,

---

38. For a full English-language version of the constitution, see http://www.zum.de/psm/weimar/weimar_vve.php.

39. On the overlap between the "discourse of defeat" and a "discourse of borders," see Conze, "Unverheilte Brandwunden," 26–27.

rather, a series of contradictory attempts to establish order. The dilemma of Germany's impossible border, although present throughout German society, was most urgent on its ideological extremes and most apparent in relation to its eastern border.

In 1918, Fritz Dieck, an ethnic German Russian, complained that "the German authorities believe that everything that comes from Russia is 'infected with Bolshevism.'"[40] The specter of Bolshevik Revolution or a monarchist conspiracy between Russians and Germans frightened Germans of various political persuasions. But fear was far from the only emotion inspired by the Bolshevik takeover in Soviet Russia. Some on the left looked eastward toward a triumphant Bolshevik regime, and many Germans on the right believed that, through German military action in the Baltic or an alliance between Germany and Russia, they could "break the ring created by Versailles."[41] Indeed, such hopes played a role in the German decision to sign the Treaty of Rapallo, in which it became the first state to recognize Soviet Russia. The East was also a source of particular concern for reasons beyond the arrival of the new communist state. As Philip Ther has pointed out, "the German Empire was built on the continuous partition of one of its neighbors. . . . Viewed from Breslau, Poznan or Warsaw, the so-called [German] unification looked more like a continuous expansion."[42] This pattern of expansion radicalized after 1914 as a result of military success that resulted in the aggressively annexationist Treaty of Brest-Litovsk that the Germans forced on the Soviets in early 1918. With the Versailles Treaty a year later, however, the eastward expansion of Germany was reversed as the newly independent Polish state was awarded formerly German territory. Gregor Thum suggests that German resentment at the loss of its status as a great power focused on the loss of the Polish territories because "Germany's imperial ambitions during the war were usually directed toward the east and therefore the decline (*Fallhöhe*) was particularly dramatic there."[43] Equally important to the facts of territorial gain or loss was the sense of instability that persisted throughout the 1914–1922 period. The eastern border of Germany did not assume its final shape until after the Silesian plebiscite of 1921, whereas uncertainty about the final placement of borders in Eastern Europe lingered at least up until the absorption of the Ukrainian People's Republic into the Soviet Union in mid-1922. This instability

40. "Bericht des Rückwanderers Fritz Dieck vom 2.8.1918." Bundesarchiv [hereafter BArch], R 1501/118388, 35.

41. Josef Bischoff, *Die letzte Front: Geschichte der Eisernen Division im Baltikum 1919* (Berlin: Schützen-Verlag, 1936), 247.

42. Philipp Ther, "Beyond the Nation: The Relational Basis of a Comparative History of Germany and Europe," *Central European History* 31, no. 1 (2003), 53.

43. Gregor Thum, "Mythische Landschaften: Das Bild vom deutschen Osten und die Zäsuren des 20. Jahrhunderts," in *Traumland Osten: Deutsche Bilder vom östlichen Europa im 20. Jahrhundert,* ed. Gregor Thum (Göttingen: Vandenhoeck and Ruprecht, 2006), 188.

allowed Germans to believe in the possibility of further change in the region. In part precipitated by frontier changes and in part by political instability, civil war, and famine, the largest number of war and postwar migrants, from German citizens leaving newly Polish provinces to anti-Bolshevik Russian émigrés, either came from Eastern Europe, or, as in the case of the Freikorps and the socialist organization Ansiedlung Ost, desired to settle in the region. And, finally, "the East" had a symbolic value as a source of utopian dreams and apocalyptic danger for the war and postwar imaginary of Germans across the political spectrum. This relationship, marked alternately by fear and longing, was an inheritance of earlier centuries, which was now radicalized by the extreme and labile politics of the war and postwar period.[44] "Ex oriente lux [light comes from the East]," as one Freikorps memoirist put it, was "a saying that hypnotized many in those days."[45]

The crisis of sovereignty had different meanings for the political moderates that controlled migration policy during this period and for the parties of the extremes that critiqued it. The most important actors in migration policy during the early years of the Weimar Republic were the Prussian Ministry of the Interior, run by Wolfgang Heine until 1920 and Carl Severing thereafter, both socialists, and the national Ministry of the Interior, governed by a succession of ministers drawn from the Sozialdemokratische Partei Deutschlands (SPD) and the liberal Deutsche Demokratische Partei (DDP). In both interior ministries, dire warnings about the dangers posed by immigration often accompanied more moderate policies toward actual migrants. This apparent contradiction resulted from attempts to weave a middle course among nationalism, practical limitations, and a commitment to humanitarian restraint. Both ministries were innovative at times—devising new strategies for securing the border or reforming citizenship or asylum policies—as they strove to put nationalist or socialist priorities into practice. At the same time, they also maintained a keen sense of the constraints confronting Germany—the financial constraints of a state hamstrung by the economic demands of war and reparations, the territorial constraints of the Versailles Treaty, and the ideological constraints of a republic often divided against itself. Both interior ministries viewed the crisis of sovereignty and the migrations that were its components and consequences as problems that threatened to spin out of control and that needed to be managed as best they could.

44. On Germany's complicated relationship with "the East," see Wolfgang Wippermann, *Die Deutschen und der Osten: Feindbild und Traumland* (Darmstadt: Primus, 2007). On the complications specific to the twentieth century, see Gregor Thum, ed., *Traumland Osten: Deutsche Bilder vom östlichen Europa im 20. Jahrhundert* (Göttingen: Vandenhoeck & Ruprecht, 2006); Gerd Koenen, *Der Russland-Komplex: Die Deutschen und der Osten* (Munich: Beck, 2005); Lew Kopelew and Gerd Koenen, eds., *Deutschland und die Russische Revolution* (Munich: Fink, 1998). More generally, see the series "West-östliche Spiegelungen. Deutsche und Deutschland aus russischer Sicht: Russen und Rußland aus deutscher Sicht," (Munich, Fink 1983–2006).

45. Erich Balla, *Landsknechte wurden wir . . .: Abenteuer aus dem Baltikum* (Berlin: Wilhelm Kolk, 1932), 16.

For those on the political extremes, however, Germany's impossible border was a symbol of the republic's failures of ideological rigor and practical efficacy. Both *völkisch* nationalists and communists believed that the crisis of sovereignty was an opportunity to be seized to forge a new relationship among the state, its citizens, and its frontiers. It was in this context that escape from the confines of Germany through emigration found its appeal. The popular emigration schemes I discuss in chapters 2 and 3 reflected a sense of utopianism and ambition largely absent from German immigration policy during this period. Frustration accompanied the collapse of these plans and the inability of the German state to manage immigration. Yet, as much as the enemies of the republic bemoaned these failures, they rarely rescaled their aims to match the practical limitations faced by the German state or its people. On the contrary, in a dangerous dialectic, frustration functioned as a productive force for ambition, encouraging yet more boldness and more discontent with the half measures of the Weimar state.

In chapter 1, I examine the wartime euphoria about German victory in the East, which inspired plans for widescale annexations and population realignments to solve the immediate problem of ethnic German suffering in Russia while also providing for the future health of the German nation. Even the practical difficulties of large-scale population displacement that appeared in spring and summer 1918 did little to dampen German enthusiasm for remaking the demographic and political map of Eastern Europe. The German defeat on the Western Front in November 1918 put an end to these far-reaching plans, even as revolutions and the postwar treaties unleashed population movements more complex than anything Germans had envisioned when victory had seemed assured.

In chapters 2 and 3, I consider the Germans who considered leaving Germany to settle either in the Baltic nations or in Soviet Russia. Members of the Baltic Freikorps believed that they could establish a German community and base for a future ascendant German state by settling in Latvia and becoming Latvian citizens. Meanwhile, Ansiedlung Ost members longed for a *terra nova* in southern Russia, where they could live as revolutionary socialists divorced from any national ties. Neither effort succeeded, but both groups—whose combined numbers approached 100,000—represented the radical destabilization of the relationship among nation, state, and territory on the political margins of Germany.

I next examine the migration of approximately 1 million Germans, Russians, and Jews into Germany during the first years of the republic. In chapter 4, I explore the state responses to German immigrants from the territories ceded to Poland, people whom the German state could neither refuse on moral grounds nor financially afford to support. In trying to decide who was worthy of state assistance, and in attempting to limit its responsibility by restricting immigration, the German state moved increasingly to embrace the *völkisch* principles of ethnic exclusion and territorial expansion. As I demonstrate in chapter 5, in encountering non-ethnic German immigrants, the state evinced little of the ambivalence that plagued it with regard to ethnic Germans. Despite the general consensus that Germany should do its best to seal its borders to foreigners, experience proved this to be unfeasible and Eastern European Jews became symbols of the impotence of Germany in controlling its territorial frontiers.

This nearly obsessive concern with Germany's boundaries provided a potent metaphor for all German interactions with foreigners, even those migrants who had already transgressed the physical German borders. In chapter 6, turning to the controversies over Russian POWs and Red Army internees in Germany, I show that Bolshevism was perceived as a kind of border crossing, that is, a transnational force with the potential to destabilize nationalist loyalties. Ironically, the fear of Bolshevism itself was the impetus for an international alliance of anti-Bolshevik forces that, by its very nature, necessitated crossing national borders. In chapter 7, I continue this examination of the imaginary of the German frontier by describing how citizenship policy and practice acted as a kind of symbolic border control. Finally, in chapter 8, I turn to the fragile and contested concept of asylum. During the early years of the republic, socialists insisted on German moral obligations to Eastern European Jews and a much broader consensus agreed to extend sympathy and temporary asylum to anti-Bolshevik Russians. In both cases, supporters of asylum argued that the territory of Germany was not solely for those who belonged to the German nation-state.

In each of these cases, migrants posed daunting practical challenges and their very existence was a visible demonstration of crisis. The image of the impossible border suggests the hesitations, paradoxes, conflicts, and imperfect compromises that formed the fabric of state practice and lived experience during these years. The fear and exhilaration inspired by migration, as well as the new grammar of social and territorial relations that emerged fitfully in the attempts to understand and control it, are the subjects of this book.

1. "German Brothers"

War and Migration

On August 1, 1914, Germany declared war on Russia, and a week of public demonstrations—both for and against the war—culminated in hundreds of thousands of Germans' marching to the palace of Kaiser Wilhelm II in the center of Berlin. The demonstration reached its emotional climax when the kaiser came to the balcony to speak to the crowd and proclaimed, "I no longer recognize parties or confessions. Today we are all German brothers, and only German brothers."[1] But which Germans did he mean? In the enthusiasm of the moment, most Germans in the crowd were probably not asking this question; however, in the ensuing years, as German troops "discovered" Germans in the Baltics, and as Germans from the Baltics and greater Russia began to immigrate to Germany, a series of related questions were increasingly posed: What did it mean to be German? How were true Germans to be recognized? What, for that matter, were the limits of Germany itself?

The outbreak of war in 1914 inspired an upsurge in nationalism and a temporary decrease in ethnic prejudice. German Jews and Poles believed that the civil peace (*Burgfrieden*) between the government and its socialist opposition would also allow them the opportunity to prove their loyalty to the Reich. As the war progressed, this brief moment of harmony collapsed amid mounting German casualties and suffering on the home front. As the situation on the home front

---

1. Ulrich Cartarius, "Zweite Balkonrede des Kaisers, August 1, 1914," in *Deutschland im Ersten Weltkrieg: Texte und Dokumente 1914–1918,* ed. Ulrich Cartarius (Munich: Deutsche Taschenbuch-Verlag, 1982), 15.

appeared increasingly unmanageable and especially after massive strikes in 1917–1918 threatened the entire political and social structure of Wilhelmine Germany, the successes of Germany on its Eastern Front grew in importance for the government and its supporters. The possibility of large-scale annexations in the Baltics and the migration of Russian and Reich Germans to the region presented an opportunity for many German military and civilian planners to solve the problems of Germans on both sides of the now-swollen Reich frontiers. The increasingly besieged state encouraged German citizens to regard victory in the east as a reward for their suffering. German victory in the east was also seen as a boon to the large population of ethnic Germans inside the Russian Empire, who were then suffering under punitive anti-German policies pursued by the desperate tsarist regime. The voluntary migrations of ethnic Germans to the Baltic states and the forced migrations of people of other nationalities to make way for them would redeem German suffering while simultaneously enhancing the colonial prospects of Germany in its northeastern borderlands. The national Interior Ministry established the Reichswanderungsstelle (RWS) in May 1918 to advertise for and coordinate the migration of Russian Germans to Germany and the territories to be annexed in the Baltics. In preparation for a potential migration that many officials estimated could reach 1 million Russian Germans, the euphoria of conquest turned to the sober realities of administration. Nevertheless, objections were cast aside as the powerful vision of a remade German-dominated Baltics continued to entrance civilian and military planners up to the final days of the war.

Citizenship and Belonging before 1913

The notion of the German *Volk* as a cultural and ethnic group solidified in the early 1800s in response to the civic nationalism then developing in France.[2] Whereas the French saw national identity as a product of the state (civic nationalism), over the first half of the nineteenth century, Prussian law increasingly elided national identity and belonging to the state. In 1842, Prussian King Friedrich Wilhelm IV replaced the existing Prussian citizenship law (which had granted citizenship to those with a permanent residence in Prussia) with a *jus sanguinis* (law of blood, i.e., descent) policy granting citizenship only to those with German ethnic heritage.[3] Despite some abortive efforts in 1848, there was

---

2. Rogers Brubaker, *Citizenship and Nationhood in France and Germany* (Cambridge, Mass.: Harvard University Press, 1992); Johannes Wilms, *Die Deutsche Krankheit: Eine kurze Geschichte der Gegenwart* (Munich: Carl Hanser Verlag, 2001), 30–37.

3. Wolfgang Wippermann, "Das Blutrecht der Blutnation: Zur Ideologie- und Politikgeschichte des Ius Sanguinis in Deutschland," in *Blut oder Boden: Doppelpass, Staatsbürgerrecht und Nationsverständnis,* ed. Andreas Dietl, Jochen Baumann, and Wolfgang Wippermann (Berlin: Elefanten Press, 1999), 10–48. Both Andreas Fahrmeir and Dieter Gosewinkel have offered less ethnocentric

no liberalization of Prussian citizenship law to make it easier for non-ethnic Germans to acquire citizenship.[4] At the same time, the statist tradition, a legacy of Prussian absolutism, maintained that belonging was a consequence of one's loyalty and service to the state.[5] From 1871 onward, the German state both encompassed many non-ethnic Germans and excluded many who claimed German ethnic heritage; also Jews living on German territory were emancipated and granted citizenship when Germany was unified. According to Dietmar Schirmer, "the newly founded Reich oscillated between the Prussian statist and the German national ideas, unable to resolve the inherent tensions between them."[6]

From the 1880s onward, Germany found itself confronting growing numbers of migrants—especially Poles and Jews—and both national and Prussian authorities began to operate with an increasingly ethnic definition of belonging. The Poles were the largest ethnic minority in Germany. The Poles living in the German Polish territories were German citizens, equaling up to 10 percent of the total Prussian population, but they were "second-class citizens," discriminated against in matters of schooling, jobs, and cultural institutions.[7] After the 1886 Settlement Law (Ansiedlungsgesetz), the German state bought Polish-owned land to settle approximately 120,000 Germans in the eastern territories with the dual purpose of preventing their migration overseas and providing a greater demographic claim to the region.[8] Seasonal Polish workers from Russia and Austria-Hungary were imported to work as farm labor on Junker estates in the east. Germans developed an extensive system of measures to keep track of and maintain control over these workers.[9] The German ambivalence toward the Polish

---

views on German citizenship in the early nineteenth century. Fahrmeir compares German and British legal mechanisms for dealing with foreigners in the first two-thirds of the nineteenth century and finds that Britain was in many cases no more liberal than Germany in its foreigner laws; Andreas Fahrmeir, *Citizens and Aliens: Foreigners and the Law in Britain and the German States, 1789–1870* (New York: Berghahn Books, 2000); Dieter Gosewinkel, *Einbürgern und Ausschließen: Die Nationalisierung der Staatsangehörigkeit vom Deutschen Bund bis zur Bundesrepublik Deutschland* (Göttingen: Vandenhoeck and Ruprecht, 2001).

4. Gosewinkel, *Einbürgern und Ausschließen*, 102–35.

5. Gregg O. Kvistad, *The Rise and Demise of German Statism: Loyalty and Political Membership* (New York: Berghahn, 1999); Dietmar Schirmer, "Closing the Nation: Nationalism and Statism in Nineteenth and Twentieth Century Germany," in *The Shifting Foundations of Modern Nation States*, ed. Sima Godfrey and Frank Unger (Toronto: University of Toronto Press, 2004), 35–58.

6. Schirmer, "Closing the Nation," 47.

7. Gosewinkel, *Einbürgern und Ausschließen*, 211; see 211–18 for a discussion of nationality conflicts in Wilhelmine Prussia and the ways in which this second-class status manifested itself.

8. Martin Broszat, *Zweihundert Jahre deutsche Polenpolitik* (Frankfurt: Suhrkamp, 1972), 142–72. For a perspective that stresses the colonial aspect of the German relationship to Poles and the eastern territories occupied by them, see Kristin Kopp, "Contesting Borders: German Colonial Discourse and the Polish Eastern Territories," PhD diss., University of California, Berkeley, 2001.

9. Bade, *Europa in Bewegung*, 222–31; Conrad, *Globalisierung und Nation*, 124–67; Broszat, *Zweihundert Jahre deutsche Polenpolitik;* Hans-Ulrich Wehler, "Polenpolitik im deutschen Kaiserreich," in *Krisenherde des Kaiserreichs 1871–1918: Studien zur deutschen Sozial- und Verfassungsgeschichte*, 184–203 (Göttingen: Vandenhoeck and Ruprecht, 1979).

borderlands as well as toward both the Poles who were German citizens and these seasonal workers anticipated the impossible border of the war and postwar periods. Often the very same agricultural barons who lobbied for an increase in Polish migrant labor also expressed anxiety about the possibility of the "Polonization" of the German frontier regions. Meanwhile, German socialists were split on whether to welcome Polish seasonal labors as potential agitators or to reject them as unfair competition.[10]

In addition, the late nineteenth century brought the large-scale immigration of Eastern European Jews. The German government sought to limit Jewish immigration and, indeed, managed briefly to seal its eastern border several times, but once it decided to import Polish seasonal labor, separating desirable and undesirable eastern immigrants became a practical impossibility. At one time, as much as 10 percent of all Prussian gendarmes were stationed on the German-Russian frontier, rules were established requiring identity cards for all immigrants, and 1,000 mark fines were imposed on smugglers who helped immigrants cross the border. Yet even such drastic measures failed to halt the immigration of Eastern European Jews to Germany.[11] Mass expulsions of Jews and Poles took place in Prussia in 1884–1885 and 1904–1906, but restrictionist campaigns foundered on fears that harsh treatment of Jewish immigrants could negatively affect the image of Germany in the world.[12] The Wilhelmine state proved itself incapable of limiting migration to the categories of immigrants it found necessary—namely Polish seasonal workers imported to work on the large Prussian estates. Although xenophobic rhetoric waxed and waned during the Kaiserreich depending largely on economic imperatives, public discourse generally presented Jews and Poles alike as "products of the backward East, speakers of inferior languages and elements of subversion."[13]

The ascendency of German ethnonationalism of the later Kaiserreich was itself in part a response to this mobility.[14] Founded in 1891, the Pan-German

---

10. Conrad, *Globalisierung und Nation*, 131–32.

11. Jack Wertheimer, *Unwelcome Strangers: East European Jews in Imperial Germany* (New York: Oxford University Press, 1987), 14–15.

12. Ibid., 36, 40. For more on the Polish expulsions in the 1880s, see Richard Blanke, *Prussian Poland in the German Empire (1871–1900)* (New York: Columbia University Press, 1981); Joachim Mai, *Die preussisch-deutsche Polenpolitik, 1885/87: Eine Studie zur Herausbildung des Imperialismus in Deutschland* (Berlin: Rütten & Loening, 1962); Oswald Hauser, "Polen und Dänen im Deutschen Reich," in *Reichsgründung 1870/71: Tatsachen, Kontroversen, Interpretationen*, ed. Theodor Schneider and Ernst Deuerlein (Stuttgart: Seewald, 1970), 291–318; Wehler, "Polenpolitik im deutschen Kaiserreich."

13. Wertheimer, *Unwelcome Strangers*, 27. Nonetheless, it is important to keep in mind that even if the Poles did make up a large percentage of (at least) the Prussian population, the 1910 census counted only 70,000 Jews, or one-tenth of 1 percent of the total population of Germany, living in the Reich. The majority of Eastern European Jews, unlike the Poles, used Germany as a way station in their attempt to migrate further westward.

14. Conrad, *Globalisierung und Nation*, 20–23.

League was symptomatic of this ethnicism; it was dedicated both to extending German power on the international stage and combating what its members saw as "Un-German" elements, such as Slavs and Jews, within Germany itself.[15] For the pan-Germans, the project of German national awakening would be incomplete as long as millions of Germans continued to live outside of the borders of the German state. Germany had, after all, been a land of emigration; millions of Germans had emigrated during the nineteenth century, with the United States as the most common destination.[16] The pan-Germans were not alone in their desire to connect overseas Germans to the metropole; one of the central arguments for German colonialism was the need to direct German emigrants to locations where they could retain a connection to Germany.[17] The pan-Germans were, however, especially interested in the connections between the German state and the *Auslandsdeutsche* in Eastern Europe. According to the pan-Germans, the Germans in Eastern Europe were vital to the Reich; as pioneers in the expansive and dangerous territory of *Slaventum,* they deserved its protection and support.[18] Under Ernst Hasse, president of the Pan-German League and National Liberal deputy in the Reichstag, the pan-Germans introduced a proposal to the Reichstag in December 1894 to impose more restrictions on foreigners attempting to gain German citizenship and simultaneously make it easier for Germans to retain their German citizenship while living abroad. Although it was defeated by labor-hungry agricultural barons loath to discourage immigration, they continued to make similar proposals in the ensuing two decades.[19]

These initiatives culminated in the citizenship law of July 22, 1913, which echoed in key ways the demands of the pan-Germans. During the fractious debates about this law, delegates from the radical right and the socialist left clashed over both the rights of people of German descent living outside of Germany and the rights of Jews who had lived their entire lives on German soil.[20] Those on the right who pushed for the liberalization of laws governing the maintenance and retrieval of German citizenship often referred to the *Auslandsdeutsche,* espe-

15. On the Pan-German League, see Roger Chickering, *We Men Who Feel Most German: A Cultural Study of the Pan-German League, 1886–1914* (Boston: Allen & Unwin, 1984); Michael Peters, *Der Alldeutsche Verband am Vorabend des Ersten Weltkrieges (1908–1914): Ein Beitrag zur Geschichte des völkischen Nationalismus im spätwilhelminischen Deutschland* (Frankfurt am Main: Lang, 1992).

16. On emigration from Germany in the nineteenth century, see Klaus Bade, ed., *Deutsche im Ausland. Fremde in Deutschland: Migration in Geschichte und Gegenwart* (Munich: Beck, 1992); Conrad, *Globalisierung und Nation,* chap. 5; Dirk Hoerder and Jörg Nagler, eds., *People in Transit: German Migrants in Comparative Perspective, 1820–1930* (New York: Cambridge University Press, 1995).

17. Bradley Naranch, "Beyond the Fatherland: Colonial Visions, Overseas Expansion, and German Nationalism, 1848–1885," PhD diss., University of North Carolina, Chapel Hill, 2006.

18. Chickering, *We Men Who Feel Most German,* 84.

19. Brubaker, *Citizenship and Nationhood,* 116.

20. Ibid., 136.

cially those living in Russia. These foreign Germans, they argued, were a vital part of the German nation and deserved the right to obtain German citizenship.[21] Hazy, but no less potent, fears of a Slavic onslaught that had their origin in the Middle Ages played a role in motivating legislators to enshrine the principle of *jus sanguinis* into law. The very real increase in immigration (especially of Poles and *Ostjuden*) during the prewar period also lent authority to these long-standing fears. Between 1890 and 1910, the number of resident foreigners had tripled—from 430,000 to 1,260,000.[22] The 1913 citizenship law was not actually more restrictive than previous citizenship practices. It merely kept in place already existing barriers to the naturalization of Jews and other easterners. Foreigners living within Germany did not gain any new rights as a result of this law, and they did not find it any easier to obtain German citizenship.[23] As had been the case prior to 1913, a resident of Germany who was born in Germany and whose parents had also been born in Germany did not automatically have a right to citizenship. The law differed from previous German citizenship practices, however, by greatly liberalizing the policies by which *Auslandsdeutsche* retained and transmitted their citizenship. Whereas previously Germans had lost their German citizenship automatically after they had resided more than ten years abroad, under the new policy they could retain their citizenship indefinitely and were able to transmit it to their children and grandchildren. For foreigners of German descent without German citizenship, the new law made it easier for them to apply for naturalization. Indeed, even those who had renounced German citizenship in favor of that of another country could apply to have their German citizenship reinstated. Rogers Brubaker has argued that the 1913 law represented the triumph of the principle of *jus sanguinis* over *jus soli* (law of the soil, i.e., residency) and thus "marked the nationalization, even the ethnicization, of German citizenship."[24]

The 1913 law was a victory for the proponents of an ethnic definition of German identity, but it was not a total triumph. The most radical clauses proposed by the pan-Germans did not succeed in the Reichstag in 1913. For example, a proposal to automatically grant citizenship to *Auslandsdeutsche* foundered in the face of opposition from groups that felt that ethnic Germans were not worthy of citizenship unless they had served in the armed forces. These groups, which ranged from the socialist opposition to the older conservative parties, argued from a statist perspective. Although they believed that the *Auslandsdeutsche* could potentially aid the homeland, they did not show much interest in supporting or protecting them until they had demonstrated such support through

21. Ibid., 116–18.
22. Ibid., 118.
23. Ibid.
24. Ibid., 114. See also Markus Lang, *Grundkonzeption und Entwicklung des deutschen Staatsangehörigkeitsrechts* (Frankfurt am Main: Verlag für Standesamtswesen, 1990), 47–49.

military service.[25] Moreover, the 1913 law might be better defined as a law of descent rather than one of ethnicity. German citizenship was dependent on the citizenship of one's grandparents, not on ethnic heritage. Finally, a proposal from the Office of the Interior that was intended to categorically deny citizenship to "ethnically foreign (*stammfremde*) elements from the East . . . or Jews who are not on our level of culture" faced heated opposition and ultimately did not find its way into the final document.[26] On the other hand, social democrats, with the support of the progressives, Poles, and to some extent the Center Party, proposed the granting of citizenship to all those born and raised in Germany.[27] Although the Office of the Interior angrily dismissed these proposals, the fact that the largest party in Germany at the time was willing to argue from the perspective of *jus soli* is not inconsequential. The tensions that played out in the construction of the citizenship law reflected the conflicts of the ever more polarized prewar state.

The Spirit of 1914

Almost exactly one year after the passage of the citizenship law, Germany went to war. Spontaneous demonstrations of nationalism greeted the onset of hostilities, and even though the myth of the "spirit of 1914" masks a wide variety of differing responses to the outset of the war, it was an undeniably powerful image of a German community united in a common struggle.[28] The outbreak of war served as a nationalizing experience, lending a tangible meaning to abstract concepts such as loyalty, sacrifice, and national identity.[29] During the heady days of August, Jewish organizations declared their unlimited support for German war plans and encouraged their members to join the military to prove their loyalty and their worthiness of equal membership in the German nation.[30] Returning the favor, the government banned several extreme anti-Semitic and pan-German publications for their incendiary statements against the Jews and recruited Jews into public positions.[31] A statist, or civic, conception of nationalism appeared to triumph over narrower ethnic definitions.

25. Gosewinkel, *Einbürgern und Ausschließen*, 278–327.

26. Ibid., 318.

27. Brubaker, *Citizenship and Nationhood*, 121.

28. Jeffrey Verhey, *The Spirit of 1914: Militarism, Myth and Mobilization in Germany* (Cambridge, UK: Cambridge University Press, 2000); Steffan Bruendel, *Volksgemeinschaft oder Volksstaat: Die "Ideen von 1914" und die Neuordnung Deutschlands im Ersten Weltkrieg* (Berlin: Akademie Verlag, 2003).

29. Verhey, *Spirit of 1914*. See also Peter Fritzsche, *Germans into Nazis* (Cambridge, Mass.: Harvard University Press, 1998), 11–82.

30. Peter Pulzer, *Jews and the German State* (Detroit: Wayne State University Press, 2003), 194–98.

31. Ibid., 196.

Along with the newly inclusive spirit toward German Jews, the nationalist enthusiasm that greeted the war also inspired hostility to foreigners. Foreigners living in Germany were either interred or expelled.[32] Meanwhile, as Germany entered the war, propaganda excoriated German enemies. German justifications for fighting the war painted it from the outset as a fight between German *Kultur* and Russian barbarism, and visions of an invasion by the autocratic and barbaric Russians helped solidify SPD support behind the war.[33] Comparisons to "Huns" and descriptions of "hordes," "swarms," and "waves" created a fearful image of Germany overrun by uncivilized Slavs intent on destroying the glories of German *Kultur,* violating the bodies of German women, and killing defenseless German children. Troy Paddock writes, "so extensive was this theme in the newspapers that in many accounts it appeared that the word 'Russian' could not appear unless accompanied by the words 'barbarism' (*Barbarei*), 'cruelty' (*Grausamkeit*) or 'foul deed' (*Schandtat*)."[34] In part, the need of Germany to underline the defensive nature of its war dictated the virulence of the propaganda attack on Russia. In the days leading up to the declaration of war, the SPD had encouraged large demonstrations against war, and the German government remained unsure about the reliability of the socialists. A defensive war against the reactionary autocratic Russian Empire would be more likely to earn socialist support than an offensive war against democratic France.[35] Thus it was in the interest of the German government to emphasize the irreconcilable differences between East and West, to encourage harshly negative propaganda about the Russian threat, and to deemphasize Germany's own expansionist plans. At the same time, the virulence of the German press coverage of Russia went further than even the state intended.[36]

The anti-Russian sentiment in 1914 had its roots in the prewar period. Al-

32. Similar kinds of internment measures were taken in other combatant countries. For more about the internment measures taken in Britain, see Panikos Panayi, *The Enemy in Our Midst: Germans in Britain during the First World War* (Oxford: Berg, 1991). For French measures taken toward the Alsatians, see Paul Smith, "The Kiss of France: The Republic and the Alsatians during the First World War," in *Minorities in Wartime,* ed. Panikos Panayi, 27–49 (Oxford: Berg, 1993). These actions against foreigners supplemented the increased surveillance of nationals. On France, see Jean-Jacques Becker, *The Great War and the French People,* trans. Arnold Pomerans (Dover, N.H.: Berg, 1985). On Britain, see David Englander, "Military Intelligence and the Defense of the Realm: The Surveillance of Soldiers and Civilians in Britain during the First World War," *Bulletin of the Society for the Study of Labor History* 52 (1987): 24–32.
33. Chickering, *We Men Who Feel Most German,* 61.
34. Troy Paddock, "Still Stuck at Sevastopol: The Depiction of Russia during the Russo-Japanese War and the Beginning of the First World War in the German Press," *German History* 16, no. 3 (1998), 371.
35. On August 28, 1914, Secretary of State Gottlieb von Jagow instructed newspapers not to discuss the German war aims but, instead, to focus on the fact that the German victory would free oppressed people from Russian autocracy and British imperialism; Wilhelm Diest, *Militär und Innenpolitik im Weltkrieg, 1914–1918* (Düsseldorf: Droste, 1970), 78–79.
36. Paddock, "Still Stuck at Sevastopol," 374.

though German attitudes toward Russia had been generally positive in the after-math of the Napoleonic wars, they declined steadily over the course of the nine-teenth century.[37] In the years leading up to 1848, German liberals, much like liberals in other European countries, viewed Russia as a dangerous colossus capa-ble of threatening progressives across the European continent.[38] During the sec-ond half of the nineteenth century, Germans of all political persuasions increasingly characterized Russians as primitive, Asiatic, and foreign to European culture, cus-toms, and politics.[39] The embarrassment of the Russo-Japanese War, in which the Russians were convincingly defeated by a non-European power, only fueled sus-picions of Russian backwardness.[40] Yet, although the Russian defeat by Japan should have reassured Germans that the Russians posed no threat, it instead had the opposite affect—by 1913, Germans from across the political spectrum began to speak more consistently of a battle for existence (*Existenzkampf*) between Ger-mans and Slavs.[41] A rhetoric of Slavic invasion was used to describe both the threat posed by the tsar and the threat of a massive immigration of "Easterners," and this specter of invading Slavic hordes helped solidify support behind the war.

As Germany first embarked on war in late summer 1914, strict censorship re-garding German annexationist war aims meant that propaganda emphasized al-most exclusively the defensive nature of the war and the need for walls and barriers between Germany and the East.[42] Nevertheless, even though these an-nexation plans rarely appeared in the press in 1914, they did circulate in gov-ernment and radical nationalist circles. As a result of German defeats in African colonial contests in 1913 and 1914, imperialist attention had turned toward Cen-tral and Eastern Europe in the final days before the war.[43] The war aims prom-ulgated by Heinrich Class for the Pan-German League in August 1914 called for territorial expansion toward both the east and the west. Class's text called for, among other things, the annexation of Belgium; the incorporation of France up

37. Lew Kopelew, "Zunächst war Waffenbrüderschaft," in *Russen und Russland aus deutscher Sicht. 19 Jahrhundert: Von der Jahrhundertwende bis zur Reichsgründung (1800–1871)*, ed. Mechthild Keller (Munich: Wilhelm Fink Verlag, 1992), 15.

38. Ibid., 49.

39. Lew Kopelew, "Am Vorabend des grossen Krieges," in *Russen und Russland aus deutscher Sicht. 19/20. Jahrhundert: Von der Bismarckzeit bis zum Ersten Weltkrieg*, ed. Mechthild Keller (Munich: Wilhelm Fink Verlag, 2000), 68.

40. Paddock, "Still Stuck at Sevastapol," 358–77.

41. Wolfgang Wette, "Rußlandbilder der Deutschen im 20. Jahrhundert: Kristallisationspunkte, Haupt- und Nebenlinien," in *Rußland und Europa*, ed. Michael Wegner (Leipzig: Rosa Luxemburg Verlag, 1995), 173.

42. David Welch, *Germany, Propaganda and Total War, 1914–1918: The Sins of Omission* (New Brunswick: Rutgers University Press, 2000), 65; Axel Schmidt, *Der deutsche Krieg*: Politische Flugschriften, vol. 7: *Die russische Sphinx* (Stuttgart & Berlin: Deutsche Verlags-Anstalt, 1914); Al-fons Paquet, *Der deutsche Krieg*: Politische Flugschriften, vol. 23: *Nach Osten!* (Stuttgart & Berlin: Deutsche Verlags-Anstalt, 1915).

43. Fritz Fischer, *War of Illusions: German Policies from 1911 to 1914* (New York: Norton, 1975), 447.

to the mouth of the Somme, including Longwy-Briey; the seizure of French and Belgian colonies in Africa; and the acquisition of the Baltics, (Russian) Poland, and the Ukraine, which would become German agricultural settlements.[44] Other leading parliamentarians and industrialists called for territorial expansion at the expense of German enemies. Matthias Erzberger of the Catholic Center Party wanted to take the Belgian and French coastline from Dunkirk/Calais to Boulogne and French mining regions, as well as either granting independence to or annexing Poland, the Ukraine, and Besserabia to remove them from the Russian sphere of influence.[45] Not all German war aims were so extravagant. Theobald von Bethmann-Hollweg, the German chancellor, wrote the September Plan in collaboration with Walter Rathenau and Karl Helffrich, the president of the German Bank, in September 1914. The September Plan focused on economic hegemony rather than annexations, but even here, the German entry into war offered important opportunities for Germany to enhance its position on the European continent.[46]

In the first days of hostility, Germany experienced surprising success in the West while the Eastern Front witnessed a brief incursion of Russian troops on to East Prussian soil. Within a few weeks, however, German forces under the command of General Paul von Hindenburg won a major victory at Tannenberg; inflicted 120,000 in Russian losses; and, in a series of encounters in September known as the Battle of Masurian Lakes, managed to expel the Russians from German territory.[47] Meanwhile, British and French forces halted the German offensive at the Marne.

The war quickly settled into a pattern that persisted for the next four years—stalemate in the West and success in the East. The two fronts, indeed, could not have been more different. The Western Front featured large-scale trench warfare and deadly but unproductive battles of attrition, whereas the Eastern Front was characterized first and foremost by movement.[48] As 1915 began, German armies stood on the border with Russian Poland; with the new year, they went on the offensive. The Battle of Masuren in February 1915 brought them back into Russia, and by the middle of March 1915, the German front lines in the East were deep

44. On the circulation of Class's war aims and the substantial participation of Hugenberg and German industry in creating the Kriegsausschuß der Deutschen Industrie (KDI), the leading organization in the right-wing war-aims movement, see Dankwart Guratzsch, *Macht durch Organisation: Die Grundlegung des Hugenbergschen Presseimperiums* (Düsseldorf: Bertelsmann Universitätsverlag, 1974), 127–28. Class's *Denkschrift* was later published with minor changes (the most important, and really only substantial, one being the decision not to annex Poland but, instead, to grant it statehood) in 1917 as Heinrich Class, *Zum deutschen Kriegsziel* (Munich: J. F. Lehmanns Verlag, 1917).
45. Fischer, *War of Illusions*, 518.
46. Jörg Brechtefeld, *Mitteleuropa and German Politics: 1848 to the Present* (New York: St. Martin's Press, 1996), 43–44; Fischer, *War of Illusions,* 520–22.
47. See Norman Stone, *The Eastern Front 1914–1917* (London: Hodder and Stoughton, 1975), for an account of the military history of the Eastern Front.
48. Liulevicius, *War Land on the Eastern Front*, esp. 14.

within Russian territory. German and Austrian troops staged an offensive in April 1915, and German troops moved into Lithuania in the north. During August 1915, Mitau, Bauska, Kowno, Brest-Litovsk, and Warsaw fell to the advancing German armies; meanwhile, further south, Entente forces pushed the Russians out of Galicia. By September, the German offense temporarily ran out of steam, and the Germans turned to administering their new territories.

As the German offensive rolled eastward, German soldiers encountered people and cultures that they saw as vastly different from their own. They were bewildered by what appeared to be a "whirlwind of human misery, dirt, disorder, disease and confusion."[49] German soldiers had expected the dirt and disorder, as the jokes printed in the *Berliner Morgenpost* in August 1914 make clear. "'Great cleaning next week. The Russian Bear will be washed.' . . . 'Insecticide transport to Petersburg through Berlin.'"[50] What was more surprising to many German observers than the poverty of the East was that the theoretically monolithic Russian bear contained a wide variety of different ethnic types: Poles, Latvians, Lithuanians, Russians, Ukrainians, Jews and also Germans. One official described the Baltics as "a cauldron, in which all kinds of peoples and currents simmered together wildly."[51] Yet in the midst of this "cauldron," soldiers also found themselves in seemingly familiar German towns and villages. Soldiers' accounts painted the German settlements they saw as islands of cleanliness and culture in a sea of barbarism; the definitive proof of German superiority lay in the order and cultivation of the Baltic Germans despite being surrounded by so much dirt and disorder.[52] The German press seemed unsure of what to make of this new territory and its inhabitants. In 1915, in the pages of the popular magazine *Die Gartenlaube,* Hedda v. Schmid described Kurland, the area with the most Germans, as a land where "German culture, German industry and, above all, *German loyalty* have always found a home."[53] At the same time, the liberal *Kriegs-Echo* was more skeptical about the region: "It is truly easy to understand that there were once Germans here. Unfortunately our troops do not see very much of this presence today. The thin German ruling class had mostly disappeared as the war drew closer, and the peasantry does not seem to be German-friendly at all."[54]

The Germans that these soldiers encountered were part of the nearly 1.8 million German speakers living in the Russian Empire.[55] In the Baltics, the set-

49. Ibid., 7.

50. Reprinted in *Kriegs-Echo,* no. 1, 1914, 15.

51. Liulevicius, *War Land on the Eastern Front,* 33.

52. Ibid.

53. Hedda v. Schmid, "Das deutsche Kurland und seine Herzöge," *Gartenlaube,* no. 36, 1915, 763. Emphasis in original.

54. "Die Eroberung Kurlands: Neues vom Feldmarschall Hindenburg," *Kriegs-Echo,* no. 49, July 16, 1915, 14.

55. Ingeborg Fleischhauer, Benjamin Pinkus, and Edith Rogovin, *The Soviet Germans: Past and Present* (London: Hurst & Co., 1986), 13.

tlers claimed descent from the thirteenth-century teutonic knights and lived a life of privilege, making up the cultural and landholding elite in the region.[56] Farther east and south in the Volga region, there was a very different kind of German settlement. The Germans there were peasants who had immigrated to Russia in the eighteenth century at the behest of Catherine the Great (herself a German).[57] Despite the very different histories of German settlement in the two regions, Germans in prewar Russia had lived a relatively privileged existence and were generally loyal to the tsar. In fact, the Baltic German elite often served in the army and staffed the highest levels of the Russian bureaucracy. One apocryphal but telling story recalled a Russian general whose greatest aspiration was to be promoted to the rank of "German."[58] Russification campaigns from the 1880s onward put pressure on the Russian and Baltic Germans, but did not make sufficient inroads to challenge their loyalty to the tsarist state.[59] Victor Doenninghaus estimates that 50,000 Russian Germans served in World War I.[60] Public attention to the Russian and Baltic Germans increased in the years leading up to the war in Germany, but as I discussed earlier, the state and many of its supporters remained decidedly cool toward these Russian citizens of German descent, and even the pan-Germans dismissed the Russian Germans as hopelessly backward.[61] Indeed, in part due to the strict censorship of the German press at the outset of the war concerning German war aims, the *Auslandsdeutsche* barely figured at all in the outpouring of propaganda that accompanied the start of hostilities. As countless wartime accounts stressed, only the war itself truly awakened Germans to their Russian and Baltic brethren.[62] German successes on the Eastern Front encouraged wide-ranging fantasizes about territorial expansion and population displacement in theoccupied territories. The *Auslandsdeutsche* provided both the excuse for these plans and the proof of their potential success.

56. On the Baltic Germans, see Andrew Ezergailis and Gert Pistohlkors, eds., *The Russian Baltic Provinces between the 1905/1917 Revolutions* (Cologne: Böhlau, 1982).

57. James W. Long, *From Privileged to Dispossessed: The Volga Germans, 1860–1917* (Lincoln: University of Nebraska Press, 1988); Fleischhauer, Pinkus, and Rogovin, *Soviet Germans.*

58. Robert Williams, *Culture in Exile: Russian Émigrés in Germany, 1881–1941* (Ithaca: Cornell University Press, 1972), 12.

59. Long, *From Privileged to Dispossessed,* 223. For more on Russification policies in the Russian Empire, see Theodor Weeks, *Nation and State in Late Imperial Russia: Nationalism and Russification on the Western Frontier, 1863–1914* (DeKalb: Northern Illinois University Press, 1996).

60. Victor Doenninghaus, *Revolution, Reform und Krieg: Die Deutschen an der Wolga im ausgehenden Zarenreich* (Essen: Klartext, 2002), 185. Due to suspicions about their loyalty, most of these served on the Turkish rather than the German front (226).

61. Henry Cord Meyer, *Drang nach Osten: Fortunes of a Slogan Concept in German-Slavic Relations, 1848–1990* (New York: Peter Lang, 1996), 87; Chickering, *We Men Who Feel Most German,* 84.

62. Williams, *Culture in Exile,* 39. See later in this chapter for the rhetoric on the awakening of Germans in the Reich to the connection between them and the Russian and Baltic Germans.

The Progress of War: Annexation and the *Auslandsdeutsche*

As the war continued on into its second and third years, the euphoria of the early months faded quickly into cynicism and foreboding. Instead of a short war, bringing the soldiers home in time for Christmas, German troops found themselves occupying strange territories in the East or trapped in trenches and dying in unprecedented numbers in the huge battles of attrition on the Western Front. The lives of Germans living on the home front changed irrevocably as well. Already in 1915, amid extreme privation and mounting casualties, the first cracks appeared in the *Burgfrieden,* and discontent mounted in Germany. At the same time as frustration on the home front grew, Erich Ludendorff, who, along with Paul von Hindenburg led the German High Command, drafted and enacted ambitious plans for the administration of the Baltics under a military dictatorship while military and civilian officials developed ever more audacious plans for wide-ranging annexations and population resettlement. The annexation plans devised by the pan-Germans and their allies met with hostility from Germans on the center and left who believed in a negotiated peace without punitive strictures. Nevertheless, the *Auslandsdeutsche* became an increasingly visible symbol of the German historical claim to territory in Eastern Europe.

In 1914 proponents of annexation had tried to keep their designs secret, but in 1915 they were the ones to break the silence about German war aims. In July 1915, Heinrich Class, the leader of the Pan-German League, and Dietrich Schäfer, the Berlin historian, with the financial assistance of Alfred Hugenberg, the right-wing publisher, established a war-aims committee, which had the express goal of being the "shock troops of the annexationist movement," to focus attention on the German-occupied territories in the Baltics.[63] By summer 1915, Germany had already conquered large swaths of Russian territory, the northern portion of which Erich Ludendorff administered through the military dictatorship Oberkommando Ost (Ober Ost); Ober Ost attempted to brutally remake the entire landscape of the Baltics, from the crops it grew to the culture it fostered.[64] Alongside the practical work of occupation and exploitation, annexationists heralded the gains that Germany could receive from its new Baltic holdings.[65] Silvio Broederich-Kurmahlen's *Das neue Ostland* (published in 1915)

63. Guratzsch, *Macht durch Organisation,* 139.
64. Ober Ost encompassed Kurland (part of modern-day Latvia), Lithuania, and Bialystok-Grodno—a space of 108,808 kilometers with a diverse population consisting of 3 million Russians, Latvians, Lithuanians, Germans, Jews, and other ethnicities; Liulevicius, *War Land on the Eastern Front,* 21.
65. Guratzsch, *Macht durch Organisation,* 365–66. In many ways, this project resembled Hugenberg's efforts in the 1880s and onward to settle Germans in the Prussian Polish territories (26–62).

was the most influential of annexationist texts, proposing the annexation of the Baltic provinces and their subsequent settlement with Germans drawn from Russia and the Reich itself. The natives of the Baltics would be Germanized or resettled elsewhere.[66] Friedrich Meinecke, a liberal-conservative historian, spoke of Kurland as an ideal "rural colony" once the Latvian natives had been displaced.[67] Annexationist ideas also found resonance at the highest levels of the state. In March 1915, in a memorandum for the chancellor's office, Friedrich von Schwerin, the president of Frankfurt/Oder and a member of the Pan-German League, proclaimed that the war presented "an opportunity—perhaps for the last time in world history—for Germany to reengage its imperial mission in the East. . . . the broad territories in the East can become a fountain of youth for Germany in the centuries to come."[68] On July 13, 1915, a conference at the chancellor's office concluded that Germans in the Baltics should be encouraged to remain there, whereas Russian Germans from the Volga and even from the territories under Austrian occupation in Russian Poland should be resettled in the eastern borderlands to provide further support for the Baltic German population.[69]

These sweeping plans did not inspire all Germans to support annexationist policies. Indeed, the issue of German territorial acquisitions through the imposition of punitive peace terms exposed a bitter fault line in German politics. By 1916, Germans had split into two camps: those who believed that Germany should seek a negotiated peace without annexations (*Verhandlungsfrieden*) and those who promoted a victory with territorial gains for Germany (*Siegesfrieden*).[70] As the sacrifices of the war intensified and casualties mounted, the rhetoric of each camp grew more extreme. The socialists (SPD) found themselves in a precarious position, supporting the state but with a membership that was uncomfortable with a war for territorial aggrandizement. In an article published in *Vorwärts* in July 1916, its internal divisions became public—some SPD officials were opposed to any annexationist demands, but others within the party were willing to agree to a limited annexationist program.[71] The socialist schism in April 1917 into the Unabhängige Sozialdemokratische Partei Deutschlands (USPD; Independent Social Democrats)[72] and the majority social democrats (the SPD) was in large

66. Silvio Broedrich-Kurmahlen, *Das neue Ostland* (Charlottenburg: Ostlandverlag, 1915).

67. Letter from Meinecke to Walter Goetz, in Friedrich Meinecke, *Ausgewählter Briefwechsel,* ed. Ludwig Dehio (Stuttgart: Koehler, 1962), 59.

68. Imanuel Geiss, *Der polnische Grenzstreifen 1914–1918: Ein Beitrag zur deutschen Kriegszielpolitik im Ersten Weltkrieg* (Lübeck: Matthiesen Verlag, 1960), 83.

69. Ibid., "Maßnahmen gegen weitere Verminderung der Bevölkerung der Provinz Ostpreußen durch die Ansiedlung rückwandernder Deutschrussen, 1915–1918," July 19, 1915 (Dok. 1), 150–51.

70. Welch, *Germany, Propaganda and Total War,* 179.

71. Ibid., 181.

72. See Hartfrid Krause, *USPD: Zur Geschichte der Unabhängigen Sozialdemokratischen Partei Deutschlands* (Frankfurt am Main: Europäische Verlangsanstalt, 1975); David W. Morgan,

measure the result of these differences. The radicalization of the war aims discussion also affected the right, and the Deutsche Vaterlandspartei (DVP; German Fatherland Party) was founded by annexationist agitators.[73] From its establishment in September 1917, the group spearheaded right-wing propaganda against socialism and peace without annexation. The foundation of these two new radical parties in 1917, the DVP and USPD, reflected the polarization of German society in general and of the war aims question in particular. It is difficult to assess the success of either side in attracting the support of the German people, but there were indications that the propaganda campaign of the annexationists was not as successful as they had hoped. At the outset of 1916, the Catholic Center Party supported the annexationist war aims of the conservatives, but it soon began to express skepticism about territorial aggrandizement.[74]

Faced with this loss of parliamentary allies, nationalists ratcheted up their agitation in support of the *Auslandsdeutsche* living in Russia, with the pan-Germans and the allied Verein für das Deutschtum im Ausland (VDA; Association for Germandom Abroad) taking the lead.[75] A series of appeals made by the VDA in 1911 and 1918 illuminates the politicization of the attitude toward foreign Germans. In 1911, the VDA had asked Germans to give money and support on behalf of German schools and religious and cultural institutions abroad, but it also emphasized that:

> Germans who are citizens of a foreign state can and should consciously fulfill the duties to their state, even as they safeguard their language and [German] nature. The republicans in Brazil and the German Russians who are true to the Tsar, the Catholics from South Tyrol as much as the Lutherans in Siebenbürgen all have a claim on our participation for the nourishment of their German nature and German spirit which resides in their homes and schools. . . .[76]

In contrast, a wartime appeal by the VDA redefined the connection between Germans on both sides of the *Reichsgrenze* in eschatological terms: "The Ger-

The Socialist Left and the German Revolution: A History of the German Independent Social Democratic Party, 1917–1922 (Ithaca: Cornell University Press, 1975).

73. Guratzsch, *Macht durch Organisation,* 147. For more on the DVP, see Heinz Hagenlücke, *Deutsche Vaterlandspartei: Die nationale Rechte am Ende des Kaiserreiches* (Düsseldorf: Droste, 1997).

74. Welch, *Germany, Propaganda and Total War,* 181. Note that Erzberger had penned his own declaration of annexationist war aims in 1914.

75. The VDA was founded in Berlin in 1908. It originated as the Allgemeine Deutscher Schulverein in 1881, working to promote German education in Germany and elsewhere. For a history of the organization, see Gerhard Weidenfeller, *VDA: Verein für das Deutschtum im Ausland. Allgemeiner Deutscher Schulverein (1881–1918): Ein Beitrag zur Geschichte des Nationalismus und Imperialismus im Kaiserreich* (Bern: Peter Lang, 1976).

76. March 1911 Aufruf by the Verein für das Deutschtum im Ausland, GStA PK, Rep. 89, Geheimes Zivilkabinett, Jüngere Periode, Nr. 15632, 2.

man people fight for their existence (*kämpft einen Daseinskampf*). . . . Thousands of those of our blood have been ripped from their hard work and ambitions and robbed of their belongings and futures without having done anything wrong. They have also fought and suffered in quiet renunciation and unbroken hope, surrounded by enemies, and true to the Fatherland. . . ."[77]

Meanwhile, German publishers distributed harrowing accounts of the suffering of Russian Germans at the hands of the tsarist regime and later under the Bolsheviks. These accounts often noted that the war had opened the eyes of Germans in the Reich to the continuity of suffering that united ethnic Germans on both sides of the border.[78]

This emphasis on suffering was not surprising because German soldiers discovered these Russian German communities just at the moment of their greatest trials. World War I displaced people throughout the combat zones in the western Russian Empire. In addition to the mobilization for war itself, scholars estimate that approximately 5 percent of the population of the Russian Empire —or over 6 million people—became refugees by 1916.[79] Much of this displacement occurred as civilians fled a brutal war and occupation, but some of it was a result of scapegoating by the tsarist regime of the Russian Germans for the failure of the Russian war effort.[80] Although they had loyally supported the tsar at the outbreak of war and many had served in the Russian army, Russian Germans were subject to increasing persecution as the war went on.[81] In December 1914, Germans and Jews living near the frontlines were deported behind the Vistula River.[82] In February 1915, German farmers were forbidden from purchasing land; moreover, those living in a 100- to 150-verst zone (1 verst = 1,067 kilometers) on the Russian western border were given up to sixteen months to sell all of their holdings at reduced prices. Other laws issued in 1914 and 1915 sharply restricted the use of the German language in public life; shortly thereafter, many Germans were involuntarily resettled to Siberia. Meanwhile, in May 1915, rioters plundered 759 German shops and homes in Moscow.[83] That same

77. July 1918 Aufruf by the Verein für das Deutschtum im Ausland, GStA PK, Rep. 89, Geheimes Zivilkabinett, Jüngere Periode, Nr. 15632, 222–23.

78. See, for example, Hans Fischer, *Nach Sibirien mit hunderttausend Deutschen. Vier Monate russische Kriegsgefangenschaft* (Berlin: Ullstein, 1915); Hans Friedrich, *Die Flucht aus Sibirien* (Reutlingen: Ensslin & Laiblin, 1916); George Jonck, *Meine Verschickung nach Sibirien, Erinnerungen und Erlebnisse eines rigaschen Buchhändlers* (Munich: J. F. Lehmann, 1916); August Kett, *Erlebnisse aus dem Jahre meiner Gefangenschaft in Russland, erzählt von A. Kett* (Regensburg: Friedrich Pustet, 1916); Alexander Geymann, *Dem Reiche der Knute entflohen: Dem Flüchtling nacherzählt* (Berlin: Scherl, 1917).

79. Gatrell, *Whole Empire Walking*, 3.

80. Long, *From Privileged to Dispossessed*, 227.

81. Long estimates that 40,000 Volga Germans served in the Russian army; Ibid., 224.

82. Sanborn, "Unsettling the Empire," 306.

83. Detlef Brandes, "Die Deutschen in Russland und der Sowjetunion," in *Deutsche im Ausland-Fremde in Deutschland: Migration in Geschichte und Gegenwart,* ed. Klaus Bade (Munich: C. H. Beck, 1992), 123.

month, an organization representing émigré Baltic Germans pleaded with the German chancellor, Theobald von Bethmann-Hollweg: "We have only one choice; to be annexed by Germany or massacred by Russia."[84]

As this statement suggests, the plight of the Russian Germans turned out to be a political boon for annexation advocates, allowing them to frame their demands not as a greedy land grab but as an attempt to save suffering ethnic Germans. The mainstream media breathlessly reported on the suffering *Auslandsdeutsche* and the hopes they invested in German occupation. One article in the *Gartenlaube* described Germans living in Riga desperately awaiting the arrival of German troops, when, "from their churches and houses, warm and homey voices (*heimatliche Stimmen*) would sound."[85] Another explained the joy in Mitau when German troops arrived: "After all of the unutterable hardships that Kurland and its cities have endured, this day was a festival of joy. The rebirth of Germandom was celebrated and hearts were filled with new hopes as the past retreated into the background for a moment." Meanwhile, other Baltic Germans were said to cry out: "Brothers, we await you!"[86] Just as tellingly, the socialist and moderate press generally ignored the *Auslandsdeutsche* altogether. Although they were comfortable explicitly challenging the territorial aggrandizement of the right, the demands for the protection of the *Auslandsdeutsche* were unanswerable.

The *Auslandsdeutsche* had a moral authority that was hard for even more moderate politicians to resist, as a speech by Bethmann-Hollweg on April 5, 1916, reveals. Under enormous pressure from both sides of the war aims debate to clarify his position, Bethmann-Hollweg finally broke his silence on the question of war aims.[87] He rejected the territorial demands of the annexationists, although not wholeheartedly agreeing to the socialists' demands for immediate peace negotiations.[88] He also insisted that Germany must serve as the protector of the Russian Germans. "It is our right and our duty to demand from the Russian government that they offer compensation for their human rights violations and open the door for our tortured and persecuted countrymen to leave Russian servitude."[89] Bethmann-Hollweg's statement of responsibility toward the Russian Germans moved him closer to the position long advocated by the pan-Germans and the VDA. This unambiguous support for the *Auslandsdeutsche* in Russia is particularly striking considering that it came at the very same moment

---

84. Letter from Otto von Veh to Bethmann-Hollweg, May 10, 1915, quoted in John Hiden, *The Baltic States and Weimar Ostpolitik* (New York: Cambridge University Press, 1987), 3.

85. Valerian Tornius, "Das malerische Riga," *Gartenlaube*, no. 8, 1916, 170.

86. Frieherrn von Behr, "Mitau," *Gartenlaube*, no. 46, 1916, 930.

87. On this pressure, see Welch, *Germany, Propaganda and Total War*, 161–94, regarding this speech, 179.

88. *Verhandlungen des Reichstags: Stenographische Berichte und Drucksachen*, Bd. 307, 856.

89. *Verhandlungen des Reichstags*, Bd. 307, 852–53.

that he was rejecting the annexationist goals also advocated by the right.[90] Beth-mann-Hollweg's commitment to the Russian Germans was tested less than three months later when 20,000 German peasants from the Volhynia region of western Ukraine, along with their farm animals, wagons, and implements, began to cross the German lines. Approximately half of them were brought to Germany, where they were put to work on farms desperately in need of labor, but another 8,000 remained in quarantine camps in occupied Poland.[91] In their wake, the War Ministry warned that the German state needed to begin planning for large numbers of Russian German immigrants.[92] On August 8, 1916, a meeting at the national Interior Ministry established that the Reich would share the cost of future Russian German migrants with the individual states where these migrants settled. These monies would be directed through the quasi-private Fürsorgeverein für Deutsche Rückwanderer (FdR; Welfare Organization for German Return Migrants). The 20,000 Volhynian peasants alone would cost 500,000 marks, but such expenses were justified by the potential benefits represented by an immigration of *Auslandsdeutsche*.[93] Proponents of the *Auslandsdeutsche* stressed the economic and cultural rejuvenation that they offered to a weary German nation. In other discussions of Russian German immigration, explicit references to the "holes in the labor force" that the *Auslandsdeutsche* could be expected to fill were a response to the very real male depopulation caused by the war.[94] In this context, the Prussian Ministry of Agriculture and Forestry spoke of the need to "win" Russian German migrants who might otherwise immigrate to North America.[95] Shortly thereafter, on March 8, 1917, the War Ministry allowed the FdR access to the Russian Germans in the POW camps, where it acted as advocates for the Russian Germans, both where they worked and in the camps themselves. The War Ministry explained the unprecedented authority granted to the FdR by stating that it was necessary "to secure their migration to Germany after the war . . . *to strengthen the future military power of the Reich.*"[96]

The *Auslandsdeutsche* were suffering, and German annexation along with the encouragement of migration—of non-Germans out of German territory and of Germans into it—would redeem that suffering for the higher cause of the

---

90. Welch, *Germany, Propaganda and Total War,* 199.

91. Kriegsministerium [hereafter KM] an Reichsamt des Innern [hereafter RAI], July 16, 1916, BArch R 1501/118385, 35.

92. KM Rundschreiben, July 5, 1916, BArch R 1501/118385, 15.

93. "Aufzeichnung über Ergebnis der am 8. August 1916 im Reichsamt des Innern abgehaltenen kommissarischen Besprechung, betreffend Regelung der bei der Rücksiedlung deutscher Kolonisten aus Wolhynien entstandenen Kosten," BArch R 1501/118385, 52–53.

94. Vereinigung für deutsche Siedlung und Wanderung, Aufruf, n.d. (most likely 1916), BArch R 1501/118385, 2; Auswärtiges Amt [hereafter AA] to the Prussian secretary of the interior, March 31, 1916, BArch R 1501/118385, 6.

95. Ministerium für Landwirtschaft, Domänen und Forsten to Staatssekretär des Innern, August 10, 1916, BArch R 1501/118385, 62.

96. KM Erlass, March 8, 1917, BArch R 1501/118385, 241. Emphasis in original.

German nation. In 1916, von Schwerin traveled to Ober Ost to examine its suitability for settlement.[97] Von Schwerin and Hugenberg then began making concrete plans for the new Ostland, Neudeutsche Wirtschaftsgesellschaft GmbH with the tacit approval of Ober Ost and in conjunction with several organizations of Baltic Germans. This new organization had a budget of 44,000 marks and a mandate to prepare for the immigration of large numbers of Germans to the Baltics.[98] In February and March 1917, German civilian planners from the Chancellery, the Foreign Office, and the Prussian and national interior ministries began concrete discussions about the future of occupied Eastern Europe.[99] The forced population displacements in the war zones due to Russian policy and the unplanned displacements caused by years of brutal conflict had left chaos in their wake. Germans, now in charge of this region, saw a golden opportunity to remake it in line with earlier annexationist dreams. German designs in Eastern Europe would be achieved using a variety of methods to displace the current non-German residents of the Baltics. Russian church and state property could simply be seized, but planners were more circumspect about using such methods on the non-Russian residents of the region. The Interior Ministry warned against a plan that called for directly expropriating Polish landowners in the Baltics and compensating them with land in the new Polish state. In response, Ober Ost recommended that financial pressure be used; the high level of debt combined with punitive taxes on Polish landowners would "encourage" them to sell to ethnic Germans.[100] Meanwhile, the peace treaty with Russia would include a clause stating that only Latvians who were still in the territories to be annexed by Germany would gain German citizenship. The huge numbers of Latvians that had been displaced during this conflict would not be able to become German citizens and, thus, could be barred from returning to their homes.[101] Finally, planners considered, but did not resolve, the question of whether Poles living in Prussia could be encouraged to move from newly German territory to a Polish puppet state.[102] Germans from the Reich and Russia would be brought in to replace the more diverse populations that had left the region, and the Russian state would pay compensation to Russian Germans for any property that they had left behind.[103]

This differentiated approach to the diverse ethnic groups in the Baltics re-

97. Liulevicius, *War Land on the Eastern Front*, 95.
98. Guratzsche, *Macht durch Organisation*, 368.
99. "Niederschrift über die Beratung vom 31 März 1917 btr. die Rückwanderung deutscher Stammesgenossen aus Rußland und sonstigen Ländern und die dieserhalb in die Friedensverträge aufzunehmenden Bestimmungen," BArch R 1501/118385, 222–30.
100. Ibid., 228.
101. Ibid., 227–28.
102. "Kommissare über die Frage der Rückwanderung und Ansiedlung deutscher Stammesgenossen aus Rußland und sonstigen Ländern," February 13, 1917, BArch R 1501/118385, 209.
103. Ibid., 211.

flected the fact that German ideas about the various people of the Baltics were
no longer as monolithic as they had been at the start of the war. In 1914, war aims
and propaganda emphasized and naturalized the "wall" between the backward
East and the cultured West, but by 1917, German propagandists viewed the
Baltics historically, stressing the long German history there as well as arguing
that the German presence had brought civilization to the other peoples in the region.[104] This new attention to history emphasized the changing shape of physical borders over time, the consistency of German presence in the region, and the
malleability of identities. In particular, the Latvians and Lithuanians became
symbols of Baltic impressionability, unlike the hopelessly primitive Russians.
Otto Blum wrote in the *Gartenlaube* that Latvians and Lithuanians were "sound
in mind and body" and were as a result "capable of being educated."[105] Meanwhile, one Ober Ost officer remarked that the Latvian "is a realistically minded
opportunist: whoever offers him the best chances he will join it. . . . If the Latvian sees that he gets further with German than with Latvian, he will very quickly
become German."[106] Befitting their supposed flexibility, the Latvians and, to a
lesser degree, the Poles were to be subject to a softer form of expropriation than
the Russians. Such ideas of Baltic malleability went hand in hand with German
fantasies about reordering the region. Adaptability and change were the slogans
of an imperialist German state interested in reordering its eastern borderlands.
History demonstrated both the long record of German involvement in the Baltics
and the susceptibility of the local Baltic population to German influence. German planners believed they could move entire populations around at will like
pawns on a chess board, and in the euphoria of the approaching victory in the
East, they believed that the defeated Russian Empire would pay for it.

Eastern Fantasies and Concrete Plans:
Brest-Litovsk and After

In March 1917, after years of growing tumult, revolutionaries in St. Petersburg
overthrew the tsar. At the urging of its French and British allies, the provisional
government of Alexander Kerensky kept Russia in the war against the Germans.
Nonetheless, the vastly overmatched Russian army lost huge amounts of territory
as the Germans went on the offensive in the summer. German forces stormed
Riga on September 3, 1917, and by mid-October, they took the Baltic islands of

104. Valerian Tornius, "Der Kampf um die Vormacht an der Ostsee," *Leipziger Illustrirte Zeitung*, 3899, March 21, 1918, 305. See also Paul Rohrbach's plans for Russian territory after the peace; for example, Paul Rohrbach, "Der Friede in Osteuropa und seine Folgewirkung nach Osten," *Leipziger Illustrirte Zeitung*, 3900, March 28, 1918. For more on Rohrbach, see Henry Cord Meyer, "Paul Rohrbach and His Osteuropa," *Russian Review* 2 (1942–1943): 60–69.
105. Otto Bloom, "Litauen—Land und Leute," *Gartenlaube*, no. 9, 1918, 117.
106. Alfred von Gossler, quoted in Liulevicius, *War Land on the Eastern Front*, 179.

Oesel, Dagö, and Moon. On November 7, 1917, the Bolshevik Revolution over-threw the teetering Kerensky provisional government, bringing a movement to power whose slogan was "bread, land and peace." The next day, the Bolsheviks proclaimed the Decree of the Termination of the War, and less than three weeks later, the Bolsheviks formally requested peace negotiations. These negotiations began at Brest-Litovsk on December 22, 1917. Prompted by Ludendorff and Hin-denburg, the German negotiators demanded the Ukraine, the Caucasus, and the Baltics. Aghast at the punitive German terms, Trotsky called off negotiations less than two months later, on February 10, 1918. Almost immediately, German troops went back on the offensive, capturing the rest of Latvia, Livonia, Estonia, Belarus and the Ukraine in short order. The Bolsheviks returned to the negotiating table by the end of the month and signed the Treaty of Brest-Litovsk on March 3, 1918.[107] The treaty brought the war in the East to a startlingly successful conclu-sion for the Germans. Russia relinquished control of Estonia, Latvia, Lithuania, Russian Poland, and much of Belarus. It also ceded some land to Turkey and rec-ognized an independent Finland and Ukraine. Contained in these territories were 54 percent of Russian industry, 33 percent of its rail system, 32 percent of its agri-culture, and 34 percent of its population.[108] Germany now had direct or indirect control over a line of territory stretching from Finland through the Caucasus.

Both before and after Germany concluded the negotiations that culminated in the uncompromisingly annexationist Treaty of Brest-Litovsk, German officials were divided as to how aggressively they should pursue an annexationist agenda.[109] Whereas Ludendorff forcefully pushed for annexing as much terri-tory as Germany could possibly lay claim, Richard von Kühlmann, the foreign minister, and his successor Paul von Hintze were substantially more moderate in their demands.[110] Assisted by Russia's weakness and its attendant desire to sue for peace at any price, Ludendorff successfully navigated the thickets of Ger-man administration and won the kaiser over to his side. Wilhelm himself was motivated not by purely administrative or military criteria; rather, he fancied himself the leader of a crusade to free Germans in the Baltics from Russian tyranny.[111] After the treaty was signed, the euphoric voices of Ludendorff and his conservative supporters overwhelmed the public sphere, although von Kühl-mann continued to voice doubts about whether the Germans were getting more

107. Separate treaties were also signed with the Ukraine and Finland on February 9, 1918. Winfried Baumgart and Konrad Repgen, *Brest-Litovsk* (Göttingen: Vandenhoeck and Ruprecht, 1969); John Wheeler-Bennett, *Brest-Litovsk, the Forgotten Peace, March 1918* (New York: W. W. Norton, 1971).

108. Liulevicius, *War Land on the Eastern Front*, 206.

109. Russian Germans played little role in the treaty negotiations; Oltmer, *Migration und Poli-tik,* 165.

110. Hans Erich Volkmann, *Die deutsche Baltikumpolitik zwischen Brest-Litovsk und Com-piègne: Ein Beitrag zur "Kriegszieldiskussion"* (Cologne: Böhlau, 1970).

111. Ibid., 98.

than they bargained for in attempting to annex a large swath of territory with so many foreign and hostile peoples.[112] In the Reichstag, the Conservative and National Liberal parties welcomed the treaty, even in its most provocative elements. In a speech on the Reichstag floor on March 15, Gustav Stresemann, a national liberal, echoed Ludendorff's maximalism, explaining that only the union of the Baltic territories with the German Empire would secure the eastern German border.[113] After the government made some efforts to assuage their concerns about the self-determination of the Baltic peoples, the more skeptical moderate parties, such as the Catholic Center and the Fortschrittliche Volkspartei (FVP; Progressive Liberal Party), also signed on to the provisions of the treaty.[114] The socialist parties in the Reichstag were more skeptical about the Treaty of Brest-Litovsk's ambitious annexationist agenda. Hugo Haase, the USPD leader, strongly condemned its harsh terms.[115] Striking workers loosely affiliated with the USPD explicitly linked their calls for more control at home with demands for Germany to refrain from forcing a punitive peace on the new Soviet Republic.[116] The more moderate SPD was conflicted about Brest-Litovsk's annexationist demands, and it abstained from the parliamentary vote called to ratify the treaty; even those SPD members wary of Lenin and Trotsky's new regime were uncomfortable with Germany's plans to annex large portions of Russian territory.[117] Fearful of government intentions regarding the annexation of the Baltic countries without the consent of the governed, the Center Party, FVP, SPD, USPD, and even the National Liberal Party pushed through a resolution guaranteeing the "truly democratic right of self-determination" for Poland, Lithuania, and Kurland.[118] The ratification of Brest-Litovsk and the concurrent passage of this resolution demonstrate the ambivalence of the more moderate parties within the Reichstag regarding the future of German occupied territories.

Civilian and military annexationists were undeterred by the doubts expressed in the press and on the floor of the Reichstag. Although they continued to discuss the timing, feasibility, and extent of the annexations and attendant population resettlement, by the time Brest-Litovsk had been dictated in winter 1918, the fact that territory would be annexed and populations resettled was no longer

112. Ibid., 119–21.
113. Ibid., 122–23.
114. Ibid., 128–29.
115. Welch, *Germany, Propaganda and Total War*, 224.
116. In the Reichstag, Haase claimed that the strikes were the result of negotiations at Brest-Litovsk being held up in January by the excessive German demands; Ibid.
117. The editorial policy of *Vorwärts* was similarly anti-annexation. See, for example, articles published in March and April 1918, such as the scathing critique of the "Baltic Barons"; "Kurland: Der Landesrat trägt dem deutschen Kaiser den Herzogshut an," *Vorwärts,* March 13, 1918; and the more moderate Alexander Libschütz, "Das Herzogtum Kurland," *Vorwärts,* April 22, 1918 (Libschütz was a former resident of Riga).
118. Volkmann, *Deutsche Baltikumpolitik,* 131.

in dispute.[119] The annexationist plans for population movement continued to focus on the Baltics. The region still controlled by Ober Ost was to be both a refuge for persecuted ethnic Germans from Russia and a new home for Germans in Germany seeking land and adventure in the new eastern German frontier. A meeting at the national Interior Ministry on March 2, 1918, the day before the signing of Brest-Litovsk, concluded that the Baltics could provide a homeland for 70,000–90,000 German families from both the Reich and the Russian interior.[120] A series of quasi-private groups including the Landgesellschft Kurland mbH, the Kurland GmbH, and the Neuland GmbH also encouraged Baltic migration among "workers, farmers, and their dependents" from the Reich, along with Russian Germans whose lives had been made untenable by anti-German repression and revolution. By July 1918, these organizations, made up of annexationists at the highest levels of the state and industry within Germany along with influential and wealthy Baltic landowners, controlled resources that totaled nearly 50 million marks of private and state funds.[121]

As civilians in Berlin prepared for the migration of Germans into the Baltics in the future, military occupation authorities confronted an emergency in the present as Poles, Balts, Germans, and Russians all sought to align themselves with the new political and geographical realities of a region now under German control.[122] Ober Ost responded on April 13 by banning the entry of Russians and Poles into its territory.[123] But even ethnic Germans, whose migration had been so prized in the preceding years, presented a problem for the state. A meeting at the national Interior Ministry on April 12 made it clear that neither the Reich nor the Baltics were prepared for an immediate immigration. A representative of Ober Ost stated that the Baltics would be able to handle large numbers of ethnic German migrants only in 1919. That said, the Interior Ministry warned that the migrants would not be willing to wait a year and thus that it was an economic and political imperative "to care for our ethnic German comrades (*Stammesgenossen*) in Ober Ost even if they cannot come to Germany itself."[124] Meanwhile, corruption and confusion defeated German attempts to institute a "solid border defense" against uncontrolled migration of both Germans and other ethnicities in the occupied territories.[125]

119. See Geiss, *Der polnische Grenzstreifen 1914–1918,* 86.
120. "Aufzeichnung über das Ergebnis der am 2. März 1918 im RAI abgehaltenen kommissarischen Besprechung über Rückwanderung Auslandsdeutscher und deutschstämmiger Ausländer," BArch R 1501/118386, 40–43.
121. Guratzsch, *Macht durch Organisation,* 370–71; Satzung der Landgesellschaft Kurland m.b.H., BArch R 1501/118387, 113–16.
122. Gatrell, *Whole Empire Walking,* 189.
123. Ober Ost Erlass, April 13, 1918, BArch R 1501/118387, 126.
124. "Aufzeichnung über das Ergebnis der am 12. April 1918 im RAI abgehaltenen kommissarischen Besprechung, betr. Aufnahme und Verwendung der aus Rußland nach Deutschland zurückwandernden reichsdeutschen und deutschstämmigen Personen," BArch R 1501/118386, 140–41.
125. Oltmer, *Migration und Politik,* 174–75.

Facing pressure from representatives of the Russian Germans, the urgent needs of ethnic Germans already on the move, and the still very much active plans for the resettlement of the Baltics and the Reich with Germans from Russia, the German government set up a central office to coordinate German migration in Eastern Europe. On May 29, 1918, the RWS was established and given the tasks of recruiting ethnic Germans, known as *Rückwanderer* (return migrants), to migrate to Germany, shepherding them to the German border, and assisting them once they arrived on German soil.[126] The RWS was to accomplish this through a network of branch offices established across occupied Eastern Europe.[127] As provided for by Brest-Litovsk, the Reich Chancellery assembled eighteen commissions led by the General Consul Dr. Gustav Wendschuh, from the Foreign Office, and Rittmeister Ernst Buchfink from the RWS, and including representatives from both the Prussian and Reich interior ministries as well as from the FdR and selected private citizens to travel throughout Russia to investigate German communities and their political reliability and practical suitability for migration to Germany and the territories in the Baltics that would potentially be annexed to the Reich.[128] The reports from the commissions along with unsolicited reports offered by ethnic German pressure groups inside Russia, such as the Pan-Russian League of Russian Citizens of German Nationality, painted a picture of communities of Germans in Russia who had maintained their German identity despite the challenges they faced: "Since they are so spread out, it is even more noteworthy that the colonists, with few exceptions, have kept their German identity and their national individuality. It is so pure that one can often distinguish between the language and customs of the Prussians and Hessens, the Swabians, the Bavarians, the Palatines and the Alsatians."[129] Even where Russian Germans had been loyal subjects of the tsar, one commissioner was quick to offer assurances that the Russian Germans "have kept their German identity almost pure in terms of language and custom. Their schools and churches are in full bloom. German teachers and German pastors have nurtured and kept their German identity in the colonies."[130] Meanwhile, an

---

126. "Bekanntmachung betreffend die Errichtung einer Reichsstelle für deutsche Rückwanderung und Auswanderung," May 29, 1918, BArch R 1501/118318, 21. For the history of the RWS and its successor organization, the Reichswanderungsamt, see Klaus Bade, "'Amt der verlorenen Worte': Das Reichswanderungsamt 1918–1924," *Zeitschrift für Kulturaustausch* 39, no. 3 (1989): 312–21.

127. BArch R 1501/118318, 50–54.

128. The commissions were provided for by Articles 17 and 21 of the Treaty of Brest-Litovsk. "Arbeitsplan für die deutschen Kommissionen zum Zwecke der Fürsorge für die deutschen Kriegs- und Zivilgefangenen sowie die deutschen Rückwanderer in Rußland," BARCH R 1501/118386, 170–71; "Dienstanweisung für die deutschen Kommissionen zum Zwecke der Fürsorge für die deutschen Rückwanderer in Russland," June 5, 1918, BArch R 1501/118387, 11–12.

129. "Die deutschen Ackerbauer Rußlands als Kolonisationsfaktor," written by the Allrussischer Verband russischer Bürger deutscher Nationalität, January 6, 1918, BArch R 1501/118385, 401.

130. "Denkschrift betreffend die deutschen Kolonisten in dem ehemaligen russischen Kaiserreich und ihre Rückwanderung nach Deutschland," GStA PK, 1 HA, Rep. 89, Nr. 13302, 7.

official from the RWS who met with representatives of the German community in Odessa assured his colleagues that "the German colonies that were established by the Russian government in southern Russia about one hundred years ago were . . . totally closed bodies."[131] These reports of pure German communities in Russia inspired Chancellor Georg von Hertling to reiterate his support for the migration of Russian Germans in a letter to the kaiser in August 1918: "In the former Russian empire—with the exception of the Baltics and Poland—there are one and a half million Russians of German descent. They have remained German according to their language, attitudes and customs. . . . Where they have not mixed [with the native population], they could represent a particularly valuable addition to our people."[132]

The acceptability of the Russian Germans often seemed to turn on how much they might have been corrupted by contact with Russians. One cavalry officer worried that the Germans held in camps with other nationalities could be affected both by the "primitive races" they were in contact with as well as the Bolshevik propaganda they had been subjected to.[133] Another official expressed concern that any migrant, regardless of his or her ethnicity, was potentially a "carrier" of revolutionary ideas.[134] Walter Jung, the director of the RWS, contrasted the Germans living in "closed communities" to those in the cities. "Here [in the cities] Bolshevik ideas could infiltrate more, and it cannot be doubted that many of these workers became Bolsheviks and, in contrast to the majority of the colonists, betrayed Germandom." As a result, it was necessary to "carefully sift through and observe all those who seek to enter Germany."[135] Tellingly, Jung contrasted Germans with Bolsheviks and not with Russians. The elective quality of Bolshevism made it different than the ethnic essentialism that adhered to the stereotype of the Russian Slav; although Germans could hardly become Russians, they could quite easily betray their German identity by becoming Bolsheviks (see chap. 6).

In a continuation of the prewar statist position that valued the well-being of the German state over the interests of foreign Germans, a few government officials made it clear that they desired as immigrants only those Germans who could be useful to Germany itself. A meeting held at the national Interior Ministry in 1916 concluded that "everyone who wants to return to Germany is not equally desirable. Instead, [we should allow] only those who represent a clear use to the German people."[136] This idea found its fullest expression in a 1918 proposal

131. Bericht über eine Unterredung mit Vertretern Odessaer deutschen Kolonisten, n.d. (visit took place March 29, 1918), BArch R 1501/118385, 236.
132. Reichskanzler to the kaiser, August 27, 1918, GStA PK, Rep. 89, Nr. 13064, 18.
133. V. Pfuehl to RAI, April 11, 1918, BArch R 1501/118386, 144–45.
134. Gatrell, *Whole Empire Walking*, 189.
135. RWS to Staatsekretär des Innern, August 1, 1918, BArch R 1501/118387, 293.
136. "Vorläufige Aufzeichnung über das Ergebnis der am 3. Oktober 1916 in RAI abgehaltenen kommissarischen Beratung betreffend Regelung der überseeischen Rückwanderung nach dem Krieg," BArch R 1501/118385, 118.

to naturalize only families with sons who could contribute to the war effort.[137] Up until this proposal, with few exceptions, the state had operated from the belief that assisting the Russian Germans would necessarily aid the Reich itself. However, here a more statist position was taken—only those of immediate and obvious use to the state as cannon fodder (along with their immediate relatives) would be granted German citizenship. It is important to note, however, that, contrary to the debate about the 1913 citizenship law, when such a sentiment was dominant and ultimately determined the shape of the resulting legislation, the proposal put forth in 1918 was tentative, immediately faced a storm of criticism, and was never actually put into practice.[138] Despite a few reservations about the political unreliability of Russian Germans or the burdens that they might place on the German state and society, in 1918 most government officials did not clearly separate the fate of the *Auslandsdeutsche* from the fate of the German state, and proposals to limit the migration of Russian Germans were political nonstarters. The financial and logistical burdens of Russian German migrations may have became increasingly clear throughout 1918; however, this did not diminish either the German sense of responsibility or the feeling that the migration to and from the East would secure the future of Germany in a new European order.

World War I brought unprecedented suffering to a German nation decimated by battlefield losses, starvation, and disease. At this time, the German state also recognized millions of ethnic Germans inside Russia, who were themselves facing displacement and persecution as in need of the protection of the German state. Meanwhile, German military and civilian planers viewed the possibility of wide-ranging annexations (already under discussion before the war began but made a tantalizing reality by the German success against the overmatched Russian army) as not merely an opportunity for expanding its frontiers but also as a means for remaking the populations within those boundaries. In this context, migration—of Germans from Germany and Russia to the Baltics, and of non-Germans from these territories—was a solution to the problems of the German people both in Germany and in Russia. By annexing and repopulating the Baltics, Germany would secure its eastern borders while also providing space for colonial expansion. This tension between expansion and defense was reproduced in a completely different context after the end of World War I, when a weakened German state with newly shrunken borders confronted a new set of challenges.

137. Preussische Ministerium des Innern [hereafter PMI] to AA, August 10, 1918, BArch R 1501/118387, 236–37.
138. Einbürgerungskommission aus Odessa an RWS, October 21, 1918, BArch R 1501/118388, 112.

As the German Empire collapsed into revolution in November 1918, one of Chancellor Max von Baden's final acts was to reassure the *Auslandsdeutsche* that Germany would protect them:

> Do not doubt the German people! . . . Those of you who have suffered and fought for your German fatherland through these difficult years of war, will not be forgotten by the new Germany. As long as it is within the power of the German state and the German people to alleviate the suffering of the war and its consequences, [Germany] shall care for the Germans abroad just as it cares for the Germans in its more narrow (*engeren*) homeland.[139]

With these words, von Baden made a promise to the *Auslandsdeutsche* that the new republic would find nearly impossible to fulfill. Millions of Germans from territories that had been under German control until the Treaty of Versailles suddenly found themselves *Auslandsdeutsche,* symbols of German defeat. Agitation on behalf of these *Auslandsdeutsche* grew in visibility and virulence in a postwar climate of defeat and resentment. And, facing its own tenuous legitimacy as a representative of the German *Volk,* the postwar state could not afford to ignore their claims.

Equally important, Weimar Germany contended not merely with the immigration of ethnic Germans but also with an onslaught of hundreds of thousands of ethnic Jews and Russians. The complicated responses to these non-German immigrants refigured the principles of ethnic solidarity and humanitarian obligation that were already present in the heady interlude between the signing of the Treaty of Brest-Litovsk and the defeat. Furthermore, the practical concerns that had already begun to weigh on the heads of German officials who were envisioning a massive immigration in 1918 gained even more salience as actual immigrants began to arrive in financially strapped postwar Germany. The very fluidity that had been a source of promise in early 1918 became an immense burden on the fledgling German republic.

139. "Der Kanzler an die Auslandsdeutschen," *Vorwärts,* November 8, 1918.

2. "Now We Were the Border"

The Freikorps Baltic Campaign

With the German defeat and revolution in November 1918, the self-confident empire that had laid claim to the Baltics was nothing more than a memory. Taking its place was a fledgling state barely able to exert control over the population living within its own shrunken borders, much less assume responsibility for the dreams of Baltic colonization that had tantalized nationalists several months earlier. The expansionist dreams fueled by the war were unattainable by the new republic, but the German Freikorps continued to fight in the Baltics through 1919, nominally invited by the Latvian state and with the tacit acceptance of the victorious allies as a bulwark against the Bolsheviks. Although the Freikorps soldiers were commanded by a general of the Reich, they were not regular soldiers but volunteers drawn to the Baltics by a complex set of motivations, including the desire to fight Bolshevism, a wish for adventure, and the dream of Baltic settlement. The Freikorps were small bands of paramilitary fighters organized around a large number of charismatic leaders. Gustav Noske, the national defense minister of the republic, authorized their formation on January 4, 1919, as allies in the fight against Bolshevik insurrection in Germany. Until they were disbanded in the aftermath of the Kapp Putsch in spring 1920, the Freikorps fought in numerous battles, from the streets of Berlin and Munich to the Polish borderlands and the Baltic plains. The number of men fighting with the Freikorps in the Baltics fluctuated and thus cannot be ascertained with any certainty, but estimates range from 20,000 to 40,000. In the Baltics, the Freikorps fought as part of the VI Reserve Korps under the command of General Rüdiger von der Goltz, who had previously assisted the Finns in driving back

Bolshevik forces. A special command established in East Prussia, the Armee Oberkommando Grenzschutz Nord (OKN), had authority over the entire mission. The Freikorps campaign in the Baltics was a muddled and violent attempt to work through long-standing fantasies of eastern expansion, fantasies that had been encouraged by the victories in the East during World War I and made more urgent by the humiliation of defeat.

Freikorps ideology in general, but especially that of the *Baltikumkämpfer*, was an attempt to come to terms with the confused legacy of defeat and revolution—the loss not only of the state but also of the dreams of territorial expansion and military triumph that died with the defeat and revolution in November 1918. These feelings of frustration and betrayal inspired by defeat became the impetus for a wild and unchecked creativity. The Baltics became the host to a variety of projects, utopias, and remappings, the energy of which belie the notion of Germany as "tired" that dominates the accounts of both the Freikorps fighters themselves and many of the historians who have written about Weimar Germany as a society desperately attempting to grasp an elusive normalcy.[1] Some members of the Freikorps chose to adopt atavistic identities, comparing themselves to seventeenth-century brigands, others aspired to acquire Latvian citizenship to become gentleman farmers on the Baltic plains, and still others believed that the campaign in Latvia could provide a base for a final effort to avenge the defeat and the humiliation of the postwar settlement. Finally, this freedom of the Freikorps in the Baltics was often a license for pillage and brutality—the Freikorps Baltic campaign was saturated in blood. This violence must be read as a key component of Freikorps creativity. The form of the territorial boundaries of Germany, the nature of its state, and the constitution of its people were all up for grabs in 1919, the year of the Freikorps' Baltic adventure. Violence was both a symptom and constitutive element of this chaos. The very contradictions of the Freikorps—a group pledged to defend the republic at the same time that many of its members conspired to defeat it, the desire to defend Germany against Bolshevism while also projecting German power outward, and the wish to assert German national identity by assuming Latvian citizenship—were symptomatic of larger paradoxes during this time of protean borders and uncertain identities.

1. On the (relative success) of demobilization, see Richard Bessel, *Germany after the First World War* (Oxford: Clarendon Press, 1993). On the quick return to "normal" gender roles after the upheaval of war, see Ute Daniel, *The War from Within: German Working-Class Women in the First World War*, trans. Margaret Ries (New York: Berg, 1997). Dirk Schumann, *Politische Gewalt in der Weimarer Republik 1918–1933: Kampf um die Strasse und Furcht vor dem Bürgerkrieg* (Essen: Klartext, 2001), discusses the anti-Bolshevik activities of the *Einwohnerwehren* in the early years of the republic and explains them as inspired by a longing for a return to normalcy. See also the work on the German revolution, in which the fateful social democratic compromises with the right are ascribed to the party's fear of revolution. Peter von Oertzen, *Betriebsräte in der Novemberrevolution* (Düsseldorf: Droste, 1963); Reinhard Rürup, *Probleme der Revolution in Deutschland 1918/1919* (Wiesbaden: Steiner, 1968).

Viewing the Freikorps' confusion of national identity and territory within this context disrupts the standard historiographical teleology that regards the Freikorps primarily as proto-Nazis or as a bridge between the Baltic military utopia articulated during World War I and the German Eastern Campaign in World War II.[2] Although the Nazis surely drew on the fantasies and resentments of the Freikorps and many Freikorps volunteers later joined the Nazi party, the Freikorps also must be read on their own terms.[3] Freikorps volunteers were motivated by a logic or, really, by several overlapping but at times inconsistent logics that diverged from the image later appropriated by Nazi idealogues: for some, a desire to settle in the Baltics and abandon German citizenship; for others, an emphasis on the expansion of German territory; and for yet others, the existential possibility of freedom on the Baltic plains. The ideology of the Freikorps, produced by defeated and humiliated soldiers for a defunct state, differed radically from that of the more self-confident eras that both preceded and followed it. The Freikorps were at the radical edge of the disarticulation of the tenuous consensus of the Wilhelmine era about the shape of German state and society.

Eastern Settlement Plans and the Motivation of the Freikorps

The Freikorps were not the first group to imagine settlement in the east as an alternative to living in a Germany hobbled by defeat. In fall 1918, Hindenburg and Ludendorff seriously considered the possibility of continuing the war from Kurland.[4] In early 1919, August Winnig, the German plenipotentiary in the Baltics, considered the creation of a Baltic state encompassing Lithuania, Latvia (Livland and Kurland), and both East and West Prussia, which would be associated with Germany but free from the strictures of the expected peace.[5] Also in early 1919, after the armistice had been signed but two months before the terms of the Treaty of Versailles were known, several leading members of the kaiser's government began to discuss the possibility of reestablishing a German state in

2. This view was first articulated by the Nazis themselves. Friedrich Wilhelm von Oertzen, *Die deutschen Freikorps 1918–1923* (Munich: Bruckmann, 1936). See also Hagen Schulze, *Freikorps und Republik, 1918–1920* (Boppard am Rhein: H. Boldt, 1969); Liulevicius, *War Land on the Eastern Front;* Robert G. L. Waite, *Vangard of Nazism: The Free Corps Movement in Postwar Germany, 1918–1923* (Cambridge, Mass.: Harvard University Press, 1952).

3. Bruce Campbell, "The Freikorps as Model and Myth in German Political Life, 1918–1935," unpublished paper presented at the German Studies Association Annual Meeting, September 18–21, 2003, New Orleans, LA.

4. Arthur Rosenberg, *Die Entstehung der deutschen Republik 1871–1918* (Berlin: Rowohlt, 1928), 126.

5. Hagen Schulze, "Der Oststaatplan 1919," *Vierteljahreshefte für Zeitgeschichte* 18, no. 2 (1970), 131.

the east, a scheme they termed the *Oststaat* plan. The planned state, which would have encompassed much of eastern Prussia, was an attempt "to save of Germandom, that which it is possible to save . . . [and when Poland fell] it would be possible to return to Germany."[6] The new *Oststaat* would be a *"Freistaat,"* invested with greater autonomy than the prewar *Länder,* and one backer even considered the affiliation of such a *Freistaat* with Poland.[7] None of these plans ever left the drawing board, and even if they had been proposed, it is highly unlikely that such a solution would have been acceptable to the Entente. Nonetheless, in their very unrealizability, these schemes reveal the desperation of their backers and their desire to find a way of expressing the German values they held most dear, even if this required jettisoning the existing German state, much of its territory, and most of its citizens.

Just as some German military and civilian leaders contemplated the establishment of an exile government, international circumstances arose to make eastern settlement attainable in a very different context. Article 12 of the armistice signed between Germany and the Allies that ended World War I states, "All German troops at present in territories which before the war formed part of Russia must . . . return to within the frontiers of Germany [as they existed on August 1, 1914] as soon as the Allies shall think the moment suitable, having regard to the internal situation of these territories."[8] In authorizing German forces to remain in the Baltics, the Allies were motivated by the rapid advancement of Soviet troops in late fall 1918. Two days after hostilities in the West drew to a close on November 11, 1918, Soviet forces began a major offensive in the Baltics. Facing exhausted and demoralized troops, the Red Army rolled through Estonia and Latvia, taking Riga on January 3, 1919.

In an agreement finalized on December 29, 1918, Winnig negotiated with Latvia to allow the organization of a Baltic German force, the Baltische Landeswehr, which would include substantial participation by volunteers from Germany. These men would join the troops of the German Eighth Army already in the Baltics, who had renamed themselves the Iron Division and were led by Major Josef Bischoff. As part of the agreement to organize this force, Winnig extracted a promise that the Latvians would allow the German members of the Landeswehr to apply for Latvian citizenship if they had served for at least four weeks.[9] Meanwhile, the Anwerbestelle Baltenland was established to enlist Freikorps volunteers for the Baltic mission. When this treaty was published in Germany on January 9, 1919, applicants immediately overwhelmed the new Anwerbestelle Baltenland offices in Berlin and other cities across the Reich.[10] The

6. Ibid., 123.
7. Ibid., 130.
8. Harry R. Rudin, *Armistice 1918* (Hamden, Conn.: Archon Books, 1967), 428–29.
9. Waite, *Vanguard of Nazism,* 104.
10. Ibid., 136.

support of the German Workers' and Soldiers' Councils for the establishment of these recruiting offices is further evidence of the widespread popularity of the Freikorps mission in the Baltic.[11] In addition to the recruitment offices themselves, specific Freikorps units placed advertisements in various German newspapers extolling the benefits of volunteering for the Freikorps campaign in the Baltics. An ad was even placed in the social democratic organ *Vorwärts* (which had been opposed to annexation during the war) promising bonuses, family allotments, and good food in addition to "excellent colonization opportunities."[12] Settlement was at the forefront of the recruitment effort. According to Defense Minister Noske, "what wasn't stated in printed advertisements, the recruitment officers promised verbally."[13]

Freikorps commanders were adamant that theirs was a mission to defend Germany and Europe against Bolshevik aggression. General Rüdiger von der Goltz, in charge of the Freikorps mission, wrote, "We were the last wall of protection for the Reich against the East."[14] Yet, despite this ostensible mission of defending Germany from an outside enemy, von der Goltz saw the Freikorps' task as one and the same, whether they fought against Russian Bolsheviks in the Baltics or German communists in Munich.[15] If the Freikorps were fighting the same enemy within and without Germany, if the German state and many of its citizens had proven treacherous, the Bolsheviks had already breached the German defenses, rendering the concept of defense versus offense relative at best. Indeed, at the time the Freikorps soldiers were first being recruited, the Treaty of Versailles had not yet been negotiated. Germans, not just the Freikorps, could not be certain which territory would or would not be included in the final shape of the new republic. Furthermore, at the same time as the Freikorps conceptualized their mission as a last line of defense against Bolshevism, they and their supporters also spoke of the Baltic campaign as an opportunity to rescue lost German prestige and escape the strictures imposed by the lost war. Winnig saw the possibility for redemption in the east, "Prestige on the seas is lost, the way to the West blocked off. But here in the East the path must be kept open—it is the path to the world. . . ."[16]

Far afield from these geopolitical concerns, both contemporary observers and Freikorps memoirists writing in the later part of the republic stressed settlement as an important, perhaps the decisive, motivating factor for the partici-

11. Hiden, *Baltic States and Weimar Ostpolitik*, 16.

12. Ad from March 10, 1919, cited in Waite, *Vanguard of Nazism*, 105. See also a similar ad that appeared in *Vorwärts*, March 16, 1919, from the Anwerbestelle Baltenland.

13. Gustav Noske, *Von Kiel bis Kapp: Zur Geschichte der deutschen Revolution* (Berlin: Verlag für Politik und Wirtschaft, 1920), 177.

14. Rüdiger von der Goltz, quoted in Oertzen, *Deutschen Freikorps*, 57.

15. Rüdiger von der Goltz, *Ernste Gedanken zum 10. Geburtstage der deutschen Republik 9.11.1928* (Berlin: Brunnen Verlag-Winckler, 1928), 13.

16. Quoted in Waite, *Vanguard of Nazism*, 101.

pation of ordinary volunteers in the Baltic Freikorps campaign. One former Freikorps soldier remarked:

> One point convinced many to go to the Baltics. The Latvian government had promised every German soldier who took part in expelling the Bolsheviks up to 80 Morgen of land to settle on. Settlement organizations that provided information both orally and in writing were represented in every formation and worked according to uniform directives of the General Commando. . . . the work took place in view of the goal of settling in Kurland.[17]

The chief of the army General Staff also stressed the importance of settlement for Freikorps volunteers: "These volunteers have come on the basis of promises that were made to them in writing from the German government—from Reichskommissar Winnig. These promises include the pledge of Latvian citizenship that will allow them to settle in Latvia without any further difficulties. If this promise had not been made, the majority of the men would not have volunteered."[18]

The treaty signed between Germany and Latvia on December 29 did not explicitly mention settlement. Nonetheless, there was a tacit understanding among the German government, the Freikorps volunteers, and the Latvian government that the latter would grant citizenship to the members of the Freikorps so they would have the opportunity to settle in Latvia in the future.[19] Meanwhile, the Baltic German landowners renewed their wartime pledge to sell one-third of their land—or enough for 15,000 people—to German settlers at prewar (and, hence, pre-inflation) prices.[20] German Freikorps would have to pay only 10 percent of the value of the land they wished to buy at the time of sale, and cooperatives established by the Baltic Germans and the Freikorps settlers would finance the remaining 90 percent.[21]

For 75 pfennig, prospective Freikorps volunteers could buy Kurt Stavenhagen's pamphlet *Die eigene Scholle in der Baltenmark* at all Anwerbestelle Baltenland offices.[22] *Die eigene Scholle* spelled out a vision of Baltic settlement that began by noting the desperate circumstances inside of Germany itself: "Millions of Germans are asking themselves the question: 'Where should we go and what should we do in order to get bread for our families?'"[23] The solution, Staven-

17. Johannes Zobel, *Schüler freiwillig in Grenzschutz und Freikorps* (Berlin: Grundel, 1932), 62.

18. Chef des Generalstabes des Feldheeres to AA, June 17, 1919, Politisches Archiv des Auswärtiges Amts [hereafter PAAA] R 21791.

19. Schulze, *Freikorps und Republik, 1918–1920,* 133.

20. Walter von Rohrscheidt, *Unsere Baltikum-Kämpfer: Die Ereignisse im Baltikum 1918 und 1919* (Braunschweig: Albert Limbach, 1938), 18.

21. The actual price was determined through a somewhat complicated formula, but it was essentially the prewar price; "Bericht über die Siedlungssituation," BArch R 8025/20, 7.

22. Anwerbestelle Baltenland, "Siedlungsmöglichkeiten im Osten," BArch R 8025/20, 21.

23. Kurt Stavenhagen, *Die eigene Scholle in der Baltenmark: Neue Existenzmöglichkeiten für Landwirte, Offiziere, Techniker, Ingenieure, usw.* (Stuttgart: Greiner & Pfeiffer, 1919), 2.

hagen argued, was emigration, and his text was an attempt to convince Germans of the merits of Baltic settlement. Similar to wartime publications on the Baltics, he emphasized that the hitherto unremarkable agricultural production of the region was not caused by the lack of fertility of the land but was a function of "insufficient cultivation as a result of unfavorable economic, political and social circumstances."[24] According to Stavenhagen, the Latvians were grateful to their German liberators and this gratitude would translate into a "friendly relationship." He added that because Germany was now a socialist republic, the republican government in Latvia would be even more welcoming toward the Germans settling in their land.[25] More important, however, than the cooperation of the Latvians was the existence of a strong German community to aid the new settlers. Although Stavenhagen emphasized that German settlers would not, at least at the outset, have an easy life in the Baltics, he promised that German solidarity would emerge triumphant and that "energetic and cooperative self-help on the part of the settlers, aided by the local German community, will overcome these difficulties."[26] Migration to the Baltics further offered the opportunity for Germans "to settle in connection with a strong Germandom that is rooted to the soil, without the danger of becoming lost to their own people."[27] Stavenhagen called on ideas of both civic and ethnic solidarity in painting this utopian vision of the "Baltenmark." The Freikorps settlers could expect German support for ethnic and emotional reasons and Latvian support for political ones, demonstrating that historiographical assumptions about the incompatibility of civic and ethnic definitions of belonging are often anachronistic when applied to this period. Verbal promises from recruiters and texts such as Stavenhagen's combined to instill a "Baltic fever" among Freikorps volunteers.[28]

But settlement was not the sole motivating force for ordinary Freikorps soldiers. There were many who were attracted by the lack of order and rules in the Baltics. Some were criminals who felt they could escape punishment by fighting in the Baltics.[29] For others, this sense of freedom took on an existential quality. Franz Nord wrote that the Baltics were a "magical center" a "new German force field (*deutsches Kraftfeld*), that could replace the lost homeland, and at the very least would provide a break in the deathly grip that encircled [Germany].[30] The Baltic plains provided not only a release from the chains that currently bound Germany but, as the phrase "force field" suggests, from boundaries altogether.

24. Ibid., 6. The idea that German work created German territory was a mainstay of many geographers and *Ostforscher* of the postwar period. See Herb, *Under the Map of Germany.*

25. Stavenhagen, *Eigene Scholle in der Baltenmark*, 14.

26. Ibid., 13.

27. Ibid., 2.

28. Gustav Noske, *Von Kiel bis Kapp*, 177.

29. Rohrscheidt, *Unsere Baltikum-Kämpfer*, 29.

30. Franz Nord, "Der Krieg im Baltikum," in *Der Kampf um das Reich*, ed. Ernst Jünger (Essen: Kamp, 1929), 63.

Erich Balla, a Freikorps soldier, explained that hearing about the Freikorps in the Baltics was "a salvation. . . . Here was once again a purpose, a goal to live for!"[31] In contrast, Ernst von Salomon, a former Freikorps soldier and later editor of the Freikorps newsletter *Reiter Gen Osten,* wrote in his memoirs that "we marched without idea, without a goal, without a purpose."[32] But for both von Salomon and Balla, when they left Germany, "We found ourselves on the other side of the world of bourgeois norms. . . . More had been broken for us than the values that we had all held, the crust that held us prisoner had also been broken. The connections broke; we were free. And our blood suddenly rose up in adventure and this blood drove us into the distance and into danger. . . ."[33]

The Capture of Riga

Freikorps began to arrive in the Baltics in large numbers during early 1919, with the ostensible mission of protecting Latvia and Europe against Bolshevism. These soldiers served either with the Baltic German *Landeswehr* or the Iron Division Freikorps. In February 1919, both these groups were placed under the command of General von der Goltz. Walter Eberhard von Medem, a Freikorps commander, described the confusing scene that greeted his Freikorps on their arrival in the Baltics: "Men, horses and carts sank up to their knees in clay. Snow and pouring rain made the ground disappear. In addition to this, the few telephone lines had been cut and the inhabitants were undependable." It was, he concluded, "a war conducted in darkness."[34] In von Salomon's words, "the forest was full of secrets."[35] The Latvians and even the Bolsheviks appear in Freikorps memoirs less as full-fledged enemies than as spectral presences. One memoirist described moving through the countryside near Mitau. He found traces of a Bolshevik presence, but there was "no enemy to be seen. Everything was empty. Deep, uncanny silence—a few crows flew overhead. . . ."[36] Another wrote of the Latvians' gaining strength at night: "The night came, and with it the strength of the Latvians. One must know it, this night overhead: pitch black, so

31. Balla, *Landsknechte wurden wir,* 16.

32. Ernst von Salomon, "Sturm auf Riga," in *Der Kampf um das Reich,* ed. Ernst Jünger (Essen: Kamp, 1931), 106. Salomon's participation in right-wing politics in Germany is complicated. He was sentenced to five years for his part in the conspiracy that murdered Foreign Minister Walter Rathenau in 1922, after 1933 rejected Nazism but was briefly imprisoned by the Americans in 1945–1946, and later in 1951 caused a controversy when he published his *Fragebogen* (Hamburg: Rowohlt, 1951), containing ironic answers to questions about his involvement in the Nazi regime.

33. Ernst von Salomon, *Die Geächteten* (Gütersloh: Bertelsmann, 1930), 83.

34. Walter Eberhard von Medem, *Stürmer von Riga: Die Geschichte eines Freikorps* (Leipzig: Franz Schneider, 1935), 46, 51.

35. Salomon, "Sturm auf Riga," 108.

36. Eugen von Engelhardt, *Der Ritt nach Riga: Aus den Kämpfen der Baltischen Landeswehr gegen die Rote Armee 1918–1920* (Berlin: Volk und Reich, 1938), 49.

that one cannot see three steps ahead. Whether or not it was organized, the Latvians changed with the coming of darkness."[37] The uncanny nature of the war was intensified by the fact that this was essentially a guerilla conflict, in which battlelines were unclear and the division between enemies and friends uncertain.[38] Bolshevik Russians, Latvians, and even former German POWs fighting on the side of the Bolsheviks collapsed into a hazy "Eastern" enemy. The Freikorps were fighting less against Bolshevism or any clear enemy than a collection of ill-defined ghosts.

Many Freikorps memoirists expressed their surprise and delight at finding German speakers in this threatening landscape. "There, above us, in the three Russian North Sea provinces, there lived Germans like us: men of the same blood, the same language, the same race. The German blood that flowed into the Baltic lands over a half a millennium earlier was still alive and fertile."[39] But this recognition was also not always what it seemed. Freikorps fighters in the Baltics, just like the soldiers who had fought on the Eastern Front during World War I, were confronted with seemingly familiar sights—German people, the German language, German architecture—that had become displaced from their usual contexts. The image of a girl who spoke German but turned out to be of another ethnicity is a staple of Freikorps accounts. For example, von Salomon described "a very lovely girl, dressed in an urban style, none of this Latvian peasant garb. We all turned our eyes. And the girl spoke German! My god, she had a melodious voice!" It turned out, however, that "No, she is a Russian. . . ."[40] Von Salomon depicted this German-Russian girl as friendly; her German speech and manners determined her friendly behavior rather than her Russian ethnicity. Confusion marks the accounts of other Freikorps soldiers as well; however, for them, this misrecognition did not always end as peacefully. Balla repeatedly described his hero's encounters with beautiful young women who were rarely, if ever, what they appeared at first glance; occasionally they seduced and betrayed him, whereas at other times, they proved a source of succor and support.[41]

Freikorps members tried to find historical reference points both for their own actions and for the strange vistas of the Baltics. Balla described a "secret power that eminated from the distant, very distant Thirty Years war," whereas Johannes Zobel saw "the living image of 1812" in the ravaged landscape.[42] Von Salomon described "units carrying *Bundschuh* flags of the Reformation's Peasant

37. Ludwig F. Gengler, *Rudolf Berthold: Sieger in 44 Luftschlägen im Bruderkampfe für Deutschlands Freiheit* (Berlin: Schliessen-Verlag, 1934), 148.

38. Medem, *Stürmer von Riga,* 46.

39. Rohrscheidt, *Unsere Baltikum-Kämpfer,* 12.

40. Salomon, *Geächteten,* 94.

41. see Balla, *Landsknechte wurden wir,* (for the former) 19–22, 126, 176, 180–81; (for the latter) 102–3, 185.

42. Ibid., 55; Zobel, *Schüler freiwillig in Grenzschutz und Freikorps,* 97.

Wars, and troops from Hamburg following the old Hansa flag, singing pirate songs, and letting their beards grow out. Before battles, a friend doffed a beret like that of *Wandervögel* or minstrels of the high Middle Ages."[43] In donning this wide variety of uniforms and flags, Freikorps fighters were reaching beyond the German state that currently existed or the one that had recently been defeated to a form of German identity that transcended loyalty to any specific state but was, instead, rooted in a pre-nineteenth-century Germanic past. To be sure, the young Wilhelmine state had sought to legitimate itself through reference to a past that predated the *Reichsgründung* in 1871, but this took on a different meaning with the loss of this state as a stable referent. These historical identities were no longer invoked to prop up the legitimacy of the state but to *replace* it.

At the same time that they adopted these varied identities in a new and strange landscape, some Freikorps fighters took concrete steps toward fulfilling their dream of Baltic settlement. As men arrived in the Baltics to fight with the Iron Division, Josef Bischoff, its commander, repeated to them the promise that, once the fighting was done, they could begin a new life as farmers in Latvia.[44] By the end of April 1919, many Freikorps soldiers had sold their property in Germany to buy land in Kurland, deciding that they would not return to Germany. These soldiers organized themselves into mutual aid societies, and some promptly began to work the land.[45] The soldiers' newspaper, *The Drum*, was filled with wild promises and practical instructions for prospective settlers. Franz Nord described the coming of settlers as if the land itself were awakening:

> The settlers advanced with wagons packed high with *Pfaff* sewing machines on featherbeds, with plows and scythes. At the front of this train, the father of [the] family rode wearing a dress gray shirt, with his weapon in the manner of the Boers resting on his thigh. Craftsmen and farmers peeled away from the Battalions. . . . Sawmills awoke after years of sleep, rusted machines creaked tiredly. . . . carts stumbled over the fields—piled with the freshly cut shingles that found a ready market throughout the area.[46]

The Freikorps also began their fight against the Bolsheviks. In mid-February, shortly after von der Goltz's arrival, he launched an offensive against the Red Army. Starting from their base in Libau, German forces took the historically German towns of Goldingen, Windau, and Mitau in quick succession. Within a few weeks, the coast of Latvia had been "liberated" from the Bolsheviks, and the Freikorps began making plans for an advance on the prize of the Baltic cam-

43. Salomon, summarized in Liulevicius, *War Land on the Eastern Front*, 236.
44. Balla, *Landsknechte wurden wir*, 34.
45. Noske, quoted in Schulze, *Freikorps und Republik, 1918–1920*, 158.
46. Nord, "Krieg im Baltikum," 80.

paign—Riga. In negotiations with the Berlin government, which was already under strong pressure from the Allies to withdraw the Freikorps, von der Goltz used the settlement hopes of his soldiers as a justification for his remaining in the Baltics. If he left, he argued, he could not guarantee that his troops would leave with him.[47] At the same time, the Freikorps not only fought against the Bolsheviks but also turned on their Latvian allies. In a coup on April 16, 1919, the Freikorps replaced Premier Karlis Ulmanis's government with one headed by Pastor Andreas Needra. Although Needra had no popular legitimacy, the Freikorps hoped that he would be more receptive to their goals, especially that of granting citizenship to the Freikorps soldiers for the purpose of settlement.[48] The coup prompted calls by the British for the recall of the Freikorps to Germany, to which the German government responded that such a recall would leave the British solely responsible for defense against the Bolsheviks. Faced with this possibility, the British backed down; the German border remained open, and Freikorps reinforcements continued to pour into the Baltics.[49]

On May 22, 1919, the Freikorps campaign in the Baltics culminated in the capture of Riga. In a Berlin newspaper article published two weeks after Riga was "liberated," Captain von Medem, the leader of the Freikorps who had led the successful attack, described the reaction when his unit freed some Germans from a Bolshevik prison:

> An ecstasy has gripped these men that can only be explained when one knows what it means to suffer undeservedly for three or more months in the hands of the Bolsheviks. . . . From the intertwined masses, first softly and then ever louder, came the spontaneous cry, that old sound: "Lobet den Herrn," and [the song] came forth from the cells that had not yet been opened. For me it was as if a powerful fugue roared forth from the prison, as if a mighty orchestra, led by a maestro, gave its highest exertion. Like a single organ blast that rises up from this miserable world, this "Lobet den Herren" sounded in my soul. God triumphs after all![50]

The gratitude of the Riga Germans impressed Ludwig Gengler so much that he wrote, "one is ashamed as a German [to experience] this high degree of love for the homeland that one usually does not oneself possess. We do not want to leave this land, we want to strengthen (*festigen*) Germandom here."[51]

So important was it to describe these scenes of thanksgiving that, writing during the Nazi era, Cordt von Brandis emphasized that all non-Bolshevik resi-

47. Schulze, *Freikorps und Republik, 1918–1920*, 143.
48. Rohrscheidt, *Unsere Baltikum-Kämpfer*, 36.
49. Waite, *Vanguard of Nazism*, 113.
50. Walter Eberhard von Medem, "Riga Himmelfahrt," *Berlin Lokal–Anzeiger* June 4, 1919.
51. Gengler, *Rudolf Berthold*, 143.

dents of the liberated Baltics expressed their gratitude: Germans, Latvians, and even Jews. Brandis used a faux Yiddishized German to describe the appreciation of the Jews to the German troops: "'Oh there they are, our friends, the Germans! Say, our brothers, the Germans, they have come to save the Jewish people!'" Quickly, von Brandis added that one soldier in particular rejected this label of the Freikorps as the saviors of the Jews: "'We have not taken a single step on account of you, you Stinker!' Adolf v. Oertzen called out in a fury."[52] Nonetheless, it is striking that von Brandis, in a memoir published in 1939, still found that the gratitude of the entire Baltic population, even the Jews, was important enough to the Freikorps' experience of the Baltics in 1919 to mention it. He even reiterated a few pages later that "Everyone, everyone—whether German, Latvian or Jewish—wanted to show their thankfulness and greet the liberators and entertain them. They fought amongst themselves to provide housing to the soldiers."[53] In a text written prior to the Nazi *Machtergreifung*, another Freikorps volunteer stated, this time without any qualifier, that "Thousands of Baltic Germans, Latvians, Jews and Russians owe their lives to them."[54] For many Freikorps fighters, the gratitude that they perceived was more important than the ethnic divisions they encountered in the Baltics.

Freikorps memoirists bitterly compared the thankfulness that greeted them in the Baltics with the misunderstanding and rejection that Freikorps fighters believed greeted them in Germany itself. Hermann Gerstmayer described how

> difficult it was in those days to find someone [in Germany] who really in his heart sympathized with the Baltic Freikorps. The German people were infected by the clamor of a press without a Fatherland, which saw anything as a betrayal that served the interests of the nation, and which dammed what upstanding German men saw as their sacred duty. In this Germany without dignity, there was no sympathy or understanding for the difficult task that the Baltic Freikorps had chosen.[55]

The "Song of the Baltic Fighters" identifies those who they believed had abandoned them: "The Heimat has made us exiles / We abroad are the ones that are free / We are alone still Reich and country."[56] Another song popular among Freikorps fighters expressed their need to feel loved and their anger at those who did not appreciate them: "The spirit is still German, that cannot be defeated /

52. Cordt von Brandis, *Baltikumer: Schicksal eines Freikorps* (Berlin: Kolk, 1939), 59.

53. Ibid., 76.

54. Georg Heinrich Hartmann, "Erinnerungen aus den Kämpfen der Baltischen Landeswehr," in *Kampf um das Reich,* ed. Ernst Jünger (Essen: Kamp, 1931), 145.

55. Hermann Gerstmayer, *Baltikumkämpfer!* (Berlin: Beltz, 1934), 77.

56. Gengler, *Rudolf Berthold,* 135.

We remain strong even in the greatest peril / Those who do not love us should die neglected."[57] It was commonplace in Freikorps memoirs to mention how they were "von der Heimat geächtet," or ostracized by the homeland.[58] In reality, government officials were much more ambivalent. Whereas Friedrich Ebert and Philipp Scheidemann called for the immediate withdrawal of von der Goltz, they also did not want to be seen as caving to Allied pressure. Thus, Berlin delayed obeying Allied orders to withdraw or restrain von der Goltz.[59] On May 26, one week after the capture of Riga, the cabinet unanimously recommended that, since Germany would not be able to offer any help to the Freikorps once the Treaty of Versailles was signed, Freikorps fighters should obtain Latvian citizenship as soon as possible.[60]

The military successes of the Freikorps against a weak and underprovisioned Bolshevik army were accompanied by violent purges directed against the newly "liberated" Latvians. No less an authority on violence than Rudolf Höss, later commandant of Auschwitz, wrote, "The battles in the Baltic states were more brutal and vicious than anything I had experienced before. There was hardly a front-line; the enemy was everywhere. Wherever the opposing forces collided, there was a slaughter until no one was left."[61] The Freikorps reportedly shot 500 Latvians suspected of aiding and abetting the Bolsheviks in Mitau. In Tukkum, 200 Latvians were killed and, in Dünamunde, 125. Approximately 3,000 died in the terror that followed the capture of Riga in May 1919.[62] Thousands more were killed in smaller engagements.[63] Most Freikorps accounts sanitize their own contribution to the violence in the Baltics, attributing all atrocities to the Latvians or Russian communists.[64] Erich Balla displaced this violence on to the Baltic

57. Zobel, *Schüler freiwillig in Grenzschutz und Freikorps*, 93. In reality Freikorps accusations that they had been abandoned by Germany oversimplified a range of reactions to their actions in the Baltics. Although the socialist press was largely critical of the Freikorps mission, this criticism was far from absolute. In February 1919, an author penned an open letter in *Vorwärts* to the Entente, arguing that the Freikorps mission could succeed only if they received assistance from the Allies; "Die Parteivorstand zu den Vorgängen in Lettland," *Vorwärts*, May 31, 1919. An article in July expressed sympathy for the Germans in Latvia in terms reminiscent of newspapers further to the right; "Zum Schutze der Deutschen in Lettland," *Vorwärts*, July 7, 1919. The liberal democratic *Vossische Zeitung* opposed the Freikorps campaign as well, but for tactical reasons rather than moral ones; "Die Entente besiegelt?" *Vossische Zeitung*, May 25, 1919; "Die neuen Kämpfe im Baltikum," *Vossische Zeitung*, June 12, 1919.
58. Zobel, *Schüler freiwillig in Grenzschutz und Freikorps*, 83.
59. Schulze, *Freikorps und Republik, 1918–1920*, 142–43.
60. Protokoll der Sitzung des RMI, May 26, 1919, PAAA R 21787.
61. Rudolf Höss, *Death Dealer: The Memoirs of the SS Kommandant at Auschwitz*, trans. Andrew Pollinger (New York: Da Capo, 1996), 60.
62. Waite, *Vanguard of Nazism*, 118–19.
63. See, for example, Zobel, *Schüler freiwillig in Grenzschutz und Freikorps*, 75.
64. For an extreme version of this, see von Medem's account of how the Freikorps peacefully disarmed a group of Latvians who had killed a Baltic landowner; Medem, *Stürmer von Riga,* 49–50.

German *Landeswehr;* nevertheless, his description of the bloody aftermath of the capture of Riga gives a sense of the brutality and strangeness of the Frei- korps' actions and worldview. Balla described the attacks of the Baltic Germans on the *Flintenweiber,* or young female communists:

> The anger of the [Baltic Germans] now rampaged through the streets of Riga. It is horrible to admit this, but it was mostly directed against young women between the ages of 16 and 20. These were the so-called *"Flintenweiber,"* mostly beautiful things . . . who spent their nights in sexual orgies and their days in orgies of vio- lence. . . . The Baltic Germans showed no mercy. They did not see their youth or their charm. They saw only the face of the devil and hit, shot, stabbed them dead (*schlugen, schossen, stachen*), whenever they saw them. Four hundred *Flinten- weiber* lay on the streets of Riga in pools of their own blood. The hobnailed boots of the German Freikorps marched calmly over the corpses.[65]

Balla rhetorically reenacted the violence he illustrated, moving from the orgies of the *Flintenweiber* to the alliterative repetition of *"schlugen, schossen, stachen"* and finally to the image of violent order triumphant with the hobnailed boots trampling over the dead bodies of the young women. Gerstmayer did not men- tion the *Flintenweiber,* but still provides a sense of the brutality of the Freikorps in Riga: "[The city] was cleaned street by street. Blood flecked the cobblestones. Blood ran in small rivlets through the streets. The dead lay strewn about, their faces filled with hate. . . . He who did not have a gun, grabbed a bayonet and let loose."[66]

Such scenes appear to contradict the descriptions of gratitude that appear alongside them. In the Freikorps imaginary, however, violence was not a con- tradiction to gratitude but, rather, its necessary complement. Violence served a cleansing function—the blood that ran through the streets of Riga was not what needed to be cleaned away; it was itself what cleaned. Balla also described the torching of a Latvian village,[67] during which, even as their homes burned around them, peasants rushed into the flames to deliver bread, butter, and milk to the Freikorps soldiers who had destroyed their homes. Balla reported, "they carried [food from their homes] and carried and let nothing remain to demonstrate their

---

65. Balla, *Landsknechte wurden wir,* 180–81. This scene recalls Klaus Theweleit's insights into the hysterical nature of Freikorps violence toward women, as well as the Freikorps belief that vio- lence against women was a means of restoring order; Klaus Theweleit, *Male Fantasies,* trans. Stephen Conway, Erica Carter, and Chris Turner (Minneapolis: University of Minnesota Press, 1987). Bran- dis also claimed to have encountered the so-called *Flintenweiber* in terms that recall Balla's account; however, he stated that he merely captured but did not kill these women; Brandis, *Baltikumer,* 174– 76.

66. Gerstmayer, *Baltikumkämpfer,* 54.

67. This destruction turned out to be entirely unnecessary because the Bolsheviks had already left before the Freikorps arrived.

gratitude and friendliness. It was a scene that touches the heart of any feeling person."[68] As Edgar von Schmidt-Pauli later explained, the motto of the Freikorps may well have been "Onward with our weapons—for the fraternity of the world and for everlasting peace."[69]

After Riga: Disillusionment and Desperation

On May 21, the day before Riga was taken, an ad appeared in the *Tägliche Rundschau* from the Anwerbestelle Baltenland promising "Kurland is the settlement land of the future. If you want your own home in the beautiful Baltics, come to the Anwerbestelle Baltenland."[70] Encouraged by their success in Riga, Freikorps fighters tried to find ways to remain in the Baltics.[71] In a telegram to the Foreign Ministry on May 28, shortly after Riga fell to the Freikorps, the German representative in Libau noted that Freikorps soldiers had already submitted "several thousand" applications for Latvian citizenship and that the Latvian government, still led by Pastor Needra, a German puppet, was ready to grant them.[72]

But Latvian policy was in reality no longer so welcoming. On June 11, Needra's government published the terms for the admission of Freikorps members into the Latvian army. It agreed to provide clothing, food, and munitions for their new soldiers as well as a daily salary of 9 marks. After demobilization, Needra also agreed to provide a one-time payment to the Freikorps soldiers. The citizenship promises that had originally motivated Freikorps settlement fantasies were conspicuously absent.[73] A letter from the undersecretary for the chancellor to the Defense Ministry explained that this omission was not accidental. The Latvians felt that "[a] massive, unorganized and simultaneous transition to Latvian citizenship appears undesirable because of its effect on public opinion."[74]

In the aftermath of their defeat at Riga, the Bolsheviks retreated from the Baltics in May. Shortly thereafter, the Freikorps turned against the Baltic peoples whom they were ostensibly protecting and invaded Estonia. The success of the Freikorps and their continued aggression led the British to renew their demands to the German government that Freikorps forces be withdrawn. British advisors arrived to train Baltic forces to fight against the Freikorps, and the Entente increased its pressure on the German government to withdraw all sup-

68. Balla, *Landsknechte wurden wir,* 111.
69. Edgar von Schmidt-Pauli, *Geschichte der Freikorps 1918–1924* (Stuttgart: Lutz, 1936), 30.
70. Quoted in Bernhard Sauer, "Die Baltikumer," Arbeitspapier des Instituts für Internationale Politik und Regionale Studien 7, Freie Universität-Berlin, 1995, 12.
71. Medem, *Stürmer von Riga,* 89–90.
72. Schulze, *Freikorps und Republik, 1918–1920,* 146.
73. Beschluss der provisorischen Regierung Lettlands, PAAA R 21790.
74. Unterstaatssekretär in der Reichskanzlei to the Reichswehrminister, June 12, 1919, PAAA R 21790.

port from them. Combined Estonian and Latvian forces scored a victory against the German Freikorps and the Baltic *Landeswehr* on June 22 in Wenden. Estonian troops, enraged by the Freikorps' violation of their sovereignty, drove them back in a series of battles lasting until July 3. Von der Goltz was forced to sign the Treaty of Strazdumuiža and withdraw from Riga with the rest of the Freikorps forces. After fighting between the forces of Needra and Ulmanis, on July 3 the British also reinstated Ulmanis, who had been deposed in the April 1919 coup, as premier.

As the Latvians grew increasingly hostile toward the Freikorps soldiers who had replaced their head of government and killed thousands of their compatriots, the Freikorps were themselves feeling yet more alienated from Germany after the republican government agreed to the terms of the Treaty of Versailles in late June. Expressing the views of many of his fellow volunteers, von Salomon wrote, "Did [the acceptance of the Versailles Treaty] not sound like a message from a distant, foreign country . . . ? A land, like an empty speck on a map, in which topographers hesitate to put in cities and towns and rivers and borders, a plump and passive land, a land without reality."[75] Von Salomon also experienced a heady sense of freedom mixed with this feeling of betrayal:

> No order held us together, neither money nor bread nor the warm flavor of our homeland bound us. We were driven by a need that we could only divine, we were lashed by a law that we could only see the shadows of. We stood in the insane confusion of danger. We were held by a new proving ground, a measure of hope, free from the ballast of deplorable demands. . . . outcasts, exiles, homeless beggars—we held our torches high.[76]

As prospects in Germany appeared increasingly bleak, the Freikorps fighters found consolation in the east. Von Medem wrote:

> The news from the German homeland was ever more desperate: bloody fights with the Spartacists on the streets of major cities, dishonorable behavior from the government and national assembly in Weimar, the insane demands from Versailles and their acceptance. For the soldiers in the Baltics, Germany sank into a dishonorable Marxist void. They increasingly clung to the Latvian state's old pledge of citizenship for the Baltic fighters and the promises of land made by the Baltic German barons. The old drive dating back to the 13th century to settle in the East was once again awakened in the Baltic fighters.[77]

75. Salomon, *Geächteten*, 126.
76. Ibid., 128.
77. Medem, *Stürmer von Riga*, 89.

Rudolf Berthold also described the revitalizing effects of the Baltic campaign: "The Bavarians have re-established their old reputation. And I will also take care that it is maintained. How small and ugly is all of this superficiality (*all dieses Äußerliche*), this rushing and grasping for money in Germany!"[78] In his statement, Berthold demonstrates the reversal of order between center and periphery. Germany was the home of *"all dieses Äußerliche"*—with its dual meaning of both "superficiality" and "exteriority"—whereas it was in the Baltics that the Bavarians had regained their old reputation. Many in the Freikorps believed that they had found a new *Heimat* in Latvia. This was a homeland that had little to do with legal status; the Freikorps settlers would, after all, have been Latvian citizens. Instead, the stories of Baltic gratitude, especially when contrasted with the thankless and treacherous homefront in Germany, which had perpetrated the "stab in the back" of the German forces that had already passed into legend, were the proof that the new German *Heimat* lay in the east, not within the old borders of Germany. In the topsy-turvy world of the Baltic campaign, the Baltics had become a new homeland, and Germany had become a foreign country.

For the Freikorps, the betrayals of the surrender and then the acceptance of the Treaty of Versailles tore a rift between the nation and the state. In a speech given eight years later, on the occasion of the tenth anniversary of the Weimar Republic, von der Goltz attempted to sum up the lessons of the war. Seeing both the treachery of the socialists and the surprising solidarity between Germans inside and outside the territorial boundaries of Germany, he argued that Germans had learned that "The consciousness of the German people has proven itself to be stronger than the consciousness of the state."[79] For von Medem, "[Freikorps] soldiers owed nothing to any German state, any commander or any army, but only to the idea and thus to themselves."[80] Balla said simply, "In the Baltic, there was no conception of the state (*Staatsidee*)."[81] All three men found the lesson of the defeat and the treachery of the new republic to be the impermanence, indeed the dispensability, of the state.

The news of the acceptance of the punitive terms of the Treaty of Versailles lent a new urgency to the Freikorps' campaign. After hearing of it, von Brandis explained to his troops that their mission in the Baltics was an attempt to rescue Germany from Entente encirclement. With (obviously) unintended irony, he expressed the fear that British soldiers wanted "[a]ll of Germany to become a concentration camp (*Konzentrationslager*)!" Instead, he stated, "Here, where we stood was the place that one could cut through the barbed wire that had been

---

78. Rudolf Berthold, quoted in Gengler, *Rudolf Berthold,* 143.
79. Goltz, *Ernste Gedanken,* 25.
80. Medem, *Stürmer von Riga,* 66.
81. Balla, *Landsknechte wurden wir,* 57.

pulled around concentration camp Germany."[82] Bischoff wrote, "it became possible and necessary to turn the German will in the direction of the Baltics in order to create a military power that could break the ring created by Versailles."[83] Von der Goltz believed that by fortifying his position in the Baltics, he could establish a base that would enable him to march on Berlin and overthrow the republic.[84] Yet although von Brandis, Bischoff, and von der Goltz were concerned with the fate of Germany, many other Freikorps members paid less attention to geopolitics and instead expressed their belief that because Germany had betrayed them they were ready to reject Germany. Von der Goltz's plans for a German coup were rejected by the Freikorps volunteers, who did not wish to abandon their plans for settling in the Baltics.[85]

Abandoning the German nation-state for some writers meant that words that had previously been used to describe territory now became separated from their earlier referents. Just as the meaning of the *Heimat* was now associated with the gratitude offered to them in the Baltics, rather than a specific place, Franz Nord wrote that *Vormarsch* now meant something quite different from its earlier, territorially bound meaning:

> "Advance" did not mean for the soldiers in the Baltics the march towards a military goal, towards a point on a map, a line in the territory to be conquered. It meant much more than this, the experience of a hard community, it meant the creation of a new excitement that raised the fighter to a higher level. It meant the dissolution of all of the bonds to a sunken and rotten world with which the true fighter no longer had any communion.[86]

According to von Salomon, Germany itself had been lost:

> Where was Germany? In Weimar, in Berlin? At one time it was on the Front, but the front collapsed. Then it was supposed to be in the homeland, but the homeland lied. It called in song and in language, but the tone was false. One spoke of a Fatherland and a Motherland, but the Negro had that too. Where was Germany? Was it with the people? But the people screamed for bread and shook their thick bellies. Was it the state? But the state searched blitherlingly for its form and found it in abandonment.[87]

82. Brandis, *Baltikumer,* 216.
83. Bischoff, *Letzte Front,* 247.
84. Rüdiger von der Goltz, *Als politischer General im Osten, 1918 und 1919* (Leipzig: Koehler, 1936), 166.
85. Charles L. Sullivan, "The 1919 German Campaign in the Baltics: The Final Phase," in *The Baltic States in Peace and War, 1917–1945,* ed. Vytas Stanley Vardys and Romuald J. Misiunas (University Park: Pennsylvania State University Press, 1978), 33.
86. Nord, "Krieg im Baltikum," 64. Incidentally, an identical quotation appears in Salmon, *Geächteten,* 79.
87. Salomon, *Geächteten,* 72.

Von Salomon listed a series of fallacies—language, the state, the people—that nationalists had claimed were the essence of national identity and found all of them wanting. National identity, indeed individual identity, he suggested, could not rest on any of these unreliable foundations. In such a place, the Freikorps soldiers themselves were both the apotheosis of German identity and its limit. "Now, we were the border."[88] Rhetorically, the phrase "we were the border" metaphorically encompassed the mixture of opportunity and despair that distinguished the Freikorps venture. On the one hand, by claiming they "were" the border, von Salomon was arguing that the Freikorps were the last line of defense for a German spirit that had been failed by the state. On the other hand, this notion of becoming the border, and indeed von Salomon's entire text, also contained within it a sense of possibility and excitement. It is important to recall how much Freikorps literature stressed the constraints around Germany. This emphasis on constraint existed before the Treaty of Versailles and played a role in the popularity of settlement fantasies, but it became noticeably more important once the Allies had dictated the punitive terms of the treaty, in which Germany was forced to cede more than 10 percent of its prewar territory and its claim to the Baltics where the Freikorps were then fighting. In the context of these feelings of constraint, much of the Freikorps literature emphasized the desire to escape, whether in the geopolitical terms of von Brandis or Bischoff or in the existential expressions of von Salomon. The defeat and the treaty were understood as limits or boundaries; however, by incorporating the limit themselves—becoming the border—von Salomon believed that he and his Freikorps comrades could transcend it.

Mutiny

Throughout summer 1919, German military and civilian leaders vacillated in their support of the Freikorps. Winnig told the National Assembly that the evacuation of the Baltics would mean "the extermination of the remainder of German culture in the Baltics." Meanwhile von der Goltz was informed by his commanders at OKN that any evacuation orders should be ignored and that, instead, he should prepare the ground for a transfer to the command of White Russian General Pavel Avalov-Bermondt. The OKN believed that a German–White Russian alliance could both defeat Bolshevism and provide a means for Germany to overcome Allied pressure. There was no clear line to be drawn between defending Germany and eastern expansion. Independent socialist delegates to the National Assembly accused Noske and the majority socialists of encouraging these plans.[89] Meanwhile, made even more desperate by the acceptance of the

88. Ibid., 74.
89. Sullivan, "1919 German Campaign," 34.

Treaty of Versailles, Freikorps volunteers continued to make plans for settling in the Baltics. Freikorps fighters filled out applications for permanent settlement in Latvia and then attended fourteen-day courses, arranged by the Baltic German landowners, in which they learned about settlement opportunities and requirements. Each applicant was promised 80 *Morgen* (approximately 70 acres) of land, assuming that he could pay the necessary 10 percent downpayment of its value.[90] Ulmanis, the reinstated Latvian premier, was unsympathetic to these plans. On July 15, 1919, a representative of the Latvian government stated that his government would not respect the promises of granting Latvian citizenship made in the treaty of December 28, 1918. Freikorps fighters became increasingly restive on learning of Ulmanis's supposed betrayal, and a group of 10,000 Freikorps assembled in Mitau on July 28 to demand the right to settle in the Baltics that they believed had been promised to them.[91] The Baltic German landowners sought to reassure the Freikorps that they did not agree with Ulmanis's decision. Nonetheless, the writing was on the wall. Hubert Gough, the Allied representative to the Baltics, informed von der Goltz that the December 28 treaty was null and void. On July 23, Foreign Minister Hermann Müller told the National Assembly that "there was no opportunity to successfully support the representatives of the Baltic Landwehr in their demands for the land that had been promised to them."[92] Knowing that he would soon be recalled, on July 12 von der Goltz secretly agreed with Avalov-Bermondt to a transfer of forces to the Russian commander. But von der Goltz soon began to have doubts about the success of this venture without at least financial support or the acquiescence of the Allies. Ten days later, he expressed his fear that events had moved beyond his control. Even if the German government did order a withdrawal, he was afraid that exuberant commanders such as von Brandis would refuse to obey it. He thus agreed to work with both the Russians and Freikorps to facilitate this transfer. Under Allied pressure, President Ebert agreed to a withdrawal but delayed actually issuing an order until August 5. A week later, the OKN called for the immediate evacuation of Freikorps troops.[93]

Feeling betrayed and abandoned, the Freikorps forces that gathered at the railway station on August 24 to board trains to take them back to Germany mu-

90. "An den Führer der 1. Schwadron vom Kornett beim Stabe Mittau," August 14, 1919, BArch R 8025/20, 27; "Fragebogen für Zukunfts-Siedler im Baltikum," BArch R 8025/20, 30.

91. "Deutschland und Lettland: Erregung unter den deutschen Soldaten im Baltikum," *Vorwärts,* July 31, 1919.

92. Schulze, *Freikorps und Republik, 1918–1920,* 158–59. This confusion of the Baltic *Landwehr* with the Freikorps—who were mostly part of Bischoff's Iron Division but also had fought with the Baltic *Landwehr*—was typical of the lack of knowledge about the Freikorps Baltic mission in Germany.

93. Noske indicated his support for the transfer of forces to the Russians. He even reportedly told one Freikorps leader that if he were twenty again "I might go along with you." Quoted in Sullivan, "1919 German Campaign," 37.

tinied under the command of Josef Bischoff, leader of the Iron Division.[94] That night, with torches ablaze, Freikorps soldiers sang "Deutschland über alles," and Bischoff told them that "We march on Riga!"[95] Bischoff gave two accounts of his reasons for leading this mutiny, the first in 1919 in a letter to the Freikorps themselves and a later one in his memoirs published during the Nazi era. The differences between the two demonstrate the evolution of the Freikorps myth in the years between 1919 and the Nazi ascension to power. In 1936, Bischoff maintained that he planned to support General Avalov-Bermondt to help establish a new Russian regime and circumvent the restrictions imposed by the victorious Allies. Because the German government "did not see this duty," he felt that for the good of Germandom he needed to take matters into his own hands.[96] Bischoff's letter to the Iron Division in the immediate aftermath of the mutiny, however, did not discuss Germandom at all; instead, it focused on the specific demands of his troops. He wrote that the actions of the German regime in abandoning the Freikorps and agreeing to the terms of the Entente meant that he was forced to take this step to defend the rights of the men under his command. Bischoff's demands in 1919, and presumably those of many of his soldiers, addressed the Freikorps' desire to stay together and fight either for the *Reichswehr* or in the Baltics and their continued hope of settlement.[97] These demands were not related to the German state, the German nation, or some greater German spirit but, rather, more narrowly with the well-being of the Freikorps alone. According to Balla and von Medem, the supposed betrayal of their hopes for settlement was the crucial factor that encouraged the mutinous Freikorps to turn their backs on both the Latvian government, which refused to give them citizenship, and the German state, which failed to support them in this quest.[98]

Hearing of the mutiny, Ebert and Scheidemann were incensed and called von der Goltz to speak to the German cabinet. There von der Goltz explained, "The Freikorps don't want to go home. Some of them want to settle and build their 'military-settler-state.'" He admitted that this was a "totally vague idea. . . . In response to my question if they had money, they stated that they would print it and live off the land. This kind of military state cannot survive in Latvia, but will in the end become a republic of thieves."[99] Archly mobilizing the specter of revolution, von der Goltz told Wilhelm Groener that he would support Bischoff "in order to defend against a 'Spartakist Action' among the troops."[100] After the

94. Schulze, *Freikorps und Republik, 1918–1920,* 159.

95. Bischoff, *Letzte Front,* 199; Sullivan, "1919 German Campaign," 37.

96. Bischoff, *Letzte Front,* 151.

97. Letter from Josef Bischoff to the Eiserne Division, August 28, 1919, published in *Die Freiwillige,* August 29, 1919.

98. Balla, *Landsknechte wurden wir,* 190–91; Medem, *Stürmer von Riga,* 94.

99. Goltz quoted in Schulze, *Freikorps und Republik, 1918–1920,* 163.

100. Goltz in ibid., 168.

mutiny on August 24, 14,000 men, along with 64 airplanes, 6 cavalry units, 56 field pieces, armored sections, a field hospital, and 156 machine guns, remained in Latvia.[101] On October 6, this remnant of the Freikorps was officially transferred to the Russian Army of the West commanded by the eccentric General Prince Avalov-Bermondt. The treaty that Bischoff signed with Avalov-Bermondt confirmed settlement rights for German troops in Latvia and granted them Russian citizenship.[102]

Avalov-Bermondt claimed to have 55,000 troops at his command, of whom 40,000 were German nationals.[103] With their transfer to the forces of Avalov-Bermondt, the Freikorps found themselves fighting alongside Russians in the final quixotic episode of the Baltic campaign. They were welcomed by Avalov-Bermondt: "You have left your homeland (*Heimat*) in order to fight in my army for a new homeland (*Heimatboden*) for the Reich."[104] The young Johannes Zobel provided a dreamlike description of Germans waking up to see the wide variety of troops surrounding them:

> Where were they? . . . And then it became clear before their eyes. They sat in a room surrounded by Kirgisen, Turmen, Sibierians and Kosaaks from the Urals, White Russians from the Ukraine and Tartars from the furthest steppe. They had all felt at home in little mother Russia (*Mütterchen Rußland*). And they were all still true children of their little father, the tsar (*Väterchen Zar*), and they would all still fight and bleed for him.[105]

Zobel admitted that "a *German* formation would of course have been better" and that "it was difficult to acclimate oneself."[106] Nonetheless, the German and Russian troops began gradually to understand one another. In particular, a shared sense of homelessness united the disparate elements in Avalov-Bermondt's army.[107] But this homelessness was not just a source of community. According to Balla, it was a "poison" that led men to even greater extremes of violence and disorder: "women were raped, men were killed in a fit of violence. Such actions proliferated like rapacious weeds (*wucherten wie geiles Unkraut*)."[108]

The German government did not know how to react to the unwillingness of the Freikorps troops to return home or to their vague plans for staying in the Baltics. Many in political, military, and diplomatic circles in Germany felt that a

---

101. Liulevicius, *War Land on the Eastern Front*, 232.

102. Schulze, *Freikorps und Republik, 1918–1920*, 184.

103. Waite, *Vanguard of Nazism*, 125. These figures were most likely inflated.

104. "Aufruf des Fürsten Awaloff zum Kampf gegen die Letten," reprinted in Ernst von Salomon, *Das Buch vom deutschen Freikorpskämpfer* (Berlin: Wilhelm Limpert-Verlag, 1938), 192.

105. Zobel, *Schüler freiwillig in Grenzschutz und Freikorps*, 69.

106. Ibid., 70. Emphasis in original.

107. Ibid.

108. Balla, *Landsknechte wurden wir*, 205.

bridge between Germany and Russia was "the only possibility to break free from encirclement by the entente powers."[109] At the same time, the state was under pressure from the Entente to prevent the continued stream of men and material to the Freikorps that prolonged fighting in the east. Despite protestations that it was unable to staunch this flow and the use of considerable delaying tactics, the German government finally put in place measures to seal the border and cut off all means of support to the Freikorps in early October. With this, the final tie between Germany and the Freikorps was broken. The Freikorps continued fighting with Bermondt-Avalov's army against the Latvians, but without the earlier supply of fresh recruits and war material, they were pushed out of the country. Retreating to German territory, the Freikorps took out their frustration and rage on the Baltic countryside and its people, burning villages and destroying farms, killing their inhabitants, and looting whatever was left. The Freikorps' violence did not spare their own men. The roads back to East Prussia were littered with Freikorps corpses wearing signs "Condemned to death because of plundering. Do not bury as a warning to the others!" that bore witness to the final spasms of disorder and violence of this already chaotic and blood-drenched campaign.[110] The remnants of the Freikorps returned to Germany during late fall and winter 1919–1920.

The response in Germany to the returning *Baltikumkämpfer* varied. In the immediate aftermath of the mutiny, the *Vorwärts* expressed sympathy for the Freikorps, who "only emigrated because they wanted to settle in the Baltics."[111] But the patience of the newspaper soon ran out once it became clear that the Freikorps had no intention of voluntarily returning to Germany. Just as nationalists located a danger in the east, namely Bolshevism, the socialist paper also associated the idea that these Freikorps fighters were dangerous with their being "Baltic" or eastern.[112] As might be expected, some nationalists expressed their support for the Freikorps fighters who had fought in the Baltics. In an article that appeared in September 1919 in the nationalist East Prussian newspaper *Deutsche Aufgaben*, one author took the German government to task for its two-faced policy toward the Freikorps. Through the Anwerbestelle Baltenland, government officials had encouraged Germans to sign up for the Freikorps and fight for the right to settle in Latvia. Now, however, the social democrats had abandoned the Freikorps. The *Deutsche Aufgaben* insisted that the German government support the Freikorps in their fight for Latvian citizenship and the right to settle there.[113] Such demands were a far cry from the

109. Schulze, *Freikorps und Republik, 1918–1920,* 172.
110. Balla, *Landsknechte wurden wir,* 229.
111. "Revolte in Mitau," *Vorwärts,* August 27, 1919. At no point, however, did the *Vorwärts* actually support the idea of mutiny.
112. Paul Witolla, "Die baltische Gefahr," *Vorwärts,* December 24, 1919.
113. "Das Siedlungsrecht der deutschen Truppen," *Deutsche Aufgaben,* September 14, 1919.

self-confident plans for annexation and expansion that nationalists had espoused a year earlier.

Speaking at one of several contentious session of the National Assembly in October, 1919, Defense Minister Noske expressed sympathy for the Freikorps soldiers in the Baltics despite his declaration that they needed to return to Germany immediately: "The motives that lead the majority of these people to remain [in Latvia] are completely respectable. They [Freikorps soldiers] fear the lack of jobs in the *Heimat*." Furthermore, he added, the Freikorps troops felt betrayed because the Latvian government had gone back on its promise of Latvian citizenship, which would have enabled them to settle there: "The Latvian government promised citizenship. The Latvian government knew also that volunteers were being recruited with this goal in mind."[114] In the same session, Gustav Stresemann, the DVP delegate expressed his agreement with Noske that the Freikorps had the right to feel betrayed in their expectations.[115] As Noske's statement makes clear, many of those who argued that the Freikorps should return in fall 1919 still believed that the Freikorps had been betrayed. Even if the Freikorps' methods were questioned, their desire to leave Germany and settle elsewhere met with widespread sympathy. On orders from the Defense Ministry, the returning Freikorps were paid and provisioned.

The embittered men who returned in Germany in late fall and winter 1919 framed the end of their campaign as another case in which a victorious and strong German army had been stabbed in the back. One former Freikorps fighter wrote, "Only as the sabotage from the Heimat began to take effect and as the Latvians in front of us were assisted by the Lithuanians behind us, did we begin to suffer setbacks. . . . For the second time in one year, Tacitus's words were fulfilled: 'Germani non nisi Germanis vinci possunt.' 'Germans can only be conquered by other Germans.'"[116] According to Brandis, the Freikorps had been stabbed in the back by the German government in bowing to the demands of the British, the German people, the German military commanders in not supporting the Freikorps, and finally the Latvians in withdrawing their permission for settlement.[117] The army disbanded Bischoff's troops against their wishes on their return. Many of them fought with the right-wing Kapp in 1920, and after the Freikorps were disbanded, many took part in the unsuccessful Nazi putsch of 1923. Many, although by no means all, of the Baltic Freikorps volunteers became Nazi supporters, and General von der Goltz campaigned for Hitler in his

114. *Verhandlungen,* Bd. 330, 2919. The National Assembly discussed the Freikorps nearly every day in summer and fall 1919, but particularly heated debates occurred on July 4, 23, 26, and 28 and on October 8–10.

115. Ibid., 2921.

116. Zobel, *Schüler freiwillig in Grenzschutz und Freikorps,* 88.

117. Brandis, *Baltikumer,* 202, 207.

unsuccessful presidential bid in 1932.[118] Even more important, the Nazis were inspired by the story of the Baltic campaign of the Freikorps volunteers, whom they saw as true German patriots who had been abandoned by a treacherous regime. The Nazis explicitly portrayed themselves as continuing along the path pioneered by these martyrs.[119]

The fantasies of eastern expansion and settlement that were tantalizingly close in spring and summer 1918 became desperate necessities in the context of a defeated and shattered Germany. Yet, as frustrated as the Freikorps were with a Germany they felt had rejected them, the hopefulness with which they approached the Baltics is striking. Their perception of rejection by the Germans in Germany and gratitude from those in the Baltics lent emotional weight to the Freikorps' rejection of their homeland for the Baltic plains.

June and July 1919 marked a turning point for the Freikorps. Allied pressure increased after the capture of Riga in May and the retreat of the Bolsheviks shortly thereafter. Meanwhile, Latvian and Estonian forces combined to defeat Freikorps forces. Most devastating of all, however, the Ebert government agreed to the punitive terms of the Treaty of Versailles. Furthermore, when the Latvian government withdrew its promise of citizenship for Freikorps troops who wished to settle in Germany, Berlin did not force Latvia to accept the Freikorps as Latvian citizens. Faced with these betrayals, the Freikorps felt ever more distant from Germany. The radical nature of this break was revealed in the August mutiny of Freikorps forces under the command of Bischoff. These forces abandoned German control altogether to fight with White Russian General Avalov-Bermondt. But without access to fresh troops or supplies and facing a reinforced enemy, the alliance with Avalov-Bermondt quickly collapsed and the remnants of the Freikorps returned to Germany in late fall 1919.

Resituating the Freikorps within its 1919 context makes the radical nature of the Baltic campaign more evident, along with the combination of hope, desperation, and violence it embodied. An almost postmodern disregard for the idea of the nation-state was accompanied by a shocking degree of violence. The Freikorps represented a particularly extreme version of the disarticulation of nation, state, and territory in postwar Germany, and the dual meaning of *boundary* and *edge* contained in von Salomon's image of the border is apt not only as

---

118. For more on the personal connections forged during their Freikorps service that persisted until the Nazi era, see Campbell, "Freikorps as Myth and Model." For more on the persistence of the Freikorps myth, see Sven Reichardt, *Faschistische Kampfbünde* (Cologne: Böhlau, 2002).

119. See the speech for the fifteenth and sixteenth anniversaries of the liberation of Riga from Bolshevism, May 22, 1935 in Berlin, BArch R 8012/39, 132–34, 81.

a metaphor for the Freikorps themselves but also for German society at that time more generally.

What did it mean to be German after defeat, revolution, and territorial revisions? What shape would the borders of Germany have in the postwar and postrevolutionary era? The Freikorps' proposed solution to the problem of the impossible border was not shared by most other Germans; however, in postwar Germany, not only the Freikorps were asking these questions.

3. Socialist Pioneers on the Soviet Frontier

Ansiedlung Ost

n his *Moskau 1920*, Alfons Goldschmidt reported on his recent visit to Soviet Russia. With respect to the train ride to Moscow, Goldschmidt observed, "It smells sweet like spring . . . and there is ever more forest, forest, forest. No land in the world has so much forest as Russia."[1] His impressions of Moscow itself were even more positive: "There is still much elegance in Moscow, and still the proletariat rule. . . . The proletariat rules the city with its own police and its own work regulations."[2] The city was overflowing with red—red banners, red flags, and red bands—and was full of singing workers, hailing their new communist idyll.[3] Goldschmidt rushed to assure critics that there was gender equality and freedom in the new Russia, that the poverty on the streets was solely a result of laziness, and that rumors that all communists were forced to dress in matching uniforms were false.[4] Goldschmidt visited a factory and reported that the conditions were clean and, even more remarkably, the food provided to the workers was plentiful, healthy, and delicious. Soviet workers could expect high wages along with the newest equipment and machines.[5]

Today, Goldschmidt's vision can be dismissed as the delusions of a communist who saw a utopian vision of progress in a Russia that was, in reality, wracked by hunger, poverty, and war. But for many workers in Germany, Goldschmidt's words

1. Alfons Goldschmidt, *Moskau 1920: Tagebuchblätter* (Berlin: Rowohlt, 1920), 22.
2. Ibid., 31.
3. Ibid., 23, 32.
4. Ibid., 25, 41–42, 37.
5. Ibid., 67–68.

were a revelation. Inspired by Goldschmidt, a group known as Ansiedlung Ost or the Interessengemeinschaft der Auswanderer-Organisationen nach Sowjet-Rußland considered a mass immigration to Soviet Russia.[6] Only a small contingent of fewer than 150 workers actually made the trip, but approximately 30,000 workers from across Germany and from a spectrum of left-socialist parties joined Ansiedlung Ost at its height, and its meetings were often attended by upward of 1,000 people interested in settling in Soviet Russia. As any observer familiar with Russia in 1920 could have anticipated, Ansiedlung Ost was doomed to failure. The 150 German workers arrived in Kolomna just at the start of a devastating famine, and faced with hostile Russian workers, hunger, and their own inadequate planning, the majority of these settlers returned to Germany embittered. Yet, even though Ansiedlung Ost can easily be dismissed as an amateurish debacle, the very unrealizability of its vision attests to its power.[7] The Ansiedlung Ost movement tapped into a strain of individual escapism unaddressed by either official communist ideology, with its emphasis on the collective goal of (German) revolution, or the cautious new German democracy. Most important, Ansiedlung Ost offers us a window onto the hopes and fantasies of a large number of German workers regarding Soviet Russia and the transformative power of revolution.

Ansiedlung Ost was possible only in 1920. It was only then, when the situation in Soviet Russia was both unsettled and relatively unknown, and when Germany's own prospects appeared so bleak, that a large number of German workers saw a colony in Russia as a preferable alternative to their lives in Germany. The members of Ansiedlung Ost saw the wide-open spaces and untouched forests of Russia as a *tabula rasa* on which they could create fulfilled and meaningful lives in a way that was not possible in the exhausted and depleted Germany that they saw around them. Much like the Freikorps, Ansiedlung Ost was motivated more by the desire to escape Germany than by a clear vision of what awaited its

6. Ansiedlung Ost was the name originally given the group when it formed in March 1919. Later that year or early the next, as it changed its emphasis to the emigration of industrial workers rather than the attempt to form an agrarian-based commune, it changed its name to the Interessengemeinschaft der Auswanderer–Organisationen nach Sowjet-Rußland. Despite the official name change, officials from the German government and members of the organization continued to use the older name in tandem with the later one. Finally in the aftermath of the Kolomna scandal, the group changed its name once again to the Proletarische Auswanderer–Organisationen nach Sowjet-Rußland (Proletarian Emigration Organizations to Soviet Russia). To simplify the discussion, I refer to the organization as Ansiedlung Ost throughout. Ansiedlung Ost members often cited Goldschmidt as an inspiration. See Bruno Grimm and E. Weber, *Russlandfahrt 1920* (Berlin: Germania, 1921), 17; Paul Fähnrich, *Kolomna: Erlebnisse von 76 Rückwanderern der Interessengemeinschaft der Auswandererorganisationen nach Sowjetrussland* (Berlin: Germania, 1921), 24.
7. See R 1501/118321 for information on other, later, localized left-wing agitations. Julia Mahnke lists later grassroots organizations that sought to emigrate eastward; none of these had anything like the national scope of Ansiedlung Ost. Julia Mahnke, *Auswanderungsvereine mit Ziel Ukraine und Sowjet-Russland in der Weimarer Republik* (Munich: Ost-Europa Institut, 1997), 77–96.

members further east. They differed from the Freikorps in their understanding of the sufficient conditions for such a utopia—whereas the Freikorps found solace in the long history of German settlement in the Baltics, Ansiedlung Ost looked to the revolution as creating a fundamentally new opportunity for German workers. The discourse of revolutionary Russia fused associations with both Russia, as a primitive and empty space, and revolution, as an event filled with utopian promise. In seeking to settle in Russia, the members of Ansiedlung Ost were attempting to take advantage of the protean nature of national borders in the aftermath of war, revolution, and territorial revisions. Furthermore, members negotiated a kind of communal identity that connected them neither with the German nor with the Soviet state. According to the citizenship guidelines negotiated by the Ansiedlung Ost leadership, settlers would be citizens of the Soviet state but without military or tax responsibilities. Instead, they would carry visas identifying them as members of Ansiedlung Ost. Ansiedlung Ost was both international and local in orientation, eschewing national identifications and state affiliations. Finally, the collapse of Ansiedlung Ost is also part of this story. The first transport of Ansiedlung Ost workers in July 1920 failed miserably. On returning to Germany, many Ansiedlung Ost members wrote embittered memoirs in which they disavowed the folly of emigration, concluding that the failure of Ansiedlung Ost was also a failure of communism and of internationalism more generally. In a bitter irony, both the returning Ansiedlung Ost settlers and critics of the mission, from the left-socialist USPD to the far right, took the failure of Ansiedlung Ost as evidence for the indispensability of the nation-state.

Locating Ansiedlung Ost

In March 1919, a group of workers and revolutionary agitators in Leipzig founded Ansiedlung Ost to prepare for their emigration to the fledgling Soviet republic in the east. The leaders of Ansiedlung Ost lamented the fact that previously the only groups making plans to settle in the east had been the Freikorps, and they consciously designed Ansiedlung Ost as a socialist "counter-weight to the [Freikorps] 'Baltic Adventure.'"[8] Groups devoted to the idea of settling in Russia began to spring up across Germany, and in December 1919, these organizations banded together to form a national organization with its headquarters in Leipzig, called the Community of Organizations for Emigrating to Soviet Russia (Interessengemeinschaft der Auswanderer-Organisationen nach Sowjet-Rußland).[9] The group lasted for less than two years, collapsing in 1921 after the news

8. "Russische technische Staatskommission für die Auswanderung nach Sowjet-Russland: Bericht über die Interessengemeinschaft der Auswandererorganisationen nach Sowjetrussland, 31 Oktober 1920," BArch R 1501/101827, 87; "Mitteilungen," *Deutsch-Russische Wirtschaftskorrespondenz* 2, no. 35 (September 19, 1920), 1.
9. "Russische technische Staatskommission," BArch R 1501/101827, 86.

spread about the disastrous first transport of immigrants to a factory in Kolomna and also as the situation inside Russia worsened with the onset of catastrophic famine in 1921–1922.

During these two years, however, Ansiedlung Ost was the largest and most successful organization of its kind in Germany. A Reichswanderungsamt (RWA) report in March 1920 estimated that the movement boasted a membership of 28,000, and other estimates ranged as high as 100,000 members organized in a network of local chapters in over twenty cities across Germany. The local groups varied in their degree of association with the Leipzig headquarters—some were direct subsidiaries, whereas others were affiliated groups that maintained a certain degree of autonomy.[10] At first, Ansiedlung Ost was imagined as primarily an agrarian settlement. But after Hugo Gumprich, one of the leaders of the organization, visited Russia in 1919 and because the movement found its greatest popularity in urban areas, this shifted to an emphasis on an industrial colony, albeit in a rural setting.[11] According to a report released in October 1920, slightly more than half of the members of Ansiedlung Ost were industrial workers, both skilled and nonskilled, from a variety of industries, from metal workers to textile workers and miners and even a small number of engineers. The rest were agricultural workers. Furthermore, fully half of the membership of Ansiedlung Ost was unemployed.[12] When Wilhelm Dittmann, the secretary of the USPD, visited the settlement in Kolomna, he met with a group of Ansiedlung Ost members; of these, forty were from the USPD, thirteen from the Kommunistische Partei Deutschlands (KPD), six from the syndicalist Kommunistische Arbeiter-Partei Deutschlands (KAPD; Worker's Party of Germany), eight members of trade unions without party affiliation, and two who belonged neither to a political party

10. *Reichswanderungsamt Rundschreiben* 189, March 17, 1920. The exact size of the membership of this organization is very hard to ascertain. A report from the Russian Technical State Commission, the Russian delegation that worked with the Ansiedlung Ost, reported that the membership in August 1920 reached 12,000. Based on the subsequent breakdown of the professions of the prospective emigrants, it seems that this number represents only the male members of the organization. Therefore, any count of the membership, and any sense of the prospective size of an emigration, must assume a somewhat greater figure; I consider 28,000 to be a somewhat reasonable guess. "Russische technische Staatskommission," BArch R 1501/101827, 89–90. It is also important to note that Ansiedlung Ost held open meetings that could be attended by nonmembers who did not want to pay the dues of membership (5 marks per month, a substantial sum for some workers during this period); thus, the membership of Ansiedlung Ost alone is not an indicator of its influence within working-class communities. In a surveillance report of a Stuttgart meeting, one observer estimated that there were over 1,200 people in attendance. "Bericht: Offentliche Versamlung, aller Interessenten für eine Auswanderung nach Sowjet-Russland . . . 10 März 1920 im Grossen Saale der Brauerei Wulle. Einberufer: Ortsrat der Vereinigung Ansiedlung Ost–Sitz Stuttgart," BArch R 1501/101826, 61–62. Julia Mahnke reports that Ansiedlung Ost had a membership of over 100,000, but her estimate is based on wildly inflated reports from anti-Bolshevik agitators and cannot be taken at face value; Mahnke, *Auswanderungsvereine.*

11. "Bericht," 89.

12. Ibid. The professions of 5,748 members are listed; the same report stated that over 12,000 men claimed membership in Ansiedlung Ost.

nor a trade union.[13] In the Reichstag elections of June 1920, the USPD polled 18.6 percent of the vote, against 1.7 percent for the KPD.[14] If Dittmann's count can be considered accurate for the organization as a whole, although the KPD was proportionally overrepresented in Ansiedlung Ost, communists by no means constituted a majority or even a plurality of its members. As for its leadership, Goldschmidt himself was a communist, but Gumprich does not appear to have been associated with any political party.

The USPD was founded in 1917 in a break with the SPD over the issue of war credits; by 1920, it was riven with internal conflicts and divisions, most significantly with regards to Russian Bolshevism.[15] Moderate USPD members never accepted the October revolution as a model for Germany, whereas the left-wing of the party looked toward the revolutionary councils in 1918–1919 as the basis for a German Bolshevik revolution. The USPD eventually split in October 1920 under Comintern pressure to adopt Grigory Zinoviev's Twenty-One Points and conform to the line set down by Moscow. In late August 1920, the party organ, *Freiheit,* published an exposé of the disastrous Ansiedlung Ost settlement in Kolomna in southern Russia. This piece was later used as evidence by those USPD members who rejected collaboration with Soviet Russia.

The KPD developed out of the revolutionary Spartacist movement in late 1918 and was itself a more radical offshoot of the USPD.[16] The KPD was banned during the Spartacist uprising of the winter 1918–1919, and in early 1920, it was still a small fringe party; it made serious electoral inroads only with the USPD schism of late 1920 and the merger of the USPD left with the KPD in December 1920.[17]

Whatever their conflicts concerning ideology and in the streets, all three of the major German socialist parties—the SPD, USPD, and KPD—sharply criticized Ansiedlung Ost. Meanwhile, party affiliation seems to itself have held little importance to the membership of Ansiedlung Ost because it was rarely spoken of in either internal documents or the memoirs of the settlers. Members of Ansiedlung Ost identified themselves as socialists, but were less interested in making finer distinctions.

13. Wilhelm Dittmann, "Die Auswanderung nach Sowjet-Rußland," *Freiheit,* August 31, 1920.
14. Geoff Eley, *Forging Democracy: The History of the Left in Europe, 1850–2000* (Oxford: Oxford University Press, 2002), 169.
15. Krause, *USPD;* Morgan, *Socialist Left.*
16. For more on this history, see Hermann Weber, *Der Gründungsparteitag der KPD: Protokoll und Materialien* (Frankfurt am Main: Europäische Verlagsanstalt, 1969). For more on the KPD in general, see Ossip Kurt Flechtheim and Sigrid Koch-Baumgarten, *Die KPD in der Weimarer Republik* (Hamburg: Junius, 1986); Klaus-Michael Mallmann and Wilfried Loth, *Kommunisten in der Weimarer Republik: Sozialgeschichte einer revolutionären Bewegung* (Darmstadt: Wissenschaftliche Buchgesellschaft, 1996); Eric Weitz, *Creating German Communism, 1890–1990: From Popular Protests to Socialist State* (Princeton: Princeton University Press, 1997).
17. Weitz, *Creating German Communism, 1890–1990,* 97–98. Weitz notes that in fall 1919 the KPD had 106,656 members and in fall 1920 it had 66,323. By early 1921, it had over 350,000 members.

"A Factory in the Forest": The Ansiedlung Ost Idyll

Taken as a whole, the Ansiedlung Ost utopia was a mishmash of various, often contradictory utopian visions. Partially agrarian or pastoral, members imagined that they were going to live in a worker's paradise, where they would run a factory according to communist principles. Propagating German culture, they also hoped to escape from the stultifying and repressive conditions within Germany itself. Hoping to have the opportunity to work hard, the emigrants also expected a land of plenty that would provide for them. Fittingly, considering their lack of knowledge about Russia and their desire to escape a Germany that itself had failed to achieve revolution, the majority of Ansiedlung Ost images of Russia were dominated by images of freedom—Russia was an open space where German migrants would be able to reinvent themselves and their society.

Repeatedly, the Ansiedlung Ost leadership stressed that it wished to have only members who were committed to Bolshevism. An article entitled "Duties" in the *Rätezeitung,* a subscription to which was mandatory for each member of Ansiedlung Ost, exhorted members to remember that they were going eastward to help build a new socialist state, not necessarily to improve their own lives: "The Organization is not here to create a better existence for its members. In no way should egoism drive you, even if this egoism is mixed with idealism. He who wants to go to Russia because he wants to find a more secure future, or to establish a comfortable life in an idyllic communist village, is unfit for the organization."[18] Yet no matter how often the Ansiedlung Ost leaders reminded their membership of their duties, these members, although certainly not devoid of an altruistic desire to aid the cause of world revolution, were at least equally interested in emigration as a way of improving their own desperate situation inside Germany. H.F. Osbahr, a returning emigrant, described the dual motivations behind the interest to emigrate to Russia: "We had all decided to undertake the trip to Russia in part out of political, and in part out of economic, motivations. On the one hand, we wanted to help Russia build Communism, because we held Communism to be an ideal. On the other hand, we wanted to improve our economic circumstances, because we were either unemployed or feared unemployment."[19]

As Osbahr suggests, the workers who were attracted to any emigration organization, but especially to one intending to settle in a place as unsettled and dangerous as Russia in 1920, unsurprisingly were from the more disadvantaged sectors of society, including over 50 percent who were unemployed. For many Ansiedlung Ost members, the fact that they were committed socialists meant

18. "Pflichten," *Rätezeitung,* April 12, 1920. The details of the mandatory subscription to the *Rätezeitung* were laid out in the "Richtlinien der Interessengemeinschaft," *Rätezeitung* 2, no. 6, 1.

19. H. F. Osbahr, *Menschenhandel: Russische Erfahrungen Hamburger Arbeiter die auf Veranlassung des Ansiedlung Vereins Ost/Sitz Hamburg nach Russland zur Arbeit auswanderten* (Hamburg: n.p., 1920), 14.

less that they wished to sacrifice themselves for the Soviet project and more that they believed that settlement in Soviet Russia offered them their best chance for a better future.

At Ansiedlung Ost meetings across Germany, speakers made all sorts of promises about the opportunities and rewards of emigration, the most elementary of which were monetary. The police in Munich reported that workers at meetings there had been promised that each settler in Soviet Russia would receive between 2,000 and 5,000 marks.[20] Other members of the organization wanted to emigrate because of the opportunity to join the Red Army.[21] Still others joined Ansiedlung Ost because they feared punishment after their participation in political uprisings in Germany.[22] Most members, however, seemed less swayed by the promise of money or their fear of government retribution and more attracted by the pictures drawn by Goldschmidt of the endless Russian forest and steppe and the orderly and clean factories run by the workers in Soviet Russia.

The first and most important part of this vision was the vast Russian landscape that awaited future German emigrants. Gumprich described the future home of the Ansiedlung Ost members: "The land consists of nine-tenths forest, mostly oak, pine, asp, larch and beech. In the wild there are bears, deer[,] . . . water birds, many birds of prey, and in the winter there are also wolves. There are wild berries, mostly strawberries, cranberries and blueberries, also mushrooms. Grass can be as much as a meter high and is the same as ours. . . ."[23] Returning emigrants also emphasized that "The question of land is unimportant; in this, Russia is immeasurably rich. . . ."[24] At a meeting of the Bremen chapter, a speaker promised his audience that, after living in Russia for two years, each worker and his family would receive their own plot of this rich land.[25]

This vision of Russia as a wide-open, untouched wilderness accompanied a belief that Russia's primitivity offered great opportunities for German settlers. Gumprich described the task that lay before the Ansiedlung Ost emigrants in Russia: "To move to a foreign land, and to work together to transform a piece of wilderness, of primeval forest, with much effort and hard work into a humane, cultured existence."[26] Goldschmidt wrote:

20. Report from Polizeidirektion München, July 26, 1920, BArch R 1507/1059, 7.

21. Polizeidirektion—Bremen report on Bremen meeting of Ansiedlung Ost, July 9, 1920, BArch R 1507/1059, 2.

22. Grimm and Weber, *Russlandfahrt 1920*, 19. The role of the KPD in the Ruhr uprising of March 1920 is discussed by Erhard Lucas, *Märzrevolution 1920*, 3 vols. (Frankfurt am Main: Roter Stern, 1970–1978); George Eliasberg, *Der Ruhrkrieg von 1920* (Bonn-Bad Godesberg: Neue Gesellschaft, 1974).

23. Hugo Gumprich, *Delegationsbericht über die Verhandlungen mit Sowjet-Russland von H. Gumprich: Referat zur ausserordentlichen Mitgliederversammlung und zum Delegiertentag am 31. August 1919 im Volkshaus zu Leipzig* (Leipzig: Verein Ansiedlung Ost, 1919), 26.

24. Grimm and Weber, *Rußlandfahrt 1920*, 6.

25. Polizeidirektion—Bremen report, 2.

26. Gumprich, *Delegationsbericht*, 27.

The Russian worker needs examples. . . . Here the Russians can learn how one saves machinery and how one works rationally. German work is German work. I don't say this to be a nationalist. The Russians say it themselves. Russian work must be "Germanized", so to speak. They desperately need that. The economic leaders in Russia know that. They praise German work, they long for German work. German work is, economically speaking, gold for Russia.[27]

Ansiedlung Ost members saw themselves as ambassadors from the cultivated and civilized West who would teach the Russian workers how to really work. One returning emigrant from Hamburg expected that "With the German love of order and German hard work (these two German characteristics are very important in Russia) the residents of Hamburg will create a masterpiece."[28] Another wrote, "We should use our model factory to teach Russian workers, and these workers who have learned from us will be sent to other factories in Russia."[29] This theme of Russia as a "primeval forest" awaiting the transformative efforts of cultured Germans echoes similar statements by right-wing proponents of emigration to the east during World War I and the Freikorps mission.

The Ansiedlung Ost leadership believed that the argument about the Russian "primeval forest" was one of their most persuasive appeals, but those who warned against emigration also emphasized the backwardness of Russia. One anonymous pamphleteer, after mentioning the experiences of Germans who had served on the Eastern Front, concluded, "He who goes to Russia today knows that he returns to a primeval condition (*Urzustand*)."[30] Whether they talked about an *Urwald* or an *Urzustand*, Germans agreed that Russia was a radically primitive place that was not only behind Germany in terms of infrastructure or technology but existed outside of the time line of modern society. Of course, depending on the perspective of the author, this was either an opportunity or a danger.

After Gumprich's visit to Russia in late 1919, Ansiedlung Ost abandoned its goal of founding an agricultural community and, instead, began to speak of an industrial colony. This shift to an emphasis on industry reflected both the composition of the Ansiedlung Ost membership, which was drawn from the industrial working class, and the perceived Russian need for the industrial talents of German workers.[31] Nonetheless, the pastoral nature of Ansiedlung Ost members'

---

27. Goldschmidt, *Moskau 1920*, 123.
28. Grimm and Weber, *Rußlandfahrt 1920*, 13. The German belief that hard work was an essential part of the German national character is discussed in Joan Campbell, *Joy in Work, German Work: The National Debate, 1800–1945* (Princeton: Princeton University Press, 1989).
29. Osbahr, *Menschenhandel*, 3.
30. Anonymous, *Was erwartet den deutschen Arbeiter in Sowjetrußland?* (Berlin: W. Wegner, n.d. [probably 1920]), 7.
31. Fähnrich, *Kolomna*, 4.

dreams survived in the image of "a factory in the forest."[32] Speakers for the Ansiedlung Ost movement emphasized the land of plenty that awaited them. One speaker at a meeting in Magdeburg in mid-1920 reportedly aligned freedom and prosperity, telling his audience: "There is no life of hunger as there is here in Germany. Bread, meat and money are available in plenty, and the worker can live free from every chain and restriction."[33] This emphasis on freedom resurfaced when the Magdeburg speaker discussed the control that workers would have over their own working conditions: "After a few years of work, which he himself controls and determines, he can enjoy the happiness of a safe and carefree existence."[34] In these reports, the ability to control one's living and working conditions appears to be as important as the freedom from material want. Note that this was not freedom *from* work. If anything, the Ansiedlung Ost utopia, true to its Marxist heritage, was a utopia *of* work. Ansiedlung Ost emigrants were not planning, or at least were not admitting to planning, to shirk work in any way. Instead, as one wrote, "Everyone had the honest desire to go to Russia and give his best to the reconstruction."[35] According to the Ansiedlung Ost guidelines, men would be expected to work six to eight hours per day and women would work four to six hours.[36]

Although they wanted and expected to work, Ansiedlung Ost members clearly expected to be taken care of. Grimm and Weber reported on their return, "Like all the others, I wanted to live in 'happy Russia, where everything is provided.'"[37] They also discussed the assurances they received: "The Russian government would provide a factory at our disposal. Plows, sowing and reaping machines, and all possible machines would be delivered. Credit would be available."[38] A Defense Ministry official wrote about other promises that were made to Ansiedlung Ost members: "They are said to work in the Kolomna factory near Moscow and receive a daily salary of 500 Rubles, as well as soldier's rations, free apartments and furnishings."[39] At the Ansiedlung Ost national conference in Berlin in December 1919, speakers made a variety of further pledges: a central kitchen (necessary because the first shipments were expected to be composed primarily of men, who could presumably not cook for themselves); shorter work

32. Grimm and Weber, *Rußlandfahrt 1920*, 13. Dittmann and Fähnrich also mentioned that the Hamburger emigrants had been promised a *Fabrik im Walde* and were bitterly disappointed with what they found instead.

33. Abschrift to Reichswehrministerium, letter reporting on agitation for emigration to Russia, July 17, 1920, BArch R 1507/1059, 13.

34. Ibid.

35. Bruno Grimm, *Klassenkampf und Arbeiterschaft: Von einem nach Rußland ausgewanderten und wieder zurückgekehrten Arbeiter* (Berlin: Germania, 1920), 4.

36. "Richtlinien der Interessengemeinschaft," *Rätezeitung* 2, no. 6, 1.

37. Grimm and Weber, *Rußlandfahrt 1920*, 8.

38. Grimm, *Klassenkampf und Arbeiterschaft*, 6.

39. Reichwehrministerium—Heeresleitung to Reichskommissar für Überwachung der öffentlichen Ordnung, July 10, 1920, BArch R 1507/1059, 10.

hours; better food; longer vacations; and schools for children, in which they would have the opportunity to train for a chosen career. The inhabitants would also enjoy free theater performances. Finally, the rights and duties of women and men would be equal in the settlement.[40]

The leadership of Ansiedlung Ost stressed that the creation of a community in Russia was necessary for the tasks that lay in front of them. Gumprich wrote in 1919, "Logically this will be a communal effort. . . . everything individual including individual prejudices must fall away, or, better put, must not be there to begin with."[41] But community was not important only to the leadership of the movement; indeed, the opportunity to live and work in a community was one of the primary motivations of the membership of Ansiedlung Ost. As one bitterly disappointed emigrant wrote on his return, "We wanted to build *a community* and run a factory in Russia based on communist principles. We believed that we could bring our wives and children later, and if not have a perfect, at least an adequate, life. We would receive good food and everything that is necessary for life."[42] This was neither a national nor an international community but, rather, something more tangible and local. Many workers believed that "every local chapter would build a community for itself [in Kolomna]. These would fan out like rays from the industrial center."[43]

In an oversight that foreshadowed later problems that the group would encounter, Ansiedlung Ost members were much more excited about moving to Russia than they were about coming into contact with Russians. Russia was a place to escape to—a "primeval forest"—and the existence of other residents of this "piece of wilderness" did not seem to enter into their consciousness. Gumprich saw the Russian peasantry as inspiringly primitive and naïve, but his was a decidedly minority opinion.[44] Instead, many Ansiedlung Ost members either saw the backwardness of the Russians as an opportunity to perform a valuable pedagogical service or ignored them altogether.

The potential contradictions between the modern revolution that had occurred on Russian soil, and provided the opportunity and impetus for the planned Ansiedlung Ost emigration, and the backward, primitive peasants they hoped to teach did not appear to trouble Ansiedlung Ost speakers unduly before they traveled to Russia. This contradiction, however, became more important after the settlers arrived in Russia, and especially once they returned, disillusioned, to Germany.

---

40. "RWA Rundschreiben Nr. 189. Betr: 'Ansiedlung Ost' in Leipzig, die Schwäbische Siedlungsgesellschaft Südrussland in Stuttgart und andere Vereinigungen, die sich die Ansiedlung in Russland zum Ziele gestellt haben," BArch R 1501/118345, 254.

41. Gumprich, *Delegationsbericht,* 27.

42. Osbahr, *Menschenhandel,* 15. Emphasis in original.

43. Grimm and Weber, *Rußlandfahrt 1920,* 6.

44. Gumprich, *Delegationsbericht,* 27.

Ansiedlung Ost was in no way designed to foster contact between Germans and Russians. According to a contract signed by Gumprich and Vladimir Milutin, a representative of the Soviet government in May 1920, the Ansiedlung Ost immigrants would become citizens of the Soviet Republic, but would not have to pay local or national taxes for five years and would also have three years before they would have to serve in the army.[45] According to another agreement, the members of Ansiedlung Ost would receive an identity card from the Russian commission that carried a visa from Ansiedlung Ost itself. These workers would become Soviet citizens, but (at least temporarily) without any of the duties required of ordinary Soviet citizens and with a special passport identifying them as members of Ansiedlung Ost.[46] Despite the warnings of emigration opponents and the attention paid by the Ansiedlung Ost leadership to this issue, most Ansiedlung Ost members did not trouble themselves to think about what citizenship they would hold when they left Germany. Formal citizenship had assumed a new importance for European states during World War I, but this did not mean that it assumed any greater importance for the working-class men and women who made up Ansiedlung Ost. The memoirs of returning emigrants did not mention identity documents or citizenship at all. Instead, both the speeches by Ansiedlung Ost agitators before the transport of July 1920 and the memoirs of returning members thereafter stressed the emotive ties among the members of the organization and the wider struggle for proletarian revolution.

In their visions of a semipastoral village community, prospective emigrants drew on a long tradition of German pastoral utopianism that crossed political divides. Yet it is important to recognize that, unlike the Freikorps settlers who looked eastward, longing to recapture the lost glory days of German hegemony in the Baltics, Ansiedlung Ost members did not see their emigration as in any way an attempt to recapture something that had been lost. In contrast to the Freikorps, resentment was not a factor for the members of Ansiedlung Ost. They did not mourn their lost security or prestige but, rather, felt that the vistas opened up by the revolution were fundamentally new. The Russian revolution had created a workers' El Dorado, one that was unlike anything that had previously existed. This was a peculiarly modern utopian vision, one that looked for

45. "Grundlagen auf welchen den Mitglieder der deutschen Interessengemeinschaft der Auswandererorganisationen nach Sowjet-Russland die Einwanderung ermöglicht und ihnen in den Fabriken und Werkstätten der R.S.F.S.R. Arbeitsgelegenheit gewährt werden soll," BArch R 1501/101826, 274. The Russian government did not have any official policy regarding immigrants before 1921; Mahnke, *Auswanderungsvereine*, 29. See also Geoffrey Hosking, *A History of the Soviet Union* (London: Fontana, 1990), 119–20. For more on the negotiations with Ansiedlung Ost from the perspective of the Russians, see Galina Jakovlena Tarle, *Druz'ja strany sovetov: Ucastie zarubeznyh trudjascihsja v vosstanovlenzii narodnogo hozjajstya SSSR v 1920–1925 gg* (Moscow: Nauka, 1968), 34–49.

46. "Ausführungsbestimmungen über die vom Obersten Volkswirtschaftsrat und der Interessengemeinschaft der Auswandererorganisationen nach Sowjet-Russland festgesetzten Grundlage vom 19. Mai 1920," BArch R 1501/101826, 275.

its answers in the future, not the past, and that incorporated such progressive features as rights for women, free vocational training for children, and free theater performances for all. Furthermore, like the utopian imaginings of Marx, their goal was "the abolition of the estrangement between man and the world, the assimilation of the world by the human subject."[47] And like Marx, this "dazzling" vision of human fulfillment and freedom was more important than the specifics of their future plans.[48] If the German revolution had not turned out to be as radical as the communists and others had wished, this does not diminish the fact that many Germans longed for a revolution not only of state but of society as a whole. Ansiedlung Ost incorporated both the hopes invested in the German revolution and the disappointment when they did not come to pass. As compensation for the failure of their dreams in Germany, the members of Ansiedlung Ost believed that the revolutionary space of newly Soviet Russia, a *tabula rasa,* was open to them as loyal members of the revolutionary proletariat.

"Desertion of the Worst Kind": Responses to Ansiedlung Ost

Despite or perhaps as a result of its popularity within the working class milieus of German industrial cities, both state officials and left-wing parties looked on the movement with suspicion. Although they differed in several obvious respects, both the National Migration Office and the KPD believed that the emigration of Ansiedlung Ost members would be a loss for some larger cause—the well-being of Germandom and the revolutionary struggle, respectively. After the defeat in November 1918, the Reichswanderungsstelle (see chap. 1) shifted its emphasis to emigration rather than immigration. In April 1919, it officially changed its name to the Reichswanderungsamt (RWA; National Migration Office), although this change of name did not reflect a substantial change in the duties that the ministry performed or the composition of its staff.[49] Recognizing German weakness and the suffering of Germans during the war and demobilization, the RWA

47. Leszak Kolakowski, *Main Currents of Marxism,* Vol. 1, trans. Paul S. Falla (Oxford: Clarendon Press, 1978), 223–24.

48. Marx explicitly avoids calling his own thoughts utopian; nonetheless, it is possible (indeed, quite easy) to find utopian resonances in many of his texts. See especially "Economic and Philosophic Manuscripts of 1844," "The German Ideology," "Manifesto of the Communist Party," and "Critique of the Gotha Program"; these can all be found in Karl Marx, *The Marx-Engels Reader,* 2nd ed., ed. Robert C. Tucker (New York: W. W. Norton, 1978). For a more general discussion of utopianism, see Ruth Levitas, *Concept of Utopia* (Syracuse: Syracuse University Press, 1990); Barbara Goodwin and Keith Taylor, *The Politics of Utopia* (New York: St. Martin's Press, 1982); Krishan Kumar, *Utopia and Anti-Utopia in Modern Times* (New York: Blackwell, 1987).

49. For a discussion of the shift in emphasis after the defeat in November 1918, see "Bericht über den inneren Ausbau der Reichswanderungsstelle in der Zeit vom 1. Juli bis 31. Dezember 1918," BArch R 1501/118318, 79–87. For a brief history of the RWA, see Bade, "'Amt der verlorenen Worte.'"

believed emigration was inevitable.[50] But "as we have the greatest interest in filling the gaps that the war has torn in the strength of our people (*Volkskraft*)," they sought to limit it through a combination of measures aimed at prospective emigrants.[51] Government officials were instructed to notify the RWA immediately whenever a prospective emigrant came to inquire about obtaining a passport or visa in order to leave.[52] At its local information offices located in cities across Germany, and through its publications such as the *Nachrichtenblatt*, a bimonthly chronicle of emigration opportunities, prospects, and scams, the RWA provided potential emigrants with information about popular destinations (especially South America). The RWA held to the belief that prospective emigrants were motivated exclusively by economic need; therefore, their advice for emigrants often contained a combination of warnings (and in many cases, sober advice) about emigration and attempts to reassure prospective emigrants that job prospects within Germany would improve.[53]

In case economic need overwhelmed the RWA efforts to discourage emigration, the organization strove to guide emigrants in directions "that best express our cultural (*völkische*) and economic concerns. Although always respectful to the complete freedom of individuals to emigrate, we must search for means to bring their interests into line with the general interest of Germany."[54] This second goal—organizing emigration in the "general interest of Germany"—was not merely a last resort, forced on government officials by the desperate situation in Germany, but also represented a particular vision of the German nation and German identity. RWA officials and private *Auslandsdeutsche* advocates imagined a world populated by Germans living under many different governments but connected to one another through their common German heritage, language, and culture.[55] Aside from this vague commitment to the German community, the RWA did not officially evaluate the caliber of emigrants or their political commitments. RWA officials were, at least in theory if not always in practice, as willing to assist Ansiedlung Ost members as they were to help conservative or apolitical emigration groups. The *Nachrichtenblatt* published articles even after the failure of the Ansiedlung Ost settlement in Kolomna about the (usually but not overwhelmingly negative) outlook for emigrants in Soviet Russia.[56] At least according to its own statements, the ministry was more concerned

50. RWS to Preussische Staatssekretär des Innerns, January 16, 1919, BArch R 1501/118318, 93.
51. Ibid., 88.
52. GstA PK, 1. HA Rep. 77, Tit. 1814, Nr. 3, 3, GstA PK, 1, HA.
53. Ibid.
54. Ibid.
55. See "Bericht über den inneren Ausbau der Reichswanderungsstelle in der Zeit vom 1. Juli bis 31 Dezember 1918," BArch R 1501/118318, 78–79, for a discussion of the need to keep these connections.
56. See, for example, "Zur Lage in Sowjetrußland," *Reichswanderungsamt Nachrichtenblatt* 3, no. 6, March 15, 1921, 219; "Die gegenwärtigen Aussichten für eine Auswanderung nach den

with the problems of rash and ill-thought-out emigration into an unknown and deeply troubled country than with the left-wing politics of the Ansiedlung Ost organization.

Reasoning that no sane person in 1920 would want to travel to Russia—a land suffering from shortages of every conceivable kind exacerbated by a blockade, engaged in fighting a civil war and then a war against Poland, and a land that had lagged well behind Germany even before the outset of World War I—RWA officials believed that the members of Ansiedlung Ost were driven by blind desperation and had been tricked by an unscrupulous leadership. They worried about the bitter disappointment that these misguided emigrants would suffer once they experienced the reality of a life in Russia, which bore scant relation to their image of Russia as a worker's paradise.[57] True to the prevailing ideology already discussed, the greatest fear of the RWA was that emigrating Germans would lose their connection to Germany. A pamphlet written in Leipzig in 1920 reflected the arguments put forth by the RWA. After listing the many ways that Russia lagged behind Germany and the many horrors that awaited any German who attempted to emigrate, it ended with the dire warning: *"He cannot come back.* There is no possible return for him."[58] An article in the *Nachrichtenblatt* that appeared days before the ship bound for Kolomna set sail warned that emigration to Russia meant the breaking of all ties to their homeland and, in this event, that "they [the emigrants] would lead a life of slavery."[59] Leaving Germany and crossing the border into another state was one thing—and certainly not without potential dangers—but the real danger for emigrants was that they would lose their connection to the German community.

Government officials disagreed about the political implications of Ansiedlung Ost agitation. The Prussian commissioner for the maintenance of public order urged calm: "We don't need to worry when left-wing radicals emigrate to Russia."[60] Yet others believed that the enthusiasm of Ansiedlung Ost members for their prospective new home had turned them into dangerous propagandists for Bolshevism: "[t]he people that are being prepared to leave are so convinced by the pretty pictures of the Soviet state that they have heard about, that they serve, in part unconsciously, as agitators for the Bolshevik ideal. Nine thousand Agitators! The danger for the German state and the people may be equal to the

Sowjet-Staaten des ehemaligen Rußlands," *Reichswanderungsamt Nachrichtenblatt* 4, no. 10, May 15, 1922, 321–22.

57. *Reichswanderungsamt Nachrichtenblatt* 2, no. 16, August 15, 1920, 544. That German workers held illusions about Russia that could be dangerous and needed to be combated was a mainstay of RWA reporting on the Ansiedlung Ost movement.

58. Anonymous, *Was erwartet,* 10.

59. "Lage in Sowjetrußland," *Reichswanderungsamt Nachrichtenblatt* 2, no. 13, July 1, 1920, 424.

60. Reichskommissar für Überwachung der öffentlichen Ordnung to the Staatskommission für Überwachung der öffentlichen Ordnung, July 19, 1920, BArch R 1507/1058, 3.

danger for the individuals who have been tricked into emigrating."[61] Again here, the issue was less the emigration itself than the potential effect it could have on other Germans, the possibility that enthusiastic emigrants would spread propaganda about Soviet Russia within Germany itself.

Although many Ansiedlung Ost members were supporters of the Communist Party, the party itself was hostile to the organization. The KPD that witnessed the growing strength of Ansiedlung Ost was not the mass party that it later became in the aftermath of the USPD collapse in fall 1920. At this time, it was still a relatively small party, and the Ansiedlung Ost movement, which had attracted 1,000 people to individual meetings, had 5,000 paying members and a larger group of supporters in the tens of thousands, represented a serious threat. Both Ansiedlung Ost and the KPD had a utopian hope for the potential of Soviet Russia, but their visions of achieving or participating in that utopia were very different. The KPD emphasized international cooperation, not international migration; communist movements in various countries could offer moral support, possibly even teaching one another valuable lessons, but they needed ultimately to effect revolution independently in their own countries. When German communists spoke of Soviet Russia, they did so in symbolic terms: "For every member of the proletariat, Soviet Russia is the symbol of a better future."[62] The promise of the Soviet Russian utopia glimmered on the horizon, spurring German communists on to greater efforts to achieve a communist revolution in Germany itself.

The Ansiedlung Ost proposal that German socialists could immigrate to Soviet Russia and in that way experience a socialist utopia without bringing about a revolution in Germany itself was a direct threat to this vision. In February 1920, *Rote Fahne* first acknowledged the growing Ansiedlung Ost movement. Despite evincing respect for the dedication and courage of the prospective emigrants, the author took a firmly negative stance toward their emigration plans. He wrote that "*Soviet Russia stands and falls with world* revolution. Without it, the Bolshevik regime is untenable and the workers there, those who emigrated as pioneers of Socialism, will come under the wheel of capitalism just like those in Ebert's republic." The very existence of Ansiedlung Ost was a sign that "The German working class is still not committed to revolutionary *struggle*. Otherwise, no one would come to the idea of emigrating—instead of first fighting to establish the concrete basis for achieving those dreams."[63] An article published a few days later stated the case against emigration even more strongly, arguing that "For party members, emigration to Soviet Russia is desertion of the worst kind, a retreat from the revolutionary front."[64] After the failure of the mission had become known, a KPD member spoke at an Ansiedlung Ost meeting to remind people of the need

61. Abschrift to Reichswehrministerium, 13.
62. "Die Auswanderung nach Rußland," *Rote Fahne*, February 27, 1920.
63. Ibid. Emphasis in original.
64. "Die Auswanderung nach Räterußland und die K.P.D.," *Rote Fahne*, March 2, 1920.

to stay and "fight here for world revolution." The Ansiedlung Ost speaker replied that, given the lack of jobs in Germany, surely it would be better for the workers to find work in Soviet Russia than "stand around unemployed here in Germany."[65]

The Kolomna Settlement

In 1919 and 1920, Ansiedlung Ost sent delegations to Russia to negotiate with the Soviet authorities in preparation for the group's migration to the Soviet Republic. A preliminary agreement in August 1919 left most of the details of the actual land transfer and supply of provisions to the colonists unclear.[66] A second delegation from Ansiedlung Ost went to Russia in March 1920. According to the Soviet historian Galina Tarle, this delegation actually met with Lenin himself in preparation for the trip.[67] The Ansiedlung Ost delegation returned to Germany in May 1920 with a contract that they had signed with the "Representative of the Chairman of the Highest People's Economic Council." Although this contract looked more official than the original draft from August 1919, it was no more concrete in its details.[68] It did not specify a time when the first group of settlers was supposed to leave Germany for Russia; nevertheless, without contacting their Soviet partners, the Ansiedlung Ost leaders decided to send the first group of workers in July 1920.[69]

Paul Fähnrich, one of the participants in this doomed first transport, reported that on the night of July 6 members in several cities got word that they should prepare for a transport to ship out in the next few days. This transport would settle permanently in Russia and prepare the groundwork for future shipments that would bring the rest of the group. The workers who were to make up the transport were told that they needed to collect 800 marks to cover the cost of the trip.[70] One week later, a group of 120 emigrants from Hamburg, Leipzig, Berlin, and Plauen had assembled in Stettin on the German coast for the journey to a factory town named Kolomna that lay several hours south of Moscow.[71] The emigrants piled onto a ship and began their journey to Russia. The mood aboard the ship was buoyant. The emigrants sang the "Internationale" and shared the food that they had brought.[72] Even though they did not have enough food

65. Zentralpolizeistelle in Karlsruhe to Reichskommissar für Überwachung der öffentlichen Ordnung, November 16, 1920, BArch R 1507/1059, 22.
66. Mahnke, *Auswanderungsvereine*, 43.
67. Tarle, *Druz'ja strany sovetov*, 35. Mahnke is skeptical of this claim; Mahnke, *Auswanderungsvereine*, 44–45.
68. BArch R 1501/101826, 273–77.
69. Mahnke, *Auswanderungsvereine*, 46.
70. Fähnrich, *Kolomna*, 4–5.
71. Ibid. Mahnke disagrees, asserting that more than two hundred men made up this group; Mahnke, *Auswanderungsvereine*, 47.
72. Osbahr, *Menschenhandel*, 4.

aboard the ship, "We still hoped for the best in Russia. Little things could not kill our enthusiasm."[73] Rumors passed through the ship about the possibility that they had been lied to, but most emigrants, loyal to Ansiedlung Ost and excited about their new lives in the Soviet workers' paradise, paid them little heed. The ship left Stettin and first stopped in Reval, part of the newly independent Estonia. After refueling, they were to continue on to Russia itself; however, because the migrants had failed to obtain transit visas, they could not leave Reval. This held up the group for several days, forcing them to stretch their already limited food supply even further.[74] The Ansiedlung Ost emigrants ignored Goldschmidt's own warnings in *Moskau 1920* about the difficulties of border-crossing[75], just as they had ignored the warnings against emigration that had come from many quarters. Members of Ansiedlung Ost did not consider national borders or distinctions to be important; this is clear from their desire to avoid military service in Russia and from their lack of attention to RWA warnings that they might lose their citizenship if they emigrated. In part this lack of attention to borders on the part of the members of Ansiedlung Ost can be explained by the fact that these borders were so new. A mere two years earlier, Reval had been a part of Russia and not in the newly independent Estonian state.

Their crossing into Russia provided the first hint that this mission would not be as easy as they had imagined. As Osbahr wrote after his return, "Even at the first station we had the opportunity to observe the difference between the circumstances in Germany and Russia. They were not favorable to the Russian."[76] At Petersburg, the group of families who were designated for an agricultural colony in the north separated from the settlers whose destination was Kolomna and who continued on to Moscow.[77] As Goldschmidt had predicted, Moscow was bedecked in red. Nonetheless, it appeared in shambles. "The city is mostly in rubble. The streets are full of disorder. There are long streets without a door or window that is not broken. The masses of houses are uncanny, as they are empty of people. When someone does appear, he moves quietly and quickly."[78] In this environment, Soviet pageantry "seemed to us to be a bitingly ironic commentary on the situation in Soviet Russia. As if a dying land could defend itself from the fall with a lot of screaming, singing and red flags."[79] A delegation tried to visit the Kremlin and receive an audience with Karl Radek, a German communist and member of the Bolshevik Central Committee, to complain about the lack of food on their trip, but were unsuccessful in reaching him.[80]

73. Grimm and Weber, *Rußlandfahrt 1920*, 10.
74. Dittmann, "Auswanderung nach Sowjet-Rußland."
75. Goldschmidt, *Moskau 1920*, 11.
76. Osbahr, *Menschenhandel*, 6.
77. It is unclear whether the group that split off was associated with Ansiedlung Ost.
78. Grimm and Weber, *Rußlandfahrt 1920*, 12.
79. Ibid., 10.
80. Osbahr, *Menschenhandel*, 7.

Finally, after a journey that had lasted over two weeks, the Ansiedlung Ost migrants reached Kolomna, an industrial town 100 kilometers southeast of Moscow. Having heard that the Russians were eagerly anticipating their arrival, the Ansiedlung Ost members expected a jubilant reception. Instead, there were "only a few begging and bargaining children" to greet them.[81] Later that day, they visited the factory in town and were shocked by the conditions they saw: "It was a jumble of old machines, parts of rails, complete disorder in a place that did not seem to be a factory building but chaos."[82] But even more surprising than the condition of the factory was the fact that Russians were still working there. When one German turned to the leader of the Russians and asked if this was the factory that they were to take over, the Russian responded that "there can be no discussion of a takeover of the factory."[83] As this news spread among the workers, they became upset and angry. They may have arrived at the expected "factory in the forest," but they had not expected this factory to already employ 5,000 Russian workers. The Ansiedlung Ost settlers became even more disillusioned when they learned that they would be sleeping on floorboards because there were neither beds nor even straw mattresses.[84] The conditions did not improve; if anything, they worsened as time went on. Fähnrich complained about the food: "Because the bread was made with an additive of straw, grains and sand, it was inedible"; "Meat that we threw away and even the dogs would not eat."[85] Food in general was a fraught issue for the Ansiedlung Ost settlers. Not only was the food itself of poor quality, but the relationship of the Russian people to food was seen as pathological. Another settler described what happened when the Ansiedlung Ost settlers attempted to throw out some rotten meat that they still had with them. "As we got to Kolomna, we threw out some meat that we had brought from Reval, because it was blue, smelled horrible and was totally rotten. About 15 girls, who had to work at the railroad, pounced on it and ate it before our eyes like scavenging animals, even though we said that they would die from it because it had gone bad."[86] For the Ansiedlung Ost settlers, whose memories of wartime food shortages were still fresh, the food situation in Kolomna was a particularly bitter irony. Fähnrich also complained about the heat and the illnesses that befell the Germans, who were unused to the primitive Russian conditions: "the Comrades became for the most part ill, they had stomach and liver pains, became unconscious and had fits, they had blood in their digestive tracts so that the doctor needed to be called and then many Comrades were taken directly to the hospital."[87] And he and other returning settlers complained about "the Rus-

81. Fähnrich, *Kolomna*, 9.
82. Ibid.
83. Ibid.
84. Grimm and Weber, *Rußlandfahrt 1920*, 13.
85. Fähnrich, *Kolomna*, 12, 13. See also Dittmann, "Auswanderung nach Sowjet-Rußland."
86. Osbahr, *Menschenhandel*, 13.
87. Fähnrich, *Kolomna*, 13.

sians." Ansiedlung Ost members accused their Russian coworkers of sabotage: "Measuring tools were stolen and the machines were turned off. . . ."[88]

In Reval, the group had accidentally encountered Wilhelm Dittmann, a member of the centrist faction of the USPD and a deputy of the Reichstag, who was traveling to Moscow with a delegation to discuss the possibility of the potential adherence of the USPD to the Communist Third International.[89] Dittmann had assisted the group in gaining the necessary transit visas to travel through Estonia. Concerned about the fate of these migrants, Dittmann visited the group and reported his findings in an article that appeared in the USPD newspaper, *Freiheit*, in late August 1920. In particular, he recorded their complaints about the combination of laziness, backwardness, intractability, and general hostility that the Ansiedlung Ost migrants observed in their Russian colleagues:

> Despite the fact that the Germans could not really work in the bad nutritional and working conditions, one German still produces as much as five Russians. . . . it is impossible to see any interest or enthusiasm in the Russians for their work. Quite the opposite; even the factory management tries to sabotage the work. After a half hour the Russian worker relaxes and spends a half hour, even sometimes a full hour, smoking cigarettes and talking, and only then does he slowly begin to work again. And so goes the entire day.[90]

By the time of Dittmann's arrival, the relationship between the Russians and the Germans had deteriorated. The Russian leader of the factory attended a meeting of the German workers, urging them to cease their selfishness, recognize the common cause of the international working class, and try to work together with the Russians. This did not meet with a warm response. Comrade Marakoff, the factory leader announced:

> Violence will only be used against those that refuse to work. Without work, no bread. I wonder why you don't want to work, why you don't want to help the revolution? (Call: "We are really counter-revolutionaries!") What do you want? Do you want a leader for each of you (the translator said leader instead of nanny, as the speaker had said). Get rid of your bourgeois prejudices and work with us Russians. ("We want to go home.")[91]

Insult was added to injury when Dittmann later spoke with a member of the Worker's Ministry in Moscow, who stated, "We can't treat Chinese Kulis and

88. Ibid., 16.
89. The other members of the delegation were Arthur Crispien, Ernst Däumig, and Walter Stöcker; Dittmann, "Auswanderung nach Sowjet-Rußland."
90. Ibid.
91. Quoted in ibid.

German workers differently." Dittmann remarked that he seemed to have little understanding of the situation.[92]

By the time Dittmann visited the Kolomna workers, they had divided themselves into two camps: those who wanted to return to Germany and those who wanted to stay and make the best of their situation. Fähnrich led the faction that wished to return. He reported to Dittmann that eighty men wanted to go back to Germany. Furthermore, of those who wanted to return, only eleven still worked in the factory; the remaining sixty-nine workers had stopped working in the factory and, by their account, were instead working on various projects to help the immediate situation of the German community. As one Ansiedlung Ost member told Dittmann, "In Germany, everything had been described very differently; they had been told that they would come into a small factory that they would manage and work in alone, that apartments would be available for everyone, and that the food would be both plentiful and good, and now they could see that none of that was true."[93] Another remarked poignantly, "[I] have spent 35 years working for socialism and emigrated to help build Russia and to serve the world revolution. But hunger makes that impossible."[94] Dittmann's report on Ansiedlung Ost ended with a warning about immigrating to Russia, and he urged Germans who were considering emigration to wait at least until Germany had established diplomatic relations with Russia and, thus, they could receive necessary supplies and provisions.[95] In a follow-up article the next day, Dittmann remarked that "Blind devotion and belief has made Soviet Russia a paradise in which all suffering of the Proletariat will have an end" but that the experiences of Ansiedlung Ost had proved this to be little more than fantasy.[96]

Ansiedlung Ost as Cause Célèbre

Dittmann's article was printed in *Freiheit* on August 31, 1920. In a pamphlet published later that year, A. Franke described the impact of Dittmann's report: "True: All of this had been said in Germany, often and from a wide variety of publications. But the radical workers had not believed it. Those who had previously spoken or written against Bolshevism could be called reactionaries or sellouts. Now one heard the same verdict, if anything even more sharply, from the mouths of radicals."[97]

92. Ibid.
93. Ibid.
94. Ibid.
95. Ibid.
96. Wilhelm Dittmann, "Die Wahrheit über Rußland," *Freiheit,* September 1, 1920.
97. A. Franke, *Die Wahrheit über Russland: Die Auswanderung nach Sowjet-Russland und das Diktat der dritten Internationale, Mitteilungen der deutschen U.S.P.-Moskau Delegierten und anderer Zeugen* (Berlin: Birn, 1920), 5. Emphasis in original. In his memoirs, Dittmann described the effect of this article, and his follow-up the next day, as a "bomb explosion." Wilhelm Dittmann, *Erinnerungen* (Frankfurt am Main: Campus, 1995), 761.

Until Dittmann's visit, most of the eyewitness accounts of Soviet Russia available to Germans came from the reports of émigrés.[98] These highly partisan and wildly differing accounts offered by emigrants of various political persuasions had the effect of reducing the credibility of any account of Soviet Russia. But, because Dittmann had impeccable socialist credentials, both the right and left took his criticisms of conditions in Soviet Russia seriously. And Dittmann's article became both a symptom of and a catalyst for the growing split in the USPD between those who wanted to work more closely with the Soviet Union, as part of the Comintern, and those who wanted Germany to find its own path to socialism.[99] Sepp Oertner, writing in *Freiheit* the day after Dittmann's article appeared, announced his own position, "*I will not lick the Russian boot—even if the foot of a Lenin or a Trotsky is in it. And I hope and expect that from our party.*"[100] At the USPD conference held in Berlin in early September 1920, the Ansiedlung Ost controversy was so significant that even supporters of an alliance with Moscow were forced to take it into consideration. Ernst Däumig, who had been on the same trip to Moscow as Dittmann and was a representative of the left wing of the party, blamed the catastrophe of Ansiedlung Ost on the emigrants and their overly optimistic expectations. In his opinion, the problems in Russia were the birth pangs of a new state and society, and "we have been quiet for too long about the fact that private organizations have spread all possible illusions about Russia to the workers."[101]

After the publication of Dittmann's damning portrait of both the Ansiedlung Ost mission and the situation in Russia as a whole, the fate of Ansiedlung Ost became a cause célèbre in Germany. Dittmann's piece was reprinted in pamphlet form by various anti-Bolshevik organizations, in *Germania,* the newspaper of the Catholic Center party, and in the RWA monthly bulletin. In the months that followed, the workers from the Kolomna colony found their way home and wrote a host of pamphlets that generally confirmed Dittmann's report on the horrible conditions and their disappointment over their attempt to found a German workers' colony on Russian soil, describing their experiences and issuing a warning to those who might consider emigration to or an alliance with Soviet Russia in the future. As one returnee wrote:

> We saw little beauty, little good and little truth, instead we saw much dirt, meanness, ruthless self-involvement. We found it bitter that we had been lied to and

98. Gerd Koenen, "Vom Geist der russischen Revolution: Die ersten Augenzeugen und Interpreten der Umwälzungen im Zarenreich," in *Deutschland und die russische Revolution 1917–1924,* ed. Gerd Koenen and Lev Kopelev, 49–98 (Munich: Fink, 1998).

99. Kai-Uwe Merz, *Schreckbild: Deutschland und der Bolschewismus, 1917–1921* (Berlin: Propyläen, 1995), 476.

100. Ibid., 115. Emphasis in original.

101. Protokoll der Reichskonferenz vom 1–3.9.1920, in *Protokolle der Parteitage der USPD,* Bd. 2 (Glashütten im Taunaus: Auvermann, 1976), 177.

betrayed. . . . Comrades, you all have a reason to be mistrustful! Pay more attention to the tricks of your so-called leaders who tell you about a Russia that is a paradise that has been healed of class struggle! Let yourself be warned before it is too late![102]

Most observers had predicted the failure of Ansiedlung Ost, and most expressed a sense of satisfaction when that failure came to pass. From the RWA to the right-wing Anti-Bolshevik Liga to the USPD, commentators used the failure of Ansiedlung Ost as yet more evidence for the backwardness of the Russian people, the destruction wrought by the Bolsheviks, and the folly of believing that there was a place for Germans in revolutionary Russia. The newspaper of the Anti-Bolshevik Liga, the *A.B.C.*, accused "Bolshevik agitators," particularly a "Herr Sliwkin" of seducing the migrants into leaving Germany and called for more aggressive measures to protect German borders against these dangerous elements.[103] But even when commentators did not blame shady foreign agitators, it was clear to everyone, not only the right, that the failure of Ansiedlung Ost was really a failure to understand the hopelessly primitive Russians. Faced with the sabotage, backwardness, and laziness of the Russian worker, one returning settler announced his discovery that "The German farmer is not like the Russian. [The German farmer] can read and write and is also organized."[104] This was also the lesson that Dittmann said Germans needed to draw from the experiences of the Ansiedlung Ost settlers. The Russians "only a few decades earlier, had been serfs." They were, he continued "two-legged animals. . . . The revolution has not been able to change these primitive men. . . ."[105] A *Nachrichtenblatt* article from August 1921 provided an update of the fate of the remaining German settlers, but did so only to reinforce the folly of settling in Russia:

> They succeeded in creating somewhat manageable circumstances. Then in early March, 1921, one night armed bands broke into many living quarters, storage areas and barns and stole from them. After the bands left, local peasants and Kirgystanis appeared that had already tried to rob the place and made off with the remaining tools and machinery. With one stroke, the entire work of the settlers was destroyed. It was pointless to remain after these events and it was also impossible to do so after so many tools had been stolen.[106]

102. Grimm and Weber, *Rußlandfahrt 1920*, 3.
103. "Zur Auswanderung deutscher Arbeiter nach Sowjetrussland: Was unternimmt die deutsche Regierung gegen bolschewistische Agenten?" *A.B.C.*, October 8, 1920.
104. Grimm, *Klassenkampf und Arbeiterschaft*, 4.
105. Dittmann, "Wahrheit über Rußland."
106. "Schlechte Erfahrungen deutscher Ansiedler," *Reichwanderungsamt Nachrichtenblatt* 3, no. 16, August 15, 1921, 613.

Commentators from across the political spectrum took the failure of Ansiedlung Ost as a lesson about the failure of communism and of internationalism more generally. An article published in the social democratic *Rheinische Zeitung*, entitled "The Victims," quoted one of the returning emigrants: "I saw Russia as heaven on earth. . . . Communism here is nothing more than betrayal and theft. We who are here and have seen the truth are no longer communists."[107] Franke added that the lesson to be drawn from Ansiedlung Ost was that "No Soviet Republic can help us. German workers must rely on themselves."[108] Grimm, too, recommended a turn inward; the Germans could not rely on the Russians for help because "The jump from 'I' to the 'International' is too large, today it is drivel. We must stay in the Nation, think in national terms, advance nationalism."[109]

The effect of the failure of the Ansiedlung Ost movement was both immediate and lasting. Two years later, the RWA began to receive queries about new emigration schemes. Remarking on the situation, one RWA official wrote that skepticism about emigration lingered among prospective emigrants because of the Ansiedlung Ost fiasco in 1920.[110]

The Ansiedlung Ost organization itself continued to exist for almost another year. At its annual meeting in October 1920, its leaders sought to defend themselves from the charges that they had been unprepared or unscrupulous, and they blamed the returning settlers for what had happened to them in Russia. One speaker accused some of them of being saboteurs: "they obviously did not have the intention of staying in Russia, but were instead corrupted by their [Ansiedlung Ost's] opponents so as to make their plans impossible."[111] Other speakers felt the need to emphasize the reality of the conditions in Russia: "The local groups of the organization must paint a very gloomy picture so that new immigrants are not disappointed."[112] The optimism of a few months earlier was gone forever. Nonetheless, the speakers continued to imagine a large and important role for Germans in Russia: "If the Germans had come to Russia earlier, there is nothing that [Pyotr Nikolayevich] Wrangel [a White Russian general] or any Pole could have done."[113] Defiant, Ansiedlung Ost vowed to send a small second transport of workers in November 1920, but there is no evidence that this ever took place. A couple of months later, rocked by the damning stories told by returning settlers, the organization changed its name to the Proletarische Auswan-

107. "Die Opfer," *Rheinische Zeitung*, October 6, 1920.

108. Franke, *Wahrheit über Russland*, 29.

109. Grimm, *Klassenkampf und Arbeiterschaft*, 8.

110. RWA to RMI, December 2, 1921, BArch R 1507/1059, 46.

111. "Zur Reichskonferenz der Interessengemeinschaft der Auswanderer nach Sowjetrußland," *Reichswanderungsamt Nachrichtenblatt* 2, no. 22, November 15, 1920, 766.

112. Ibid.

113. "Bericht über die Reichskonferenz der Interessengemeinschaft der Auswanderer-Organisationen nach Sowjet-Russland, am Sonntag den 10. Oktober," BArch R 1501/101826, 85–286.

derer-Organization nach Sowjet-Rußland (Proletarian Emigration Organization to Soviet Russia) and changed its goal from settlement in Russia to the mere support for the economic reconstruction of the Soviet state.[114] Shortly thereafter, the group broke apart amid recriminations, debts, and legal proceedings.[115]

The communist *Rote Fahne*, which had initially lambasted the group for its betrayal of socialist principles, now attacked the critics of Ansiedlung Ost, defending the Soviet project in Russia as well as its own reputation. One author in the *Rote Fahne* bitterly reflected on Dittmann's betrayal: "Everything that the Anti-Bolshevik League had said better and finer, is now said by the *sick, petty bourgeois* Dittmann, *fatter, dumber* and, what barely seems possible, even *meaner*."[116] Paul Levi, who had accompanied Dittmann to Russia and became a leader of the Communist Party after the breakup of the USPD, responded more substantively to Dittmann's accusations, arguing that (1) the communists had, from the first, warned German workers against such an ill-planned venture; (2) the communist workers in Kolomna had behaved themselves in an exemplary manner and continued to work, whereas only the noncommunist, SPD, and USPD workers had abandoned the colony and sought to return home; and, finally, (3) that Dittmann had a vendetta against the communists and was using the situation in Kolomna to attack them.[117]

A year later, the *Rote Fahne* updated its readers on the fate of the Kolomna settlement. The reporters P. Neumann and E. Friesland visited the settlement and reported that "the work was of the same exactness and precision as in a similar German factory. . . . we did not find any of the dirt and disorder that had made such a bad impression on Wilhelm Dittmann a year earlier. . . . every German worker will recognize the conditions there, as they are the same as those that one sees everyday in the large German industries."[118] Although the Russians had apparently learned to tolerate the Germans and relations between the two groups had improved, they described a life in which the Germans mainly kept to themselves. The authors of this article marveled at the ability of the thirty-five remaining emigrants in Kolomna to maintain their German way of life, symbolized by the cleanliness of their working and living spaces.[119] They expressed the opinion that "the room and board has been described as sufficient by the workers themselves . . . relatively speaking, good. . . . we are convinced that the workers in Berlin would happily trade their apartments with these," but at the same

114. RWA to RMI and AA, January 10, 1921, BArch R 1501/101826, 359.
115. RWA to RMI, May 20, 1921, BArch R 1507/1058, 31.
116. Franke, *Wahrheit über Russland*, 20. Emphasis in original.
117. "Gen Paul Levi schreibt uns," *Rote Fahne*, no. 171, September 1, 1920.
118. "Zur Lage der Arbeiter in Sowjet-Rußland," *Rote Fahne*, August 10, 1921. There is some doubt about the trustworthiness of this account of the success of the Ansiedlung Ost settlement; this report came at the same time as published reports of the devastating Russian famine and Maxim Gorky's desperate call for Western aid for the starving Russians.
119. Ibid.

time they stopped short of openly advocating the emigration of more Germans to Russia.[120] Although the *Rote Fahne* continued to espouse internationalism and an alliance with Moscow, it had ironically adopted a position not so very far from that of the RWA prior to the emigration—viewing the worth of Germans abroad in their ability to maintain their German essence.

———

Like so much else in the years 1914–1922, Ansiedlung Ost was the product of a combination of uncertainty, utopian yearnings, and frustration. Uncertain of their prospects in Germany and unclear as to the nature of revolutionary Russia, the migrants to Soviet Russia imagined that they were coming to an empty and open land. The members of Ansiedlung Ost were drawn by a utopian vision of the opportunities for them in a revolutionary idyll. And frustration played an important role at both the beginning and end of this doomed venture. Frustrated by both their individual prospects and those of the German revolution more generally, members of Ansiedlung Ost saw emigration as a last desperate chance.

The failure of Ansiedlung Ost was used as evidence for the impossibility of internationalism. The contradiction between the modern, revolutionary worker's paradise they had expected and the poor and primitive land and people that they found drove many of the returning Ansiedlung Ost settlers to embrace a chauvinistic nationalism and to abandon their previous ideals. Commentators from the USPD to the reactionary right drew the conclusion that primitive Russians made change in Russia impossible—revolution had not changed the essence of the Russian people. *Rote Fahne* was left in the position of defending Soviet Russia; ironically, it did so by describing the German community that the settlers had managed to create there and refraining from mentioning any kind of solidarity, revolutionary or otherwise, between the Germans and Russians.

The members of Ansiedlung Ost shared with the Freikorps soldiers a conviction that freedom could be found in the east. For both groups, the protean and porous borders of the postwar world offered an opportunity for freedom and escape. Indeed, it is striking how often both words appear in the texts of these two groups, as different as their membership and ideology were.

Yet most Germans were not willing or able to leave Germany. They, too, were highly aware of the fluid and porous nature of the Germany frontiers, but for them this nature contained threat rather than promise. The uncontrolled frontiers of Germany were particularly problematic for the new republican state. For the German state to assert its legitimacy, it needed to seal its borders effectively not only against those Germans who sought to leave and resettle elsewhere but, more important, against the hundreds of thousands of foreigners who sought to enter Germany in the first years of the republic.

120. Ibid.

4. "We Who Suffered Most"

The Immigration of Germans from Poland

A s a result of the Treaty of Versailles, Germany was forced to hand over the provinces of Posen and West Prussia (Westpreussen) to Poland. A realignment of population accompanied this realignment of territory, and by the end of 1921, between 500,000 and 750,000 Germans (or between one-half and two-thirds of the German population) in the newly Polish provinces of Poznań and Pomorze had left for Germany.[1] German authorities confronted them with a mix of trepidation and resignation. The response of Germany to the immigration of Germans from Poland is a story of the country's coming to terms with the metaphorical and practical consequences of its defeat. The German state could not morally refuse the rights of these former German citizens to settle in German territory and receive government aid, but it also could literally not afford to pay for them. The moral claims of the Polish Germans rested on their status as living symbols of the injustices meted out at Versailles and the suffering of the German nation as a whole. As such, they were able to profit from the powerful appeal of victimization in the political and social culture of the Weimar Republic.[2] From re-

---

1. For the lower figure, see Richard Blanke, *Orphans of Versailles* (Lexington: University Press of Kentucky, 1993), 32–33; for the higher figure, see Hermann Rauschning, *Die Entdeutschung Westpreussens und Posens* (Berlin: R. Hobbing, 1930). As Blanke notes, figures for the migration of Germans living in Poland are difficult to arrive at, not least of all because of the highly politicized nature of these figures. For example, Poles had reasons to undercount these refugees, whereas Germans often overcounted them. Furthermore, the malleability of national identity in the region meant that many people changed the identity they reported for reasons beyond national conviction.

2. Greg Eghigian, "The Politics of Victimization: Social Pensioners and the German Social State in the Inflation of 1914–1924," *Central European History* 26, no. 4 (1993), 401.

turning soldiers and war widows to potential welfare recipients, a complex and powerful connection between suffering and martyrdom operated as a moral basis upon which claims could be made on the state.[3] Indeed, nationalists often represented the German nation itself as a victim, suffering at the hands of internal and external enemies. German nationalists claimed that the territorial concessions mandated by the Treaty of Versailles had turned Germany into "a mutilated body, bleeding from a thousand wounds,"[4] and one of the most resonant founding myths of the German republic was the stab-in-the-back story told by German conservatives to justify their defeat in the war, which was itself a story of betrayal, suffering, and victimization.[5]

At this time of social, political, and economic weakness, the state nonetheless had to balance the claims of the Polish Germans with fiscal and logistical feasibility. In performing this balancing act, it came to embrace two key axioms of the *völkisch* right: (1) the triumph of ethnicity over citizenship as the key criterion for recognizing German identity and (2) the need for the German state to financially and culturally support German communities beyond its borders. These two precepts were not necessarily dominant at the end of the war or even in the immediate aftermath of the Treaty of Versailles. Rather, the radicalizing effect of the treaty resulted from a cascading set of emotional and material obligations and frustrations as the local and national state attempted to cope with a massive and inescapable flood of immigrants. Much like the emigrant utopian dreams of German expansion, which were ultimately crushed by material constraints (see chaps. 2–3), the flood of refugees from the eastern territories encouraged another utopian vision—that of a German nation that encompassed the lost Polish territories. Thus, German revanchist fantasies became a justification for keeping the Germans in Poland from moving to Germany, and German imperial aims ironically evolved as an consequence of the limits of German resources.

Suffering and the Polish Germans

The Germans living in the territories ceded to Poland included many bureaucrats and settlers who had been enticed to the region by the policy of land grants and

3. Robert Whalen, *Bitter Wounds: German Victims of the Great War, 1919–1939* (Ithaca: Cornell University Press, 1984); Bessel, *Germany after the First World War;* Deborah Cohen, *The War Come Home: Disabled Veterans in Britain and Germany, 1914–1939* (Berkeley: University of California Press, 2001); Karin Hausen, "The German Nation's Obligations to the Heroes' Widows of World War I," in *Behind the Lines: Gender and the Two World Wars,* ed. Margaret Hignonet, Jane Jenson, Sonya Michel, and Margaret Weitz, 126–40 (New Haven: Yale University Press, 1987); David Crew, *Germans on Welfare: From Weimar to Hitler* (New York: Oxford University Press, 1998), esp. 205.
4. Hans-Dietrich Schulz, "Deutschlands 'natürliche' Grenzen," in *Deutschlands Grenzen in der Geschichte,* ed. Alexander Demandt (Munich: C. H. Beck, 1991), 63.
5. For more on the *Dolchstoßlegende,* see Boris Barth, *Dolchstoßlegenden und politische Desintegration: Das Trauma der deutschen Niederlage im Ersten Weltkrieg 1914–1933* (Dusseldorf: Droste, 2003).

employment that made up the aggressive attempt of the Kaiserreich to Germanize its Polish borderlands.[6] As early as November 1918, the unstable situation in Poland and the defeat of the German army gave rise to fears of a massive immigration of Germans from Polish territory to Germany.[7] These fears were not unfounded, as the Polish insurgency unleashed a wave of immigration from Posen that began even before New Year's Day 1919.[8] A larger migration of these Germans from the Polish territories began in May 1919 after the publication of the terms of the Treaty of Versailles. German government officials were the first to leave. In July, a second wave of Germans joined them, driven by fears of a Bolshevik invasion. Compared to the Germans who came in the following years, the 1919 emigrants were relatively well off. Although 60 percent required some sort of assistance from the Red Cross, most of them had a destination (most often their relatives). The migration appeared to subside at the end of 1919, but it increased sharply again in mid-1920 as Germans in Poland realized the financial and political consequences of their loss of the privileged status they had enjoyed under the kaiser.[9] Estimates for the total number of migrants varied wildly and were almost certainly overstated. In April 1921, the Red Cross counted 285,866, not including children under the age of fourteen, for 1920 alone; however, officials recognized that the precision of that number was undercut by the fact that many migrants failed to contact the Red Cross for assistance.[10] In 1924, the German Consulate in Posen claimed that 846,828 migrants had left Poland for Germany in the previous five years.[11] Although the emigration abated somewhat after 1923, it never entirely ended, and by 1931, only 330,000 of the original 1.2 million German residents of the Polish Territories remained in Poland.[12]

The Germans in Poland were not the only group of Germans who emigrated to the Reich after the German defeat in World War I; approximately 150,000 Germans also left the provinces of Alsace and Lorraine for the Reich.[13] Despite the lack of any state control over their immigration, the Alsatians were relatively easily integrated into the now smaller German state. There are several reasons

6. Broszat, *Zweihundert Jahre deutsche Polenpolitik;* William Hagen, *Germans, Poles & Jews: The Nationality Conflict in the Prussian East, 1772–1914* (Chicago: Chicago University Press, 1980).

7. Red Cross to AA, November 22, 1918, BArch R 1501/118388, 17.

8. See Rainer Schumacher, "Die Preussischen Ostprovinzen und die Politik des deutschen Reiches, 1918–1919: Die Geschichte der östlichen Gebietsverluste Deutschlands im politischen Spannungsfeld zwischen Nationalstaatsprinzip und Machtanspruch," PhD diss., University of Cologne, 1985, 22–41.

9. Minutes for meeting at the Red Cross Central Committee in Berlin, February 28, 1921, GStA PK, I HA, Rep. 77, Tit. 1146, Nr. 98, Bd. 4.

10. Red Cross to PMI, April 15, 1921, GStA PK, I HA, Rep. 77, Tit. 1146, Nr. 98, Bd. 4.

11. Deutschen Konsulat Posen (DKP) to AA, October 21, 1924, PAAA R 82229, 91.

12. Oltmer, *Migration und Politik,* 99. Because it was in the interests of the Polish state to undercount the number of Germans in Poland and in the interests of the Germans to overcount them, these numbers, too, must be taken with a degree of skepticism.

13. Ibid., 94.

for this. First, the Alsatians emigrated very early, with almost 120,000 of the total 150,000 arriving in the first months after the armistice and before the Treaty of Versailles was even signed. Later arrivals, such as the majority of the Germans coming from Poland, encountered a growing economic and housing crisis that was not as apparent in late 1918–1919. Furthermore, the immigrating Alsatians were largely state employees, who often continued to be employed by the state, or workers in the mining industry, where there were serious labor shortages after the war, whereas, the population that emigrated from Posen and West Prussia was largely rural. Moreover, from November 1918 it was clear that Alsace-Lorraine would be returned to France and that this situation would not change in the near future. In contrast, the German eastern border was uncertain until after the 1921 plebiscite in Upper Silesia, and in addition to this sustained uncertainty, the Polish Germans were pawns in the minority politics of Eastern Europe in a way that the Alsatians never were.[14] And, finally, in the wake of the long-term imperialist interest of Germany in Eastern Europe and its recent experience of eastern conquest, many Germans felt particularly aggrieved that they had to give up territory to a new Polish state. In this context, the plight of the Germans in Poland became a symbol of the more general suffering of the German nation.

During the war, German military and civilian planners had viewed annexation and migration as means of ameliorating the suffering of both the Russian Germans and the German nation as a whole (see chap. 1). After the war, migration was no longer the solution to German suffering but, instead, the *Auslandsdeutsche*—both those who had been German citizens up until Versailles and those who had never set foot on German territory—became powerful symbols of German suffering and, damningly, of the inability of the German state to protect them. The *Auslandsdeutsche* were visible everywhere in German postwar political culture. Over 1 million new members joined the VDA.[15] And it was joined by a host of new, more overtly political organizations, such as the Deutscher Schutzbund (DS), which claimed to support the social, cultural, and political unity of Germans "strewn across the entire globe" through the promotion of national "thoughts" and "feelings" among the German people both outside and, especially, within the German borders.[16] Its leaders saw themselves as representing "not the German nation as state, but rather the German people wherever they live."[17] The Deutscher Ostbund, which specifically represented the interests of the Polish Germans, counted 1 million members in over 450

    14. Ibid., 94–96.
    15. Rainer Münz and Rainer Ohlinger, "Auslandsdeutsche," in *Deutsche Erinnerungsorte,* ed. Hagen Schulze and Etienne François (Munich: C. H. Beck, 2001), 376.
    16. Volker Mauersberger, *Rudolf Pechel und die 'Deutsche Rundschau': Eine Studie zur konservativ-revolutionären Publizistik in der Weimarer Republik (1918–1933)* (Bremen: Schünemann Universitätsverlag, 1971), 44.
    17. "Was der Deutsche Schutzbund ist und was er nicht ist," *Der Tag,* January 9, 1921.

local groups.[18] In addition, geographers and historians founded the field of *Ost-forschung*, which took as its subject the "East," especially those areas with a substantial history of German presence.[19] *Ostforschung* advocates not only sought to provide support for German claims to territories that had belonged to the Reich before 1918 but also to lay claim to areas of German settlement that had never been part of any German state in Eastern Europe.[20]

The VDA and DS were part of the *völkisch* movement, which shared several precepts:

1. Germans were under threat around the world. As one author wrote in *Deutsche Post aus dem Osten,* a publication dedicated to the Germans from the east, "An iron press squeezes us together and teaches us that the rest of the world is suspicious of us and hates us."[21]
2. The German state should work on behalf of all Germans, regardless of where they lived or what their citizenship was.
3. The state, especially in its present weakened form, could only do so much. Therefore, all Germans needed to cooperate on behalf of Germandom because the nation had greater value than the state.

Not yet the biological logic of the national socialists, these beliefs resembled the ideology of the prewar pan-Germans, but with much broader public support. Perhaps more important than ideology,[22] the *völkisch* movement was dominated by a mood of resentment and threat inherited from the prewar pan-Germans but given an extra impetus by the defeat, revolution, and the loss of German prestige and territory. These Germans saw in the defeat of Germany a reason to believe the most paranoid claims made by the right and to eschew a state-centric form of nationalism in favor of one that privileged the nation above and beyond the state. A pamphlet published by the Reichsstelle für Heimatdienst (National Office for Homeland Services) demonstrates the degree to which the state itself signed up for these goals. The author, Dr. Gottfried Fittbogen, stated baldly that "The peace dictated at Versailles has taught us that the German Volk is greater than the Ger-

18. Kurt Göpel, "Die Flüchtlingsbewegung aus den infolge des Versailler Vertrages Abgetretenen Gebieten Posens und Westpreußens und ihre Bedeutung für die deutsche Volkswirtschaft," PhD diss., University of Giessen, 1924, 60–61.

19. On *Ostforschung* in the early years of the republic, see Burleigh, *Germany Turns Eastward,* 22–32. On the work of geographers, see Herb, *Under the Map of Germany;* Murphy, *Heroic Earth.*

20. Burleigh, *Germany Turns Eastward,* 25.

21. "Die Politik der deutschen Post," *Deutsche Post aus dem Osten,* 1920.

22. The precepts that governed the *völkisch* movement never coalesced into a clear philosophy. Indeed, Ulrich Herbert has suggested that it was the very flexibility of *völkisch* ideology that allowed it to be so popular. Ulrich Herbert, "'Generation der Sachlichkeit': Die völkische Studentenbewegung der frühen zwanziger Jahre in Deutschland," in *Zivilisation und Barbarei,* ed. Frank Bajohr (Hamburg: Christians, 1991), 128.

man state. Germans who had previously been part of the state were violently torn from that state, but remain members of the Volk regardless. Belonging to the Volk and belonging to the state are not the same (*Volks- und Staatszugehörigkeit decken sich nicht*). Belonging to the Volk is more important."[23]

Völkisch politicians saw the national radicalization of the German people as a consolation for the humiliation of defeat. As the author in the *Deutschvölkisches Jahrbuch* put it, the suffering of the war had at least one salutary effect: "It [Germandom abroad] has lost strength, it has lost dear property, it has had to sacrifice, but it had won what appeared impossible years earlier, the increased attention and willingness to help from the motherland. And in all the storms that buffeted it and that came from the hatred of the enemy, it has itself become more 'national' than it was prior to the war."[24] The connections between Germans within and outside the frontiers of Germany were forged in shared suffering—suffering was both the content and form of solidarity. Poems such as "The Refugee" by Leonhard Schrickel described Germans thrown to the mercy of foreign powers:

> *My father was German, my mother was German*
> *As is my life and my suffering:*
> *Driven from my fields, hounded from my home,*
> *Now I am poor and alone:*
> *"Come my wife, come my child, we must leave."*[25]

As this suggests, familial metaphors dominated the poetry dedicated to the refugee. The poem "The Refugee's Last Hope" by August Sperl depicted a family of refugees running to their mother as a metaphor for the relationship of the German nation to the refugees:

> *No, you cannot cast us out,*
> *Your children, your only.*
> *And in your arms and lap*
> *We will lament our misery—*
> *Oh mother, oh mother!*[26]

23. Gottfried Fittbogen, "Was jeder Reichsdeutsche vom Grenz und Auslandsdeutschtum wissen muss," draft published by the Reichszentrale für Heimatdienst, 1923. To little avail, the Auswaertiges Amt sought to soften this rhetoric, in particular objecting to Fittbogen's characterization of the prewar period as one in which Germans cared little for the *Auslandsdeutsche* and his claim that belonging to the people was more important than belonging to the state. AA to the Reichszentrale für Heimatdienst, July 21, 1923, PAAA R 60002.

24. F. F. "Zukunft und Ziele des Auslandsdeutschtums," *Deutschvölkisches Jahrbuch* 1920, 165.

25. Flüchtlingsfürsorge des Bundes der deutschen Grenzmarken-Schutzverbände, n.d. (probably 1921), BArch R 1501/118460.

26. Ibid.

Sperl's statement that "No, you cannot cast us out" was a plaintive warning, both calling on the emotions of the reader and proposing a model of familial responsibility owed by Germans in Germany to these German refugees. In similar but less poetic terms, the *Berliner Volkszeitung* reminded its readers that "we must not forget that those who have been torn from their homes and livelihoods by fanatical Poles have neither committed a crime nor bear any other responsibility for their fate, but have rather been persecuted only because they are German (*um ihres deutschen Volkstums willen*)."[27]

The suffering German refugee embodied an insistent and unfulfillable demand. Recognizing the potency of their claim, Germans from Poland emphasized their victimization when they interacted with officials. One letter from the Verein verdrängter Deutscher aus Polen (Organization for Displaced Germans from Poland) in Hamborn began, "We who suffered the most as a result of war can see what a large part of our comrades in sorrow (*Leidensgenossen*) continue to endure, such as the poor mother and her sick children, who live in pitiful circumstances, or the father, who would love to work but cannot find a job and so cannot bring his family here, or entire families who live in a single room."[28] Meanwhile, organizations such as the Deutscher Heimatbund Posener Flüchtlinge (German Homeland Society for Refugees from Posen) and their supporters in the parliament demanded compensation from the German state for the suffering endured by these refugees in the name of Germany and Germandom.[29] Their supporters insisted that the amelioration of the suffering of the Polish Germans was a moral issue. The president of Brandenburg called refugee assistance a matter of honor, whereas the president of Frankfurt-Oder argued flatly that to ignore the needs of the Germans immigrating from Poland would constitute the "political bankruptcy" of the Prussian state.[30]

This rhetoric of suffering underwrote a huge apparatus of refugee assistance. As of February 1919, the German Red Cross was responsible for providing aid for ethnic German refugees from Poland using funds provided by the federal government as well as money raised through periodic appeals to the compassion of the German people.[31] The Red Cross offices in Berlin directed the nationwide effort through a network of aid commissioners in each state and province. Red Cross commissioners attached to the German consulates in the annexed territories evaluated the persecution claims of potential German immigrants and

---

27. "Die Nöte der Flüchtlinge: Um des deutschen Volkstums willen!" *Berliner Volkszeitung*, February 10, 1921.

28. Hilfsbund für Elsass-Lothringen Ortsgruppe Hamborn & Verein verdrängter Deutscher aus Polen, Hamborn to the RAM, July 28, 1921, BArch R 1501/118462.

29. *Verhandlungen*, Bd. 335, 155; *Verhandlungen*, Bd. 363, 282.

30. Regierungspräsident, Frankfurt a/O to PMI, Januar 24, 1919, and Agreement from the Oberpräsident der Provinz Brandenburg und von Berlin, January 31, 1919, GStA PK, I HA, Rep. 77, Tit. 1146, Nr. 98, Bd. 1.

31. PMI to the RMI and regional governments, July 25, 1919, BArch R 1501/118443, 150.

administered the "emigration trains" that took Germans into the Reich. On the border, the Red Cross operated temporary sanitary quarantine camps for incoming Germans.[32] By the middle of 1920, the number of incoming Polish Germans was so large and the lack of housing in Germany so great that the quarantine camps, which had been designed for stays of no longer than a week, became the homes of Germans for months at a time. As a result, the Red Cross established more permanent *Heimkehrlager* near the border in cooperation with the newly established Reichskommissariat für Zivilgefangene und Flüchtlinge (RKZF; National Commission for Civilian Internees and Refugees), a department of the national Interior Ministry.[33]

The *Heimkehrlager* contained only those refugees without a destination; those with family or other contacts inside the new German borders went directly to their destination. The camps were mostly wooden barracks that had formerly served as internment or POW camps. They had schoolrooms, church services, and a small police force run by the refugees themselves. The refugees received clothes, food, and a small allowance. Residence was voluntary, and Polish Germans were free to leave at any time.[34] The goal of these camps was to find housing and jobs for the refugees as quickly as possible, but the increasingly long stays of their residents inspired fears that the immigrants would become lazy, politically unreliable, or engage in "immoral sexual relations."[35] To facilitate the process of finding jobs and housing, in 1921 and 1922 the Red Cross set up new camps (*Verteilungsstellen*) spread out across Germany for people who were unmarried or had small families and who were thus easier to place. Even after refugees left the camps, they continued to receive aid. Should a refugee not be able to find work, she or he was eligible for national and local unemployment assistance, and because the needs of the refugees were greater than those of other unemployed people, refugees received payments of up to 150 percent of the payments made to other Germans. Refugees could also take advantage of special support for students, former German officials, and the sick.[36] Finally, both the Red Cross and private organizations, such as the Deutscher Ostbund, aided in the housing search (or built housing specifically for the refugees), and the national Finance Ministry operated a special bank that provided loans to enable

32. Red Cross—Flüchtlingszentrale Ost to Red Cross Central Committee, October 27, 1919, GStA PK, I HA, Rep. 77, Tit. 1146, Nr. 98, Bd. 1.

33. Bekanntmachung betr. die Übertragung der Geschäfte der Reichszentrale für Kriegs- und Zivilgefangene auf den Reichsabwicklungskommissar, 7.12.1920, in *Reichs-Gesetzblatt* 1920, S. 2032. These camps were in Celle, Eydtkuhnen, Guben, Güstrow, Hameln, Hammerstein, Havelberg, Lamsdorf, Lechfeld, Lerchenberg, Lockstedt, Nordholz, Pr. Holland, Sagan, Zeithein, Zittau, Zossen, and Wünsdorf; Göpel, "Flüchtlingsbewegung," 84–85.

34. Göpel, "Flüchtlingsbewegung," 86–94.

35. Ibid., 96.

36. On the provisions for aid to former German officials from the annexed territories, see Interessenvertretung der Beamten gefährdeter Gebiete & Arbeitsgemeinschaft der Reichsbeamten und Lehrerschaft to AA, August 11, 1921, PAAA R 82223, 234–35.

refugees to get back on their feet.[37] As of July 28, 1921, Germans from Poland could claim restitution for the losses that they incurred as a result of Polish persecution.[38]

Noting the financial burdens posed by the refugees, in November 3, 1919, Matthias Erzberger, the national finance minister, informed the Prussian Interior Ministry that he could "not recognize a duty for the Reich to care for the Germans living in the territories to be ceded to Poland (*an Polen abzutretende Gebiete*) who have been injured."[39] As a result of the overwhelming pressures that the national and Prussian states felt from *völkisch* pressure groups as well as their own sense of responsibility, his call for fiscal restraint fell on deaf ears. And even Erzberger could not entirely reject responsibility for the Polish Germans, admitting that it was still necessary to assist those "in truly desperate circumstances."[40] The unanswerable charge of Polish German suffering meant that denying aid was not politically feasible. As the migration grew in 1920, attempts to limit it were generally limited to the bleak portraits painted by the Red Cross of its inability to help the Polish Germans and its urging them to remain in Poland.[41] Instead, the predominant concern of national and Prussian authorities was with apportioning the burden of responsibility and making sure that only the right people were being assisted.

Even though the Red Cross was supposed to be in charge, local officials repeatedly complained that the financial and logistical responsibilities for the refugees were unclear and that they were being overburdened as a result.[42] A July 1919 effort by the Prussian Interior Ministry to redirect the flow of migrants away from regions with particularly severe housing shortages succeeded only in raising complaints from areas that had previously been free of migrants.[43] The taxing efforts to provide aid for the Germans from Poland engendered resentment against them, and calls to local governments for solidarity with the displaced German refugees were often ignored.[44] Meanwhile, refugee organizations complained that Polish Germans were treated rudely and that overlapping spheres of responsibility meant that no one was really aiding the

---

37. Minutes of the November 25, 1919 meeting at the Deutsche Bank, GStA PK, Rep. 77, Tit. 1146, Nr. 98, Bd. 1.

38. *Verdrängungsschädengesetz,* July 28, 1921; *Reichs-Gesetzblatt* 1921, 1021. Few payments were actually made to Polish Germans. As of October 1922, only 2,728 of 49,432 restitution claims had been accepted; Göpel, "Flüchtlingsbewegung," 157.

39. Reichsministerium für Finanz (RMF) to the PMI, November 3, 1919, BArch R 1501/118459.

40. Ibid.

41. German Red Cross Central Committee, November 25, 1920, BArch R 1501/118459.

42. Reichsschatzminister to RMI, January 10, 1920, BArch R 1501/118444, 219.

43. PMI to provinces & Berlin police, August 14, 1919, GStA PK, I HA, Rep. 77, Tit. 1146, Nr. 98, Bd. 1.

44. Breslau, police president to Regierungspräsident, Breslau, February 19, 1921, GStA PK, I HA, Rep. 77, Tit. 1146, Nr. 98, Bd. 4.

migrants.[45] Those who failed to respond to these demands were accused of "an unwillingness to remain true to the German nation."[46]

Prussia, the largest state and the state to which the Polish provinces had once belonged, argued with the national government about how to apportion financial responsibility for the Polish Germans. A national cabinet decision on August 20, 1919, divided the costs for the care of the Germans from Poland between the national and Prussian states; however, in July 1920, Prussia insisted that the Reich be forced to pay for the care of the Polish Germans, arguing that, because the Reich had signed the Treaty of Versailles ceding the territories to Poland, it bore the responsibility for the care of the people displaced as a result. National officials countered that, because the refugees were Prussian citizens, the costs should at a minimum be shared between Prussia and the national state.[47] Clearly, neither the German nor Prussian government wanted to bear the sole burden of the Germans emigrating from Poland; on the other hand, both saw them as deserving of support.

In addition to the ongoing arguments about the apportionment of the financial and logistical burdens of refugee care, officials wrestled with the question of who among the refugees were eligible for assistance. As was the case across Central and Eastern Europe, the relationship among ethnicity, language, and citizenship was problematic in the territories ceded to Poland. The Polish Minorities Treaty granted former German citizens born in what was now Polish territory the right to opt for Polish citizenship.[48] Article 91 of the Treaty of Versailles gave every person who had lived in the former German Polish territories as of January 1, 1908, the option of choosing German or Polish citizenship, with those who failed to claim German citizenship automatically becoming Polish citizens on January 10, 1922, two years after the treaty went into effect. Former German officials and those who had moved to the Polish territories in 1908 or later did not have the right to Polish citizenship.[49] The two treaties left the practical details of these policies to be worked out later. This left the residents of the former Prussian territories in an unclear situation, with confused officials uncertain about their citizenship status.[50] As a result, citizenship could not guide officials in deciding who deserved admittance and assistance.

45. Deutscher Heimatbund Posener Flüchtlinge to Reichsregierung, March 18, 1920, BArch R 1501/118444, 252; Deutscher Heimatbund Posener Flüchtlinge to Reichsregierung, April 13, 1920, BArch R 1501/118459.

46. Verein ostmärkischer Flüchtlinge to the Prussian Landesversammlung, May 12, 1920, GStA PK, I HA, Rep. 77, Tit. 1146, Nr. 98, Bd. 2.

47. PMI to the RMF, July 2, 1920, BArch R 1501/118459.

48. "Treaty of Peace Between the United States of America, the British Empire, France, Italy, Japan and Poland," The American Journal of International Law 13, no. 4, Supplement: Official Documents (Oct. 1919): 423–40, here 426–27.

49. Ralph Schattkowsky, Deutschland und Polen von 1918/19 bis 1925. Deutsch-polnische Beziehungen zwischen Versailles und Locarno (Frankfurt am Main: Peter Lang, 1994), 106.

50. Regierungspräsident Marienwerder to the Deutsche Passstelle, Bromberg, March 8, 1921, PAAA R 82221, 283.

Rather than asking immigrants their individual preference or aiding all immigrants who had been German citizens prior to the establishment of the Polish state, the Red Cross stated in August 1920 that only refugees of German descent (*Deutschstämmige*) from Poland were worthy of receiving full assistance from the Reich.[51] The director of the Bromberg Red Cross office explained that the difference between Poles, who were to be refused entry, and Germans could be ascertained by looking at their names, endorsing a distinction based on ethnicity.[52] As for what should be done with the Poles, the leader of a Polish German advocacy group stated baldly that "our goal is to care only for those of German descent. Anyone else should be sent to a concentration camp (*Konzentrationslager*)."[53] In November 1920, the Red Cross refused to go that far, but it still explained that refugees of Polish descent were not to receive aid and were to be turned over to the border police, regardless of whether they had once been citizens of the Reich.[54] The German Red Cross routinely questioned immigrants not about their current or former citizenship but, rather, about their ethnicity (*Stammeszugehörigkeit*).[55] The Foreign Office explained that, although former German citizens of the "Polish race" had the right to opt for German citizenship, this did not give them the right to assistance from the Reich or Prussia.[56] Even when citizenship status was finally regulated in 1922, the national and Prussian interior ministries argued that those of German descent were to be handled in the same way, regardless of whether they possessed German or Polish citizenship, and that those of Polish descent were to be barred from national or Prussian assistance, regardless of their citizenship status.[57] Thus, in the laws and policies of the national and Prussian states as well as the Red Cross, ethnicity trumped both current and former citizenship as the salient category for apportioning aid.

The Baltic and Russian Germans

The German emphasis on descent and suffering also legitimated the claims of postwar ethnic-German immigrants from the Baltics and Russia. During the war, the German state had encouraged the immigration of Russian Germans to Germany through the Reichswanderungsstelle (RWS; National Migration Office), which recruited German return migrants, shepherded them to the German bor-

51. Flüchtlingszentrale Ost to the RMI, August 4, 1920, BArch R 1501/118463.
52. Meeting between the Foreign Office, interior ministries of Prussia and the Reich, Red Cross and other governmental and non-governmental agencies in charge of the refugee problem, August 4, 1920, GStA PK, I HA, Rep. 77, Tit. 1146, Nr. 98, Bd. 2.
53. Ibid.
54. *Red Cross Bulletin*, no. 13, November 10, 1920, 5, BArch R 1501/118450.
55. PMI to Red Cross, March 23, 1922, GStA PK, I HA, Rep. 77, Tit. 1146, Nr. 98, Bd. 5.
56. AA to PMI and RMI, July 6, 1921, PAAA R 82223, 171.
57. RMI to AA, December 23, 1922, PAAA R 82226, 200.

der, and assisted them once they entered Germany. The end of the war meant the dismantling of RWS efforts to encourage the immigration of Russian Germans, but it did not mean that they ceased to come. Between 1917 and 1922, an estimated 120,000 Russian and Baltic Germans came to Germany. For approximately half of these migrants, Germany was just a temporary stopover on the way to North or South America.[58] Both the transmigrants and those who wished to settle more permanently on German soil pushed the limits of the *völkisch* consensus that had come to dominate policy toward the Polish Germans. Unlike the Polish Germans, the Russian and Baltic Germans had never been German citizens, and therefore the decision to assist them could have a basis only in their shared ethnicity, not a legal obligation. The inability of both the national and Prussian states to refuse their claims speaks to the importance of ethnicity in the immediate postwar period.

In July 1919, as the Freikorps were being pushed out of the Baltics, warnings about as many as 100,000 potential refugees from the region began to reach Berlin.[59] The Defense Ministry argued that "As the Baltic Germans . . . have reason to fear for their lives, we cannot deny them entry to Germany."[60] The Prussian and national interior ministries were more conflicted about how or whether to limit their entry. The national Interior Ministry official policy was to try to limit these migrants as much as possible, due to the insufficiency of the funds allocated to their care.[61] Wolfgang Heine, the Prussian interior minister, expressed frustration at reports that Baltic migrants who were not German citizens were being allowed over the East Prussian border.[62] At the same time, both ministries felt that ethnic Germans (*Deutschbalten*) were their responsibility, even calling for negotiations with the Entente to protect both German citizens and ethnic Germans who neither had nor had ever had German citizenship.[63] Much as in the case of the Germans from Poland, suffering gave the Baltic Germans a claim to support that could not be denied, even in the absence of sufficient funds to care for them.

In late summer 1919, Baltic migrants began reaching Germany and, after a short time in quarantine camps on the border, were officially under the care of the Baltischer Vertrauensrat and the FdR.[64] By January 1920, these private organizations had proven themselves incapable of providing sufficient care, and to

58. Jochen Oltmer, "'The Unspoilt Nature of German Ethnicity': Immigration and Integration of 'Ethnic Germans' in Wilhelmine and Weimar Germany," *Nationalities Papers* 34, no. 4 (2006), 435.

59. Kriegsministerium to RMI, July 18, 1919, BArch R 1501/118443, 94.

60. Reichswehrministerium to the PMI, October 22, 1919, BArch R 1501/118443, 288.

61. RMI to the AA, RMF, Reichswehrministerium, Reichswirtschaftsministerium, RAM, PMI, etc., October 25, 1919, BArch R 1501/118443, 215.

62. Heine to the RMI, November 29, 1919, BArch R 1501/118443, 351.

63. Minutes of the November 4, 1919, meeting at the RMI regarding the Baltic refugees, BArch R 1501/118443, 263.

64. RWA to RMI, September 27, 1919, BArch R 1501/118443, 189.

keep Baltic and other ethnic German migrants from becoming burdens on local states, Erich Koch-Weser, the Reich interior minister, reluctantly agreed to provide aid. Koch-Weser explained that this support was justified by the fact that although they "are not German citizens, they are close to us on account of their German descent, German language and custom, and suffered, as carriers of Germandom, the loss of their entire holdings when they were driven from their homes."[65] He sought to limit the impact of this decision by restricting aid to cases of "dire emergency."[66] Once such an exception was granted, however, the case for limiting aid became almost impossible to make. After all, even though local officials were repeatedly admonished to be as strict as possible in their judgment of who was deserving of assistance, it was exceedingly difficult to keep them from being generous with the state's money. The state found itself repeatedly called on to do such things as setting up a bank fund for temporary support and providing short-term housing and restitution for losses at the hands of the Bolsheviks in the Baltics.[67] Matching the National Interior Ministry assistance, the Prussian Interior Ministry extended some aid to those of German descent but without German citizenship who migrated to Germany during and after World War I.[68]

Although Koch-Weser's explanation seems to imply that there was a united community of Germans that transcended the current border and that those living in Germany would welcome the Russian Germans with open arms to their German *Heimat,* the complaints expressed by the immigrants themselves reveal the difficulties of actual interactions between the two groups. One author in *Deutsche Post aus dem Osten* complained:

> When you read the writings about us, you sometimes get the impression that a newly discovered people, some sort of wild tribe, has been discovered. . . . We are supposed to be called "German foreigners." Why not "Also-Germans," "Just-Germans," or "Still-Germans"? A sign of difference must be there, otherwise— God help them!—we could be confused with the "Germans," or, what would be even worse, could get some benefits as "German." Yes, our old homeland is even now truly German; we understand them and love them also when they err. Still it is difficult and sometimes unbearable when one has been persecuted in Russia as a German, and then in one's homeland seen or treated as a Russian or at least as a "foreigner."[69]

65. RMI to all Landesregierungen, January 9, 1920, GStA PK, 1 HA, Rep. 77, Tit. 1146, Nr. 74, Beiheft 4, Bd. III, 229.
66. Erlass RMI, January 9, 1920, BArch R 1501/118444, 40.
67. RMF to Reichsministerium für Wiederaufbau, February 11, 1920, BArch R 1501/118444, 105; Red Cross to RMI, February 14, 1920, BArch R 1501/118444, 110.
68. PMI to the Oberpräsident in Cassel, July 17, 1920, GStA PK, I HA, Rep. 77, Tit. 1146, Nr. 74, Beiheft 4, Bd. III, 2918.
69. *Deutsche Post aus dem Osten*, March 28, 1920, 1.

In the face of such skepticism, Prussian and national officials repeatedly intervened to stress the importance of aiding ethnic Germans. In early 1920, the Prussian Welfare Ministry reminded the oberpräsident of Cassel that Russian Germans were ethnic German "brethren" deserving of assistance, emphasizing that the suffering endured by these Russian Germans justified their receipt of welfare benefits. Answering the objections that these Russian Germans neither were German citizens nor had immediate ancestors who had been German citizens, the Welfare Ministry explained that Cassel was looking at the word *German* in too much of a "legal-technical" sense and that the word needed to be understood as something "cultural-ethnographic."[70] Three years later, national Interior Minister Rudolf Oeser, a liberal, stepped in to protect foreign Germans from having to pay foreigner taxes, as well as the higher prices levied on foreigners in theaters, spas, and hotels. Although he offered little in the way of legal assistance, explaining that Article 276 of the Treaty of Versailles prohibited the differential treatment of foreigners of different ethnicities, confidentially he sought to enlist *völkisch* organizations to educate their fellow Germans to make "individual exceptions" for those of German ethnicity.[71] Furthermore, he reminded state governments, wherever possible, to be lenient or to try to find loopholes to assist ethnic Germans.[72]

These examples demonstrate the lengths to which the Prussian and national governments were willing to go to support foreign Germans, as well as the skepticism they received from recalcitrant local governments and private facilities, which were more skeptical about a "cultural-ethnographic" conception of German identity. At the same time, they also reveal the limit of national and Prussian support for the foreign Germans. After all, the officials made no mention of extending citizenship rights en masse to all those of German ethnicity, which would have obviated the need for an extension of aid to a new category of people. In effect, these decisions established the refugees of German descent as currently and temporarily in need of assistance but not (or at least not yet) German citizens. Ethnic Germans did receive preferential treatment in naturalization policy, but they were not automatically granted German citizenship (see chap. 7).

In January 1921, the Reconstruction Ministry argued that Russian Germans should be eligible for restitution in extreme cases as long as they had not applied for foreign citizenship but had "handled themselves like German citizens" during the war.[73] But this was a step too far for both the Interior Ministry and the

---

70. Prussian Minister for Volkswohlfahrt forwarded to the Oberpräsident of Cassel on June 20, 1920, GStA PK, Rep. 77, Tit. 1146, Nr. 74, Beiheft 4, Bd. III, 291.

71. RMI to VDA, Bund der Auslandsdeutschen, Deutscher Schutzbund, January 18, 1923, PAAA R 60002.

72. RMI to AA, January 18, 1923, PAAA R 60002.

73. RMI to Reichsministerium für Wiederaufbau, January 4, 1921, BArch R 1501/118445, 185.

Finance Ministry, which ultimately decided to reject these claims.[74] In doing so, they had to contend with charges that they had abandoned their "strong moral responsibility" to care for such Germans.[75] The finance and interior ministries could resist these demands only by emphasizing the inability of the state to fulfill them, and their insistence on their own poverty compromised both their moral and practical authority.[76] The ethnic Germans had moral authority on their side, whereas those who opposed extending aid to them had only weakness.

Instead of denying requests for aid outright, the state preferred to provide financial and other incentives to convince the immigrants to leave or not migrate in the first place. In August 1920, the national Interior Ministry agreed to give 300 marks and free train passage to Baltic Germans who wished to return to their homelands.[77] Unable either to meet or ignore the demands of the Baltic Germans, the state was in effect bribing them to leave. Of course, once the Baltic Germans succeeded in obtaining this assistance, it was impossible for the state to avoid a cascading effect in which other Germans, such as those from the rest of Russia and the overseas colonies, demanded similar aid.[78]

Limits and Expansion

As the number of migrants rose through 1920, the German state had actually expanded its financial responsibility by building *Heimkehrlager* and extending an increased amount of aid to ethnic German immigrants who had never been German citizens. The state was captive to a kind of political blackmail, in which the suffering of ethnic Germans gave them an unimpeachable claim to German resources. The turning point came in 1921; the growing size and cost of the Polish German migration forced the question of aid, with many officials arguing that the migration of Germans from Poland to Germany was doubly bad: (1) it only increased the financial pressure on the German state and the German people, and (2) it counteracted the claim of Germany to the territory lost to Poland in 1919.[79] In this new understanding, the suffering of German displaced persons was no longer a symbol of the collective suffering of the German nation but rather a factor contributing to that suffering. The German exodus from Poland was now redefined as a national tragedy that required draconian countermeasures.

74. Minutes from a meeting held in the Reichsministerium für Wiederaufbau, February 11, 1921, BArch R 1501/118445, 252.

75. Minutes from a meeting of the Arbeitsgemeinschaft für (nichtamtliche) Flüchtlingsfürsorge, December 5, 1921, PAAA R 60379.

76. RMF to Reichsministerium für Wiederaufbau.

77. Erlass RMI, August 21, 1920, BArch R 1501/118445, 56.

78. Bund der Auslandsdeutschen: Gruppe Oberschlesien to RMI, November 18, 1920, BArch R 1501/118445, 111.

79. Reichsarbeitsministerium (RAM) to the Thuringian Staatsministerium, April 5, 1921, BArch R 1501/118460. See also the Thuringian Staatsministerium to the RAM, December 28, 1920, GStA PK, I HA, Rep. 77, Tit. 1146, Nr. 98, Bd. 3.

By 1921, the Red Cross was responsible for a huge network of camps, and the national and local states continued to provide assistance even after refugees found housing and jobs. All of this cost money. In January 1921, the national Finance Ministry authorized 17,000,000 marks toward the cost of refugees from the Polish provinces and the Rhineland.[80] One month later, the national interior minister estimated that for 1921 the portion of these costs might come to 52,500,000 marks for the Reich, the same amount for Prussia, and a further 15,300,000 marks for local governments. Adding in the monies needed for housing refugees who worked in industry and mining, which totaled 20,000,000 marks, the Reich looked forward to spending a total of over 80 million marks for refugee assistance for 1921 alone.[81] Although the amounts needed for refugee assistance were small compared to the larger financial crisis that the German state faced by 1921, both the national and Prussian states had increasingly little patience for the demands of the Polish Germans.[82] Yet, no matter how much money the state provided, the refugees and their supporters complained that it was not enough.[83] Caught between financial penury and moral obligation, desperate officials at the German Red Cross even welcomed the Polish government's punitive emigration tax, stating that if emigrants faced losing 50 percent of their property to the Polish state, it might cause them to reconsider leaving Poland.[84] But the Polish government could not be relied on to do the heavy lifting for Germany. Starting in 1921, the national and Prussian states, and in particular the respective interior ministries, tried to limit immigration through a two-pronged campaign: increasingly strict limits on the eligibility of German immigrants from Poland for state assistance, and a simultaneous effort to support German communities in Poland and (later) elsewhere in Eastern Europe.

Up until 1921, the attempts of the Red Cross to limit costs were mostly limited to publishing biweekly bulletins containing ever longer lists of people who had tried to swindle their way into receiving charity that they did not deserve.[85] But under pressure from the national and Prussian states, the Red Cross now tried to put the brakes on as spending threatened to spiral out of control.[86] In March 1921, it released new guidelines recognizing three categories of refugees: (1) those who had been forced to leave by the Polish government, (2) those whose life and health were threatened by ethnic conflict, and (3) those whose economic livelihoods were

80. RMF to the Reichshauptkasse, January 20, 1921, BArch R 1501/118460.

81. RMI to the RMF, February 9, 1921, BArch R 1501/118460.

82. For more on this general financial crisis, see Gerald Feldman, *The Great Disorder: Politics, Economics and German Society in the German Inflation, 1914–1924* (New York: Oxford University Press, 1993).

83. Note the complaints in "Mangelnde Fürsorge für die vertriebenen Ostmärker," *Der Tag,* April 8, 1921.

84. Meeting Minutes—Red Cross Central Committee, February 28, 1921, BArch R 1501/118460.

85. See the bulletins collected in BArch R 1501/118450, beginning in August 9, 1919.

86. PMI to Reichskanzlei (RK), February 12, 1921, GStA PK, Rep. 77, Tit. 1146, Nr. 98, Bd. 3.

compromised by the fact that they were ethnic Germans. People who did not fit these criteria were reminded that they had a duty to remain in Poland.[87] In addition, the national Interior Ministry sent out letters to state governments begging them to remember that monies should not exceed the agreed-on limits and that, should there be some *"extraordinary"* circumstance that made larger expenditures necessary, this should take place only after the most *"careful"* review.[88] Two months later, the national Interior Ministry restricted aid to only those who had lost their homes, rejecting claims by those who had merely lost their jobs.[89] Despite this attempt to inject a degree of control into the aid system, in many cases aid to the jobless continued.[90] In August 1921, Koch-Weser suggested that visas for immigration to Germany should be given only to those who could prove that they had been displaced.[91] In addition, the Prussian Interior Ministry reminded local governments that they needed to check with the German consulates in Poland to make sure that anyone to whom they offered residency met the legal burden of being truly displaced.[92] Such stern warnings, however, could not mask the fact that the national and Prussian states appeared unable to reject responsibility for these refugees. Should the refugees demonstrate an adequate level of suffering—and accounts never ceased to describe in great detail the degree to which they had suffered—the state would and could not deny them assistance.

The degree to which this was the case is demonstrated by the German response to the immigration of ethnic Germans from famine-stricken southern Russia in 1921 and 1922. The famine was caused by a combination of forced requisitions and bad harvests, and it devastated southern Russia, causing up to 20 million people to suffer from hunger, over 5 million of whom died. Saratov Province, where the Volga German settlements were concentrated, was particularly hard hit. The famine unleashed a flood of migrants from the affected areas, with up to 20 percent of the German population of the region, or about 74,000 people, fleeing to other parts of Russia or other countries where they might be able to find food.[93] As news of the famine reached Berlin, the national Interior Ministry immediately sought to avert the expected flood of refugees into Germany.[94] This hesitancy to aid the refugees, however, was challenged by the Foreign Office, the RWA, and the Prussian Interior Ministry, which all preached understanding

87. Deutscher Rotes Kreuz (DRK) to PMI, March 29, 1921, GStA PK, I HA, Rep. 77, Tit. 1146, Nr. 98, Bd. 4.

88. RMI to sämtliche Landesregierungen, March 2, 1921, BArch R 1501/118460. Emphasis in original.

89. RMI to the RAM, May 28, 1921, BArch R 1501/118461.

90. See, for example, Zentralstelle für öffentliche Arbeit to the AA, June 8, 1921, BArch R 1501/118461.

91. RMI to the AA, August 17, 1921, BArch R 1501/118462.

92. Runderlass PMI, August 27, 1921, PAAA R 82224, 10.

93. James W. Long, "The Volga Germans and the Famine of 1921," *Russian Review* 51, no. 4 (1992): 510–25.

94. RMI to AA, August 9, 1921, BArch R 1501/118389, 283.

for the suffering of the Russian Germans. The RWA warned that the German population would not understand why Russian Germans "are left to starve at the German border, whereas swarms of foreign elements, especially *Ostjuden* . . . are regularly granted hospitable admission in[to] Germany, with the government referring to humanitarian obligations."[95] Arguments similar to those used by the Polish and Baltic Germans regarding their suffering because of their German identity during World War I were also marshaled on behalf of the Russian Germans.[96] The Foreign Office obtained the cautious assent of the national Interior Ministry to treat the Russian Germans in the same manner as German citizens "so long as the number of refugees did not reach overwhelming proportions."[97] In October 1921, the Prussian Interior Ministry ruled that all ethnic Germans should receive aid according to the Red Cross guidelines for Germans coming from Poland.[98]

On December 6, 1921, a transport of Volga Germans arrived at Frankfurt-Oder; of the approximately 600 people who boarded the transport, two had died and 115 needed to be hospitalized at an unprepared municipal hospital. By the end of the month, 241 people had been quarantined.[99] This debacle tested the already limited patience of the national Interior Ministry as well as the local authorities, which were forced to take care of the Russian Germans. The national Interior Ministry initially withdrew its already grudging consent for the admittance of Russian Germans. In response, an article in the *Deutsches Abendblatt* accused the government of allowing "Germany to become the El Dorado of [Jewish] privateers, so there is no longer any place for our starving German brethren (*Volksgenossen*)."[100] As a result, the national Interior Ministry reluctantly allowed this particular group to receive aid from the state, although, at a press conference on December 29, the ministry restated its general policy of refusing the entry of Russian German hunger refugees.[101] But this was not enough and it continued to face opposition from the Foreign Office, nationalists in the Reichstag, and the press.[102] Moreover, groups of Russian Germans that found

95. RWA to RMI, August 19, 1921, BArch R 1501/118389, 306.

96. Arbeitsgemeinschaft für das gesamte (nichtamtliche) Flüchtlingswesen to RMI, July 4, 1921, BArch R 1501/118446, 54.

97. AA to the Reichsfinanzministerium (RFM) and Reichszentralstelle für Kriegs- und Zivilgefangene, October 27, 1921, BArch R 1501/118446, 17.

98. PMI to RMI, March 29, 1923, BArch R 1501/118446, 239.

99. RMI to AA, December 10, 1921, PAAA R 82224, 86; Oltmer, "'Unspoilt Nature of German Ethnicity,'" 437.

100. "150 000 Wolgadeutsche Verhungert! 4000 deutsch-russische Flüchtlinge an der russisch-polnischen Grenze—Die Regierung verhindert die Einreise," *Deutsche Abendblatt,* December 27, 1921.

101. AA to RMI, etc., December 14, 1921, PAAA R 82224, 87; Minutes of the Meeting on December 17, 1921 at the AA about Russian Germans, PAAA R 82224, 90–95; "Pressekonferenz am 29.12.1921 [zur] Stellungnahme des RMI zu der Frage der Einwanderung der deutschstämmigen Kolonisten aus dem russischen Hungergebiet nach Deutschland," BArch R 1501/118389, 411–12.

102. *Verhandlungen,* Bd. 370, 3248; AA (Heilbrun) to RMI, January 4, 1922, BArch R 1501/118389, 599.

their way over the border were not consistently refused entry or aid.[103] Ultimately the national Interior Ministry capitulated, accepting that, if the Russian Germans could not be helped in Russia itself, "the possibility of their immigration to Germany will be reconsidered."[104] Even in this situation—faced with noncitizens from thousands of miles away who were suspected of carrying disease during a growing financial crisis—the German state could not say no. Suffering retained its power as a claim on German resources.

In tandem with this not particularly successful attempt to tighten aid inside Germany, in 1921 the German state began a wide-ranging program to provide assistance to German communities in Poland itself. German rhetorical support for the idea that ethnic Germans should remain in Poland was nothing new. On October 24, 1919, Hugo Graf von Lerchenfeld, from the Foreign Office, informed the Reichstag that the German government would support the rights of former German officials in Poland to stay in Poland to keep the "German character" of the region and thus provide an argument for the revision of the Treaty of Versailles.[105] In addition, those who did leave were often branded as traitors by those who remained. The police president in Breslau chastised emigrating Germans for failing to pay proper attention to their national duty to remain in Poland and maintain a German claim to the region.[106] The welfare commissioner at the German Consulate in Posen said that Germans who left Poland simply did not *"love their homeland."*[107] The Red Cross echoed this language, claiming that Polish Germans had a moral responsibility to remain in their homelands and provide assistance to the German nation from afar.[108] Following a similar logic, Walter Jung, the director of the RWA, stated those of German descent abroad were "important mediators" for the German state in the regions where they lived.[109]

Despite these moral arguments discouraging emigration because of its potentially deleterious effect on the German state, except for an abortive October 1919 proposal to send 100 million marks to support German communities in Poland, the German state offered little in the way of practical aid to Germans in

103. RMI to AA, January 26, 1922, BArch R 1501/118389, 484.
104. RMI Entwurf einer Antwort der Reichstagsanfrage No. 1322. January 20, 1922, BArch R 1501/11389, 605; "RMI Besprechung mit einer Reihe von Ressorts und sonstigen Dienststellen stattgefunden, die an der Wolgadeutschen-Angelegenheit interessiert sind., PAAA R 82224, 188–90.
105. *Verhandlungen,* Bd. 330, 3388.
106. Breslau, police president to Regierungspräsident, Breslau, February 19, 1921. GStA PK, 1 HA, Rep. 77, Tit. 1146, Nr. 98, Bd. 4.
107. Deutscher Fürsorgekommissar beim DKP to RK, October 5, 1921, BArch R 1501/118463. Emphasis in original.
108. Richtlinien zur Handhabung der Fürsorge für die aus den abgetretenen Grenzgebieten Preußens stammenden Flüchtlinge im Deutschen Reich 1921, BArch R 1501/118461.
109. RWA to AA, October 30, 1920, BArch R 1501/118389, 57. See also a similar argument made on behalf of the Romanian province of Bessarabia; RMI to RWA, October 27, 1920, BArch R 1501/118389, 44.

Poland until 1921.[110] On February 26, 1921, the Foreign Office released a shocking report, claiming that between 200,000 and 400,000 Germans had already left the former German territories in Poland.[111] A second report from the general consul in Posen a week later suggested that the number of emigrants from the former German territories might be as high as 500,000, with more on the way should Germany fail to act.[112] These dire statistics made the issue of maintaining a German community in Poland a critical issue. Alarmed, the cabinet, in a meeting on March 15, 1921, agreed with the suggestion of the Foreign Office to do everything possible to stop the migration of Germans from Poland.[113] Five days later, on March 20, 1921, the residents of Upper Silesia conducted a plebiscite to determine whether the region would belong to Germany or Poland. After a hard-fought campaign, they decided by a margin of 60 to 40 percent to remain a part of Germany. In response, the Allies supported Poland in calling for a division of the province into Polish and German sections. The plebiscite and its aftermath underscored both the impotence of the Weimar state and its need to maintain a demographic presence in Poland to justify revanchist claims.

The practical meaning of the March 15 cabinet decision became clear on April 6, when the Foreign Office proposed a plan to massively increase support for ethnic Germans in Poland. In designing this plan, the cabinet explained that previous measures, such as the tightening of visa and passport restrictions and a more narrow application of the definition of *refugee,* were "insufficient because [they were] negative." Instead, they maintained, "the struggle against emigration can only be successful when it positively (in other words, materially) supports the Germans in the territories that were ceded to Poland."[114] This campaign of economic and cultural support for the Polish Germans had two important benefits for the German state. First, the presence of Germans in western Poland lent support to German territorial claims on the region. Second, the campaign of support envisioned in this 1921 meeting was supposed to be cheaper than supporting the refugees when they got to German soil. "From the time they arrive until they are able to assimilate into the German economy, the Germans from Poland are a serious burden on the Reich. Given the relation between Poland's currency and ours, they will cost us more here than they will if we support them there."[115] The initial plans developed at this meeting envisioned 1 million marks being provided equally by both the Prussian and national states, with

110. "Niederschrift über die Sitzung vom 20 Oktober 1919 über die Erhaltung und Förderung des Deutschtums in den Ostprovinzen," PAAA R 30860, K038013–K038018.

111. "Die Abwanderung in Posen und Westpreussen," report, February 26, 1921, PAAA R 82221, 230–36.

112. DKP to AA, March 2, 1921, PAAA R 82221, 243.

113. Cabinet meeting, March 15, 1921, BArch R 43 I, Nr. 380, Bl. 29.

114. Meeting at the AA, April 6, 1921, PAAA R 82223, 18–19.

115. Ibid., 19.

Fig. 1. Exhibition: Germany and the Peace Treaty, September 1922. BArch, Plak 002-008-005/ Pfeffer, S. Reproduced with permission.

an additional 1 million marks to follow each month.[116] By the end of 1921, 9 million marks had been sent to Poland. This money was distributed through the aid commissioners to various German organizations in the region.[117] These quasi-covert means were necessary because the German state could not afford to be seen to be meddling in the affairs of a foreign state. Originally, officials assumed that this money could be found by saving money on aid to refugees. This turned out to be impossible, but the attempt shows how the aid to German communities in Poland was closely tied to the frustration at providing assistance to the huge number of Polish German refugees. This frustration at the limits of German financial resources and the burdens caused by the Polish Germans contributed to revanchist politics in the Polish borderlands.

On April 25, 1921, state officials, Reichstag delegates, and private Germandom organizations that met to discuss funding for Germans abroad imagined

116. "Aufzeichnung über die Besprechung betr. Einschränkung der Auswanderung Deutscher aus Polen am 6.4.1921 im AA," PAAA R 30860, K038031.

117. Norbert Krekeler, *Revisionsanspruch und Geheime Ostpolitik der Weimarer Republik: Die Subventionierung der deutschen Minderheit in Polen* (Stuttgart: Deutsche Verlagsanstalt, 1973), 50.

the world as a series of concentric circles: the first circle consisted of the current borders of Germany, the second circle added the territory that Germany had lost at Versailles, and the third circle added the other parts of the world in which Germans lived. This notion of concentric circles rested on a false simultaneity—the current frontiers of Germany existed at the same time as its former ones, each constituting a separate circle of responsibility, with the second encompassing the first. Oddly, as they drew the map, the second circle (which was supposed to contain German territory as of 1914), included parts of Czechoslovakia and even Scandinavia. As much as this notion of geographic circles appeared grounded in history, history was actually just an occasional alibi for what was a more fanciful and imperialist vision of a transnational German community.[118] The 1921 program to support German organizations in Poland laid the groundwork for a more far-reaching German imperialism that went well beyond the 1914 German borders. By the later 1920s, German state aid to German communities in Poland and elsewhere had grown into a huge concern.[119]

As 1922 wore on, with no end to the flood of Polish Germans in sight and with the financial situation in the Reich deteriorating, the national Interior Ministry continued to cast about for ways to limit the number of new Polish German immigrants. The officials followed the ground rules established in 1921—greater restriction on admittance and aid combined with financial incentives to remain in Poland. Throughout fall 1922, the national Interior Ministry tried repeatedly to reduce the amount of assistance given to Polish Germans in Germany with the goal of decreasing the number of new immigrants, but it was stymied by the opposition of groups representing the refugees.[120] A ban on emigration transports from November 10 to December 15, 1922, succeeded primarily in arousing anger, fear, and "unwelcome political effects" among aspiring ethnic German immigrants in Poland.[121] On November 11, 1922, the parsimonious national Finance Ministry agreed to increase assistance to Germans who remained in Poland, with the explanation that it was necessary to avoid further immigrants at all costs.[122] On April 1, 1923, special assistance for ethnic German refugees was halted, and they were thrown back on the meager resources of local poor relief. Although citizenship had been explicitly ignored by officials involved in assistance in 1920, and although German officials had encouraged Germans in Poland not to opt for German citizenship, now citizenship was used as an excuse for the restriction of aid—German citizens who returned to Germany from abroad

118. Aufzeichnung der Ergebnisse der 25 April 1921 abgehaltenen Besprechung im Reichstagsgebäude, PAAA R 30860, K038042–K038047.
119. Many of these efforts, however, met with little success. John Hiden, "The Weimar Republic and the Problem of the Auslandsdeutsche," *Journal of Contemporary History* 12 (1977), 274.
120. RMI Rundschreiben, October 2, 1922, PAAA R 82225, 334; RMI Rundschreiben, October 12, 1922, PAAA R 82225, 368; RMI Rundschreiben, November 14, 1922, PAAA R 82226, 55.
121. DKP to AA, November 27, 1922, PAAA R 82226, 120.
122. RMF to AA, November 11, 1922, PAAA R 82226, 62.

would be eligible for continued assistance, but not ethnic Germans without German citizenship.[123] Tellingly, no exceptions for "dire emergency" were granted, as had been the case previously.

Restricting aid to Germans who emigrated while increasing assistance for those who stayed in Poland initially did little to stem the tide of immigrants. The number of residents in the camps increased steadily through 1922, and despite the fall 1922 ban on immigration, the number of residents in the camps, a rough measure of recent immigrants, reached a high point of 36,899 in December. Even the German financial crisis and an August 1923 ban on further intake in the camps appeared to have only a limited impact on the ethnic German migration from Poland; in September 1923, 25,223 migrants could still be counted in the camps. Nonetheless, the increasing stability of the postwar European situation and the sheer fact that most potential migrants had already left eventually led the migration to diminish, and in May 1925, the Red Cross managed to shut the final *Heimkehrlager*.[124]

———

The immigration of Germans from Poland and Russia presented the German state with a series of choices—should the Germans immigrants from the annexed territories receive governmental assistance? What about Germans from territories that had never been part of the Reich? If so, how should German identity be defined—based on citizenship or ethnicity? In answering these questions, the state embraced two key precepts of the *völkisch* right: support for the German communities outside the borders of Germany and an emphasis on ethnicity as the crucial factor defining German identity.

Triumphant wartime military and civilian officials had developed wide-ranging plans to remake the ethnographic map of Europe by settling Russian Germans in the newly won Baltic territories. After the defeat, the suffering of, first, the Germans in Poland and, then, the German nation as a whole justified the further development of a *völkisch* conception of German identity and the responsibility of the state. The expanded notion of the German state's responsibility for Germans and lands beyond its borders developed during the war was reawakened by the 1921 plans for supporting German communities in Poland. The 1921 plans simultaneously reflected German understanding of their present-day weakness and a projection of future strength. On the one hand, these plans came about as a result of fears that excessive immigration already had, and would continue to, negatively affect the state. On the other, these plans for supporting German communities abroad reached beyond the 1914 boundaries of Germany

123. PMI to RMI, March 29, 1923, BArch R 1501/118446, 239.
124. Oltmer, *Migration und Politik*, 115; Aufzeichnung über die Ressortbesprechung vom 8 August 1923 im AA, PAAA R 82228, 160.

imagining a time when Germany could once again fulfill more ambitious territorial dreams. Germany's current boundaries, or even its 1914 frontiers, were irrelevant to this plan.

As the deadline for applying for German citizenship arrived in January 1922,
the German state found itself in the seemingly peculiar position of encouraging
Germans in Poland not to opt for German citizenship.[125] The Foreign Office
echoed *völkisch* arguments that they should remain Polish citizens in Poland
and thus provide support for the German claim to these territories. Polish citizenship was thus advanced as a means of supporting the interests of Germandom. In doing so, German government officials echoed the Freikorps soldiers,
who in 1919 saw no contradiction between obtaining Latvian citizenship and
maintaining their Germanness abroad. Ethnic German identity was divorced
from territorial location and citizenship.

From this deterritorialization of German identity, of which the Polish Germans were both a cause and a symptom, we might conclude that borders had become irrelevant to the German state; after all, ethnic Germans, regardless of their
territorial location or their citizenship, could lay claim to its resources. Even the
government attempts to limit access to those resources were driven by a *völkisch*
logic that explicitly ignored the current frontiers of Germany and implicitly ignored its past ones. But the potential irrelevancy of political boundaries did not
mean a concomitant comfort with fluidity. Indeed, German efforts to support
German communities abroad were attempts to control population mobility.

Further, in the first years of the Weimar Republic, Germany also contended
with Jewish and Russian immigration that reached proportions similar to that of
the ethnic Germans. Whereas the immigration of Polish and Russian Germans
presented a conflict between moral responsibility and material resources, the
immigration of other ethnic groups was widely opposed for both moral and financial reasons. But, although Prussian and national officials embraced a *völkisch*
definition of German identity in dealing with ethnic Germans from Poland, citizenship and border control policies did not necessarily move in the same direction. Restrictions on the naturalization of non-ethnic Germans were loosened,
the Prussian Interior Ministry accepted the suffering of *Ostjuden* as grounds for
their tolerance; some members of the *völkisch* right even argued that Germany
should protect non-Bolshevik Russia POWs from communist recruitment and
persecution. The hesitations and contradictions in German responses to non-
ethnic German immigrants reveal the difficulty that Germany had in coming to
terms with the complex world created by war, revolution, new borders, and mobile populations.

125. The state released guidelines by which Polish Germans could opt for German citizenship
only in December 1921, little more than a month before the option deadline; RGBl., 1921, S. 1491.
This was done purposefully to minimize the number who would opt for German citizenship; Schattkowsky, *Deutschland und Polen*, 187.

5. "A Flooding of the Reich with Foreigners"

The Frustrations of Border Control

The first total war and the first world revolution created a European refugee crisis of unprecedented proportions. John Hope Simpson estimates that as a result of this crisis 9.5 million refugees wandered the European continent.[1] Of these, 1.5 million refugees settled temporarily or permanently on German soil in the few years between the end of World War I and the onset of the hyperinflation in 1923 that effectively ended the flood of refugees into Germany. This immigration began during the war, as ethnic Germans fled to Germany as a result of a combination of wartime chaos and the tsar's repressive policies, and increased markedly in 1919 in the aftermath of the Russian Revolution and the German defeat, when a more heterogeneous group of immigrants began crossing the German eastern border. The massive and unprecedented size of the postwar migration taxed the moral and financial capacity of both Germany individually and the world community at large. The attempts of local and national officials in Germany to respond to the postwar refugee crisis demonstrated the conflict between the utopian expectations encouraged by the war, in particular the dreams of eastern expansion (see chap. 1) and the reality of scarcity and poverty after the defeat. The arrival of so many refugees in such a short period of time unleashed a crisis for the state because it could neither adequately seal and control the German borders nor provide for refugees that arrived.

The inability of the state to seal the borders in the first years of the Weimar period had profound consequences for the fledgling democracy. Timothy

1. Simpson, *Refugee Problem*, 62.

Mitchell suggests that the legitimacy of the state as a seemingly transcendent entity lies in its capacity to project itself through the performance of such everyday tasks as minting currency, designing uniforms, and, not least, patrolling the state territorial frontiers.[2] According to Mitchell, the control of the frontier is one of the most important functions of the state: "By establishing a territorial boundary and exercising absolute control over movement across it, state practices define and help constitute a national entity."[3] If we accept that the power of the state lies in its ability to perform such functions satisfactorily, then the *failure* of the state to guard its frontiers adequately, as in the case of Weimar Germany, also has metaphorical consequences that are at least as damaging as the practical problems posed by the refugees. The powerlessness of border guards to control the massive movement of people crossing the German eastern frontier contributed to the sense of weak state legitimacy. Commentators on the nationalist right found ample evidence to excoriate both the Weimar national and Prussian state governments for their inability to regulate the quantity and quality of the immigrants that crossed into German territory. Indeed, the Weimar state was caught in a devastating spiral—its lack of an aura of authority caused its critics to constantly hammer at its incapacity to control immigration, which contributed to its loss of yet more authority. The maintenance of the border was surely not the only arena in which its critics charged that the young Weimar state had failed. Nonetheless, as the republic weathered political challenges from the left and the right, its hesitations and missteps in border policy were a constant reminder of its fragility. Moreover, in the wake of the failure of the state to control immigration, government officials and nationalist deputies to the Reichstag used stereotypes about Eastern European Jewry to describe the immigrants, contributing to a dangerous and self-reinforcing process in which the failures to control immigration were projected on to Eastern European Jews and anti-Semitic stereotypes imbued immigration policy with an increased sense of threat.

The Scope of the Refugee Crisis

Several factors intertwined to create the refugee crisis after World War I. The creation of new states in Eastern Europe based on the principle of national self-determination unsettled millions of people who found themselves living in the "wrong" state. The patchwork of Eastern European nationalities was a singularly inadequate canvas for the imposition of a model of national territory that imagined groups concentrated in areas with recognizable borders. Furthermore, with the collapse of the Russian Empire, millions of former subjects of the tsar

2. Timothy Mitchell, "The Limits of the State: Beyond Statist Approaches and Their Critics," *American Political Science Review* 85, no. 1 (1991), 81.

3. Ibid., 94.

fled civil war and Bolshevik control. These Russian refugees constituted a new category—the "stateless person." Finally, the Armenian genocide and its diasporic aftermath also contributed to the migratory movements across Europe in the immediate postwar years. The Weimar Republic was primarily affected by these first two phenomena: the creation of new states in Eastern Europe and the Russian Revolution.

Germany had the largest number of refugees of any Western European state in the immediate postwar period. There were several reasons why Germany was such an attractive destination for many refugees, even those not of German descent:

1. The defeat of Germany and the collapse of the Wilhelmine state meant that its borders were controlled only in the most perfunctory way.
2. The economic woes and inflation in Germany (even if they had not yet reached the proportions of the hyperinflation of 1922–1923) meant that foreigners with either hard currency or items to sell could live relatively cheaply.
3. The German state was loathe to invite Allied retribution by taking drastic actions to limit or punish illegal immigrants.
4. The number of Russian POWs in Germany at the end of World War I was already over 1 million, and many of them refused to return to Russia.
5. And finally, due to simple geography, Germany was the first Western country that refugees reached moving westward from Russia.

It is exceedingly difficult to ascertain definitively the number of refugees who came to Germany during and after World War I.[4] A memorandum commissioned by the Reichstag in 1920 and published in 1922 estimated that the number of immigrants to Prussia from October 1919 to May 1920 was 219,310.[5] This number is

4. Looking at census figures, Gosewinkel states that the percentage of people with foreign citizenship and speaking foreign languages in 1925 was 2.1 percent, compared to 7.5 percent in 1900. Gosewinkel, *Einbürgern und Ausschließen*, 339. There was no census in Weimar Germany before 1925. According to these figures, the postwar German state was a much more homogeneous one than it had been prior to 1919. But leaving aside the fact that many immigrants probably tried to avoid the census altogether, this figure is misleading when used as evidence for the immediate postwar period because the vast majority of refugees had moved on or been repatriated by 1925, due largely to the German hyperinflation of 1922–1923. Whereas the limited inflation prior to that period created a situation that was relatively beneficial for foreigners who possessed hard currency and goods to sell, the hyperinflation and the breakdown of civil and economic order that resulted caused many migrants to leave Germany. Furthermore, the *Ostjuden* were, generally, using Germany as a way station for the United States and Palestine, and their numbers decreased as well. The loss of the territories in the east, and the large number of Polish speakers who had lived there, further distorts this figure.

5. "Reichstag Denkschrift über die Ein-und Auswanderung nach bzw. aus Deutschland in den Jahren 1910 bis 1920," *Verhandlungen*, Bd. 372, 4405–7. This figure included foreigners of every nationality, including Germans. The majority of immigrants were listed as originating in Poland (in

extremely low, and even at the time, many officials did not take it seriously. As one official in the Prussian Interior Ministry wrote when asked to carry out this count, "it seems totally impossible to establish accurately a figure for the people who have immigrated without appropriate papers. It is precisely these people who avoid police control, as we have already experienced with the failure of the registration regulations."[6] The majority of refugees arrived in Germany in 1919, when Russia plunged into full-scale civil war and the territorial revisions mandated by the Treaty of Versailles went into effect.[7] The number of *Ostjuden,* a group that figures prominently in the discourse on migration if not necessarily in the number of immigrants, is difficult to determine. The Jüdisches Arbeiterfürsorgeamt (Jewish Workers Welfare Agency) claimed that 100,000 Jews had immigrated; however, 40 percent either returned to their home countries or went further, so only 55,000–60,000 remained on German soil. In 1921, the Prussian Interior Ministry cited a slightly higher figure of 70,000, which came to be widely accepted.[8] In any case, the highest proportion of these Jews lived in Prussia, with approximately 20,000 in Berlin. Cities outside Prussia had significantly smaller numbers, with only 400 families of *Ostjuden* in Munich and only 800–1,000 people in Stuttgart.[9] Waves of refugees fleeing the Russian Revolution and ensuing civil war arrived in 1919 and 1920. The onset of widespread famine in Russia in 1921 resulted in the arrival of yet more refugees from Russia. Hans-Erich Volkmann estimates that by 1922 there were as many as 600,000 Russian refugees resident in Germany.[10] After 1922–1923, the number of Russians in Germany began to decline precipitously due to the increasing stability in the Soviet Union and the economic problems and accompanying political turmoil in Germany during this time.[11] Yet, even with this decline, the number of Russians in Germany did not dip below 150,000–200,000 during the entire Weimar period.[12]

---

particular former German areas such as Posen, East and West Prussia, and Silesia) or Alsace-Lorraine and thus may be assumed to be of German origin. Of the Poles, 17,722 were listed as originating in "Russian Poland."

6. Prussian Interior Ministry to the Reich Interior Ministry, March 8 1921, BArch R 1501/113328, 307.

7. Skran, *Refugees in Inter-war Europe,* 34.

8. Maurer, *Ostjuden in Deutschland, 1918–1933,* 65.

9. Ibid., 66.

10. Hans-Erich Volkmann, *Die russische Emigration in Deutschland, 1919–1929* (Würzburg: Holzner, 1966), 4. Claudena Skran posits a slightly different chronology. She describes a population with dramatic fluctuations during 1920–1923. She states that there may have been as many as 500,000 refugees in Germany in fall 1920, but that this number declined precipitously to a quarter of a million as many of them moved further west. During 1922, many refugees returned to Germany to take advantage of the inflation and the cheaper living costs this afforded to those with hard currency and then, with the onset of hyperinflation and the ensuing instability, many of them left again for France; Skran, *Refugees in Inter-war Europe,* 35. Volkmann's chronology is convincing because of the range of factors he takes into account.

11. Volkmann, *Russische Emigration in Deutschland, 1919–1929,* 10.

12. Ibid., 6.

Historians and contemporary observers agree that by far the largest concentration of Russians was in Berlin, but the specific number of refugees was the subject of heated debates during the 1920s and afterward. In 1921, an article in the *Berliner Tageblatt* claimed that there were 100,000 Russians living in Berlin.[13] This number surely grew in the following years. Newspaper articles written in the aftermath of the assassination of Vladimir Dmitrievich Nabokov in April 1922 cited a figure of 250,000 émigrés in Berlin.[14] In June 1923, the German Embassy in Copenhagen estimated that 360,000 Russians were living in Berlin.[15] In the same year, the Internationale Gemeinschaft zur Förderung der Heimatlosenfürsorge also cited this figure,[16] and a Catholic charity, the Päpstliches Hilfswerk, estimated that there were 300,000 Russians in the capital.[17]

The number of migrants and the speed at which these people were displaced from their homes was unmatched by any previous crisis; in addition, the postwar refugees were qualitatively different from any group of exiles that had preceded them. Up until 1914, the open borders that had predominated worldwide meant that migration was, from a legal standpoint at least, without major consequences.[18] This changed with the war. The war brought with it the reimposition of restrictions that had largely been abolished in the preceding decades. The institution of passports and visas meant that citizenship status now came to be of everyday importance for anyone who wished to cross a border. After the war, these restrictions were not relaxed. Instead, inspired primarily by the fear of Bolshevism, European states from Germany to the United Kingdom not only kept these "temporary" wartime restrictions but actually made them even more extensive.[19] Moreover, just as European governments were erecting these barriers to entry against foreigners, they were faced with a refugee crisis that was truly a Europewide phenomenon. The new states of Eastern Europe were inundated with refugees, and Western European capitals also became centers of the refugee diaspora (see chap. 8). The refugees that arrived in Germany and elsewhere during this period were in possession of a wide and confusing array of documents—baptismal records, documents certifying military service, passports

13. *Berliner Tageblatt*, December 24, 1921.

14. "So geht es nicht weiter," *Berliner Lokal-Anzeiger*, March 29, 1922; "Russisches Flüchtlingsleben in Berlin," *Der Tag*, April 6, 1922. V. D. Nabokov was a liberal politician and the father of Vladimir Nabokov, the writer.

15. German Embassy in Copenhagen to the Auswärtiges Amt, June 19, 1923, PAAA R 83582, 50.

16. Bettina Dodenhoeft, *"Laßt mich nach Rußland heim": Russische Emigranten in Deutschland von 1918 bis 1945* (Frankfurt am Main: Peter Lang, 1993), 9.

17. Volkmann, *Russische Emigration in Deutschland, 1919–1929*, 4.

18. Part of the reason for the relatively open borders in Europe prior to World War I is that most migrants did not intend on settling permanently in Europe but were headed for the United States, which operated as an "escape-valve" that absorbed the vast majority of migrants; Marrus, *Unwanted*, 39.

19. Ibid., 92.

issued by states that no longer existed, identity papers issued by community or charity organizations, and so on—but they were not citizens of any extant state. For a variety of reasons, the Russians were, for the most part, accepted in their host lands with less of the friction that greeted the other national minorities. The responses of European governments to these refugees displayed generally good intentions, even though the enormity of the crisis outpaced the ability of these governments to manage it.[20] Meanwhile, the League of Nations played an important, albeit mostly symbolic, role in guaranteeing the well-being of the Russian refugees.

The Frustrations and Failures of Border Control

The massive number of refugees inspired widespread fears about an inundation of the Reich by foreigners. Looking back from 1923 at the immediate postwar years, Interior Minister Rudolf Oeser spoke of a "flooding of the Reich's territory with foreigners." Oeser regarded this flood as part of a "massive migration of foreign elements from the East," which had begun during the war but achieved "vigorous (*rege*)" proportions during 1919.[21] The Deutsche Gesellschaft für Bevölkerungspolitik (German Society for Population Politics) wrote to the national Interior Ministry about the deleterious effects that this migration would have on the German population: "Since the end of the war, a great migration (*Abwanderung*) from Russia and the former Russian section of Poland to Germany has begun. From month to month, this migration is becoming culturally and economically more dangerous for the German people."[22] In February 1920, police in Frankfurt-Oder wrote a letter to the Prussian border-police headquarters admonishing officials to defend the border and providing a list of the hardships that migrants from the east were inflicting on the German people—everything from a worsening of the housing shortage and an increase in the pressure on the food supply to unscrupulous merchants to the importation of Bolshevik ideas.[23] These accusations against immigrants from Eastern Europe recycled familiar anti-Semitic stereotypes that long predated the Weimar era.

Anti-Semitic nationalists imagined Germans and immigrants engaged in a zero-sum competition for Germany's scant resources. The anti-Semitic Deutschsoziale Partei published a pamphlet asking Berliners, "How much longer do you

20. Skran, *Refugees in Inter-war Europe*, 111; Marrus, *Unwanted*, 120–21.

21. RMI to the Reichzkanzlei, January 21, 1923, BArch R 43 I/594, 76.

22. Deutsche Gesellschaft für Bevölkerungspolitik to the RMI, April 9, 1920, BArch R 1501/114049, 135.

23. For a representative list, see Zentralpolizeistelle Osten, Frankfurt/Oder to the Landesgrenzpolizei on February 5, 1920, BArch R 1501/114049, 13. These stories ranged from the seemingly banal to the ridiculous. One story circulated in the right-wing press that Jewish immigrants running a factory were using cats, dogs, and garbage to create aspic. Maurer, *Ostjuden in Deutschland, 1918–1933*, 134.

want to be treated like foreigners in your own city? How much longer will you accept thousands of Galizian, Polish and Russian Jews arriving and taking your homes, your food and the clothes off your backs? Do you want to stand by until all of Berlin has become judeified and you are thrown out?"[24] In summer 1919, several Deutschnationale Volkspartei (DNVP) deputies provocatively posed the question: "60,000 Eastern Jews. . . . Is it right to hold the borders of the East open in a time when we do not have sufficient food for our own German population and a large emigration of Germans from the Fatherland appears unavoidable?"[25] This inquiry was typical of a growing tendency on the part of German right-wing nationalists to juxtapose German suffering and Jewish immigration and predation.

The national Interior Ministry response to this inquiry is telling. The ministry accepted that these Jews were not desirable immigrants, insisted that border guards had not knowingly allowed Jews into the country, and defensively reiterated: "The relevant national and state offices are united in believing that for the time being, as a result of Germany's internal difficulties immigration must be avoided whenever possible. The crossing of the Eastern border into Germany is regulated by specific passport regulations. In addition, the German representatives in the Eastern territories have been warned about immigration to Germany."[26] That is, on the one hand, the national Interior Ministry echoed the strident rhetoric of the right in denouncing the immigration of eastern Jews; on the other hand, beyond explaining that Jews needed passports and stating that they had warned neighboring countries about the immigration, it did not undertake many of the drastic policies suggested to stem this immigration.[27] The ministry was caught between competing priorities: the well-being of its citizens, its own financial and personnel limitations, and its desire not to harm the world image of Germany (see chap. 8). Given the impossible situation in which the Interior Ministry found itself, it is not surprising that it failed to satisfy nationalist critics.

Prussia was the state with the most immigrants, the state with the longest eastern border, and the most powerful state in the republic. Thus, the Prussians set the de facto immigration and border policy for the entire Reich. The Prussian interior ministers—Wolfgang Heine until after the Kapp Putsch in March 1920 and Carl Severing thereafter—were the most important individuals in

24. Deutschsoziale Partei poster, n.d., Landesarchiv Berlin [hereafter, LAB] Pr. Br. Rep. 30, Berlin C, Tit. 95, 21642, 151. The Deutschsoziale Partei was an anti-Semitic party founded in 1889 by Max Liebermann von Sonnenberg, former army officer and agitator.

25. Nr. 513 Anfrage Nr. 192, July 7, 1919 from the DNVP deputies D. Mumm, Biener, Deglerk, Knollmann, Laverrenz, Oberfohren, Traub and Wallbaum, BArch R 1501/118392, 48. According to Maurer, it was a common tactic of nationalist deputies to discredit the ability of the German government to restrict or, they implied, even count the numbers of Jewish immigrants; Maurer, *Ostjuden in Deutschland, 1918–1933,* 233.

26. Nr. 924. August 14, 1919, BArch R 1501/118392, 158.

27. Ibid.

charge of migration. Both of them were social democrats, and as such, the supposed leniency of Prussia made it a lighting rod for criticism from the nationalists in the more conservative *Länder* and in the right-wing press. But, contrary to the nationalist accusations, the Prussian border police tried desperately to locate migrants and stop them from entering German territory. Prussian efforts to limit the size of the foreign population concentrated on trying to enact an effective border control, but, because of both the lack of personnel and the size of the refugee population, they were unable to do so.

Faced with what Prussian officials believed was only the beginning of a massive invasion of Bolsheviks and Jews, a Prussian *Erlass* (order) dated January 27, 1919 (less than three months after the cessation of hostilities) attempted to seal the border in both directions to all who could not prove their German identity beyond doubt.[28] But this proved impossible; three months later, a variety of national and Prussian officials met at the Foreign Ministry and concluded, "[e]xperience shows that despite the closing of the border, foreigners crossed in droves." These officials blamed corrupt Polish and German border guards for the lack of success in sealing the borders, but with only nine hundred officers expected to patrol the 2,000-kilometer eastern frontier, it was soon clear that control of the German border would not be easily achieved.[29]

Uncertainty about the final borders of Germany persisted until the Treaty of Versailles was signed in June 1919. Although the principles underlying border control—namely the desire to seal the border—did not substantially change as a result of the treaty, the task of patrolling the German frontier was complicated considerably by the Polish German immigration. Officials did not know how to distinguish Germans (who deserved entry) from other migrants (who did not). One report warned that people coming from the east who claimed to be returning German citizens were most likely Jews who were lying to evade capture at the border.[30] As a frustrated Foreign Office official wrote in 1922 about the failure of border-control measures, "the stream [of people] from the East continues without hindrance."[31]

28. A report of a meeting on May 17, 1919, at the RMI about the recall of German troops from Kurland and Lithuania and the expected migration of the population there to the German eastern border refers to this *Erlass;* BArch R 1501/118392, 15. References continued to be made to this *Erlass* and to the need to close the border once and for all. For example, in a letter from Carl Severing, the Prussian minister of the interior, to the presidents of local governments, including the president of police in Berlin, Severing makes clear that he wants both better surveillance of the border and the railways and more tightly enforced registration regulation; GStA PK, 1 HA, Rep. 77, Tit. 1814, Nr. 3, 207–8. It is unclear exactly how an immigrant's German identity would have been proven "beyond a doubt."

29. Auswärtiges Amt on April 10, 1919, BArch R 1501/114061, 47. Regarding the number of border guards, see the report of a meeting held at the RMI with the RMI, PMI, Reichsjustizministerium, and AA in attendance, December 22, 1919, BArch R 1501/114048, 192.

30. RWA to RMI February 8, 1920, BArch R 1501/114049, 15.

31. Summary of the entry visas granted to Russian citizens during 1922, BArch R 43 I/594, 19.

Despite Prussian attempts to end corruption at the border and increase the number of soldiers assigned to border patrol, Heine wrote in 1920 that "it is impossible to seal the Eastern border without any holes."[32] He and other officials called for a variety of approaches for managing the problem of illegal immigration. A meeting held at the national Interior Ministry on November 1919 ended with the suggestion that a station be erected *behind* the border to seize people who managed to cross the border "without control."[33] Echoing this suggestion, in February 1920 a Prussian border-control official in Königsberg called for the erection of three concentric cordons at the border, each one designed to catch immigrants who managed to slip through the previous border.[34] In both solutions, officials believed that establishing a new, more easily manageable border inside of German territorial frontiers would function more effectively than patrolling the actual border. But it does not appear that such proposals, or other calls for increased surveillance of the railroads, succeeded.[35] Instead, files of the Prussian and national interior ministries and border police are filled with accounts of frustrated officials who could not even manage to count the people they believed to be streaming across the border. Neither Prussian nor national officials ever found a successful means of sealing the eastern frontier; the flood of refugees eventually abated on its own.

Expulsion was considered but largely rejected as a solution to this problem. As part of a Western European trend of expelling Jews who had migrated during and immediately after the war, Prussia carried out individual deportations of Eastern European Jews to Poland during 1918–1921.[36] Illegal immigrants were occasionally seized at the border and either interned or sent back to Poland. In 1920, 11,458 people were seized on the Eastern border, of whom 6,169 were immediately expelled. However, the April 1920 statistics note that only 62 of the 862 who were seized in April 1920 were Eastern European Jews, the group about whom authorities were most concerned. Moreover, there was little to keep expellees from returning to German soil at a later time.[37] In 1923, the Bavarians

32. PMI to the Zentralpolizeistelle Osten February 13, 1920, BArch R 1501/114049, 42.

33. Report of the results of a meeting held on November 12, 1919, at the RMI about measures to take with regard to the stronger flow of refugees from the Baltics, GStA PK, 1. HA, Rep. 77, Tit. 1146, Nr. 74, Beiheft 4, Bd. III, 152. See also the grab bag of measures—ranging from internment to registration and from border control to railway surveillance and deportations—proposed by the Prussian government in February 1920; Prussian government statement regarding deportation or internment of foreigners from the east, BArch R 1501/114049, 120–32.

34. Königsberg Landesgrenzpolizei Ostpreuβen to the Landesgrenzpolizei Osten, Berlin, February 25, 1920, GStA PK, 1 HA, Rep. 77, Tit. 1814, Nr. 3, 29.

35. Zentral-Polizeistelle Osten (Frankfurt/Oder) to the Landesgrenzpolizei in Berlin, February 22, 1920, GStA PK, 1 HA, Rep. 77, Tit. 1814, Nr. 3, 36b.

36. Maurer estimates that Prussian authorities deported 3,900 Eastern European Jews (15 percent of the total number of deportations) between 1922 and 1932; Maurer, *Ostjuden in Deutschland, 1918–1933*, 398.

37. Christiane Reinecke, "Riskante Wanderungen: Illegale Migration im britischen und deutschen Migrationsregime der 1920er Jahre," *Geschichte und Gesellschaft* 35 (2009): 89.

unilaterally expelled all of the Eastern European Jews in its territory who could not positively prove that their presence benefited the Bavarian state. However, the Bavarian Jews did not necessarily leave Germany altogether.[38] Plans for a national expulsion of Polish Jews were developed in spring 1919, but they foundered on the fear that this would negatively affect the world opinion of Germany at the very time when delegates were deciding its fate at the Paris Peace Conference.[39] Furthermore, given the massive amount of German resources that would be needed and the refusal of Poland to accept deported Jews, large-scale deportations were not a practical reality.[40] Immigrants from Russia were equally difficult to deport. An order by the Soviet government in December 1921 stripped all anti-Bolshevik Russians of their Russian citizenship. Once this happened, they could no longer be sent back to Russia, and at the same time, it was also doubtful that another country would take them.[41]

Although the Prussian Interior Ministry insisted on its right to deport foreigners who had become "burdensome," its ability to control deportation was limited. Deportations were carried out by the police in local communities without oversight from the Interior Ministry and were often a product of local interests that had little to do with Prussian or national concerns.[42] This meant that deportations were both arbitrary and ineffective. Because the deportations took place only from a specific locality, as one frustrated member of the Prussian border guard complained in 1920, illegal immigrants would merely "disappear in order to reappear later somewhere else or with another name."[43] At most, foreigners left more restrictive states to resettle in ones that were more lenient.[44] Moreover, Prussian deportation regulations released in October 1921 made it illegal to deport foreigners who had been living in Prussia

38. Rainer Pommerin, "Die Ausweisung von Ostjuden aus Bayern 1923—Ein Beitrag zum Krisenjahr der Weimarer Republik," *Vierteljahrshefte für Zeitgeschichte* 34 (1986): 311–340.

39. Protokoll der Sitzung über die jüdischen Ausweisungen im Auswärtigen Amt am 10 April 1919, PAAA R 78705, L348582–348706.

40. Heine to Staatsministerium, February 23, 1920, PAAA R 70705, L348721–348232.

41. "Besprechung über die vom PMI vorgelegte Denkschrift über die in Deutschland befindlichen Ostausländer, 10 Januar 1923," PAAA R 78705, L348516–L348517.

42. Oltmer, *Migration und Politik,* 65–67.

43. Landesgrenzpolizei Ostpreußen in Königsberg to Landesgrenzpolizei Osten in Berlin, February 25, 1920, GStA PK, 1 HA, Rep. 77, Tit. 1814, Nr. 3, 29. An attempt to address this concern was made in an *Erlass* from the Prussian government on November 17, 1920. In cases of expulsion, the president of the local government was supposed to inform the presidents of the other Prussian local governments so as to avoid a situation in which those who were expelled from one community just moved to the next. Considering the time that an expulsion procedure took and the fact that the expellee could easily change his or her name and avoid detection, it is doubtful that this measure was actually effective. Furthermore, if the expelled foreigner went to a different state, he or she could avoid this altogether (119).

44. Indeed, Saxon officials complained that the Bavarian policy of expelling foreigners meant only that more of them would come to neighboring states such as Saxony; Saxon Interior Ministry internal report, April 30, 1920, Sächsisches Hauptstaatsarchiv [hereafter SächsHStA] Ministerium des Innern [hereafter MInnern] 11718, 82.

since April 1914, providing a check on prior practices.[45] From January through October 1921, Prussian authorities ordered 1,640 deportations, in 1922, 1,558, in 1923, 4,036, and 1925, 2,741, primarily for the use of fake identity documents. These numbers were quite small in comparison to the numbers who had crossed the border.[46] Deportations appeared to be just as ineffective as border control.

The internment of the *Ostjuden,* the group of foreigners considered most dangerous, was a hotly debated approach to combating the dangers of immigration. Anti-Semites both within and outside the government argued that the establishment of internment camps was the only measure that could solve the problem of Eastern Jewish immigration.[47] Foreign Jews were interred in the Wünsdorf camp near Zossen in Brandenburg in the aftermath of the Kapp Putsch in 1920, but public protests led to their release after one week.[48] In February 1921, the Prussian Interior Ministry announced the opening of the Stargard camp in Pomerania, which was designed to hold 2,700 detainees. The camp was designed to hold only those aliens who had no residence permit, those who had received a deportation order but had not left Germany, and those convicted of a wide variety of minor crimes. It was not intended to solve the entire Eastern Jewish "problem," which many within and outside the government had called for, and even the Jewish press was relatively quiet about its existence.[49] Although the establishment of the Stargard camp reveals that the Interior Ministry was responsive to concerns about Jewish immigrants from Eastern Europe, it did not go nearly as far as many on the right would have liked.

In addition to such punitive strategies as deportation and internment, regional and national officials considered registration as a means of control. In January 1919, Prussia made it mandatory for foreigners to register with the police within forty-eight hours of their arrival in that state; throughout the year, other states followed with similar laws.[50] According to the Saxon Ministry of the Inte-

45. Reinecke, "Riskante Wanderungen," 92.

46. Ibid., 93.

47. Inquiry from September 27, 1921, *Verhandlungen,* Bd. 369, 2667. This is one particular example, but internment was suggested by nationalists several times from 1919 onward. Once deportations were no longer an option in 1921, the internment discussions became more serious; Maurer, *Ostjuden in Deutschland, 1918–1933,* 416–35.

48. Dirk Walter, *Antisemitische Kriminalität und Gewalt: Judenfeindschaft in der Weimarer Republik* (Bonn: Dietz, 1999), 70.

49. Yfatt Weiss, "Homeland as Shelter or as Refuge?: Repatriation in the Jewish Context," *Tel Aviver Jahrbuch für deutsche Geschichte* 27 (1988), 205–6. What criticism there was of the camp came from SPD, USPD, and KPD delegates; Maurer, *Ostjuden in Deutschland, 1918–1933,* 427–31. As a result of this criticism, in July 1921 only Jews who were to be deported because of crimes they had committed could be interned in the Stargard camp. The camp remained in existence in this limited capacity until 1923 (432–33).

50. Prussia enacted such a registration policy January 31, 1919. Baden followed with its policy on May 22, 1919, and Bavaria on May 23, 1919. The Saxon "Meldepflicht der Ausländer und Staatenlose" followed on July 1, 1919. SächsHStA, MInnern 11718, 4, 21, 15, n.p.

rior, the registration of foreigners and stateless persons was designed to combat the disruption of public order caused by these foreigners: "The insubordinate and disruptive activities of many foreigners that live unregistered in the Reich without any identification has become a very disturbing danger for public peace, order and security."[51] Yet, despite the threat of heavy fines and imprisonment for foreigners who did not register with the police, in Saxony at least these laws seemed to have little effect except to arouse the ire of Austrian Germans who frequently crossed the border and resented the inconvenience they faced in fulfilling this requirement.[52] Raids in the Scheunenviertel in Berlin, an area with a high concentration of *Ostjuden,* aimed to capture unregistered immigrants, but these appear to also have had little efficacy in controlling the problem of unregistered foreigners.[53] Frustrated by their failure to control immigration on their own, regional officials began to call for a centralized agency to collect and manage the registration of the thousands of foreigners.[54]

Heeding these calls, in October 1920 the National Commission for Civilian Internees and Refugees, an agency otherwise concerned with managing the *Heimkehrlager* for former German citizens from the Polish territories, developed plans for a national registration agency.[55] According to the commission, this nationwide registration and tracking system "in which the foreigners are captured, registered and placed under permanent surveillance will have the effect of rendering these foreigners harmless to the interests of the [German] people."[56] The commission and the local officials who called for this system believed that foreigners, by definition, compromised the "interests of the German people." To ease this burden, the commission proposed an elaborate system of registration and tracking. Each foreigner would register with the local police

51. Letter from the Saxon Interior Ministry to the Dresden Police Headquarters, March 6, 1919, SächsHStA MInnern 11718, 6.

52. The ineffectiveness of the threat of fines and imprisonment is referred to in a letter from the Saxon Interior Ministry to the Reichskommissar für Zivilgefangene und Flüchtlinge, February 22, 1921, SächsHStA MInnern 11718, 102. The resentments of Austrian Germans appears in a letter from the Saxon Interior Ministry to the government of Aue relaxing the registration requirement for the Austrian Germans, referred to in SächsHStA, MInnern 11718, 31.

53. Reinecke, "Riskante Wanderungen," 90–91.

54. The Bavarians had established their own central agency by April 1920; Saxon Interior Ministry (SMI), April 30, 1920, SächsHStA MInnern 11718, 82. For a sample of Bavarians' pride in their agency, see the Bavarian report from August 23, 1920, on the efficacy of foreigner control, SächsHStA, MInnern 11718, 85–89. For more on this attempt to improve registration practices, see the notes from a meeting held in the RMI about police measures to handle the immigration of foreigners, held on February 16, 1920 (the continuation of a meeting held on December 22, 1919), BArch R 1501/114049, 44.

55. This agency remained in existence until October 31, 1924, when it was deemed no longer necessary because the tide of migration had subsided. For more, see the records of the agency collected in BArch R 1501/18401.

56. Reichskommissar für Zivilgefangene und Flüchtlinge, Denkschrift betr. Abänderung der Bestimmungen über die Meldepflicht und die Behandlung der Ausländer, October 30, 1920, SächsHStA MInnern 11718, 91.

and receive an identity card complete with name, description, picture, and, when possible, fingerprint.[57] A national database would house these identity cards. In consultation with one another, local authorities would assign each foreigner a tracking number, and in this way, the foreigner could be followed as he or she moved through Germany.[58] The police would then be able to arrest any foreigner who sought to avoid registration and place him or her in an internment camp.[59]

This was a bureaucratic utopia in which Weimar authorities would possess the means and ability to track all residents of the Reich, but it was a utopia of a peculiar sort. Even though the entire justification for this registration plan rested on a belief that foreigners presented a burden on the German nation, the commission proposal did not actually solve this problem. Instead, this plan is almost a parody of Mitchell's theory that the power of the state is constituted through its performance of a set of mundane tasks. Here, the commission was proposing that national and local officials coordinate in administering a hugely taxing system of national registration, but it sought only to count these "burdensome" foreigners, not to discipline or expel them. In Mitchell's terms, the commission would then present the appearance of effectiveness and thus maintain the state aura of legitimacy, but in no way did it seek to actually control these supposedly disruptive and destructive foreigners. As it was, the Saxon Interior Ministry responded to this plan with guarded enthusiasm; although it welcomed such a system in theory, it was unsure whether its costs were "proportional to the goal" of foreigner registration.[60] Indeed, this skepticism appears to have been warranted because neither the commission nor any other agency actually enacted such a system of national registration.

Officials swung back and forth, calling for border control, deportations, and registration as alternative solutions, but none of these strategies worked particularly well at stemming the problem of illegal immigration from the east. Ironically, the largest number of refugees probably arrived during 1919, not because the border was better sealed after that year (although this may certainly have had an effect) but because that was the height of the postwar turmoil, with new borders being established and the Russian civil war at its height. An ironic consequence of the German inability to keep track of those who crossed the border was a tendency to overestimate the problem and also not to realize when the situation was abating.

57. Ibid., 96–97.
58. Ibid., 95–96.
59. Ibid., 99.
60. SMI to Reichskommissar für Zivilgefangene und Flüchtlinge, February 22, 1921, SächsH-StA MInnern 11718, 101.

Ostausländer/Ostjuden: The Conflation of the Foreigner and the Jewish Problem

Although the flow of refugees began to taper off after the European convulsions of 1919, nationalist anxieties about immigration did not diminish.[61] Indeed, officials used the words *Ostjuden* (eastern Jew) and *Ostausländer* (eastern foreigner) synonymously, and stereotypes about Eastern European Jews served as models for the entire migration from the east.[62] Although Jews made up only approximately 15 percent of the Russian immigrants, German authorities believed that the majority of the immigrants who arrived in Germany after the end of the war were Jews.[63]

A description of the migration from the east and the difficulty of border controls often shaded quickly into a diatribe about the horrors of Eastern European Jewry and employed stereotypes about Jews that long-predated the current refugee crisis. In one of Otto von Bismarck's first public addresses in 1847, he characterized the Russian Jews as "backwards, prone to political subversiveness and motivated to immigrate solely by the desire for financial gain in Germany."[64] These three charges—backwardness, political agitation, and profiteering—formed a remarkably stable set of stereotypes of Eastern European Jewry that remained salient for much of the next century, increasing in virulence with the increase in Jewish immigration after 1880. Portions of this image waxed and waned according to political circumstances; for example, after the 1905 Revolution, the supposed radicalism of the *Ostjuden* received increased scrutiny. Furthermore, the rise of racial science in the later part of the nineteenth century irrevocably changed certain aspects of this stereotype; for example, the associa-

61. As discussed earlier, it is very difficult to ascertain the actual number of immigrants, but if we take the figures for Russian émigrés (the largest number of non-German refugees in Germany; see chap. 8) as representative, 1919 was the year of the greatest refugee immigration. According to Ludger Heid, anti-Semitic agitation against the *Ostjuden* reached a fever pitch in late 1920; Ludger Heid, *Maloche—nicht Mildtätigkeit: Ostjüdische Arbeiter in Deutschland 1914–1923* (Hildesheim: Georg Olms, 1995), 158.

62. Maurer, *Ostjuden in Deutschland, 1918–1933,* 161–66. Paul Weindling, *Epidemics and Genocide in Eastern Europe, 1890–1945* (Oxford: Oxford University Press, 2000), explores this connection more systematically (see chap. 6).

63. I arrived at this percentage by dividing 70,000 (Maurer's estimate for the number of *Ostjuden* that immigrated to Germany after 1914) by 500,000 (Raeff's estimate for the number of Russians in Germany); Maurer, *Ostjuden in Deutschland, 1918–1933,* 65; Marc Raeff, *Russia Abroad: A Cultural History of the Russian Emigration, 1919–1939* (New York: Oxford University Press, 1990), 24. Reichskommissar für Zivilgefangene und Flüchtlinge, "Denkschrift für die Staatskommission für öffentliche Ordnung betr. die Abänderung der Bestimmungen für die Meldepflicht und die Behandlung der Ausländer," October 30, 1920, BArch R 43 I/594, 3. The completely exaggerated number of 1 million *Ostjuden* that had immigrated to Germany appears in RWA to RMI from February 8, 1920, BArch R 1501/114049, 19.

64. Wertheimer, *Unwelcome Strangers,* 24.

tion of Jews with backwardness led to suspicions that they also carried disease.[65] Anti-Semites in Wilhelmine Germany never managed to halt Jewish immigration; nonetheless, their incessant focus on the dangers posed by Eastern European Jews forced the few defenders of Eastern European Jewry into a defensive stance.[66] As a result of this constant pressure, no one in Germany either before or after World War I argued that the immigration of Eastern European Jews would benefit Germany and should be welcomed.

Post–World War I anti-Semitic stereotypes fell into four categories: Jews taking scarce resources (including housing and food) away from deserving Germans; unscrupulous Jewish businessmen destroying German economic well-being; Jews spreading disease; and, finally, Jews fomenting revolution and unrest.[67] All these claims resonated with prewar anti-Semitic stereotypes, but they achieved a new potency in the face of German weakness in the aftermath of war and revolution. According to the nationalists and even many socialists, the defeated German people and the precarious German state could ill-afford the activities of this predatory minority. Furthermore, in the wake of revolution, concerns about the danger of Jewish political radicalism gained in plausibility. Finally, many Germans believed that an economically weakened Germany could not tolerate the profiteering of the Jews and that a starving German nation, recently recovered from the devastating influenza epidemic, needed to take the accusations that Jews carried disease more seriously than in the past.[68] In a meeting held at the Foreign Ministry in April 1919, a representative of a Jewish aid organization complained that before the revolution Jews had been accused of spreading typhoid but that now they were being accused of spreading Bolshevism.[69]

Officials from the socialist Prussian Interior Ministry and right-wing nationalist pressure groups alike argued that there was a necessary and dangerous connection between German hardships and the presence of foreigners on German soil, often using the vague term *lästig* ("burdensome") to describe a diversity of dangers blamed on foreigners. An internal memorandum from the National Commission for Civilian Internees and Refugees in 1920 blamed "burdensome foreigners" (*lästige Ausländer*) for a range of offenses ranging from profiteering from the misery of destitute Germans, inciting revolution, and taking precious housing and food.[70]

65. Ibid., 25. For an account of German epidemiology and the associations that both scientists and politicians made regarding the susceptibility of Jews to disease and their role as carriers of epidemics to the German people, see Weindling, *Epidemics and Genocide*, esp. 3–72 for the pre–World War I period.
66. Wertheimer, *Unwelcome Strangers*, 35.
67. Maurer, *Ostjuden in Deutschland, 1918–1933*, 128–45, 110.
68. Weindling, *Epidemics and Genocide*, 71.
69. "Protokoll der Sitzung über die jüdischen Ausweisungen im Auswärtigen Amt am 10 April 1919," BArch R 1501/114061, 47.
70. "Denkschrift für die Staatskommission für öffentliche Ordnung betr. die Abänderung der Bestimmungen für die Meldepflicht und die Behandlung der Ausländer," PAAA R 83812, 10. The

These accusations are the same as those made against the *Ostjuden,* and they deserve to be analyzed a bit more closely. First of all, foreigners were accused of committing illegal acts—even foreign-born ethnic Germans, who were not supposed to engage in profiteering or other criminal behavior. Second, foreigners were considered to be a source of subversive ideas and propaganda; although these political activities of foreign nationals were not necessarily illegal, they represented behaviors that many officials did not encourage for Germans either. Finally, foreigners were blamed for taking precious jobs, housing, and food away from needy Germans. Even if an immigrant refrained from profiteering and disseminating Bolshevik ideas, he or she could hardly be expected to abstain from consuming food and other resources. In other words, the mere presence of so many foreigners from Eastern Europe in Germany made them burdensome.

Although generally officials used the term *Ostausländer* to refer to all migrants from the east, they did occasionally draw distinctions among different groups of foreigners. In February 1920, the Prussian government issued a position paper that argued that Germans faced threats from poor Jews, who preyed on Germans as a result of their weakness, and from rich Russians, whose threat came from their economic strength.[71] Nevertheless, although the Interior Ministry recognized these two potential burdens, the Russian danger was an afterthought compared with the much more urgent threat posed by Jews. In this position paper, only one of twelve pages was explicitly devoted to the Russians, whereas the other eleven blamed the Jews for endangering the "peace, order and security" of the German people.[72] The brief mention of "rich Russian refugees who increase the food shortages in Germany through their luxurious style of living," was followed by a lengthy discussion of the dangers posed by "the Eastern European immigration of mostly Jewish confession."[73] The Prussian government was not unsympathetic to the Jews, arguing that they were drawn

term *lästige Ausländer* appears throughout discourse on foreigners in the Weimar Republic. For a few examples of the use of this term by a wide variety of officials, see the letter of the Bavarian Ministry of the Interior to the RMI's Abwicklungsstelle für russ. Kriegsgefangenen und Zivi-Interniertenlager, December 28, 1921, Bayerisches Hauptstaatsarchiv [hereafter BayHStA] MI 71624, n.p.; letter from Landrat Wiedenbrück to Severing, April 21, 1920, GStA PK, Rep. 77, Tit. 1814, Nr. 3, Bd. 1, 45; Reichstag Inquiry, January 24, 1922, *Verhandlungen,* Bd. 370, 3336; protocol of a meeting held at the RMI regarding the treatment of Russian POWs who did not want to return to Soviet Russia, January 10, 1921, R 1501/112383, 262. Note as well that these accusations mirror those presented in the "Frustrations and Failures of Border Control" section in this chapter. The term *lästige Ausländer* was so widespread that the *Rote Fahne* published an article saying that, instead of the *Ostjuden,* the true "burdensome foreigners" were the German capitalists; "Der lästige Ausländer (Eine aktuelle Legende)," *Rote Fahne,* September 22, 1920.

71. The Russian émigrés were by no means all rich, but this image was pervasive in public discourse (see chap. 8).

72. Explanation of the Prussian government regarding the deportation or internment of Eastern immigrants, February 26, 1920, BArch R 1501/114049, 126.

73. Ibid., 125, 129.

to Germany because of its culture and because they faced persecution from the Poles and Russians.[74] Nonetheless, it held the *Ostjuden* responsible for profiteering (*Schieberhandlung*), currency speculation, and unscrupulous business practices.[75] *Profiteering* was a commonly used code word for Eastern Jews, and with the use of this word, a wide range of anti-Semitic stereotypes and dangers adhered to the image of the foreigner.

The emphasis on foreigners and profiteering was shared by the commissioner of civilian internees and refugees, who argued that the fight against profiteering (*Schiebertum*) depended on a more strenuous control of foreigners.[76] And even in relatively tolerant Saxony, the Interior Ministry addressed the "unscrupulous" behavior of foreigners who engaged in profiteering.[77] In fact, while the Saxons had not been particularly concerned about Jews when they discussed the dangers posed by foreigners in early 1919, two years later, Saxon Interior Ministry officials singled out *Ostjuden* as particularly threatening.[78] Considering the number of words spilled to describe the hazards supposedly posed by the *Ostjuden* compared to the relative absence of energy devoted to the Russian émigré "threat," the peril of the "overwhelmingly needy Eastern European Jews" was clearly seen as a much more present and pressing danger. Both government officials and newspaper columnists were generally tolerant of the Russian émigrés (see chap. 8), in stark contrast to both the anti-Russian screeds that had dominated wartime propaganda and the bellicose rhetoric employed by nationalists and even many apparently more moderate officials regarding the Eastern European Jews. Furthermore, even when officials made it clear that the German nation actually faced several different kinds of threats from various immigrant groups, they generally classified these threats according to ethnicity. Jews posed one kind of threat, and Russians posed another. The Prussian position paper did not, for example, distinguish between long-term and short-term immigrants or between immigrants with German cultural ties and those without them. Instead, ethnicity was the most important factor for determining the dangers represented by migrant groups.

Befitting an arena where policy was often conflicted in its design and ineffectual in its application, the conclusion to this chapter is necessarily ambivalent. Be-

74. Ibid., 125.

75. Ibid., 122–23.

76. Denkschrift of the Reichskommissar für Zivilgefangene und Flüchtlinge, October 30, 1920, 92.

77. Sächsisches MI to the Reichskommissar für Zivilgefangene und Flüchtlinge, February 22, 1921, SächsHStA MInnern 11718, 101.

78. When the Saxons initially enacted a registration law in early 1919, officials complaining of the dangers posed by foreigners singled out one group for special mention—the Czechs. Because Saxony lay just over the border from the new Czechoslovak state, the *Polizeidirektion* in Dresden

cause of the failure of border-control measures, Germany was faced with a huge number of refugees after World War I. Officials at both the national and local levels contended with the practical challenges and public provocation that these refugees represented. Both the refugee situation itself and the ambivalence and hesitations of the German government in addressing it contributed to the sense of crisis in Germany.

This sense of crisis had several dangerous consequences. First, as Mitchell suggests, the perceived inability of the state to limit immigration contributed to a sense of its impotence. Right-wing critics repeatedly used the failure to control the border to challenge the authority of the new republic. Second, both commentators in the popular press and officials equated the problem of migration with Jewish migration. In a dangerous cycle, critics of the lax German borders used stereotypes about Jews to affirm the dangers of immigration, and at the same time, the dangers posed by migrants were translated as problems posed by all Jews.

The potent fears awakened by the specter of the uncontrolled German frontiers combined with the real rapid and unprecedented migration into Germany. Once again, ethnicity was a dominant category for determining the right of entry and the right to assistance from the German state. Polish Germans benefited from their claim to represent the suffering of the German nation and their ethnicity. In contrast, Jewish immigrants met long-standing German anti-Semitic imagery of predatory Jews that had been magnified by the perceived dangers posed by the flood of foreigners.

But ethnicity was not the only lens through which the border and immigration crisis was viewed. Next, we explore the Bolshevik threat in official and popular discourse of the period. Bolshevism's promiscuous appeal—Russians, Jews, and Germans were all susceptible—undermined the ethnic categories that were otherwise so central to Germany's policy toward immigrants.

---

warned that Dresden and other cities near the borders could become "the capital of Czechoslovak agitation in Germany." Polizeidirektion Dresden to SMI, March 18, 1919, SächsHStA MInnern 11718, 7. The ministry's letter on the same topic from March 6, 1919, did not include any references to a specific ethnic group; SächsHStA MInnern 11718, 6. When this topic was addressed in 1921, it was clear that the suspect foreigners were Jews; Czech agitators did not warrant any mention. Sächsisches MI to the Reichskommissar für Zivilgefangene und Flüchtlinge, February 22, 1921, SächsHStA MInnern 11718, 101.

6. Anti-Bolshevism and the Bolshevik Prisoners of War

I n the months after World War I, terror of a Bolshevik invasion and infestation held Germany in its grip. Erich Köhrer, an official with the German mission in Latvia and Estonia, wrote, "Death comes from the East, ruin rages towards Europe. As once cholera came from Asia, so, too, the Bolshevik plague, which now threatens the West, is a fully Asiatic phenomenon; and it is certainly no coincidence that thousands of Tartars and Chinese are to be found among the troops that the Soviet government has unleashed against Europe."[1] In a pamphlet entitled "Die Asiatisierung Europas," Paul Schiemann stated that Bolshevism was a form of "spiritual death that has held the people of Asia in its grasp for millennia, and now stands as a smirking ghost before the gates of Europe, cloaked in the finery and sparkle of European ideas. The world of culture has become blind and allows itself to be deceived by this finery."[2] The pamphleteer Joseph Schülter could not restrict his description of Bolshevism to one metaphor, describing it as an "Asiatic plague"[3] and also as a storm cloud now spreading westward across Europe: "This cloud arose in the East. Russia is its birthplace. In Russia, you can find the evidence of its horror and the destruction that the

1. Erich Köhrer, *Das wahre Gesicht des Bolschewismus: Tatsachen-Berichte-Bilder aus den baltischen Provinzen November 1918–Februar 1919* (Berlin: Verlag für Sozialwissenschaft, n.d. [1919?]), 1.
2. Paul Schiemann, *Die Asiatisierung Europas: Gedanken über Klassenkampf und Demokratie* (Berlin: Kommissions, Alexander Grübel, 1919), 9.
3. Joseph Schülter, *Der Bolschewismus und seine Gefahr für Deutschland!: Vortrag gehalten am 13.4.1919 im Windhorst-Bunde, Bonn* (Bonn: Kommissions, Rhenania, 1919), 33.

storm has left in its wake."[4] During the height of the Sparticist uprising in December 1919, the socialist *Vorwärts* warned, "Germany, guard your house! The Russian plague lurks at the gate!"[5]

Such statements would also have been familiar to prewar and wartime Germans, who also feared an imminent invasion by Russian Slavs (see chap. 1). Although the postwar terror of Bolshevism reflected earlier anxieties about a Slavic invasion, these statements are couched in a language of mobility and invisibility, reflecting a crucial distinction between the fear of a Russian invasion and of a Bolshevik infiltration. German stereotypes of Russian Bolsheviks after 1918 shared many characteristics with prewar stereotypes about Slavs, but postwar conceptions regarding Bolsheviks and Bolshevism differed in two crucial respects. First, Bolshevism was transmissible; although Germans could not become Slavs, the German population was susceptible to Bolshevik propaganda. Second, because Bolshevism could not be limited to any one ethnic group, it was difficult to know how to identify Bolsheviks among the larger population. These fears of Bolshevism added to the already volatile mix of stereotypes and anxieties unleashed by the massive migrations. Indeed, it is the specific kind of terror reflected in this language of disease, ghosts, and clouds—namely, the perceived ability of Bolshevism to transform the Germans themselves—that helps explain both the panic felt by many German officials about the massive immigration from the east and the acceptance that *anti*-Bolshevik Russian émigrés found in Germany between 1919 and 1922.

Etienne Balibar's concept of the interior frontier enables us to understand what was at stake in the discussion of Bolshevism in Weimar Germany. Drawing on the writings of Johann Gottlieb Fichte, Etienne Balibar argues that nation-states patrol two kinds of borders: the exterior frontier or physical borders (see chap. 5), and what Balibar terms the interior frontier or the purity of a nation.[6] The penetration of contaminants into the interior frontier is even more difficult to monitor and regulate than an invasion of the external frontier. Although it is the responsibility of the state to maintain control over the exterior frontier, the vigilance of both state authorities and the people is required to counteract threats to the purity of the nation. Germans fearful of the power of Bolshevism to seduce vulnerable members of the *Volk* expressed a twofold fear: not only was the German national community now contaminated by a foreign presence, but these German Bolsheviks were also no longer able to defend the German nation against further infection.

4. Ibid., 5.
5. *Vorwärts,* December 29, 1918.
6. Etienne Balibar, "Fichte and the Internal Border: On Addresses to the German Nation," in *Masses, Classes, Ideas: Studies on Politics and Philosophy before and after Marx*, 61–84 (New York: Routledge, 1994).

In their descriptions of Bolshevism, German officials often drew on the metaphors of epidemics and disease that had become common in the years leading up to World War I. During that period, such metaphors were often applied to immigrants, especially the *Ostjuden*.[7] Paul Weindling attributes the growing German obsession with hygiene both to advances in biological science and to social concerns regarding population mobility.[8] And, Weindling maintains, the "the medical techniques of disinfestation, fumigation, and disinfection" and the stereotypes of Jews as vermin in need of eradication culminated in Nazism.[9] In addition to this language of biological threat, anti-Bolshevik commentators also turned to uncanny images of "clouds," "waves," "swarms," and "ghosts" to demonstrate the supposed danger posed by Bolshevism in postrevolutionary Germany. Indeed, much like the rhetoric of disease and often overlapping with it, Bolshevism itself provided an available and highly compelling language for talking about the permeability and dispensability of borders that haunted the imagination of post–World War I Germans. Although both hygiene advocates and anticommunists worked to erect barriers against these invisible and transmissible foes, the concern over porous borders did not, *pace* Weindling, necessarily lead to the virulent racism of the Nazis. Instead, the fear of Bolshevism often complicated prewar racial stereotypes. Although the discourse of anti-Bolshevism borrowed many of the terms that had adhered to the prewar Russians, the perceived transmissibility of Bolshevism meant that Bolshevism could not be limited to any one ethnic group. Instead, Bolsheviks and anti-Bolsheviks alike sought international alliances against their ideological enemies. At one and the same time, Bolshevism inspired authorities to seek to shore up the frontiers and to transcend them.

Anxieties about the potential of Russian POWs to spread Bolshevism among the German people reached a crisis point in fall 1920 after 65,000 Red Army soldiers were interred on German soil during the Russo-Polish war. Camp commanders, the Prussian and national interior ministries, and a host of commentators and Reichstag deputies located across the political spectrum feared that the Russians would escape the camps and foment revolution in Germany or pillage the countryside, they were also afraid that German communists would spread propaganda among the imprisoned soldiers, and they were even afraid that fanatical Bolsheviks in the camps would infect apolitical Russian soldiers with communist ideology. In other words, German authorities expressed their concerns about the POWs as fears about the crossing of borders.

7. For the prewar association of Ostjuden and disease, Weindling, *Epidemics and Genocide*, 70–72.

8. Ibid., 103.

9. Ibid., 400.

The Russian Prisoner-of-War Camps: Patrolling the Borders of Bolshevik Infiltration

World War I marks the first time that European states were asked to contend with massive numbers of POWs. One account estimated that there were as many as 6.6 million POWs held by all combatants in the war. In Germany alone, there were 1 million POWs in 1915 and as many as 2.4 million on German soil at the cession of hostilities in 1918.[10] Despite months of attempts after the March 1918 Treaty of Brest-Litovsk to arrange prisoner exchanges between the Soviets and the Germans, 1.2 million Russians, or one-half the total number of POWs, were still held in Germany when the armistice between Germany and the western Allies was signed in November of that year.[11] The great majority of these Russians worked as forced laborers in industry and, especially, agriculture, representing one attempt by the wartime state to respond to both the labor shortages created by the army and the demands placed on the labor market by the war.[12] Erich Ludendorff estimated in December 1917 that 650,000 POWs were employed on the land and 230,000 worked in factories.[13] By the end of the war, 1.5 million POWs were employed in Germany.[14]

During World War I, German officials had sought to use these prisoners to advance German political goals. In 1915, the War Ministry began holding POWs of non-Russian nationalities in separate camps from the Russian prisoners, with plans to turn these POWs into an anti-Russian force under German command. These schemes came to nothing, but they prefigured postwar plans (also unsuccessful) to use Russian POWs against the Soviets.[15] As part of this, the FdR was allowed access to ethnic Germans in the camps with the goal of encouraging their migration to the soon-to-be annexed Baltics or the German mainland (see chap. 1). These political machinations aside, Germans primarily regarded the Russian POWs as barbarians. But their primitiveness was not seen as threaten-

10. Uta Hinz, "'Die Deutschen Barbaren' sind doch die 'Besseren Menschen': Kriegsgefangenschaft und gefangene 'Feinde' in der Darstellung der deutschen Publizistik 1914–1918," in *In der Hand des Feindes: Kriegsgefangenschaft von der Antike bis zum Zweiten Weltkrieg*, ed. Rüdiger Overmans (Cologne: Böhlau Verlag, 1999), 339. On POWs in Germany more generally, see Uta Hinz, *Gefangen im Grossen Krieg: Kriegsgefangenschaft in Deutschland, 1914–1921* (Essen: Klartext, 2006).

11. Johannes Baur, "Zwischen 'Roten' und 'Weissen'-Russische Kriegsgefangene in Deutschland nach 1918," in *Russische Emigration in Deutschland 1918 bis 1941*, ed. Karl Schlögel (Berlin: Akademie, 1995), 94.

12. The ones who worked in agriculture generally lived on the estates where they worked. For a discussion of the issues that arose as a a result, see Jochen Oltmer, "Zwangsmigration und Zwangsarbeit: Ausländische Arbeitskräfte und bäuerliche Ökonomie im Ersten Weltkrieg," *Tel-Aviver Jahrbuch für Deutsche Geschichte* 27 (1998), 158–64.

13. In Baur, "Zwischen 'Roten' und 'Weissen,'" 94.

14. Oltmer, *Migration und Politik*, 274.

15. Williams, *Culture in Exile*, 55.

ing; rather, their backwardness represented an opportunity for Germans to teach them about culture and cleanliness and also to demonstrate their own superiority.[16] Germans did express some concerns about the POWs and their contacts with German women, but even while German newspapers expressed fears about the infidelity of German women on the home front, they also told passionate stories of Russians and Germans falling in love under difficult circumstances. The press might have despaired of the moral failings of German women, but they did not seem to blame this on the Russians, who were generally portrayed as sympathetic and tender.[17] Wartime discourse about the Russian prisoners was not consumed with the fears of the prisoners breaking out of the camps and spreading disease and dangerous political ideas that became so important after the war ended.

During the war, most Russians were already employed outside the boundaries of the camps, meaning that the camp border was crossed daily. Moreover, many POWs, especially those employed in agriculture, did not live in camps at all.[18] Prior to the end of the war, the 1.5 million POWs employed in industry or agriculture could be found in approximately 750,000 different workplaces strewn across the Reich, meaning that POWs were constantly in contact with Germans.[19]

Nonetheless, in the early Weimar Republic, both the press and state authorities imagined a previously intact camp border that was in danger of being transgressed. The rhetoric of border violation that dominated postwar discussion was not an inevitable result of the large number of POWs in Germany (in fact, that number decreased). Instead, the shift in discourse between the war and the period afterward resulted from the widespread perception of the vulnerability and political instability of Germany.

With the outbreak of revolution in early November 1918, some members of the local councils appeared in the POW camps and ordered the release of the prisoners. In response, the Berlin Workers' and Soldiers' Councils (Arbeiter- und Soldatenräte) issued an order on November 9, 1918, the day the republic itself was declared, stating that "all prisoners of war, including the Russians, are to be captured immediately and brought to the nearest military facility (barracks, internment camps)."[20] Despite the fear that the POWs would become embroiled in German internal affairs, with few exceptions the Russians in the camps did not become involved in the political turmoil in Germany during 1918–1919. Instead, many Russian POWs took advantage of the chaos in Germany during and after

16. Hinz, "'Deutschen Barbaren,'" 346, 357.

17. Lisa Todd, "Sexual Treason: State Surveillance of Immorality and Infidelity in World War I Germany," PhD diss., University of Toronto, 2005.

18. Although this had been tolerated before, an October 1915 order officially allowed the boarding of POWs on individual farms; KM to Stellvertretende Generalkommandos, October 23, 1915, GStA, Rep. 87B, Nr. 16099.

19. Oltmer, *Migration und Politik*, 278.

20. Order cited in Baur, "Zwischen 'Roten' und 'Weissen,'" 94.

November to leave and return to Russia. In addition, the German state continued to transport POWs to the German border so that they would find their way back to Russia. Unfortunately, the lack of rail connections between the German and Russian train systems meant that POWs had to cross the border on foot, walking for miles in the bitter cold without food.[21] The Allies halted these transports in January 1919, but by this point, the number of Russian POWs held on German territory had decreased by almost half, from 1.2 million to 650,000.[22]

During the war, the War Ministry had controlled the camps. In January 1919, after several months without clear authority, the prisoners came under the control of two overlapping agencies: the Reichsstelle für Kriegsgefangene und Zivilinternierte (National Office for Prisoners of War and Civilian Internees), which was led by a representative from the Foreign Office and the Prussian Defense Ministry, and the Abwicklungsstelle für russische Kriegsgefangene und Interniertenlager (Settlement Office for Russian POWs and Internment Camps) in the national Interior Ministry.[23] Although these agencies claimed an official mandate over the camps, in reality a hodgepodge of national and local officials were left with de facto responsibility over the camps. For example, the shortage of troops to defend the camps meant that Prussian and national border police were often called in to oversee them. The revolution left many camps in the charge of younger and, it was argued, less disciplined guards. The German acceptance of the terms of the Treaty of Versailles, limiting its army to 100,000 men, only exacerbated this problem. Faced with this situation of unclear authority and potentially untrustworthy guards, many officials expressed alarm about the potential actions of the these POWs. As much as this fear borrowed from earlier discourses about a potential Russian invasion, it also revealed a nascent sense of international alliances arranged around support for or opposition to Bolshevism. To explore how this discourse functioned, let us examine one example in some detail.

In March 1919, the Headquarters of the Zentralstelle Grenzschutz Ost (Prussian Eastern Border Patrol) warned the War Ministry (later Defense Ministry) that "According to all available reports, the majority of Russian POWs in Germany have been strongly infected with Bolshevism. The people are under the influence of Spartacist propaganda, and it is important to recognize the great danger that these elements might take part in a later Communist putsch in Germany." The official went on to describe the threat posed by these prisoners:

---

21. Ibid., 95.

22. Johannes Zelt, "Kriegsgefangene in Deutschland: Neue Forschungsergebnisse zur Geschichte der Russischen Sektion der KPD," *Zeitschrift für Geschichtswissenschaft* 15, no. 4 (1967), 621.

23. On the authority of the Reichsstelle für Kriegsgefangene und Zivilinternierte, see PAAA R 901/86451, n.p.; *Reichsgesetzblatt,* January 2, 1919. Regarding the authority of the Abwicklungsstelle, see Baur, "Zwischen 'Roten' und 'Weissen,'" 99.

According to many Russian, German-oriented (*deutschgesinnte*) officers, the
alliance of the Russian POWs with the [German] Spartacists, which is planned
for May, would mean the same thing for Germany as the Soviet-Chinese have
meant for Moscow and St. Petersburg, in other words, a rule of tyranny by violent radicals who had been inflamed through their long captivity and the lack
of adequate food. As a result of propaganda and their sudden release, a raving
fury could develop against all non-Communist Germans such that our people
(*Bevölkerung*) would be subject to a true rule of terror.[24]

He metaphorically traveled first eastward to Moscow and Petersburg, suffering
under the tyranny of the "Soviet-Chinese," and then returned to Germany, elid-
ing Russia and Germany as both subject to Soviet threat while also invoking a
strict territorial system, in which the east remained the source of danger and the
west was powerless in its grip. Thus, Moscow was menaced by the "Soviet-Chinese" at the same time that Russians (or, more precisely, those Russians who do
not fall into the category of the "German-oriented officers") were threatening
Germany. In this rhetorical system, Russians could be both the victims (of people from further east) and persecutors (of Germans to their west).

This official's description of Russian POWs with a "raving fury" hearkens
back to images of a Russian or Bolshevik invasion that circulated during and after
World War I. But there was a key difference—he was not merely afraid that the
Russian POWs would escape but also that they could join up with the German
Spartacists. In other words, his fear was ultimately not one of a Russian invasion
but one of an international Bolshevik alliance. The enemy was not merely external (i.e., a question of invasion from Russia or even from Russian camps on
German territory) but one in which questions of internal and external seemed irrelevant—the German Spartacists and the Russian communists would have common cause against "all non-Communist Germans." National distinctions seemed,
if not irrelevant, certainly less important; after all, the German official had received his information about this threat from "Russian, German-oriented officers." As this official groped toward an understanding of non-Bolshevik Russians,
he equated German-oriented and anti-Bolshevik. And just as there were German-oriented Russians, this official also emphasized the potential alliance between the Russian Bolshevik prisoners and their German allies, who could assist
them in exercising this fury on the defenseless German populace. The geographical imaginary of the letter reflected a nascent sense of international alliances arranged around the support of or opposition to Bolshevism.

Poorly defended borders were often blamed for allowing Bolshevik con-
tamination. One official with the War Ministry explained that the potential escape of the POWs posed a dual threat. "If the planned mass breakout succeeds,

24. Zentralstelle Grenzschutz Ost to KM, March 29, 1919, BArch R 43 I/233, 70.

one section of the prisoners will plunder their way back to Russia, while another group will—on the basis of the connections that they have made with Spartacists and Bolsheviks in Germany—get arms [from their German allies] and be turned to revolutionary purposes."[25] At the same time, this official warned that the release of the POWs might actually result from overly excited German communists who had already in November "claimed the prisoners as their brothers and then set them all free."[26] The very absence of clarity about whether German or Russian communists were to be blamed demonstrated the association between Bolshevism and the transgression of borders. The Interior Ministry of Württemberg suggested that to halt revolutionary agitation it was imperative to restrict the "free movement" of the POWs. Indeed, any movement of the POWs, even when they assembled for transports to return to Russia, could easily turn into "pure Communist demonstrations."[27] A meeting of POW camp commanders also concluded that the greatest danger for Germany lay in POWs who "rove aimlessly through the countryside."[28]

The reality of Russian Bolshevik involvement in German internal affairs was much less dramatic than these stories of a Bolshevik-Spartacist alliance suggest. During the short-lived Bavarian Soviet Republic in April 1919, Major Johann Strauß, appeared at the nearby POW camp and called on the inmates to join the Red Army. Motivated more by the suffering in the camp than political fervor, 120 Russians appeared to have joined him, but the vast majority elected to stay in the camp. Those who left the camp were given Bavarian military uniforms and served exclusively as guards. As retribution for this behavior, during the White terror that accompanied the end of the Soviet Republic, fifty-three Russians serving with the Red Army were taken prisoner near Pasing, a suburb of Munich, tortured, and shot.[29] In early 1920, during the communist uprising in the Ruhr, there were rumors of a "Russian company" that fought on the side of the communists, and reports circulated of six Russians who were taken prisoner and two who were killed during fighting in Bochum.[30] But beyond a few isolated incidents, there is little evidence of a sustained alliance between the Russian POWs and German communists.

In addition, anticommunist accusations that the communists were trying to use the POWs for their own purposes were somewhat disingenuous. Noske and Russian émigré leaders drew up plans to recruit an anti-Bolshevik army from

25. KM Unterkunfts-Departement, April 2, 1919, BArch R 43 I/233, 75.
26. Ibid.
27. Württemberg Interior Ministry to RMI, December 2, 1920, BArch R 1501/113320, 36.
28. "Protokoll des Besprechungsergebnisses mit den Lagerkommandanten der russischen Kriegsgefangenenlager am 2, 3, 4 Februar 1920 im Herrenhause zu Berlin," BArch R 1501/112396, 101.
29. Heinrich Hillmayr, *Roter und Weißer Terror in Bayern nach 1918* (Munich: Nusser Verlag, 1974), 136–37.
30. Baur, "Zwischen 'Roten' und 'Weissen,'" 99.

the POW camps. Ebert ultimately refused to support this plan, but it continued to be funded by Russian émigrés.[31] During the March 1920 putsch orchestrated by the disgruntled journalist Wolfgang Kapp and his nationalist allies, rumors filled the Berlin press that anti-Bolshevik Russian officers in the camps had supported Kapp's forces. These accusations were not without some truth; General Vasili Biskupsky, Kapp's main contact with émigré Russian officers in Berlin, had signed agreements with Kapp promising support for the putsch in return for subsidies for his own plans to use the POWs against the Bolsheviks.[32]

One obvious solution to the perceived danger posed by the Russian POWs was a prisoner exchange with Soviet Russia or the White armies fighting the Soviets. Sending the POWs back to Russia would have both removed this supposedly threatening group from German soil and also would have satisfied the desires of most of the prisoners themselves. Furthermore, hundreds of thousands of Germans were being held in Russian/Soviet prisons, and a prisoner exchange would have been the easiest way to get them back to Germany.[33] Prisoner exchanges had begun after the signing of the Treaty of Brest-Litovsk in early 1918, and even though Germany and Russia severed diplomatic ties after the German revolution, they continued until January 1919. At this point, the Allied Armistice Commission forbade future transfers out of the fear that returning Russians would become Bolshevik soldiers, even though a few days before these transports were ended, the Bavarian minister for military affairs warned that the defense of Germany against Bolshevism demanded the immediate transport of all Russian POWs back to Russia.[34] By April, the Allies changed their minds about prisoner transports and demanded the repatriation of the Russian POWs to anti-Bolshevik forces fighting in Russia. The Germans were caught between conflicting priorities. On the one hand, they no longer wanted the responsibility of caring for hundreds of thousands of enemy soldiers at a time when their own resources were so strapped. On the other, they feared that repatriating Russian POWs to the White armies might lead to reprisals against the German soldiers still being held by the Bolsheviks. Moritz Schlesinger, the director of the

31. Williams, *Culture in Exile*, 88–90.

32. Ibid., 99. A White Russian office in Berlin quietly recruited some POWs to fight in Avalov-Bermondt's army (the same army that the Freikorps soldiers found themselves fighting in) up to October 1919; Volkmann, *Russische Emigration in Deutschland, 1919–1929,* 65. After the collapse of this army, approximately 12,000 soldiers were interned in East Prussia; Baur, "Zwischen 'Roten' und 'Weissen,'" 96.

33. Georg Wurzer states that 167,000 German and 2,111,146 Austro-Hungarian soldiers were held in Russian prisons; Georg Wurzer, "Das Schicksal der Deutschen Kriegsgefangenen in Russland im Ersten Weltkrieg: Der Erlebnisbericht Edwin Erich Dwingers," in *In der Hand des Feindes: Kriegsgefangenschaft von der Antike bis zum Zweiten Weltkrieg,* ed. Rüdiger Overmans (Cologne: Böhlau Verlag, 1999), 363.

34. Bayerisches Ministerium für militärische Angelegenheiten to the Staatsministerium für Verkehrsangelegenheiten, January 14, 1919, BayHStA Ministerium des Äusseren [hereafter, MA] 104118.

National Office for Prisoners of War and Civil Internees, was in charge of negotiating such exchanges, but he was trusted by no one and his attempts at negotiation went nowhere.[35] Throughout 1919 and early 1920, attempts to send the remaining Russian POWs back to Russia officially stalemated, although prisoners of war themselves often took the initiative to leave the camps, either to return to Russia or to join the burgeoning Russian émigré population in Germany itself. Some Russians married German women and planned to stay in Germany and build lives there.[36] Finally, in April 1920, Germany signed a treaty with the Soviet government to restart the prisoner exchanges, and soon ships began to send 5,000 Russians POWs per week back to Russia. At this point, the German government estimated that approximately 200,000 POWs remained in Germany, two-thirds of whom were housed in the camps.[37]

The Russo-Polish War and the Escalation of Tension

After a year of border skirmishes, in April 1920 Józef Piłsudski, the Polish chief of state, invaded Soviet Ukraine. A successful Soviet counterattack brought the Russians to the edge of Warsaw, but a Polish offensive that summer sent the Red Army into retreat. The Polish advance led between 65,000 and 90,000 Soviet soldiers to cross the East Prussian border to avoid being taken prisoner by the Poles.[38] According to the 1907 Hague Convention, which regulated the legal status of POWs, these soldiers were to be treated as civilian internees rather than POWs.[39] The Russo-Polish war became a turning point in German discourse about the POWs. Suddenly, Germans no longer faced Russian POWs who were merely potential Bolsheviks but also a large number of Red Army soldiers on German soil. And because they were civilian internees and not POWs, they were allowed access to Viktor Kopp, the Soviet government representative in Berlin. The internment of the Red Army soldiers only fueled the image of "border-cross-

---

35. Williams, *Culture in Exile*, 83–84.

36. RWA to the Kriegsministerium (Unterkunfts-Departement), May 26, 1919, GStA PK, 1 HA., Rep. 77, Tit. 1146, Nr. 74, Beiheft 4, Bd. III, 60; Kriegsministerium Fürsorgeabteilung für zurückgekehrte Kriegsgefangene to the RMI, July 24, 1919, GStA PK, 1 HA., Rep. 77, Tit. 1146, Nr. 74, Beiheft 4, Bd. III, 61.

37. In a report of a meeting held in the RMI on December 13, 1919, the number of POWs in Germany was estimated as 200,000. Approximately one-third were said to be housed where they worked, primarily in agriculture, and the balance was housed in thirty-five camps spread throughout the country; BArch R 1501/112395, 256.

38. Baur, "Zwischen 'Roten' und 'Weissen,'" 96. Baur cites two figures. The estimate of 65,000 is provided by the Reichszentralstelle für Kriegs- und Zivilgefangene and that of 90,000 appears in Soviet sources.

39. Ibid. For more on the legal status of POWs, see Stefan Oeter, "Die Entwicklung des Kriegsgefangenenrechts: Die Sichtweise eines Völkerrechtlers," in *In der Hand des Feindes: Kriegsgefangenschaft von der Antike bis zum Zweiten Weltkrieg*, ed. Rüdiger Overmans, 41–59 (Cologne: Böhlau Verlag, 1999).

ing Bolsheviks" that had coalesced among German officials in 1919 and early 1920. German anxieties about these potential border crossings—the Bolshevik commissars and ordinary Russian soldiers, communists in Germany and those in the camps, and even the fear of a spread of disease and plunder—reached a fever pitch in the months after these internees entered Germany, culminating in an impassioned debate in the Reichstag in December 1920.

Internal German political tensions fueled the perception that the interned Soviet forces posed a critical danger to the German Republic. In the aftermath of the abortive right-wing Kapp Putsch in March 1920, German communists in the Ruhr Valley seized the moment and staged a coup of their own. The popular militancy that had forced Kapp from Berlin escalated to offensive actions designed to press for demands unfulfilled by the revolution less than two years earlier. The Red Army, a workers militia in the Ruhr, managed to attract between 50,000 and 100,000 volunteers and briefly repelled the security police, the army, and the Freikorps before being crushed.[40]

In early 1920, Germany appeared on the verge of revolution. The potentially destabilizing effects of the Russo-Polish war and the internment of the 65,000–90,000 Bolshevik soldiers a mere few months later had to be taken seriously. Further increasing the sense of urgency throughout summer 1920 as the Russo-Polish war raged, German communists prepared to welcome the Red Army on to their soil by making banners and learning Russian.[41] Meanwhile, the KPD organized sabotage against the Polish forces operating near the German border.[42] In September, the *Rote Fahne* published a greeting from interned members of the Russian Red Army to the German proletariat that proclaimed their "unshakeable certainty" in "our collective victory." The greeting concluded, "In every moment, you can count on our readiness, on our love for the German proletariat," further fueling the German authorities' sense of being under siege.[43]

The defense and interior ministries believed that the Bolshevik commissars were particularly dangerous sources of Bolshevik contagion in the camps; they feared that the fatigue of the interned soldiers would leave them susceptible to

---

40. For more on the March uprisings, see Lucas, *Märzrevolution 1920;* Eliasberg, *Ruhrkrieg von 1920.*

41. Aleksandr Vatlin, "The Testing-Ground of World Revolution: Germany in 1921," in *International Communism and the Communist International 1919–43,* ed. Tim Rees and Andrew Thorpe (Manchester, UK: Manchester University Press, 1998), 119.

42. For more on these and other KPD actions on behalf of Soviet Russia, including protests in 1920 and 1927 involving hundreds of thousands of Germans marching under the banner "Hände Weg von Sowjetrussland" and 600,000 Germans who took to the streets after the signing of the treaty of Rapallo, see Heinz Habedank, *Geschichte der revolutionären Berliner Arbeiterbewegung: Von den Anfängen bis zur Gegenwart, Vol. 2: Von 1917 bis 1945* (Berlin: Dietz, 1987), 152; Günter Rosenfeld, *Sowjetrussland und Deutschland 1917–1922* (Berlin: Akademie, 1960), 398.

43. *Rote Fahne,* September 29, 1920.

Fig. 2. Soviet Civilian Internees in the Wünsdorf Camp, ca. 1920–1922. BArch, Bild 146-1995-051-29/Frankl, A. Reproduced with permission.

the commissars' Bolshevik infection.[44] Kopp's Soviet mission in Berlin was a further source of concern. Due to the fact that these were not technically POWs, Kopp was allowed to visit with the internees and both Prussian and national Interior Ministry officials believed that he used those visits to distribute Bolshevik propaganda.[45] But, although the commissars might transmit Bolshevik ideas to ordinary prisoners and Kopp could inflame the commissars, some officials were even more worried about the connections between Russian and German communists. The police president in Berlin accused German communists of "con-

44. RMI to Reichskommissar für Kriegs- und Zivilgefangene [hereafter RKKZ], September 27, 1920, PAAA R 83811; Reichswehrministerium to the RMI, AA and the RKKZ, October 18, 1920, PAAA R 83811, Bd. 2.
45. Report of a meeting held at the RMI, April 17, 1920, BArch R 1501/113319, 2. In addition to the examples mentioned here, see a report from the Landesgrenzpolizei Ost, November 27, 1920, BArch R 1501/113328, 81; PMI to the RMI, AA, etc., November 18, 1920, BArch R 1501/113328, 71. See also Aktenvermerk der RMI, November 30, 1920, BArch R 1501/113320, 21.

ducting a lively Communist propaganda" among the camp inhabitants by masquerading as members of Kopp's office to gain access to the prisoners, and the commander of an internment camp in Hameln reported that communist prisoners returned from their work outside the camps with food packages.[46] In addition, an official in Hannover warned that "incendiary Russian language pamphlets are being produced, in which the internees are directed that the time will come when the Red Army and the German Communists will fight together."[47] The Prussian border guard in East Prussia feared that Bolsheviks might escape from the internment camps and, using their connections with "the local radical left parties," might spread turmoil across Germany.[48]

This network of already established connections between Russian and German communists across the camp border rendered the border itself meaningless. Even when officials did not discuss Bolshevism, they were still concerned with the potential dangers of the porous camp border. The Hannover mayor described Russians who escaped the nearby Hameln camp and "wander[ed] around trading, begging, and stealing" from the local population. He wrote, "When a group of these ragged (verlumpte) figures appear begging at the home of a farmer, they are rarely refused a gift out of fear." Prisoners were sighted on numerous occasions killing cows from neighboring farms. Furthermore, he noted that these prisoners could spread infectious diseases such as typhoid in the surrounding population.[49] In Bremen, police painted a portrait of Red Guards roaming through the countryside, spreading disease and terror.[50]

Moreover, German officials often complained about the inadequacy of the camp border itself. The mayor of Hannover observed that "the barbed wire is rotten and rusted and it is easy to break through it."[51] Others blamed the guards at that camp, who had primarily been recruited from the ranks of the unemployed, for failing to patrol the boundaries of the camp sufficiently.[52] An inquiry in the Reichstag in July 1920 connected the hazards that the POWs and internees presented with the danger by the porous eastern German border.[53]

As German anxieties about the POWs grew stronger through fall 1920, complaints increasingly focused on the fact that troops were not allowed to shoot at

46. Polizeipräsident in Berlin to RMI, August 24, 1921, BArch R 1501/113329, 18; Aktenvermerk der RMI, November 30, 1920, BArch R 1501/113320, 21.

47. Hannover Oberpräsident to the Ministry of the Interior for Niedersachsen and AA, October 4, 1921, PAAA R 83811, Bd. 2.

48. Report from the Landesgrenzpolizei Ostpreussen on the Arys POW camp, September 5, 1920, PAAA R 83811, Bd. 2.

49. Hannover Oberpräsident to the Ministry of the Interior.

50. Polizeidirektion Bremen to the Reichsministerium für die Überwachung der öffentlichen Ordnung, BArch R 1501/113319, 339.

51. Ibid.

52. RMI to the Reichsjustizministerium, October 20, 1920, BArch R 1501/113319, 184; Reichstag inquiry, October 19, 1920, Reichstag Verhandlungen, Bd. 364, 498–99.

53. Reichstag inquiry, July 30, 1920, Reichstag Verhandlungen, Bd. 363, 232.

the prisoners unless they were directly threatened.[54] The restriction on the powers of the camp guards seemed outmoded and inadequate to combat this new threat. As a result, in October police forces stationed near the POW camps received instructions to remain on alert during the night in case of disturbances at the camps, and the camp commanders themselves were told to verify the integrity of the barbed wire around the camps.[55] A bulletin published by the Heeresabwicklungsamt in late November allowed guards to use weapons against prisoners in cases of an attempted breakout or any "evasive action after dark."[56] A week later, the Heeresabwicklungsamt claimed that, because the interned Red Guards were civilian internees, they could be punished by the German courts if they conducted Bolshevik agitation.[57]

Even these new powers failed to reassure Germans who were fearful about both the potential for a Russian-led Bolshevik uprising in Germany and about the potential abuses of the commissars against anti-Bolshevik prisoners in the camps themselves. Despite the nearly obsessive attention paid to the failure of border control and the alleged spread of Bolshevism between Russians and Germans, no border could ever be completely reliable, not because of the failure to find sufficient guards but because the border could separate only the Russian POWs and Soviet internees from the German population—actual alliances could not be untangled so neatly. Both the German and Russian populations were themselves split between Bolsheviks and anti-Bolsheviks, and no camp fence could solve this problem. The border became a tangible symbol of its own futility.

An incendiary article in the right-wing *Deutsche Zeitung* in December 1920 described the persecution of anti-Bolshevik POWs at the hands of interned Bolsheviks, precipitating a heated debate in the Reichstag. Discussion opened on December 17, 1920, with an *Interpellation* by the right-wing DNVP delegates Oskar Hergt and Wilhelm Henning, and for two days, representatives from across the political spectrum accused their opponents of attempting to propagandize in the camps and using the POWs to achieve their own political goals. August Beuermann, another DNVP delegate, spoke about the mutual support from Red Army soldiers and German communists: "These people surround us and are [ready] to insert themselves into the internal political situation of Germany."[58] Ludwig Haas of the DDP painted a terrifying picture of what would happen if the 15,000 prisoners held in his home state of Baden were to be released: "If they wanted to and had arms, 15,000 men would be in the position to

54. Reichstag inquiry, October 19, 1920, *Reichstag Verhandlungen,* Bd. 364, 498–99.

55. "Chefbesprechung über die Russenlager, 18 Oktober 1920," BArch R 43I/236, 35.

56. Bekanntmachung from November 22, 1920, mentioned by the Heeresabwicklungs-Hauptamt, December 6, 1920, BArch R 1501/113320, 82.

57. Ibid. The Heeresabwicklungs-Hauptamt is referring to a Bekanntmachung from November 29, 1920.

58. *Reichstag Verhandlungen,* Bd. 346, 1788.

make all of Baden into a Russian Republic."[59] Meanwhile, Kurt Rosenfeld, a
USPD delegate, accused the German government of "want[ing] to make White
Guardists out of the Red Guardists, ready to fight against the Soviet government
in Russia or with the reaction against the republic of Germany." He went on to
claim that the government was working with anti-Bolshevik officers in the camps
to spread propaganda and accused the DNVP of wishing to turn the interned
Red Army soldiers into strikebreakers.[60] His accusations were echoed by a *Rote
Fahne* article, which claimed that the entire spectacle of communist agitation in
the camps was a cover for the nationalists' own attempts to spread propaganda:

> The DNVP wants to bring the imprisoned members of the Red Army under the
> political influence of Russian counter-revolutionaries in order to turn them into
> cannon fodder for new White attacks against Soviet Russia. This explains their
> protests against "Communist intrigue" in the Russian camps and against the
> Communist propaganda of Viktor Kopp. They want to create free space for their
> counter-revolutionary agitation in the camps.[61]

Beyond the issue of politicization lay the question of protection and international asylum. Hergt and Henning of the DNVP argued that the Germans had
a responsibility to protect the anti-Bolshevik POWs for three reasons: (1) the
prisoners were being held on German soil; (2) Victor Kopp, the Soviet representative in Berlin, "and his comrades" were themselves active in Germany; and
(3) the POWs were suffering so greatly. Hergt and Henning decried in particular that noncommunist Russians were subject to "the most brutal abuse (*brutal-
ste Vergewaltigung*)" in the camps.[62] These three justifications combined a sense
that national rights were being violated (this was taking place in Germany) and
that more universal human rights were being violated (the abuse of the non-
communist Russians). Hergt and his fellow DNVP deputies alluded to a common
destiny for German and Russian anti-Bolsheviks. Whereas currently only the
anti-Bolshevik Russians faced the wrath of the commissars, the subversive activities of the Bolsheviks would soon threaten Germany itself.[63]

Haas, the DDP deputy, also referred to asylum rights in his defense of the
non-Bolshevik POWs, but he framed this issue as one of abstract legal principles
rather than calling on the particular anti-Bolshevik sympathies that the DNVP

59. Ibid., 1797.
60. Ibid., 1791–92.
61. *Rote Fahne,* December 17, 1920.
62. Reichstag Interpellation, November 22, 1920, *Reichstag Verhandlungen,* Bd. 364, 634. The
discussion began on this *Interpellation* on December 15, 1920.
63. It is interesting to contrast this *Interpellation* with another one made by Henning little
more than a year later on January 24, 1922, in which he asked, "Is it [the German government] willing to take the homes of the *Ostjuden* and give them to the Volga Germans?" *Reichstag Verhandlungen,* Bd. 370, 3336.

had attempted to mobilize. Haas specifically rejected German involvement in the activities of the Russian counterrevolutionaries, something promulgated by the DNVP, speaking instead of the German responsibility to protect them as potential victims of Bolshevism. During a portion of the debate concerning whether the POWs should be subject to military or civilian law, as they had been since the time of the revolution, Haas stated that "according to my understanding, they should be treated according to the principles of asylum law (*Asylrecht*)."[64] For Haas, the Germans had a unique indebtedness to the concept of asylum because of their recent history. "We all have a special motive to recognize the right of asylum because, perhaps with the exception of the extreme Left, we all share the strong sentiment towards Holland, which refused to deliver the former German Kaiser to the Entente."[65] Thus Haas equated the German and Russian demands of asylum—if Germans appreciated the asylum provided for Wilhelm II, they should provide a safe haven for Russians in danger of persecution.

When Reichstag deputies from the DNVP called for the protection of Russian POWs from Soviet propaganda and persecution, when officials within the War Ministry recognized the evidence provided by anti-Bolshevik Russians within the camps, or when a USPD delegate claimed that the German government had an interest in turning "Red Guards" into "White Guards," they were acknowledging ideological allegiances that transcended the narrow confines of ethnicity. Furthermore, both left- and right-wing deputies saw themselves as powerless to prevent the machinations of their enemies. Rather than putting forth positive suggestions for improvement, they produced accusations of the failure of the government to guarantee the safety of anti-Bolshevik Russians that compromised the aura of state authority. For example, the guards were said to be young and inexperienced or incompetent, but no serious attempt was made to replace these guards. They were, instead, used as symbols of the incompetence and perfidy of the Weimar state. One implicit lesson of the POW controversy in the early Weimar Republic was that an international, ideologically motivated enemy required an international and ideologically motivated reaction. A second lesson was that the German state was ill-prepared to mobilize such a response.

The Aftermath

Despite the anxieties expressed during late 1920 about Russian POWs and civilian internees, the number of Russians actually held in Germany steadily declined. A large number of them simply left the camps, either joining the large number of Russian émigrés then arriving in Berlin and other large cities or re-

64. *Reichstag Verhandlungen*, Bd. 346, 1795.
65. Ibid., 1796.

turning to their homes in the east. For example, a count by the national Interior Ministry in March 1921 registered approximately 30,000 Russian POWs and internees in Germany held in twelve camps, with another 40,000–50,000 described as "escaped."[66] By the end of March, the official prisoner transfers ended, and the welfare centers established by the German and Soviet governments in one another's capital for the processing of POWs were closed.[67] In June 1921, one official claimed that only 1,160 prisoners had chosen to remain in Germany because of their opposition to Bolshevism. By this point, German commentary on the Russian POWs had shifted from fears about their political activities to concern with finding jobs for those prisoners who remained and with dissolving the camps.[68]

The conclusion to the story of the POWs is ironic, considering the fears on both sides about the crossing of borders and potential alliances between forces in Germany and Soviet Russia. In May 1921, a treaty was signed between the Soviet and German governments that expanded the welfare centers in each capital and the ties between the two countries. This represented a hesitant step in the process of negotiation that ended with the Treaty of Rapallo. When Germany signed the Treaty of Rapallo in April of 1922, it became the first Western country to provide the Soviet Union with diplomatic recognition, effectively ending the possibility of a unified worldwide anti-Soviet coalition.

The rhetoric of Bolshevik infiltration expressed concerns about the destabilization of borders and identities. Russians could be Bolsheviks, but so, too, could Germans. These identities were contingent on circumstance and proximity rather than being fossilized in the amber of racial essentialism—when German officials worried about the potential spread of Bolshevism, they expressed this fear as one of contact and influence, not of fundamental differences. Authorities were also unsure about the direction in which this influence might occur. As several officials stressed, German communists could infect Russians as well as the reverse. The equality of the transmission meant that every contact had the potential to be infectious, but it also meant that, at least in theory, even the Russians could be saved. German authorities mentioned situations in which anti-Bolshevik officers had convinced soldiers in the Red Army to switch sides.[69] Thus, the management of the camps was fundamentally an issue of controlling who prisoners or internees came into contact with—in other words, of border

66. Report of Russian POWs as of March 15, 1921, BArch R 1501/113321, 52. The exact figures are 837 officers, 237 women, 115 children, and 29,905 soldiers.

67. Williams, *Culture in Exile,* 109.

68. Präsident des Reichsamts für Arbeitsvermittlung to Landesarbeitsamt Niedersachsen, June 21, 1921, GStA PK, 1 HA, Rep. 77, Tit. 4036, Nr. 9, 62.

69. PMI to RMI and AA, November 18, 1920, BArch R 1501/113328, 69.

control. As a result, the border was fetishized as a site of passage between Bolsheviks and non-Bolsheviks.

The illusion of border control was destined to fail because Bolsheviks and non-Bolsheviks could be found on both sides of the wire fences that demarcated the boundaries of the POW camps. This complicated landscape of belonging and allegiance fostered the fear of border crossing while simultaneously making cross-border alliances a matter of necessity.

Germany could not control who crossed its territorial boundaries, and Bolshevism could be transmitted regardless of attempts to control the fences of the POW camps. Thus, border control, in both senses, failed. Yet, if Germany could not police its frontiers, the German authorities could regulate who was allowed membership within the German national community. In the midst of this thicket of new identities and a fragile state, citizenship policy and citizenship practice became a highly charged arena for German officials concerned with defining the new state and its citizens. Anxieties about the failures of border control increased the stakes for German policymakers enacting citizenship regulations for the new republic. In the next chapter, I explore how national and regional officials shaped citizenship policy and practice to meet the challenges presented by porous borders, malleable identities, and a weak state.

7. "A Firm Inner Connection to Germany"

Naturalization Policy

n 1922, Aron Genkin applied for German citizenship. Genkin was a Jewish Ukrainian doctor who wanted to become a German citizen so he could be licensed to work as a doctor in Germany and thus better support his fiancée, a German war widow, and her three children. He initially submitted his naturalization application in Thuringia, which approved it and sent it to the other *Länder* for approval, as was required by the citizenship law of 1913. The Bavarians advised the Thuringians that they did not intend to support Genkin's naturalization because he belonged to an "alien nation that is foreign to culture (*fremdstämmige und kulturfremde Nation*)."[1] As a result, his application was forwarded to the Reichsrat; a majority of delegates from each of the German states would have to vote to grant him citizenship if he were to be naturalized. Genkin's fiancée, Maria Berenz, hearing of the possible rejection of his application, appealed directly to Friedrich Ebert, the German chancellor:

> I have struggled most terribly for eight years [since the death of her husband in 1914 on the front] and I am both spiritually and physically at the end of my strength. Herr Dr. Genkin, a noble man who is respected by all who know him and a selfless friend to my children, has come and wants to help us, four victims of the war. Herr Reichspräsident, shouldn't one greet this generous deed with generosity? Shouldn't the German state give this man citizenship so that he can

1. Bavarian Interior Ministry (BMI) to the Thüringen Interior Ministry, February 7, 1923, BayHStA MA 100317. Emphasis in original. The first mention of Genkin's case is made in RMI to Thüringisches Ministerium der Volksbildung from April 25, 1922, BayHStA MA 100317.

fulfill the responsibilities that he has already taken upon himself with the engagement, and that he finds sacred? Here the state can also fulfill its sacred duty towards four war victims who would otherwise be doomed. . . ."[2]

Despite Berenz's passionate appeal, there is no evidence that Ebert actually intervened in this case. Instead, the Reichsrat denied Genkin's application in a close 5 to 4 vote, with Prussia voting with the Bavarians against naturalization. According to the Bavarian representative to the Reichsrat, Genkin's application was rejected because his stated intent of helping his fiancée and her family, although noteworthy, was a private interest secondary to national concerns.[3] For the five states that voted against Genkin's naturalization, the link that Berenz had tried to invoke between the suffering of her family and the duties of the state was unconvincing.

Shortly thereafter, the Thuringian representative, with Prussia's support, brought the case back to the Reichsrat. Berenz again wrote a letter in support of her fiancé's application, this time to the Thuringian representative to the Reichsrat. This time Berenz changed her tactic: instead of emphasizing the suffering of her family, she wrote about how great a provider Genkin was, ending by noting that "it is not Herr Dr. Genkin's fault that he is of Jewish descent; he has a very noble-minded disposition and is a true friend of Germany."[4] In this later vote, the Prussian representative changed his mind and voted to grant Genkin citizenship. According to the Bavarian representative to the Reichsrat, Prussia's change of heart was based on the fact that Genkin had been admitted to the exam to get a German medical license, thus proving he was worthy of becoming a naturalized German citizen.[5] In other words, what appeared to have changed the vote of the Prussian representative was a decision on the part of other German authorities that Genkin was acceptable on his own terms.

Even those who opposed Genkin's citizenship application recognized that he was an upstanding man whose naturalization would substantially alleviate the suffering of a war widow and her three young children. Furthermore, as a trained doctor, Genkin was a highly educated man, who appeared to hold no objectionable political views.[6] Genkin, moreover, had lived in Germany for years and spoke fluent German.[7] His personal character was not at issue during this debate; nor

2. Maria Berenz to Ebert, March 9, 1923, BayHStA MA 100317.

3. Bavarian Representative to the Reichsrat to the Bavarian Justice Minister, May 12, 1923, BayHStA MA 100317.

4. Maria Berenz to the Thuringian Representative to the Reichsrat, May 3, 1923, BayHStA MA 100317.

5. Bavarian Representative to the Reichsrat to the Bavarian Justice Minister, May 17, 1923, BayHStA MA 100317.

6. If there had been even the slightest suspicion that Genkin was a communist, this would certainly have come up in the deliberations regarding his application, as it did for so many other citizenship applicants.

7. If Genkin had not spoken German, he could not have passed the medical licensing exam. According to the Thuringian Ministry for Education, Genkin had lived "at least ten years without pause" in Germany. Thuringian Ministry of Education to the RMI, June 14, 1922, BayHStA MA 100317.

was there any reason to suspect that a denial of his citizenship application would have caused him either to end his relationship with Berenz or leave German soil. Nevertheless, his citizenship application inspired heated controversy. Several German states tenaciously sought to deny him the right to German citizenship, whereas others argued just as passionately that he deserved membership in the German national community. In the pages that follow, I explore the highly divisive debates about citizenship policy and practice that convulsed the German republic in its first years. In other words, I investigate the reasons behind the initial rejection and ultimate acceptance of Genkin's naturalization application.

Although the citizenship law of 1913 and its *jus sanguinis* definition of German belonging remained in effect throughout the Weimar period, actual citizenship practice was much more heterogeneous. A complex set of concerns motivated local and national officials; a homogenous ethnic community was one, but by no means the predominant, interest. In both theory and practice, officials held to seemingly contradictory beliefs in the determinative power of ethnic belonging, the responsibilities of ethnic solidarity, and a sense of the possibility for cultural assimilation. Germans from across the political spectrum —save for the extreme left—shared a belief that citizenship should be available only to those who had proven their German identity. Nonetheless, there was a striking lack of agreement as to which attributes—ethnic or cultural—constituted this slippery notion of German identity. New naturalization regulations drawn up in 1921 reflected two contradictory developments in the postwar period. On the one hand, they liberalized the unspoken practice of denying Jews and Poles citizenship until at least the second generation of residence, due to the political clout of the socialists, particularly in Prussia and Saxony. On the other hand, the newfound interest in the *Auslandsdeutsche* (foreigners of German descent; see chap. 4) and concerns about the immigration of "undesirables" from Eastern Europe (see chap. 5) drove conservatives in Bavaria and elsewhere to emphasize ethnicity as the primary basis for citizenship claims. This debate tested the fragile equation of ethnicity and culture that formed the basis of the 1913 German citizenship law. In the early Weimar Republic, disparate cultural and ethnic definitions of the German nation competed with one another on both the national and Länder levels. The virulence and insolubility of these disagreements spoke to the deep and bitter lack of consensus about the meaning and boundaries of the German nation in the first years of the fledgling Weimar Republic.

Citizenship Policy

In establishing new citizenship policies and practices for the Weimar Republic, both national and local state officials dealt very little with the practical challenges of immigration and the refugee crisis. In the early years of the republic, even social democratic Prussia approved only slightly more than half of the citizenship applications it received. Between 1921 and 1923, the number of citizenship applications that Prussia approved increased by 250 percent—from 6,953 to 17,848.[8] Based on these figures, no more than 30,000 people applied for citizenship in Prussia in any given year and most of these were ethnic Germans from Eastern Europe. Yet in those same years hundreds of thousands of foreigners arrived on German soil (see chap. 5). Very few of these new immigrants —and especially the Eastern European Jews, who inspired the most fear in German officialdom—actually applied for German citizenship.[9] Nevertheless, although few of these new migrants were actually applying for citizenship, the migration crisis increased pressure on the state to define the symbolic limits of the German national community, and the national citizenship regulations that were drawn up in 1920 and implemented in 1921 justified their limitations on new naturalizations through references to the influx of foreigners and the demands that they placed on Germany.[10] In 1923, the Bavarian interior minister used the "flood of immigrants" to explain the necessity of a restrictive naturalization policy:

> I need to constantly stress the economic difficulties created by the flood of immigrants of foreign descent, in particular, the ways in which they create pressure on the market for jobs and apartments. The danger is even greater since a large portion of these foreigners have built their existence on the destruction of the economic life of Germany and would not be able to advance if Germany were a healthy nation. It is tempting to think that granting citizenship only to those foreigners from the East who have been in Germany for years and have "adapted themselves to German culture" is without great consequence. However, we must not forget that the renewed immigration of Eastern elements has provided fresh blood to this community and so the cases of foreigners from the East must be dealt with even more carefully.[11]

As this quote suggests, the tangible benefits that citizenship conferred on foreigners, such as state unemployment benefits or voting rights did not play a role in the official discussion of naturalization. Considering the facts that most for-

8. Gosewinkel, *Einbürgern und Ausschließen,* 359. The relatively liberal policies of the first years after the war became stricter very quickly. Gosewinkel does not note the percentage of applications by *fremdstämmige Ostausländer* that were approved and whether (or how) this changed over this period.

9. Donald Niewyk writes that the obstacles that Eastern European Jews faced in gaining citizenship meant that only a small minority ever submitted naturalization applications. Donald L. Niewyk, *The Jews in Weimar Germany* (Baton Rouge: University of Louisiana Press, 1980), 16.

10. Guidelines sent from the RMI to the *Länder,* BArch R 1501/112384, 237, 239.

11. BMI to the Bavarian Representative to the Reichsrat, September 15, 1923, BayHStA MA 100317.

eigners who were denied citizenship remained in Germany and that most recent immigrants did not even submit naturalization applications, what did citizenship mean for Weimar Germans?

Citizenship exists at the symbolic crossroads of the state and its citizens. Mitchell's theory that the performance of tangible tasks by the state functions to project an aura of its transcendence above the very social forces that constitute it is useful in exploring the importance of citizenship for states, especially fragile ones such as the Weimar Republic.[12] Even in cases in which the granting of or refusal to grant citizenship will have little tangible effect on the state or its citizens, in the process of adjudicating citizenship cases, the state is simultaneously constituting and reinventing its image and, thus, itself. Mitchell's attention to the symbolic role of state projects usefully illuminates a peculiar but rarely mentioned quality of citizenship: although citizenship is ostensibly about defining who is or is not part of a state, it rarely, if ever, actually corresponds to the composition of the people living within the borders of that state. States generally have neither the military strength nor the moral imperative to deport foreigners who manage to get over the border. Because of this fundamental lack of correspondence between the population of a state and those accorded the rights of citizenship, citizenship is never only a question of legal membership within a community, nor is it solely an issue of civic behavior and self-understanding.[13] Citizenship is quite literally about an *imagined* community; rather than representing the actual composition of society, it represents its ideal.

Because of the national convulsions of the war and the postwar period, Weimar Germans were particularly aware of the symbolic quality of citizenship policy—the disjuncture between the population claiming German cultural or ethnic identity and the population currently residing within German borders. Those who held to a notion of citizenship solely defined by descent and those who promoted the possibility of an acquired connection to German culture were arguing about this ideal vision of the German national community. Seeing citizenship in this light helps explain one of the otherwise confusing aspects of citizenship rhetoric—that debates about citizenship often emphasized the competition for scarce resources within Germany, even though immigrants (who, for the most part, could or would not be deported) would continue to compete for these resources whether or not they were citizens.

Due to the inability of Germany to police its borders and its reluctance to deport noncitizens, citizenship policies and practices could not actually control the

12. Mitchell, "Limits of the State," 77–96.

13. For representatives of these two poles, see Brubaker, *Citizenship and Nationhood,* esp. 22 (his explicit statement to this effect) and Aihwa Ong, "Cultural Citizenship as Subject Making: Immigrants Negotiate Racial and Cultural Boundaries in the United States," in *Race, Identity and Citizenship: A Reader,* ed. Rodolfo D. Torres, Louis F. Míron, and Jonathan Xavier Inda (Oxford: Oxford University Press, 1999), 262.

number or types of foreigners within Germany. Furthermore, Germans were willing to tolerate the presence of many more foreigners than they were willing to grant citizenship to. Indeed, in a letter to the Interior Ministry in Mecklenburg, the Bavarian Ministry of the Interior referred to its twenty-year waiting period for all non-ethnic German immigrants from Eastern Europe (*fremdstämmige Ostausländer*) as a "test period," implying its at least theoretical willingness to grant citizenship if, after this twenty-year term, this "Eastern immigrant" had proven his or her connection to Germany.[14] Similarly, when the Saxon representative to the Reichsrat complained of the hardships induced by the stringent citizenship policy of the Reich, the National Interior Ministry replied that "there is an important difference between tolerance of immigration and the granting of citizenship" and that many residents had not yet proven themselves worthy of citizenship, even though they were allowed to continue to reside in Germany.[15]

Thus, citizenship policy was self-consciously not an attempt to control the number or types of foreigners living on German soil. Rather, citizenship policy functioned as a battleground on which German officials debated the meaning of the German nation. Citizenship policy and practice were freighted with the symbolic burden of compensating for the unsuccessful boundary maintenance that so frustrated Germans during this period.

The opening salvos in this conflict began almost immediately after the founding of the republic. According to the 1913 citizenship law, candidates for naturalization in the German Reich submitted their applications to local offices, where they were reviewed and then forwarded for approval to the interior ministries of the province in which the naturalization candidate lived. In 1919, Heine articulated some guiding principles for the adjudication of citizenship applications in Prussia, negotiating a fine line between statist and ethnic definitions of German citizenship. On the one hand, he stated that it was a national duty to universally repatriate those who immigrated to Germany from former German territories in Poland or Alsace-Lorraine. With regard to others seeking naturalization, he noted that they surely did not do so for their own personal gain because there was little a weakened Germany could give them; therefore, they must be motivated by "a firm personal connection to the German state."[16] Heine called for the naturalization of all applicants who had served in the war or had sons who had served, including Jews and Poles.[17] The right-wing government in Bavaria, which took power after the crushing of the communist

14. Letter from the Bavarian Interior Minister to the Mecklenburg Interior Minister, May 18, 1923, BayHStA MA 100317.
15. Letter from the Bavarian Representative to the Reichsrat to the Bavarian Interior and Exterior Ministers, September 24, 1923, BayHStA MA 100317.
16. Heine to the Staatsrat für Anhalt in Dessau, May 31, 1919, SächsHStA, MInnern 9725, 14.
17. Ibid. See also Gosewinkel, *Einbürgern und Ausschließen*, 353.

Räterepublik in spring 1919, opposed Heine's proposed naturalization policy, claiming that such liberal rules would lead the Reich to be overwhelmed with Eastern European Jews, with dangerous consequences for German national and economic interests.[18]

This conflict between the two largest states in the republic led to a conference in 1920 to draft national guidelines for determining the citizenship of those immigrants who arrived in Germany after the end of war.[19] In light of the growing numbers of migrants from the east, the guidelines of the Interior Ministry took a cautious approach to the granting of citizenship.[20] Keeping in mind the housing, food, and work shortages that plagued the new republic, they instructed local governments "only to accept people that demonstrate a positive population growth in a political, cultural and economic respect." The most important criterion of suitability for citizenship was a foreigner's "way of life, namely in Germany itself, that expresses a sufficient understanding for the German way of life and for his public-legal responsibilities in the federal state and the community."[21] Positive indicators of an applicant's worthiness included: "Birth in Germany and an upbringing according to German methods and in a German environment, having a German mother or marriage to a German in combination with a long-term, trouble-free life in Germany."[22] German ancestry was an important test of an applicant's suitability for German citizenship. But the ministry guidelines also listed other factors, such as residence in Germany and exposure to German methods of child-rearing and education, implying that ancestry alone was not a sufficient basis for a citizenship claim and that culture had an important role in forging this connection to Germany. The guidelines further specified that an applicant should be able to "prove that he possesses a German character (*Eigenart*) and the ability to fit into the German cultural community. Here too, it is certain that foreigners of German descent are more likely to fulfill this standard than others."[23] The phrase "more likely" reflected a certain ambivalence—descent was important but not the sole determinative factor. Rather, German descent was salient mainly insofar as it made one "more likely" to have internalized German culture.

Moreover, as interesting as what the national Interior Ministry guidelines say is what they did not say. A draft that circulated among the German states a year earlier contained two clauses that did not appear in the final document: the first would have strictly forbade granting citizenship to foreigners from the east of non-German descent, and the second would have bestowed citizenship on

18. Gosewinkel, *Einbürgern und Ausschließen*, 354.
19. Guidelines sent from the RMI to the *Länder*, June 1, 1921, BArch R 1501/112384, 237–40.
20. Ibid., 237.
21. Ibid., 239.
22. Ibid.
23. Ibid., 240.

only the second generation of this group of foreigners, thus continuing the prewar policy. These two clauses foundered in the face of opposition from the Prussians, whose representative objected that "such clauses would signal a return to Prussia's earlier Poland policy and must be avoided. The applications of *fremdstämmige Ostausländer* must be reviewed along the same principles applied to other applications."[24] Interesting as well is the fact that the final version of the policy guidelines did not reflect the Heine's willingness to grant citizenship to the men who had fought in the German army.

As it was, the citizenship guidelines so painstakingly argued over in late 1920 had little effect on naturalization policy in the individual states. Despite its absence from these citizenship guidelines, service, including but not limited to military service, and cultural assimilation both played a role in the adjudication of citizenship cases.[25] Moreover, after the guidelines went into effect, conflicts about the worthiness of *fremdstämmige Ostausländer* for citizenship continued, pitting the principles of cultural assimilation and ethnic determinism against one another as before. There was no marked difference between the handling of citizenship cases before and after the release of the guidelines in 1921.

Social democrats and their allies controlled the Prussian state, which also had the largest number of foreigners in the Reich throughout the early Weimar period. As previously noted, Prussian naturalization practice tended to recognize the potential for the assimilation of foreigners to a greater degree than that of Bavaria, which insisted on longer residency periods than Prussia. Yet to say that Prussia was more accepting of non-ethnic Germans does not mean that its representatives entirely ignored ethnicity in adjudicating naturalization applications. Indeed, Prussian officials turned to the FdR to verify applicants' German descent.[26] The Prussian Interior Ministry also routinely assumed that non-ethnic German applicants were trying to get German citizenship solely for reasons of expediency. For example, the police president of Berlin accused the "Russian-Polish factory worker, Abraham Halpern, Jewish religion, of only wishing to keep his job to avoid deportation and separation from his German wife."[27] Despite Halpern's marrying a German woman, the police president was doubtful that he demonstrated a sufficient "firm inner connection" to Germany. He did not sympathize with Halpern's desire to maintain his livelihood and family; this desire was deemed an entirely individual motivation and, as such, was viewed with suspicion.

24. Report on the results of a meeting at the RMI about many questions regarding the law for citizenship in the Reich and the states, September 3, 1920, BayHStA MA 100317.

25. Gosewinkel, *Einbürgern und Ausschließen*, 356.

26. See the case of Frommert for an example in which the FdR was called in to attest to an applicant's German descent; GStA PK, Rep. 77, Tit. 226b, Nr. 1F, Bd. 2.

27. Police President to the Oberpräsident zu Charlottenburg, February 29, 1919, GStA PK, Rep. 77, Tit. 226b, Nr. 1H, Bd. 2. It appears that Halpern had married a German woman whose parents "would not have understood if he had been deported" and had to take their daughter.

Nonetheless, non-Germans (even Jews) could receive the approval of the Prussian state for their citizenship application. In 1920, Württemberg forwarded to the Prussians the application of Aisik Borodowisch, a Jewish factory owner, who had resided in Germany since 1903 and had unsuccessfully applied for citizenship in 1908, 1909, 1911, and 1916. Citing his military service and the fact that he did not signify a danger to the public order, the Württemberg minister of the interior recommended that Borodowisch be granted citizenship, a recommendation with which the Prussian Interior Ministry agreed.[28] The police president of Berlin forwarded the application of the Jewish doctor Helene Eliasberg to the Prussian Interior Ministry after she submitted recommendations from the Charité Hospital and the Ministry for Science, Art and Public Education.[29]

Yet even applicants who, on the basis of their names at least, appeared to be of German descent were sometimes denied citizenship because they were considered to be "alien (*wesensfremd*) to Germandom." In December 1921, a local official recommended that the Prussian Interior Ministry reject the application of Johann Müller, a miner, because he was barely competent in the German language, despite his long-term residence in Germany. Moreover, this official presumed that Müller applied for citizenship only to avoid the regulations that applied to foreigners and was actually considering returning to Russia for work.[30] Much like Halpern, Müller's desire to secure his livelihood was considered a factor against recommending his application. Also, in several cases, various federal states contested the citizenship applications of suspected communists despite the fact that they were of undisputed German descent.[31]

28. Letter from the Württemburg Ministry of the Interior to PMI, September 20, 1920, and PMI to the Württemberg Ministry of the Interior, November 9, 1920, GStA PK, I. HA., Rep. 77, Tit. 226b, Nr. 1B, Bd. 3.

29. Application sent from the polizeipräsident in Berlin to the Prussian Interior Ministry, February 17, 1919, GStA PK, 1. HA., Rep. 77, Tit. 226b, Nr. 1E, Bd. 1. The Interior Ministry response is not recorded.

30. These reasons were actually used to describe an application from Syllies, but the letter from the Regierungspräsident in Münster to PMI from December 21, 1921, describing the case states that the same factors applied for the case of Müller, GStA PK, 1. HA, Rep. 77, Tit. 226b, Nr. 1, Bd. 41.

31. See, for example, the case of Alfred Schoft, a communist of German descent, who was denied citizenship by the Bavarians on the grounds that his citizenship would create a danger to public order. Bavarian representative to the Reichsrat (Nüßlein) to the Bavarian Minister of Justice, October 22, 1922, BayHStA MA 100317. See also PMI to SMI, May 19, 1921, regarding the citizenship of Paul and Reinhard Richter, SächsHStA MInnern, 9816, 20. The Saxons' response to this letter, specifically their contention that membership in the Communist Party did not suffice as grounds for the denial of a citizenship application, is also interesting in this regard; SMI to PMI, June 6, 1921, SächsHStA MInnern, 9816, 23. See also the multiple objections to the citizenship application of Johann Werner, who participated in the March 1921 communist uprising; PMI to SMI, June 29, 1921, SächsHStA MInnern, 9816, 39; Württembergisches Ministerium des Innern to SMI, May 31, 1921, SächsHStA MInnern, 9816, 40; Lübeck Stadt und Landamt to SMI, May 28, 1921, SächsHStA MInnern, 9816, 41.

At the same time, those who were of German descent could surmount obstacles that a non-German could not hope to overcome. In 1919, the Prussian interior minister approved the naturalization of the Russian citizen of German descent, Johann Bergerack, despite his robbery conviction and ten-day jail sentence in December 1914. The local official who sent the application to the Prussian Interior Ministry wrote, "[a]s a German returnee, Bergerack is to be considered a desirable addition to the population. I am approving his application considering his unobjectionable conduct since he was punished." Based on this recommendation, the Prussian Interior Ministry approved his application.[32] Similarly, Anna Donat, an unemployed factory worker of German descent from Russia, was judged a desirable addition to the population despite the fact that she had been in Germany only since 1916 and was unemployed at the time of her application.[33] Finally, even though he was a "known homosexual," the Berlin police president recommended an applicant named Milsch because he was both of German descent and had served honorably in the war, receiving the Iron Cross and behaving, to the knowledge of the police president at least, "morally" during the time of his service.[34]

Although Prussia was more willing to grant citizenship to applicants of German descent, descent was only one criterion, albeit an important one. In general, it appears that Prussian officials followed Heine's dual citizenship policy, which viewed citizenship as a privilege based on German descent and public utility. They favored those who had performed military service, or, as in the case of Eliasberg, the doctor, other publicly useful tasks. At the same time, the Prussian Interior Ministry was wary of applicants whose applications for citizenship appeared to be motivated by personal gain. A lofty and "firm inner connection" to Germany was considered the crucial criterion for the award of citizenship, not the more limited personal goals of improving one's own life or that of one's family.

The case of Moritz Estersohn, a Russian citizen who applied for Prussian citizenship in 1919 after over twenty years of residence in Germany, represents one intriguing instance in which the Prussian Interior Ministry challenged local officials' rejection of an applicant for German citizenship. Precisely because it was not a clear-cut situation, the Estersohn case illustrates some of the tensions that underlay citizenship policy in the early Weimar Republic. Estersohn first submitted his application for naturalization in 1919. After the local government in Arnsberg rejected his application in August 1919, the Prussian Interior Ministry inquired as to the reasons for the rejection, noting that, according to his name and religion,

32. Cöpenick Regierungspräsident to PMI, July 9, 1919, GStA PK, 1. HA., Rep. 77, Tit. 226b, Nr. 1B, Bd. 3. The application was approved, according to a stamp, on August 22, 1919.

33. Regierungspräsident in Potsdam to PMI, May 21, 1919, GStA PK, 1. HA., Rep. 77, Tit. 226b, Nr. 1D, Bd. 2. The application was approved, according to a stamp, on August 16, 1919. It is unclear from this letter if Ms. Donat was married or single, but because special mention was made by the Potsdam Regierungspräsident of her lack of employment, it is more likely that she was single.

34. Police President to PMI, July 29, 1918, GStA PK, 1. HA., Rep. 77, Tit. 226b, Nr. 1M, Bd. 3.

he appeared to be of *"German* nationality."[35] The mayor of Hagen, where Estersohn was living, responded that while serving in the army Estersohn had been
punished for insubordination and the theft of some potatoes. Furthermore, the
mayor emphasized that Freikorps units had arrested Estersohn and used this as
proof that he "belonged to political circles that wanted to destroy the peace of the
population." The mayor added that Estersohn had originally been Jewish and had
converted only in 1898.[36] Even in the face of these seemingly damning allega-
tions, the Prussian government still considered forwarding Estersohn's application
to the other German states for approval. The Prussian commissioner for public
order challenged this apparent leniency toward Estersohn, reiterating the objections initially raised by the mayor of Hagen that Estersohn was a communist, a
Jew, and a thief, adding that he was a profiteer besides.[37] Estersohn was rich
enough to hire his own lawyer, who responded to these accusations by noting that
his client had served two and a half years in the army, although he had been a
Russian citizen at the time. Furthermore, the lawyer denied that Estersohn was
a communist, affirming that he belonged, instead, to the SPD.[38] The records do
not indicate whether the Prussian government ultimately awarded citizenship to
Estersohn, and even if it did, it is highly doubtful that Bavaria or other more conservative states would have approved his application. Nonetheless, the bureaucratic exchanges over Estersohn's citizenship case continued through at least
mid-1921. The Prussian Interior Ministry could not decide if he was (1) successful businessman, long-term resident, and war veteran versus (2) Jew, communist
war profiteer, and thief.[39] Caught between these two potential Estersohns, it
seemed unable or unwilling to choose between them.

Each federal state was required to submit a list of potential citizenship applicants for review by the other federal states, which were allowed to raise objections to those they considered undeserving of citizenship in the Reich. In
cases of disagreement, the Reichsrat, the upper house of parliament comprising
representatives from each of the federal states, decided applicants' citizenship
status by a majority vote.[40] In the Reichsrat, the German states tended to split
between those that held to the more conservative Bavarian line, such as Würt-

35. PMI to the Regierungspräsident in Arnsberg, August 31, 1919, GStA PK, 1. HA., Rep. 77,
Tit. 226b, Nr. 1E, Bd. 1. Emphasis in original.

36. Mayor of Hagen to the Regierungspräsident in Arnsberg, October 6, 1919, GStA PK, 1.
HA., Rep. 77, Tit. 226b, Nr. 1E, Bd. 1.

37. See, for example, Staatskommission für die öffentliche Ordnung to PMI on September 28,
1920, GStA PK, 1. HA., Rep. 77, Tit. 226b, Nr. 1E, Bd. 1.

38. Ellinghaus to PMI, 14 December 1920, GStA PK, 1. HA., Rep. 77, Tit. 226b, Nr. 1E, Bd. 1.

39. Estersohn's business success was not explicitly discussed, but I am assuming that he was at
least relatively successful because he could afford a lawyer, something that most applicants did not
seem to have.

40. This process was laid out in § 9 of the Reichs- und Staatsangehörigkeitsgesetz from 1913
and was left unchanged after World War I. See also Oliver Trevisiol, *Die Einbürgerungspraxis im
Deutschen Reich, 1871–1945* (Göttingen: Vandenhoeck & Ruprecht, 2006).

temberg, and those that followed a more liberal policy, such as Prussia and Saxony.[41] Although the Reich guidelines set a ten-year residency minimum for the acceptance of citizenship applications from those of non-German descent, the Bavarians applied their own standard of a twenty-year waiting period to the applications of *fremdstämmige Ostausländer,* routinely rejecting applications from other federal states that did not fulfill this criterion.[42] The Saxons and Prussians repeatedly complained to the national Interior Ministry that Bavaria prevented them from exercising their own citizenship policies by using its veto power to enforce its more restrictive guidelines.[43] Saxony, in particular, objected to the Bavarians' heavy-handed use of their veto power in the Reichsrat. The Interior Ministry of the SPD-USPD coalition that governed Saxony during the first years of the republic repeatedly submitted citizenship applications to the other German states for approval, even when the applicants had been in the country fewer than twenty years or were otherwise likely to provoke Bavarian opposition. Opinion was divided in Saxony about this strategy. Although the Dresden District Office complained about the Bavarian veto policy, some within the ministry argued that Saxony should not recommend the naturalization of foreigners who were inevitably destined for a Bavarian veto.[44]

The case of Johann Goluchowski demonstrates the lengths to which Robert Lipinski, the Saxon interior minister, was willing to go to protest Bavarian intransigence.[45] Goluchowski had served in the German army for a little more than one year during the war but, as an illiterate and unemployed Russian Pole who had lived in Germany only since 1910, otherwise appeared ill-suited for German citizenship, especially according to the strict Bavarian standards. When the Leipzig authorities forwarded his case to the Interior Ministry for approval in November 1919, they noted their reservations regarding his naturalization.[46]

41. See, for example, the heated debate between Saxony and Bavaria in 1922–1923, BayHStA MA 100317.

42. BMI to the Bavarian Foreign Ministry, December 9, 1921, BayHStA MA 100317. In this letter, the official also writes that one needed to be careful because even some with German names were not necessarily Germans. Thus, it was necessary to check which schools the applicant had gone to, whether he spoke German and "seemed German," and so on. This requirement was established by the Bavarians at least as early as 1922; a letter from von Spreti to the Badische Staatsministerium, Ministerial Abteilung für Präsidialische, Reichs- und Auswärtige Angelegenheiten from that year references this; BArch R 1501/108045, 12. The Prussians raised their minimum residency requirement in 1921 to fifteen years and in 1925 to twenty; Gosewinkel, *Einbürgern und Ausschließen,* 356.

43. PMI to RMI, February 17, 1923, and SMI to RMI, May 17, 1922, BayHStA MA 100317.

44. For the position of the Dresden district office, see a letter from the Dresden Kreishauptmannschaft to the Ministerium des Innern, January 23, 1922, SächsHStA MInnern 9725, 56; internal memo from October 27, 1920, SächsHStA MInnern 9710, 249.

45. Lipinski was a member of the USPD until it disbanded in late 1920, after which he joined the SPD. Lipinski was minister of the interior for the first few months of the republic and then again between July 1920 and February 1923.

46. Kreishauptmannschaft Leipzig to Sächsisches Minister des Innern, November 28, 1919, SächsHStA MInnern 9710, 255. The Kreishauptmannschaft Leipzig sent a later warning about Goluchowski, n.d., SächsHStA MInnern 9710, 348.

Nonetheless, in a May 1922 letter to the Leipzig District Office, Lipinski stated that he saw no reason to deny Goluchowski citizenship. Lipinski regarded Goluchowski's lack of employment as temporary, and he countered accusations that Goluchowski did not speak German by stating that he spoke enough German to have served in the army. Lipinski even explained Goluchowski's criminal conviction from early 1922 as a minor setback, one that was more than offset by his otherwise unblemished record.[47] Lipinski's promotion of Goluchowski's application reflected his resolute refusal to accept the citizenship criteria that Bavaria sought to impose on the other German states. Furthermore, since by 1922 it was more than clear that Goluchowski had no hope of approval from Bavaria, Lipinski's insistence on Goluchowski's candidacy for naturalization can also be seen as an attempt to test the patience of the Bavarians.[48]

Even Bavaria, it is important to keep in mind, did not deny Jews access to German citizenship. At least in theory, an Eastern European Jew could apply for citizenship after a twenty-year residency period. The Bavarians claimed that this time frame represented the minimum time necessary for an Eastern Jew to acquire German cultural values.[49] In practice, this did not necessarily mean that the Bavarian government would actually grant citizenship to Jews who had fulfilled this residency period. Yet it does make clear the importance in the political climate of the early Weimar Republic of phrasing opposition to naturalization in terms of a residency requirement rather than a total ban on citizenship for Eastern European Jews. Even the Bavarian twenty-year waiting period was itself a departure from prewar practice, in which immigrant Jews were not usually able to gain citizenship until the third generation of residence in Germany. Put another way, had the Bavarian state proposed a twenty-year residency requirement in 1913, this would have been a very progressive stance, but seven years later, the twenty-year requirement represented the extreme nationalist position.[50] Occa-

47. SMI to Kreishauptmannschaft Leipzig, May 17, 1922, SächsHStA MInnern 9711, 19.

48. Lipinski's own skepticism regarding Goluchowski's chances for naturalization may be guessed at by the way that he ended his letter: "the Ministry of the Interior has no objections to including him in the monthly list [of people sent to the other *Länder*] for the goal of naturalization." Lipinski surely had no illusions that Goluchowski would actually be granted citizenship; he merely stated that he was worthy of inclusion on the monthly list; ibid. For other examples along the same lines, see the handling of the cases of Haber and Gewürz; letter from the Sächsisches Innenministerium to the Kreishauptmannschaft Chemnitz, November 8, 1921, SächsHStA MInnern, 9710, 356. See also the case of the widow Tumpowsky and her daughter. Tumpowsky had moved to Germany before 1870, and her daughter had been born in Germany. Tumpowsky's two sons had served in the military and had been naturalized. Despite the fact that the local authorities feared that both Tumpowsky and her daughter could become burdens on the state, the ministry recommended their naturalization, claiming that the potential burden was not sufficient grounds for denying their applications; letter from the SMI to the Kreishauptmannschaft Leipzig, January 17, 1923, SächsHStA MInnern, 9711, 83.

49. BMI to the Bavarian Representative to the Reichsrat, September 15, 1923, BayHStA MA 100317.

50. Trevisiol makes the point that in the Kaiserreich the Bavarians had been the liberals and

sionally when faced with a non-German citizen who had lived for a long time in Germany, the Bavarians relented and allowed him or her to be naturalized. For example, David Linick, a prosperous Jewish businessman who had resided in Germany for eighteen years and "had an understanding for the German way of life and German customs (*deutsches Wesen und deutsche Sitten*)" was awarded citizenship in 1921, despite initial Bavarian objections.[51] Similarly, in 1921, even Bavaria was willing to approve Hermann Rieder's citizenship application when Baden, his state of residence, offered his son's already approved application for German citizenship, his daughter's marriage to a German citizen, and Rieder's own active involvement in Jewish aid organizations as evidence of his commitment to Germany.[52] Clearly if involvement in Jewish aid organizations could be considered a positive criterion for citizenship, then the meaning of a commitment to the German cultural community was more complicated than it appears at first glance.

Tensions between the cultural and ethnic definitions of German citizenship continued through the remainder of the Weimar Republic. This was most clear in the relatively liberal state of Prussia. In 1925, the Prussian government agreed to the Bavarian demand that foreigners from the east be subject to a twenty-year waiting period before being considered for citizenship.[53] Two years later, Albert Grzesinksi, the new Prussian minister of the interior, sought to replace the category of *Deutschstämmigkeit* ("German descent") with *Kulturdeutscher* ("cultural German"). In doing so, he explicitly sought to remove the barriers to the naturalization of Jews, and as such his definition of *Kulturdeutscher* included connections to family members residing in Germany, birth or upbringing in German-speaking regions or settlements, attendance at German schools, German names, and adherence to "German customs and language."[54] Against the opposition of most of the other German states and most of the national ministries, Grzesinski also rejected a fifteen- or twenty-year waiting period and sought to reinstate the ten-year waiting period for citizenship applicants from the east that had prevailed at the outset of the Weimar Republic.[55]

While officials of the new republic agreed that German citizenship should be limited to those who could prove their German identity, the highly contentious

the Prussians the promoters of a more restrictive naturalization policy; *Einbürgerungspraxis im Deutschen Reich, 1871–1945.*

51. After a letter from Baden describing the situation, the BMI relented in a letter dated May 4, 1921, BayHStA MA 100317.

52. BMI June 24, 1921, BayHStA MA 100317.

53. Gosewinkel, *Einbürgern und Ausschließen*, 356.

54. Ibid., 361.

55. Ibid., 362.

debates surrounding naturalization reflected a lack of unanimity regarding the combination of ethnic and cultural factors that constituted German identity. The Bavarians were committed to an ethnically defined vision of the German nation, but Saxon interior minister Lipiński insisted on the possibility of assimilation, even for a Russian Pole with little command of the German language and a criminal record. Yet even Bavarian advocates of an ethnic standard allowed for the possibility of assimilation after twenty years of residence, and even Saxon socialists accepted the ten-year standard residency requirement. Attitudes toward ethnicity and culture existed along a spectrum, rather than representing hard and fast extremes.

Although the Saxons and the Bavarians shared more than they often admitted, the very virulence of this debate was also instructive. Conservative nationalists in particular insisted that these questions of naturalization were so central to the future of the German nation and the German state that no compromise was possible. In this way, citizenship policy became caught in the same dynamic of extremism and paralysis that poisoned the political life of the republic more generally. In addition, regardless of the particular standard they applied, German officials were reluctant to grant citizenship to any but the most "deserving" applicants. Even when some officials believed in the theoretical possibility of assimilation, few foreigners could actually meet this high burden of proof in practice. Foreigners might be able to remain in Germany, but entry to the German national community was limited to a small minority.

Nevertheless, the restrictive citizenship policies did little to counteract the influx of immigrants. Ironically, as a result of both their failure to adequately patrol the border and their parsimonious naturalization policy, Germans found themselves confronting exactly what they most feared—a huge population of foreigners on German soil. As we have seen, few Germans were particularly hospitable to these foreigners; but, even though Germans by and large did not welcome foreigners, they often tolerated them. In the next chapter, we examine both the hesitant recognition of the right to asylum for Russians and Eastern European Jews and the limits of this tolerance in the politically fraught atmosphere of the early Weimar Republic.

8. Tolerance and Its Limits

Russians, Jews, and Asylum

I n the Weimar Republic, Germans argued about whether belonging was determined by ethnicity, parentage, or culture, but the fundamental belief that belonging to the German state was a function of German identity was undisputed. During this period, the number of "useful" foreigners, such as those imported to work on the eastern estates, shrank as a result of German economic difficulties and territorial losses. Furthermore, the sense of the collective victimization of the German nation and the individual suffering of its citizens mobilized xenophobic and anti-Semitic sentiment. In this climate of insecurity and hostility, the massive immigration from Eastern Europe during the first years of the republic was blamed for a variety of woes. Jews, in particular, faced prejudice from a wide swath of the German public sphere, and anti-Semitism motivated everything from street violence to the attempt by several German states to increase the waiting period for naturalization for foreigners from the east from ten to twenty years (see chap. 7). By almost every measure, post–World War I Germany was not an propitious place to be a foreigner of non-German descent.

Yet, despite the litanies of frustration and anti-immigrant screeds that appeared almost daily in major newspapers and despite anti-foreigner legislation, asylum and tolerance were not absent from German public discussions about migration. The Prussian Interior Ministry refused to deport Eastern European Jews, and the socialist newspaper *Vorwärts* largely supported the Prussians in this effort, despite the extreme pressure brought to bear on Prussia from the less liberally inclined national Interior Ministry. Even more strikingly, Russian émigrés received both sympathy and support from Germans across the political spectrum. These gestures of tolerance have been noted but also simultaneously dismissed by other historians.[1] For example, in her exhaustive study of the *Ostjuden* in Weimar Germany, Trude Maurer remarked that, although "the Socialists were the most decisive opponents of Anti-Semitism," they "did not do enough against it."[2] This is surely true, the socialists could have done more, but considering the widely held hostility toward the *Ostjuden,* why did socialists both within the government and in the popular press insist that Germany should provide asylum to the suffering *Ostjuden?* Why, moreover, did even the nationalist right express sympathy for anti-Bolshevik Russians on German soil?

Neither Jews nor Russians were welcomed by most Germans, and neither group gained a legal right to asylum; yet attitudes toward both groups bear witness to the existence of tolerance in the Weimar public sphere. This tolerance operated within the liminal space between two separate debates. The first encompassed the question of who belonged to the German state—the ethnicization of German identity (see chap. 5) and the issues of citizenship and naturalization (see chap. 7). The second dealt with the issue of residency in German territory. German conservative nationalists commonly conflated the two issues, arguing that the German state and the territory it occupied should serve only those who belonged to the German nation. Socialists more commonly emphasized the difference between territory and belonging. For them, the German state had a responsibility to protect foreigners who had been persecuted and forced to flee to Germany, even if they were not of German descent. Yet even conservative nationalists occasionally admitted a distinction between German identity and German territory. For instance, anti-Bolshevik Russians were supported in their demands for asylum by a wide range of Weimar parties, including those on the right. Such tolerance toward the Russians belies any simple notion of German xenophobia during this period.

The existence of tolerance is itself somewhat surprising considering the widespread condemnation of foreigners, especially from the east, of non-German descent. In addition, it is worth examining why the Russian refugees were so much

---

1. For an example of the dismissal of the existence of any German policy of asylum, see Jochen Oltmer, "Flucht, Vertreibung und Asyl im 19. und 20. Jahrhundert," in *Migration in der europäischen Geschichte seit dem späten Mittelalter,* ed. Klaus Bade (Osnabrück: IMIS Beiträge, 2002), 107–34. On German hostility toward the *Ostjuden* during the Weimar Republic, see Maurer, *Ostjuden in Deutschland, 1918–1933;* Heid, *Maloche—nicht Mildtätigkeit.* More generally, German historians often dismiss all German interactions with foreigners as xenophobic. See, for example, Panikos Panayi, *Ethnic Minorities in Nineteenth and Twentieth Century Germany: Jews, Gypsies, Poles, Turks and Others* (New York: Longman, 2000); Karen Schönwalder, "Invited but Unwanted?: Migrants from the East in Germany, 1890–1990," in *The German Lands and Eastern Europe: Essays on the History of their Social, Cultural and Political Relations,* ed. Roger Bartlett and Karen Schönwalder, 198–216 (New York: St. Martin's Press, 1999).

2. Maurer, *Ostjuden in Deutschland, 1918–1933,* 225. An even stronger castigation of the socialists for their appropriation of anti-Semitic tropes in the Wilhelmine period can be found in Lars Fischer, *The Socialist Response to Antisemitism in Imperial Germany* (Cambridge, UK: Cambridge University Press, 2007).

more successful than the Jews in mobilizing support on their behalf. Whereas the *Ostjuden* found few defenders other than the communists and social democrats, the Russian émigrés could look to supporters from across the political spectrum. Even the names most often applied to each group are instructive. Russians in Germany were referred to as "emigrants" or "refugees," descriptions that stressed the dangers that they had fled from, whereas Jews were more often called "immigrants," emphasizing their intrusion into German society.

The discrepancy in the treatment of the Jews and the Russians cannot be explained by numbers alone—there were 70,000 Eastern European Jews in Germany, but there may have been as many as 500,000 Russians, and thus we might assume that the Russians would be thought to pose the greater threat. Economic status also does not suffice as an explanation for the differing attitudes toward the two groups; both the Russian and Jewish refugees were largely destitute and dependent on charity.[3] Finally, although pre–World War I German society had an undeniable strain of anti-Semitism, anti-Slavic sentiment was also present in prewar Germany and the anti-Russian propaganda of the war years had heightened German suspicions of their Slavic neighbors. Anti-Polish sentiment, moreover, remained highly visible throughout the Weimar period.[4]

We can understand the differences between the treatment of the two groups as a function of the ways in which their requests for tolerance were framed. Even the socialists, who were clearly sympathetic to the Eastern European Jews, did not dispute that they were a burden at a time when the beleaguered German nation could ill afford any additional strain. They justified their calls for tolerance on abstract notions of human suffering and German moral responsibility. By contrast, the much greater population of Germans who supported the rights of the Russians argued simultaneously (1) that these Russians would remain solely within their own community, thus posing no threat to Germany, and (2) that Germans were duty bound to protect anti-Bolshevik Russians because of a *Schicksalsgemeinschaft* ("shared destiny") between these two peoples. The idea of a *Schicksalsgemeinschaft* originated with the nineteenth-century German Russophiles who romantically imagined a kinship between the two peoples, but it gained a new meaning after World War I when it was used to reference a shared experience of suffering and loss.[5] Rather than arguing on the basis of mere altruism, German defenders of the Russians stressed that protecting the Russians also meant protecting themselves.

3. On the destitution of the Russians despite their image as rich people living off of their accumulated riches, see Doedenhaft, "*Laßt mich nach Rußland heim,*" 14; Volkmann, *Russische Emigration in Deutschland, 1919–1929,* 11–12; Skran, *Refugees in Inter-war Europe,* 33.

4. Kopp, "Contesting Borders."

5. On the nineteenth-century conception of a *Schicksalsgemeinschaft,* see Gerd Koenen, "Der deutsche Russland-Komplex: Zur Ambivalenz deutscher Ostorientierung in der Weltkriegsphase," in *Traumland Osten: Deutsche Bilder vom östlichen Europa im 20. Jahrhundert,* ed. Gregor Thum (Göttingen: Vandenhoeck & Ruprecht, 2006), 29–34.

Asylum and the Eastern European Jews

Throughout the republic, anti-Semitism and anti-foreigner sentiment formed a dangerous and mutually self-reinforcing spiral (see chap. 5). Eastern European Jewish immigrants were blamed for everything from causing the worsening of the housing shortage and the increasing pressure on the food supply to being unscrupulous merchants and importing Bolshevik ideas. Yet, despite the hostility directed toward Eastern European Jews during the Weimar Republic, few measures were taken against them either on the national level or in Prussia, the state where the greatest number of them resided. Repeated calls for deportation or internment resulted in little in the way of practical actions to limit the number of *Ostjuden* on German soil. And, despite the absence of a national asylum law, the Prussian state explicitly accepted their right to sanctuary from persecution in Eastern Europe. The acceptance of Eastern European Jews in Weimar Germany was always tenuous and to a great degree can be attributed to the sheer inability of the state to patrol its border. Yet the very hostility of public and official opinion toward the presence of Eastern European Jews in Germany makes it that much more remarkable that socialist officials and journalists publically supported the tolerance of Eastern European Jews.

In part, the recognition of the right of Eastern European Jews to stay in Germany resulted from a fear that expelling the Jews would damage the international reputation of a weakened Germany. In particular, the Foreign Ministry believed that Jews exercised a significant influence over U.S. foreign policy, and therefore public pressure for the deportation of *Ostjuden* needed to be resisted "in the interests of the re-establishment of Germany's political, economic and cultural relationships with the outside world."[6] Nevertheless, any acceptance that Eastern European Jews received as a result of international *diktat* was clearly begrudging at best. Wolfgang Heine and Carl Severing, the social democratic interior ministers for the Prussian government in the first years of the republic, shared the concerns of the world community for the fate of the Jews, but they also believed that assisting the Jews might have detrimental effects on the German nation. In balancing these two imperatives, they arrived at a determination that Prussia must grant asylum to the *Ostjuden*. Heine's November 1919 *Erlass* on the problem of Jewish immigration was a testament to his ambivalence and that of his party. On the one hand, he argued that many immigrants, if perhaps not all, had been prompted to leave their homelands for legitimate reasons: "they didn't just leave, but were driven out under the pressure of the political situation."[7] On the other hand, Heine believed that their

6. Report by Dr. Wendschuh of a January 7, 1923, meeting to discuss foreigners in Germany, PAAA R 83581, 176. See also "Protokoll der Sitzung im AA 10 April 1919, Betr: jüdische Ausweisung," BArch R 1501/114061, 47.
7. Prussian *Erlass* November 1, 1919, GStA PK, 1 HA, Rep. 77, Tit. 1814, Nr. 3, 190.

presence would necessarily put additional pressure on finite German resources. He concluded that the suffering of the Jews in a sense trumped that of the Germans. "Despite the suffering of the German population . . . it is impossible to forcibly deport the *Ostjuden* currently living in Germany, even when they have snuck across the border and do not possess legitimate papers. This is because the situation in their homelands presents a danger to their lives."[8] According to Heine, these immigrants possessed a lower level of culture, they should not be encouraged to immigrate, and they should be kept separate from Germans whenever possible; nonetheless, except in cases in which they committed crimes, he stated that these Jews had to be tolerated "out of humanitarian concern."[9] Heine reassured Jewish aid organizations that even unemployed Jews would not be deported as long as they did not present a burden to the state.[10]

The national Interior Ministry, the Foreign Office, and the Justice Ministry harshly criticized Heine's asylum policy. Erich Koch-Weser, the national interior minister, dismissed Heine's human rights argument and asserted that Germany "did not have the least moral obligation" to tolerate these "most undesirable immigrants of foreign descent (*fremdstämmige Ausländer unerwünschtester Art*)."[11] Instead, he maintained that shortages in housing and food among German citizens and the need to provide assistance for ethnic German refugees made it impossible for the German government to tolerate yet more foreigners on its soil.[12] In response to such criticism, Heine and his successor, Carl Severing, released amended *Erlasse* throughout 1920 and 1921.[13] At first, they sought to deflect concerns that the *Ostjuden* would steal resources from needy Germans by arguing that they would be provided for by Jewish aid organizations.[14] But the ministry soon abandoned this pretense; an *Erlass* released by Severing on November 17, 1920, stated baldly that the presence of the *Ostjuden* was harmful to the interests of the German people. Unable or unwilling to justify asylum on material grounds, Severing retreated to the moral high ground, arguing that, despite all that the German people had suffered, humanity (*Menschlichkeit*) dictated that the "right to asylum (*Asylrecht*)" could not be denied to the *Ostjuden*.[15]

The social democratic newspaper *Vorwärts* supported Heine's and Sever-

8. Ibid.

9. Ibid.

10. Heine to Arbeiterfürsorgeamt der jüdischen Organisationen Deutschlands, April 29, 1919, PAAA R 78705, L348708.

11. RMI to Reichskanzler December 10, 1920, BArch R 1501/114048, 182.

12. Ibid., 181.

13. The dates of these orders were February 20, 1920; June 1, 1920; November 17, 1920; February 28, 1921; June 25, 1921; and August 17, 1921. Severing succeeded Heine in April 1920, in the aftermath of the Kapp putsch.

14. Prussian *Erlass*, June 1, 1920, GStA PK Rep. 77, Tit. 1814, Nr. 3, 47.

15. Prussian *Erlass*, November 17, 1920, GStA PK Rep. 77, Tit. 1817, Nr. 4, 119.

ing's asylum policy while simultaneously sharing its tentativeness. *Vorwärts* consistently opposed anti-Semitic agitation, although the newspaper generally sought to avoid the topic of the *Ostjuden*.[16] Its few statements on the issue of Eastern European Jews in Germany articulated their rights in terms similar to Heine's asylum order. For instance, shortly before the release of Heine's original *Erlass*, in October 1919, a front-page article by Fritz Spiegelberg addressed the issue of foreigners in Germany.[17] Even more than the article itself, which was an attack on Bolshevik agitators who threatened to enter and destabilize the already precarious German economic and political situation, the responses of *Vorwärts* readers suggest that Heine's measures accorded with wider social democratic opinion toward foreigners. One critic reminded Spiegelberg that Germans had invited foreign workers on to German soil during the war and owed them equal treatment on this basis.[18] Georg Davidsohn, a SPD Reichstag delegate, wrote to *Vorwärts*, addressing the issue of asylum specifically; Davidsohn stated that, to a greater degree than other European countries, Germany contended with large numbers of political refugees. As social democrats who had themselves been persecuted under the Hohenzollerns, he argued, they had the duty to protect these foreigners.[19] Both of Spiegelberg's critics asserted that Germany in general and social democrats in particular had a moral duty to care for foreigners, especially Jews fleeing persecution in Eastern Europe. Illustrating the potency of this argument about moral responsibility within socialist circles, Spiegelberg was twice forced to justify himself in response to these critics, strenuously denying that he was an anti-Semite and claiming that he supported the right of asylum for those who were truly persecuted.[20]

Later articles marshaled a variety of reasons to support the tolerance of Eastern European Jews on German soil. One author pointed out that many of these Jews had come to Germany as a result of German attempts to recruit workers for its munitions industry during the war.[21] Another noted that General Erich Lu-

---

16. See, among others, "Juden, Freimaurer und Sozialdemokraten: Ein Kapitel zur Volksverdummung," *Vorwärts*, August 5, 1919; "Antisemitismus und Wohnungsnot," *Vorwärts*, January 31, 1920; "Schlagt die Juden tot!" *Vorwärts*, February 1, 1920; "Die Juden-Razzia: Ein militärischer Mißgriff," *Vorwärts*, April 1, 1920; "Judenhetze mit Seitengewehren," *Vorwärts*, April 6, 1920; "Judenhetze als Wahlpropaganda," *Vorwärts*, May 14, 1920; "Ostjuden einst und jetzt," *Vorwärts*, July 30, 1920; "Das Ostjudenproblem," *Vorwärts*, October 8, 1920; "Die jüdische Eisenbahn," *Vorwärts*, November 13, 1920. Interestingly, "Antisemitismus und Wohnungsnot" argued that the *Ostjuden* were less to blame than the "Baltic barons" and "Russian nobles" for the housing crisis in Germany at the time. Here *Vorwärts* sought to turn anti-foreigner sentiment against a group of foreigners who had found support on the right.
17. "Grenzen des Gastrechts," *Vorwärts*, October 27, 1919.
18. "'Grenzen des Gastrechts,'" *Vorwärts*, October 30, 1919.
19. "Grenzen des Gastrechts," *Vorwärts*, November 13, 1919.
20. "Grenzen des Gastrechts," *Vorwärts*, November 10, 1919; "Grenzen des Gastrechts," *Vorwärts*, November 21, 1919.
21. "Ostjuden in Deutschland," *Vorwärts*, October 22, 1921. This author made the same humanitarian arguments as the article from October 1920. Approximately 35,000 of the Polish forced

dendorff had once welcomed the *Ostjuden* when he had sought their support against the Russians.[22] But, most consistently, these articles returned to the argument that Germany had a moral duty to protect all victims of persecution, including Eastern European Jews. Echoing the position articulated by Spiegelberg's critics and by Heine in 1919, one article argued that as socialists and, thus, believers in equality and humanity (*Menschlichkeit*), they owed a particular duty to help those who were suffering. "We German Social Democrats should not force these fleeing *Ostjuden* over the border into Poland, where military courts and pogroms await them."[23] This article and others stressed the suffering that Eastern European Jews had faced. One article emphasized that these Jews had suffered from the "most ghastly misery" and a "world historical catastrophe."[24] Another referred to the "pogroms and forced military recruitment" that had forced Jews to leave Eastern Europe.[25] A third article claimed that "before all else, it must be said that all of these people are *refugees* from the most horrific suffering that can be imagined," going on to describe in detail their victimization at the hands of Bolshevik, Polish, and Ukrainian forces.[26] These arguments echoed the arguments made on behalf of the Polish Germans that suffering gave the sufferer a claim on the resources of the German state (chap. 4).

The communist *Rote Fahne* also played with the language of martyrdom and suffering, demonstrating the widespread appeal of this rhetoric in Weimar Germany. In an article from September 1920, the paper published what it called "a true legend," which described the fate of a Jew wandering to different countries —including Germany, Switzerland, and Hungary—being rejected in each of them, and ultimately being killed in Hungary. The author appealed to the same potent tropes of victimization and sacrifice. The Jew's dying words were said to be "Father, *don't* forgive them, as they know what they do."[27] Although this vision of the Jew as Christ-figure found little resonance outside communist circles, the use of the image of the Jewish martyr referenced the potent emotional hold of images of suffering across the political spectrum.

These appeals to German moral responsibility to people who were suffering

---

laborers working for Germany during the war were Jews; Maurer, *Ostjuden in Deutschland, 1918–1933*, 86; Heid, *Maloche—nicht Mildtätigkeit*.

22. "Ostjuden einst und jetzt," *Vorwärts*, July 30, 1920.

23. "Das Ostjudenproblem," *Vorwärts*, October 8, 1920.

24. Ibid.

25. "Ostjuden in Deutschland."

26. "Das Ostjudenproblem." Emphasis in original.

27. *Rote Fahne*, September 22, 1920. Emphasis in original. Another article from November 1920 took issue with the omnipresent phrase *burdensome foreigner* (lästige Ausländer) that was used to describe Jews or Russians, arguing that the "The German revolutionary proletariat has every reason to say clearly to the republican government, 'For us, the Russian comrades are not foreigners rather [the foreigners are] the German capitalists.'" *Rote Fahne*, November 19, 1920.

marked a shift from the pre-1914 period, in which utility had been the main criterion for the toleration of immigrants.[28] Arguments for Jewish utility were not just absent from the arguments made on behalf of Eastern European Jews by the Weimar socialists; defenders of Eastern European Jews actually agreed with their critics that granting asylum to Jews would take precious resources from the German nation. The best argument that one author in *Vorwärts* could come up with to defend against this charge was to claim that the Eastern European Jews would be supported by German Jews and, so, were unlikely to burden overstretched German resources.[29] The social democratic defenders of asylum operated rhetorically from a defensive crouch that conceded large portions of their opponents' positions. They neither answered accusations about the unsuitability of the Jews for life in Germany nor proposed solutions for the danger they or other refugees supposedly posed to hard-working but destitute Germans. Rather, the defenders of asylum emphasized the universal humanitarian duty to shelter victims of persecution. The ambivalences of the Weimar-era SPD with regard to the *Ostjuden* represents a continuity with their Wilhelmine-era counterparts. In the years before 1914, the SPD had dutifully defended Jews against anti-Semitic attacks but were hardly Philosemites themselves, often deploying anti-Semitic stereotypes in their own writings.[30] Socialist fears at being too closely associated with Jews continued in the postwar period.

Whatever their rhetorical hesitations, it is especially striking, then, to see both the Prussian Interior Ministry and *Vorwärts* consistently adhering to the policy that *Ostjuden* were deserving of asylum on German soil. The very defense of the Jews at this time of heightened anti-immigrant and anti-Semitic sentiment was an act of significant moral courage; however, the socialist reliance on abstract pleas to tolerance and humanity and their acceptance of anti-Semitic stereotypes about the harm caused by immigrant Jews did little to defuse the arguments of their opponents. By accepting that Eastern European Jews were a burden on the German nation, socialists implicitly set up a competition between tolerance (framed as a theoretical obligation) and resentment toward a group that even they believed was harmful. Thus, it is unsurprising that socialists proved ineffective in mobilizing public opinion behind their arguments. Members of the DNVP and more extreme right-wing groups derided the socialists for their weakness, equating tolerance with impotence.

28. Wertheimer, *Unwelcome Strangers*, 178. For more on the concept of utility and German immigration policy, see Ulrich Herbert, *Geschichte der Ausländerbeschäftigung in Deutschland, 1880 bis 1980: Saisonarbeiter, Zwangsarbeiter, Gastarbeiter* (Berlin: Dietz, 1986), 74; Sassen, *Migranten, Siedler, Flüchtlinge*, 110–13.

29. "Ostjuden in Deutschland."

30. Fischer, *The Socialist Response to Antisemitism in Imperial Germany*. See also Rosemarie Leuschen-Spiegel, *Sozialdemokratie und Antisemitismus im Deutschen Kaiserreich* (Göttingen: Vandenhoeck & Ruprecht, 1978).

Asylum and the Russians

More than 500,000 Russians settled temporarily or permanently in Germany as part of the postwar refugee crisis (see chap. 5). Of these, approximately 360,000 were concentrated in the capital, which during this time had a population of approximately 3.7 million. Thus, if only for a brief period, the number of Russian immigrants living in Berlin was almost 10 percent of the total population of the city. Ilja Ehrenburg, a member of the Russian émigré community wrote:

> I don't know how many Russians there were in Berlin then. Probably very many —one heard Russian being spoken all over. Dozens of Russian restaurants were opened—with Balalaika, with Salmon, with Gypsies, with Bliny, with Schachlyk and, naturally, with the obligatory excitement. There was a cabaret. Three daily papers and five weeklies were on offer. Within a year, seventeen Russian publishers began to operate.[31]

During the 1920s, Germans often referred to Berlin as "Russia's second capital," to Charlottenburg (the neighborhood that was a center of the Russian colony) as "Charlottengrad," and to the Kurfürstendamm as the "NEP-ski Prospekt." Some Berliners went so far as to refer to their city as "Berlinograd."[32] Bus drivers, on entering the Russian neighborhood, would announce that they were now entering "Rußland." One diplomat remarked that "A small Petersburg was gradually taking shape in Berlin,"[33] and a German crime novel from the early 1930s that took place in the Berlin émigré community was titled *Petersburg am Wittenbergplatz*.[34]

The Germans did not greet these Russian émigrés with open arms. Housing shortages were a particular point of conflict, and the murder of the leading Russian liberal politician V. D. Nabokov (father of the famous writer) inspired widespread German hostility toward the Russians. Yet the German response to this group of foreigners never reached the levels of hostility inspired by the *Ostjuden*. Indeed, the socialist newspaper *Vorwärts* even questioned why it was that the

31. Ilja Ehrenburg, "Zwei Jahre lebte ich hier in Angst und Hoffnung," in *Berliner Begegnungen: Ausländische Künstler in Berlin, 1918–1933, Aufsätze, Bilder, Dokumente,* ed. Klaus Kändler (Berlin: Dietz, 1987), 47.

32. Karl Schlögel, *Berlin–Ostbahnhof Europas: Russen und Deutsche in ihrem Jahrhundert* (Berlin: Siedler, 1998), 14. On the renaming by the Germans of the Kurfürstendamm as the "NEP-ski Prospekt," see Wladimir Majokowski, "Das Heutige Berlin" (1923), in *Berliner Begegnungen: Ausländische Künstler in Berlin, 1918–1933, Aufsätze, Bilder, Dokumente,* ed. Klaus Kändler (Berlin: Dietz, 1987), 33.

33. Wipert von Blücher, *Deutschlands Weg nach Rapallo: Erinnerungen eines Mannes aus dem Zweiten Gliede* (Wiesbaden: Lines, 1951), 15.

34. R. G. Batalin and Gerhard Lindau, *Petersburg am Wittenbergplatz: Roman* (Detmold: Meyer, 1931).

German public seemed so undisturbed by its Russian émigré population, noting that "the Pan-German press blames the *Ostjuden* for [the German] housing shortage. . . . It is remarkable that they have not written a word about the over two hundred thousand Russian emigrants in Germany."[35] Instead, Robert Williams writes in his history of the Berlin colony, "in general, German policy toward the Russian community in the 1920s was one of toleration."[36] Williams's claim is confirmed by Wipert von Blücher, an official in the Foreign Office during the 1920s. In his memoir, Blücher stated, "We accepted them as guests, even though there were some among them who had been openly hostile to Germany (*deutschfeindlich*) during the war."[37]

The Russian colony is difficult to fit into established paradigms. They excited neither great enthusiasm nor great anxiety. They did not want to assimilate, and the majority remained in Germany for only a brief time. Political activists among the Russians wanted to influence German politics, but by and large they did not succeed.[38]

For most historians, the Russian émigrés are a mere footnote to the developing complex relationship between Germany and Soviet Russia. Nevertheless, it is their lack of impact on the historical record that is perhaps what is most intriguing about the Russian émigrés; the relative absence of xenophobia in the German discourse on the Russians renders this response crucial for historians of the Weimar period and of the response of Germany to migration in general. Thus, the question remains: If so many Germans were so afraid of a Russian invasion and so concerned about immigration, why were they not more disturbed by this massive and unprecedented number of Russians settling on German soil?

It is important to mention that Russian émigrés largely received a tolerant reception in many of their adopted homes across the European continent.[39] In Paris, they were seen as "impractical, exotic and frenetic," imbued with "more than a touch of the suffering Slav soul," and as such they were largely left alone by French authorities.[40] In Prague, Russians found a welcome reception, in which the Czechoslovak "Russian Action" led by President Tomás

---

35. "Zweihunderttausend russische Emigranten!" *Vorwärts,* May 19, 1921. Manfred Georg made a similar point in "Aus meinem Merkbuch. I. Die Emigranten," *Berliner Volkszeitung,* March 29, 1922.

36. Williams, *Culture in Exile,* 146.

37. Blücher, *Deutschlands Weg nach Rapallo,* 15.

38. Kellogg argues that the Russian émigrés were crucial to the evolution of Nazi ideology; Michael Kellogg, *The Russian Roots of Nazism: White Émigrés and the Making of National Socialism, 1917–1945* (Cambridge, UK: Cambridge University Press, 2005).

39. Karl Schlögel, ed., *Der grosse Exodus: Die russische Emigration und ihre Zentren 1917 bis 1941* (Munich: Beck, 1994); Raeff, Russia Abroad.

40. Robert Johnston, *New Mecca, New Babylon: Paris and the Russian Exiles, 1920–1945* (Kingston, Canada: McGill-Queen's University Press, 1988), 3.

Masaryk, a Russophile, used state coffers to provide support for thousands of Russians.[41]

This toleration extended beyond bemused detachment and was crucial to the development of an international regime of refugee protection under the auspices of Fridtjof Nansen, the former polar explorer. The fledgling League of Nations appointed Nansen High Commissioner on Behalf of the League in Connection with the Problem of Russian Refugees in Europe in 1921, with the mandate to coordinate the various initiatives of national governments and private agencies that sought to manage the European refugee problem.[42] Nansen's signature achievement was the establishment of an identity document for refugees who had had been rendered stateless by a Soviet order in 1921. In 1922, he instituted the "Nansen passport," which was granted by the government in which a stateless Russian resided but did not confer citizenship rights on that person. This was the first time that stateless people had any sort of legal identity. Although no state was obligated to accept holders of a Nansen passport, by 1923 thirty-one governments had agree to recognize the passport as legal identification.[43] In essence, the Nansen passport was an anti-passport, a recognition that the stateless person was not a citizen of the host country but also that this individual could not be deported because he or she was not a citizen of any other country. Moreover, although the Nansen passport allowed a Russian émigré to leave a state to go to another that would admit him or her, it offered no guarantee that he or she could return.[44] The Nansen passport enabled the stabilization of the European refugee situation and was possible only because the governments that recognized it did not believe that the Russian refugees posed a major threat.

Thus, the lenient stance of Germany was not unique. But, just as French tolerance was predicated on a sense of Russian exoticism and Czech tolerance was based on a sense of Slavic fellow-feeling, German acceptance of the Russian émigrés must be understood in the context of specific national circumstances. Moreover, regardless of its exceptionality, the terms of the acceptance of the Russian émigrés tell us a lot about how German observers understood immigration, Bolshevism, and national identity more generally. Two factors allowed German observers, both within and outside the local and national governments, to tolerate the émigrés. First, because of the powerful rhetorical connection be-

41. Zdeněk Sládek, "Prag: Das 'russische Oxford,'" In *Der grosse Exodus: Die russische Emigration und ihre Zentren 1917 bis 1941*, ed. Karl Schlögel, 218–33 (Munich: Beck, 1994); Sam Johnson, "'Communism in Russia Only Exists on Paper': Czechoslovakia and the Russian Refugee Crisis, 1919–1924," *Contemporary European History* 16, no. 3 (2007): 371–94.

42. Marrus, *Unwanted*, 89.

43. By the end of the decade, this number rose to over fifty and the Nansen passport was extended to Armenians refugees as well; Torpey, *Invention of the Passport*, 128.

44. Ibid.

tween Bolshevism and border transgression, German observers in diverse are-nas—from the popular press to local Berlin bureaucrats and officials at the For-eign Office—assumed that anti-Bolshevik Russians respected an invisible and unspoken border between their community and the German population of Berlin. This respect obviated the need for the elaborate border defenses that were proposed (although not necessarily enacted) to defend against the sus-pected Bolsheviks in the camps or undesirable (read Jewish and/or Bolshevik) immigrants from the east. Second, German observers felt a sense of common cause with the Russians as either victims of Bolshevism or as defeated people more generally; this allowed the Russians to escape the condemnation directed at Jewish immigrants. When Germans sympathized with the Polish Germans, this was, in essence, a form of self-pity; the Polish Germans were believed to have suffered an extreme version of the fate that all Germans were subject to after Versailles. When a small number of Germans sympathized with the *Ostju-den,* this was justified on the basis of universal human rights. But the Russian émigrés were both self and other—reminders of what the Bolsheviks were ca-pable of while also never being seen as German or even as potentially German. German tolerance was predicated simultaneously on the Russians' perceived disinterest in assimilation and the German sympathy with their plight.

Carl Zuckmeyer's memoirs of Berlin in the 1920s equated the Russian émi-grés with communists and bathed both groups in a romantic glow. "Berlin was much intrigued by the various types of Russians who added special nuances to its rich spectrum—the exiles who lived on what diamonds they had smuggled out, or earned their keep as waiters, peddlers, decorators and gigolos; the Bol-sheviks, who had just come to power; and the other assorted revolutionaries still fighting for power, all of whom appeared to us in a thoroughly romantic light."[45] Zuckmeyer praised "the everlasting influence of the Eastern Russian tempera-ment upon Berlin's cultural life," remarking that "We never knew or cared whether the invasion was one of Tsarist *noblesse* or Bolshevist libertarianism. We loved the Russians and felt a kinship with them in our intellectual and moral aspirations, and in our own libertinage."[46] Although few newspaper reporters or government officials shared Zuckmeyer's "love" for the Russians, they did agree about the lack of threat posed by the émigrés. The Berlin dailies treated the Rus-sians relatively calmly, when they noticed them at all. In December 1921, the *Berliner Tageblatt,* a liberal mass-circulation daily, situated the Russian émigré community within the proud Berlin tradition of accepting immigrants and asylees from the Huguenots onward and argued that Germans should look on

45. Carl Zuckmeyer, *A Part of Myself,* trans. Richard Winston and Clara Winston (New York: Harcourt Brace Jovanovich, 1970), 232. For a similar treatment, see Alfred Döblin, "Russisches The-ater und Reinhardt, 20.12.1921," in *Ein Kerl muß eine Meinung haben: Berichte und Kritiken 1921–1924* (Olten: Walter, 1976), 31–32.

46. Zuckmeyer, *Part of Myself,* 233.

this immigration as a reason for pride: *"The Emigrants in Europe concentrate themselves in Berlin* as a result of their instinct that Germany will play an important role in the cultural and economic rebuilding of Europe."[47] In a similar vein, an article that appeared in *Der Berliner Westen* in July 1923 explained that the Russians were a crucial part of postwar Berlin: "The capital of the Reich would not be the Berlin of the postwar period had it not been overwhelmed by the Russian immigration."[48] The author did not deny that there had been some friction with the native Berlin population, who jealously observed the new Russian shops that catered almost exclusively to a Russian clientele. "But despite the Berliners' aversion to the immigrant wave from the East, the Russians have managed to establish themselves. And the Berliner . . . has managed to accept them."[49] The most striking feature of these pieces is their tone; there is nothing of the defensiveness with which the (very few) pieces that supported the *Ostjuden* were written.

An article from the moderate-right *Kölnische Zeitung* in 1922 clarified why Russians deserved more tolerance than Jews. Russians stayed in their own communities and most often could be seen at cultural events put on by their countrymen, such as theater events and concerts. Their only danger to the rest of Germany lay in the possibility that Bolsheviks were hiding among them. The Jews, on the other hand, were dangerous because of their ability to blend in. Although they were recognizable when they first immigrated due to their distinctive dress and dirty homes, within a generation they had managed to hide their true identities and had almost completely blended in. "The East remains for a long time, even if it likes to hide itself. Even now, sometimes, when one looks at famous men who appear in flawless shimmering shirts and modern tuxedoes at premieres, one sees in unthinking gestures or an unwatched tone of voice reminders that . . . hidden in the gleam of civilization is the past of persecution."[50] The problem for this author, ultimately, was the crossing of borders—Russians were harmless because they were content to stay within the confines of the Russian enclave.

Indeed, if borders were to be crossed, Germans expected that they would be the ones to do the crossing. The *Der Berliner Westen* article described clothing stores, bookstores, cabarets, theaters, and cafes, unthreatening resources newly available for patronage by curious Germans, where they more likely than not would be served by officers and aristocrats.[51] Similarly, Zuckmayer described the Berliners' fascination with "exiles who lived on what diamonds they had smug-

47. "Die russischen Emigranten in Berlin," *Berliner Tageblatt,* December 24, 1921. Emphasis in original.
48. "Die russische Kolonie in Berlin," *Berliner Westen,* July 20, 1923.
49. Ibid.
50. "Ostjudentum in Berlin," *Kölnische Zeitung,* December 31, 1921.
51. "Russische Kolonie in Berlin."

gled out, or earned their keep as waiters, peddlers, decorators and gigolos."[52] The dwindling fortunes of the Russian émigrés provided an ironic opportunity for fantasies of German class mobility.

The public face of the émigrés was that of predominately wealthy and nationalist Russians; a common metaphor found both in contemporary accounts and in histories of the community is of a pyramid with the base cut off.[53] Nonetheless, Bettina Dodenhoeft points out that, despite this image, "the social situation of the émigrés was very poor. A few could afford glorious villas in the Tiergarten or in Grünewald, but the majority were housed in dormitories and shared housing."[54] The *International Review of Labor* agreed: "The Russian refugees come from the most diverse groups, but find themselves in pitiable circumstances, without money, without clothing, most without the knowledge of the language of the land in which they have arrived, and without the ability to pursue a job and totally unsuited for settlement in a foreign land."[55] Claudena Skran also makes the point that "Contrary to popular stereotypes, the typical Russian refugee was not a princess or an ageing archduke"; instead, defeated anti-Bolshevik soldiers, accompanied by family members and other civilians escaping the chaos of the revolution and civil war "constituted [the] core" of the emigration.[56] Nevertheless, the German image of the Russians largely ignored the poverty of much of the Russian community in their midst.

The Russian émigrés were defined by what they were not; namely, they were seen more as the antithesis of the Bolsheviks than as actors in their own right. The Bolsheviks were a vision of a possible dystopian (or, for others, utopian) modernity, but the émigrés were fossils of a time past.[57] The Bolsheviks threatened to overturn the social order, but the émigrés maintained social distinctions even in the difficult conditions of the diaspora. The Bolsheviks were the party of the working class, but the émigrés were (it was believed) aristocrats and high-ranking officials. When Germans talked about the potentially Bolshevik Russian POWs, there was a near-obsessive concern with policing the borders of the camps; however, metaphors such as "Russian Berlin," the Russian "colony," and "Charlottengrad" described a community that was discrete and self-contained. In the years immediately after the revolutions in Russia and Germany, Germans ignored the reality of the émigré experience in favor of the construction of a fanciful counterimage to the all-too-real Bolshevik threat.

52. Zuckmeyer, *Part of Myself,* 232.
53. See Williams, *Culture in Exile,* 112.
54. Dodenhoeft, *Laßt mich nach Russland heim,* 14.
55. *International Review of Labor,* cited in Volkmann, *Russische Emigration in Deutschland, 1919–1929,* 11–12.
56. Skran, *Refugees in Inter-war Europe,* 33.
57. On the Russians as relics of the past, see Julius Eckart, "Die neue Völkerwanderung/Russische Flüchtlinge," *Vossische Zeitung,* January 3, 1922; Hans von Rimscha, *Russland jenseits der Grenzen 1921–1926: Ein Beitrag zur russischen Nachkriegsgeschichte* (Jena: Frommann, 1927), 135.

This metaphor of self-containment also rendered the émigré community politically harmless in the eyes of the state. Indeed, when government officials noted any political danger lurking in the Russian community, they focused almost exclusively on the Bolshevik presence, which was, until the signing of the Treaty of Rapallo in 1922 at least, negligible compared to the size of the anti-Bolshevik community.[58] The Russian community in Berlin was highly politicized and included a range of groups that represented the spectrum of Russian prerevolutionary politics.[59] Despite the fact that in 1921 the vast majority of Russian immigrants in Germany were anti-Bolsheviks, Severing's report on Russian political activities in Berlin expressed concern only about recent immigrants' potentially spreading Bolshevik propaganda.[60] Similarly, the national Interior Ministry sought to combat the problem of communism in Germany by restricting the presence of Russians in the country using measures to keep Russians from entering Germany and by keeping Germans from traveling to Russia.[61] Neither the Prussian nor national states tried to similarly control the political activities of those on the right, even though they were well aware of them. The Foreign Office collected regular reports on the émigré political scene, even if the tangled web of alliances and feuds among various Russian émigré organizations often left them confused. Yet no one ever acted on this information either to support or stymie the political organizations of the anti-Bolshevik émigrés, and on the issue dearest to the émigrés, withholding German recognition of the Soviet regime, they were ultimately unsuccessful.[62] The German government tolerated the Russian émigrés precisely because it did not take them seriously.

Across the political spectrum, many Germans sympathized with the Russians as victims of Bolshevism. In 1922, Julius Eckart, a Baltic German who edited the liberal *Die Grenzboten* and was an informant on Russian affairs for the Foreign Office, preached understanding for the refugees. Although many of them did not have appropriate visas or passports, he wrote, "the great majority of them were not in a position to leave the area of Bolshevik control 'in an orderly manner.'" In this regard, Eckart's plea resembles the appeals on behalf of the *Ostjuden* that balanced appeals to human rights and German suffering. Eckart, however, went even further to emphasize the common cause and common suffering of Germans and Russians. Seeing these "pathetic" souls led him to imag-

58. Schlögel, *Berlin–Ostbahnhof Europas,* 136–58.

59. For an overview of Russian political parties in the diaspora, see Claudia Weiss, "Russian Political Parties in Exile," *Kritika* 5, no. 1 (2004): 219–32.

60. PMI to the Regierungspräsidenten and the Polizeipräsident in Berlin, January 6, 1921, GStA PK, 1 HA, Rep. 77, Tit. 4036, Nr. 9, 26.

61. "Über Maßnahmen auf dem Gebiete des Paßwesens gegen das Zusammenarbeiten der deutschen Kommunisten mit den russischen Bolschewisten," BArch R 1501/1132328, 36.

62. These reports are collected in PAAA R 83578–83584 for the period from March 1922 to March 1925.

ine "how it would have been for *us*."[63] According to Eckart, the suffering of the Germans should make them more sympathetic to the Russians, not less. He describes a *Schicksalsgemeinschaft* of shared suffering among those defeated in the recently concluded war. Although, of course, the needs of Germans in Germany should be met first, "one must never forget that the refugee, if he obeys the laws of the land, enjoys the right of asylum among every cultured people."[64] This sense of a shared burden of suffering also influenced the socialist *Vorwärts*'s coverage of the Russians. One author asked readers to empathize with both the Russian and German "homeless" and narrated tragic stories about refugees of both ethnicities.[65] In similar terms, Dr. Otto Färber, a Catholic activist, also sympathized with the suffering of the Russian refugees as "martyrs to their love of the Fatherland. . . . They also have the ever present danger of losing the best members of the community, their national culture and their inner connection to the homeland."[66] Although Färber does not make the explicit comparison with the suffering of the Germans that the *Vossische Zeitung* or *Vorwärts* did, Färber commiserated with the Russians as people who have lost a homeland, echoing a common trope of the *völkisch* critique of the Weimar Republic. Färber's article betrays no great love or even knowledge of Russia itself; the specific character of this homeland is irrelevant to him. Färber is able to sympathize with the Russian émigrés because the category of Russian nationalist had become emptied of its own meaning, a meaning that had previously been considered highly dangerous and suspect.

The Russian emigrants benefited in concrete ways from German sympathy. Although there were countless calls for the expulsion of Jews who did not have proper paperwork, officials were far more understanding of the difficulties that the émigrés suffered. As a result of a Soviet order on December 15, 1921, most Russian emigrants in Germany lost their citizenship as of June 1, 1922. On June 6, 1922, despite the existence of official diplomatic ties between Germany and Soviet Russia, the national Interior Ministry sent a letter to the governments of the various federal states admonishing them that "refugees should not be sent to the consulates or representatives of the Soviet Republic in Germany for the purposes of obtaining a passport." Instead, they were directed to go to Sergei Botkin's Russian delegation, which had been issuing passports to Russians in Germany since March 1920.[67]

63. Eckart, "Neue Völkerwanderung/Russische Flüchtlinge." Emphasis in original.
64. Ibid.
65. "Bei den Heimatlosen," *Vorwärts*, February 13, 1921.
66. Otto Färber, "Die russische Emigranten und wir," *Allgemeine Rundschau*, no. 14, April 8, 1922, 163.
67. RMI to the Landesregierungen (and PMI), June 6, 1922, PAAA R 83579, 108.

Gastrecht and the Border Transgressions of the Nabokov Assassins

German willingness to commiserate with the Russians as victims of Bolshevism was dependent on the belief that the Russians posed no threat to German interests or the German people. This sense of Russian isolation was tested by the assassination of V. D. Nabokov at the Berlin Philharmonic in March 1922. Because it took place on German soil, even though no Germans were victims or (except for the watchman) even witnesses, the assassination served as a clarion call to the potential dangers of the Russians living in Germany.[68] From the communist *Rote Fahne* to the right-wing *Deutsche Allgemeine Zeitung,* the German press reaction was unanimous; by carrying out the assassination on German territory, the Russian assassins—and by extension, the émigré community as a whole—had failed to respect the borders of *Gastrecht,* the set of formal and informal expectations that governed the conduct of foreign guests and their German hosts. Because it framed the assassination as a border transgression, this reaction demonstrates again the importance that the expectation of the respect for borders had for tolerance in the first place.

On the evening of March 28, 1922, the Berlin organization of the exiled Russian Kadet Party organized an event in the Berlin Philharmonic. A speech by Pavel Miljukov, the leader of the group, who was visiting from Paris and had served in Alexander Kerensky's Provisional Government, was the climax of the evening. Unknown to Miljukov, two embittered Russian former cavalry officers were sitting among his supporters in the audience, waiting to assassinate him as he descended the podium. Peter von Schabelski-Bork and Sergius Taboritzky had arrived in Germany in 1919 and in 1920; they had moved to Munich, then the German headquarters for the most radically anti-Bolshevik Russians and Germans. According to their testimony after their arrest, after reading about Miljukov's speech in a newspaper several days earlier, Schabelski-Bork and Taboritzky had hurried to Berlin intending to kill him. They were particularly angry with Miljukov because he had purportedly insulted the honor of the Empress Alexandra. Arriving in Berlin on the afternoon of March 28, they settled into a hotel, where they loaded seven bullets into each of the 2 pistols they had brought from Munich.[69]

Miljukov's supporters, including many other high-ranking members of the

68. Similar in some ways to the assassination of Walther Rathenau two months later, the assassination of V. D. Nabokov in the Berlin Philharmonic served to discredit the Russian right in the eyes of many Germans. The comparison of the two assassinations is made by Johannes Bauer, *Die Russische Kolonie in München 1900–1945: Deutsch-russische Beziehungen im 20. Jahrhundert* (Wiesbaden: Harrassowitz, 1998), 188.

69. Generalstaatsanwalt beim Landgericht I, May 29, 1922, GStA 1. HA, Rep. 84a, Nr. 55580, 16–17.

Kadet Party and few non-Russians, filled the Philharmonic.[70] Taboritzky and Schabelski-Bork found seats in the second row of the orchestra, although they did not sit together out of the fear that they might be recognized. Schabelski-Bork, in fact, was so convinced that a neighbor was staring at him that he furiously took notes throughout Miljukov's hour-long speech. At ten o'clock, Miljukov finally concluded and, after waiting for the considerable applause to die down, descended the left side of the podium toward a group of invited guests. As he did so, Schabelski-Bork ran toward him, brandishing his pistol and crying, "For the Family of the Tsar and for Russia!"; he fired five shots toward Miljukov.[71] Schabelski-Bork was immediately grabbed by two Kadet politicians, including V. D. Nabokov, and wrestled to the ground.[72] Taboritzky then suddenly sprang into action and fired several shots at Nabokov, who fell bleeding and lifeless to the floor. Three other bystanders suffered minor injuries. In the confusion, Schabelski-Bork reached the podium, where he tried to give a speech justifying his actions. He was quickly apprehended by audience members, who took away his pistol and subdued him until the police arrived.[73]

These dramatic events in the Philharmonic unfolded only a few days before the German and Soviet governments signed the Treaty of Rapallo. As a result of this treaty, Germany became the first European government to extend official recognition to the Soviets. The treaty actually had a far more devastating impact on the Berlin Russian community than did the Nabokov assassination or the outrage it inspired. After the treaty was signed, the Russian émigrés could no longer even pretend to have an influence on German politics, and Berlin increasingly became instead the center of the Soviet presence in Western Europe.[74]

Nonetheless, the Nabokov assassination produced an outcry in the German press across the political spectrum, indicating both the limits and terms of the German acceptance of the Russian presence. After the assassination, the sense of outrage in the German popular press was expressed as anger directed toward the émigrés' illicit border transgression. For the socialists and communists writing in the *Vorwärts, Freiheit,* and *Rote Fahne* or speaking in the Reichstag, this

70. Williams has argued that the Kadets excited the least interest among the Russian political parties located in Berlin; Williams, *Culture in Exile,* 224. Furthermore, judging by the list of witnesses attached to the police report of the event, all (or at least the majority) of the attendees were Russian; Generalstaatsanwalt beim Landgericht, May 29, 1922, GStA 1. HA, Rep. 84a, Nr. 55580, 16–17.

71. Witnesses were divided on how many shots Schabelski-Bork actually fired at Miljukov, LAB A Rep. 358, Nr. 264 (Film 402), Bd. 2.

72. In his novel *The Gift: A Novel* (New York: Putnam, 1979) and parts of his memoir, *Speak Memory* (New York: Grosset & Dunlap, 1960), Vladimir Nabokov, V. D. Nabokov's son, addressed the years he spent in exile in Berlin.

73. Generalstaatsanwalt beim Landgericht I, May 29, 1922, GStA 1. HA, Rep. 84a, Nr. 55580, 17–18. Taboritzky denied firing any shots in his statement to police on April 29, 1922; LAB A Rep. 358, Nr. 264, Bd. 2, 170.

74. Williams, *Culture in Exile,* 200.

was manifested in a fear that Russian and German reactionaries might join forces. Right-wing papers such as the *Deutsche Allgemeine Zeitung* and *Berliner Lokal-Anzeiger* were more concerned that the Russians had violated the terms of *Gastrecht* and had crossed both the implicit boundary of acceptable behavior and the physical border of the German community, committing a crime on German soil.

As might be expected, some of the strongest reactions to the events came from the left-wing newspapers. These papers attempted to draw attention to the role of Munich as a center of reaction and to the alliances between German and Russian reactionaries. As a result of the assassination and the possible connection between the assassins and wider Russian monarchist circles, the Berlin police shut down a monarchist convention coincidentally meeting during this time in the Rotes Rathaus. On the morning after the assassination, an article appeared in the *Rote Fahne* that attempted to draw readers' attention to the larger context of monarchist plotting in Germany and the complacency of the German government in allowing the reactionaries to operate so brazenly on German soil. "This much is already known, the murder is *an act of political revenge.* And the German government bears a not small portion of the blame for this, as it has *given free reign to the Russian monarchist plots,* by allowing [monarchist] congresses to take place."[75] Shortly thereafter, an article in *Die Freiheit* read, "The planning for the murder that took place in the Philharmonic *was hatched in Munich with the collaboration of German Monarchists, and it is certain that the money* [to fund the assassins] *came from the pockets of German counter-revolutionaries.*"[76] The socialist *Vorwärts* emphasized that the murder was another "link in the chain of a long-prepared and extensive worldwide criminal organization." The assassins themselves were part of a "Munich nest" consisting of an alliance of Russian, German, and Hungarian reactionaries.[77] The term *Munich nest* provided a concrete location for the forces of reaction. The Russian Revolution (as well as the short-lived communist republics based in Budapest and Munich) had created a deterritorialized reactionary force—an ironic international alliance of nationalists. Munich was, not without justification, considered by many on the left to be the physical and spiritual homeland of the reactionaries.[78] By becoming rooted in this new homeland and joining forces with like-minded anti-Bolsheviks of other nationalities, the Russian reactionaries had managed to reestablish their connection with a community that could provide them with strength. Furthermore, by identifying Munich as the birthplace of

75. "Ein russischer Monarchistenmord in Berlin," *Rote Fahne,* March 29, 1922. Emphasis in original.
76. "Die Hochburg der russischen Monarchisten," *Die Freiheit,* March 31, 1922. Emphasis in original.
77. Williams, *Culture in Exile,* 210.
78. Bauer, *Russische Kolonie in München 1900–1945,* 11.

monarchist plots, the left managed to localize the source of this danger while adding another unauthorized border crossing to the accusations leveled against the plotters. Their anger was directed not only toward the threat posed by the Russians in Germany but also toward the reactionary Bavarians menacing the liberals and socialists in Berlin.

The uproar about the assassination culminated in two days of socialist and communist speeches in the Reichstag that focused on the activities of the Russian émigrés. Wilhelm Koenen, the USPD delegate, began by discussing the "large apartments" and "high standard of living enjoyed by the émigrés."[79] Koenen further decried the double standard applied to Bolshevik and anti-Bolshevik political activities, accusing the German authorities of tolerating the "subversive (*staatsfeindliche*) relationship" between the German and Russian monarchists.[80] Mirroring the fear of German anti-Bolsheviks about an alliance between German Sparticists and Russian POWs, Germans on the left were now convinced of a dangerous international reactionary alliance. The next day, a communist delegate raised the issue of the double standard applied to political agitation in Germany—communists were punished, but anti-communists were tolerated. But his speech was given at the end of the day and, aside from a smattering of applause from the communists, appeared to excite little response.[81] This is not surprising; although the question of fairness toward left-wing agitators was of great interest to the communists themselves, it was not an issue that moved the members of other parties nearly as much. But it is still telling that no conservative rose to defend the Russians. The left-wing newspapers and Reichstag delegates were not the only ones to react critically to the assassination of V. D. Nabokov.

Although the nonsocialist press avoided talking about monarchist conspiracies, it was still concerned with the potentially dangerous consequences of the large Russian presence in the German capital. Manfred Georg, writing in the liberal-democratic *Berliner Volkszeitung* the day after the assassination, cataloged the resentments and complaints about the émigrés, ranging from their high standard of living to their hypocritical nationalism (while plundering their own people) to their alliance with the German radical right:

> They drink and boast in luxury restaurants with the riches that they have plundered from the Russian people (even during the war, the patriots!) and brought to Germany. They whisper and conspire, take apartments from the natives, form "nationalist organizations," mingle with the anti-republican parties of the right, write, smear and babble in our newspapers and disturb our political networks. They defend the Kapp-Putsch, spit on the rest[,] . . . infatuate and seduce our

79. *Verhandlungen,* Bd. 354, 6903.
80. Ibid., 6904.
81. Ibid., 6970.

student youth[,] . . . conduct Monarchist propaganda and, for their own purposes, try to destroy our negotiations with Soviet Russia.[82]

An article in the *Berliner Lokal-Anzeiger*, a conservative mass-market daily, that appeared on the day after the assassination was entitled "It Cannot Continue": "A portion of our Slavic guests seems to feel so at home in Berlin that they forget that one can easily misuse *Gastrecht*."[83] The author then noted the extent to which the Russians had established themselves in western Berlin: "The Russians have their own theaters in Berlin, their own restaurants, their own newspapers; when one sees certain post offices in the West [of Berlin] one could also say that they have their own post offices."[84] The author expressed a certain amount of sympathy with these victims of "the depths of human suffering," but emphasized that they needed to understand that "Germany must demand that its laws and its order are upheld and that Berlin should not be turned into a scene of violent shootings and foolish political demonstrations. . . ."[85]

The reactionary *Deutsche Allgemeine Zeitung* sought to shift the blame for the murder to the Weimar state, which, the author argued, had granted the right of asylum to refugees from every country. Although the *Deutsche Allgemeine Zeitung* did not argue that the right of asylum should be denied altogether, the author wrote, "It must be demanded from foreigners that stay with us and take advantage of our hospitality that they do not misuse the refuge that has been offered to them."[86] In addition, for the first time, after the Nabokov assassination observers explicitly connected the Russian émigrés with the generally perceived problem of foreigners living in Germany. An article in the *Kölnische Zeitung* that appeared a few days after the assassination stated that the attack was a result "of allowing foreigners to travel without appropriate supervision."[87]

The assassination in the Berlin Philharmonic demonstrated the capacity for political violence, and thus the danger, of the Russian émigrés. German commentators made much of the fact that the Russians had violated the law of *Gastrecht* and had abused the generosity of the German people. They pointed to the fact that the Russians had managed to prosper while the Germans around them seemed to be suffering. For example, an article in the *Kölnische Zeitung* on the Russian colony that appeared in the aftermath of the assassination used Russians taking precious housing from needy Germans as an example of the consequences of allowing so many foreigners to live in Germany.[88] Commenta-

82. Manfred Georg, "Aus meinem Merkbuch. I. Die Emigranten," *Berliner Volkszeitung*, March 29, 1922.

83. "So geht es nicht weiter," *Berliner Lokal-Anzeiger*, March 29, 1922.

84. Ibid.

85. Ibid.

86. "Die Mordtat der Russen," *Deutsche Allgemeine Zeitung*, April 3, 1922.

87. "Unsere politisierenden Fremden," *Kölnische Zeitung*, April 1, 1922.

88. Ibid. The problem of housing was one of the areas in which Russians did incur German re-

tors also stressed that this act of violence was particularly deplorable because it had happened on German soil and outside of the confines of the Russian colony. The *Deutsche Allgemeine Zeitung* warned that "the bullet that hit Nabokov could just have easily killed a German. German soil must not be used by foreigners for the carrying out of their political differences."[89]

The *Berliner Lokal-Anzeiger* framed the act of assassination explicitly as a violation of "the border . . . that separates politics from foreign guests [which] must be *unconditionally respected!*"[90] This rage against border violation was remarkable considering that, although the assassination took place in the Berlin Philharmonic, judging from the list of witnesses at the trial, Miljukov's lecture was almost exclusively attended by Russians.[91] Taboritzsky and Schabelski-Bork did apparently shoot into the crowd (although, miraculously, Nabokov was the only fatality), but their chances of hitting a German were practically nonexistent.

The official investigation of the assassination attempt focused on Taboritzky and Schabelski-Bork's potential co-conspirators. Indeed, the police in the small town of Bad Elster arrested a group of traveling Russian musicians immediately after the assassination on the suspicion that they might have been in some way connected to the crime.[92] With more justification, the Munich police focused its investigation on Theodor von Winberg, the former stable master of the tsar and a monarchist agitator who had lived in the same hotel as Taboritzky and Schabelski-Bork. The police had sufficient grounds to suspect von Winberg, including that he had traveled to Berlin at the same time as the assassins, where he had "accidentally" run into them at his nephew's home; had given them large sums of money on more than one occasion; and had even several months earlier given Schabelski-Bork the Browning pistol he used in the attack.[93] Von Winberg was brought in on more than one occasion for questioning, and the police also questioned many of von Winberg's friends and acquaintances about his relationship with the accused.[94] Police and prosecutors also examined copies of Russian

sentment. See BArch R 1501/114048 for letters among German government officials and from private groups (such as the Wohnungsverband Groß Berlin) from 1919 complaining about the housing shortage and the role of foreigners in exacerbating the problem. The Russians were specifically mentioned as a group with enough money to buy houses and apartments that would otherwise go to needy Germans.

89. "Mordtat der Russen."

90. "So geht es nicht weiter." Emphasis in original.

91. Generalstaatsanwalt beim Landgericht I, May 29, 1922, GStA 1HA, Rep. 84a, Nr. 55580, 19. In the course of the investigation, the only (non-Baltic) German witnesses to the shooting interviewed by the Berlin police was Georg Brunkow, the security guard at the Philharmonic; LAB, A Rep. 358, 264, Bd. 1–2.

92. Letter from the Polizeipräsidium in Bad Elster to the Polizeipräsidium in Berlin, April 5, 1922, LAB A Rep. 358, Nr. 264, Bd. 1, n.p.

93. Munich police interrogation of Theodor von Winberg, March 30, 1922, LAB A Rep. 358, Nr. 264, Bd. 2, 11–29.

94. After the interrogation of March 30, 1922, von Winberg was called in again on April 3, 1922; LAB A Rep. 358, Nr. 264, Bd. 2, 186–90. In addition to all this circumstantial evidence, von

monarchist tracts during their investigation.[95] Nevertheless, in part because they never found any hard evidence linking Schabelski-Bork and Taboritzky to wider monarchist circles, prosecutors did not mention these possible connections at the trial. On July 7, 1922, the two conspirators were found guilty; Schabelski-Bork was sentenced to twelve years and Taboritzsky to fourteen years jail time.[96] In giving its reasons for this decision, the court was careful to state that the judgment was not motivated by the politics of the defendants. In fact, the court actually admonished the defendants for failing to consider "how their act would sully their own ideals."[97] Despite these protestations of sympathy, the court believed that only a harsh punishment could hinder further political murders, especially, they noted, "for foreigners who, like the defendants, misuse German *Gastrecht*."[98] Implicit in this decision was the assumption that there was the possibility of not misusing *Gastrecht;* as long as Russians continued to respect these boundaries on their behavior, they were welcome to stay.

———

Although this chapter begins with a discussion of tolerance, what was really at stake in the first years of the Weimar Republic was not tolerance per se. Ide-

———

Winberg's own conduct was highly suspicious. He attempted to publish an article in the *Münchener Neueste Nachrichten* (the editors decided against publication) defending Schabelski-Bork and Taboritzky's act; LAB A Rep. 358, Nr. 264, Bd. 2, 131–32. Von Winberg ended his second interrogation with a plea for mercy that almost amounts to an admission of guilt: "I swear, even when you don't believe it, that a jail sentence would be the same thing as a death sentence for me. Since I fled my homeland, I have done so much, in particular living through the revolution, that I could physically not survive another detention." LAB A Rep. 358, Nr. 264, Bd. 2, 190. See also the interviews with Josefine Trausenecker, the maid at the hotel, on April 1, 1922, LAB A Rep. 358, Nr. 264, Bd. 2, 37–38, and with Konstantin Engalitscheff on April 5, 1922, LAB A Rep. 358, Nr. 264, Bd. 2, 203–5, among others.

95. See LAB A Rep. 358, Nr. 264, Bd. 2, 191–203.

96. GStA, 1. HA, Rep. 84a, Nr. 55580, 152. Decision from Landgericht I in Berlin, July 7, 1922. On June 16, 1926, the Prussian Staatsministerium reduced their sentences to eight years for Schabelski-Bork and nine years for Taboritzky. On April 16, 1927, it was decided that, because the two assassins had already served out half their sentences, they were to be released on parole; Amtliche Veröffentlichung from the Prussian Justice Ministry, April 16, 1927, GStA, 1. HA, Rep. 84a, Nr. 55580, 206. The case continued to receive official attention during the Nazi period. On February 8, 1940, the national justice minister decided to return Taboritzky's rights that he had lost with his conviction and the next day issued an order sealing Taboritzky's criminal record; Auslandsstrafregister, December 9, 1941, LAB A Rep. 358, Nr. 264, Bd. 3, n.p. This decision may have been made on the grounds that Taboritzky was of German descent; letter from the Gaugericht Berlin to the Generalstaatsanwalt bei dem Landgericht Berlin, November 25, 1941, LAB A Rep. 358, Nr. 264, Bd. 3, n.p. Intriguingly, Taboritzky's possible Russian German background played no role during the investigation or during his trial, perhaps because he spoke German poorly. Indeed, when Taboritzky failed to file an appeal during the allowed period, his lawyers argued that this was a result of his lack of knowledge of the German language. Zweiter Strafsenat, Reichsgericht (Leipzig), Beschluss, September 27, 1922, LAB A Rep. 358, Nr. 264, Bd. 3, 17.

97. Ibid.

98. Ibid.

ologies such as humanitarianism and anti-Bolshevism in certain contexts disrupted the ethnic or national essentialism that was otherwise so dominant in postwar Germany. After all, even the right argued that the German state should protect the anti-Bolshevik Russians on its soil. The problem with German asylum policy was not simply a question of the failure of Germany to provide a "haven for the persecuted."[99] Instead, the success or failure of German asylum policy during this period hinges on the discourse of sympathy and competition. The advocates for the Eastern European Jews never managed to convince many Germans, or even themselves, that sympathizing with the *Ostjuden* would not affect their own well-being. In contrast, the Russian émigrés enjoyed a much wider range of support because their advocates managed to connect their suffering with German suffering, drawing on the notion of a *Schicksalsgemeinschaft*.

Although contemporary discussions of German foreigner and immigrant policy often decry the lack of altruism in German state practice, altruism is, in fact, a highly unstable basis for policymaking. The failure of the socialists to attract a wider basis of support for their position of tolerance for the *Ostjuden* was, at least in part, a result of the purely altruistic discourse in which they structured their appeal. Germans were urged to tolerate the presence of the *Ostjuden* despite what they would do *to* Germany rather than because of what they could potentially do *for* Germany. At issue here was not a deficit in altruism but, rather, the acute awareness, even among those on the left, of the finite and already overstretched resources of Germany. The socialists were unable to connect tolerance of the *Ostjuden* with potential gains for the German nation. The wider support garnered by the advocates of the Russian émigrés attests to their success in framing their arguments in terms of German self-interest—helping the Russian émigrés also strengthened the German fight against Bolshevism. Tolerance was not a foreign concept to Weimar Germans; however, in the economically and politically unstable situation of early Weimar Germany, sympathy alone was not enough.

99. Wertheimer, *Unwelcome Strangers*, 178.

Conclusion

The Legacy of Crisis

Although 1922 marked the conclusion of the critical era charted in this book, in the end none of the questions about the meaning, location, or practicality of the borders of Germany were settled. With the inflation and the currency stabilization, many of the migrants living on German soil moved on to more hospitable countries or returned to their lands of origin. In the following years, unease about migrants and, in particular, anxieties regarding the *Ostjuden,* were a steady drumbeat in the German press. Even as Gustav Stresemann pursued a policy of appeasement with the West, as chancellor he directed an expansion of aid toward Germans abroad with the goal of maintaining the Reich claim to territory lost to Poland at Versailles and of establishing connections with ethnic Germans in even more far-flung locales.[1] *Völkisch* ideologues and geographers developed ever more aggressive images and narratives to justify German claims in Eastern Europe.[2] With the depression, anti-Semitism and anti-foreigner sentiment again exploded into public consciousness and political action with devastating consequences.

It is worth returning here to Hannah Arendt's argument that it was the trauma of statelessness that led to the greater horrors of totalitarianism. According to Arendt, nineteenth-century liberals equated the establishment of nation-states with the arrival of constitutional government, and, as such, the

---

1. Krekeler, *Revisionsanspruch und Geheime Ostpolitik;* Hiden, *Baltic States and Weimar Ostpolitik.*

2. Herb, *Under the Map of Germany.*

nineteenth-century nation-state was "based on the rule of law . . . against the rule of arbitrary administration and despotism." But the nation-state always existed in a sort of tension between its twin loyalties to the nation and to the rule of law. The war and postwar crisis completed "the transformation of the state from an instrument of law [to] an instrument of the nation. . . . the nation had conquered the state."[3] This conquest had grave consequences for both the people who had no state to call their own and the nation-states themselves.

The system of national states devised at Versailles and laid uncomfortably over the ethnic mélange of Eastern and Central Europe created a population of rightless minorities and stateless individuals that subsequently could not be managed within a set of gerrymandered international institutions and guarantees. National minorities were the first group to feel the wrath of the victory of the nation-state as a form of political organization. Arendt claims that the minority treaties, ostensibly designed to protect the political expression of those people caught in nation-states designed for other national groups, were, in fact, a recognition that "only nationals could be citizens; only people of the same national origin could enjoy the full protection of legal institutions" whereas non-nationals required extra guarantees from international bodies.[4] The minorities protected by the minority treaties were only partial outsiders in the post-Versailles order; they did belong to some state, even though they required protection above and beyond the authorities of that state. The people rendered stateless by the war, postwar settlements, and revolution were much more troubling. Once Europe was faced with people who did not belong to any government, "it turned out [that] no authority was left to protect [these rights] and no institution was willing to guarantee them."[5] In this situation, the stateless did not necessarily lose their freedom—in fact, Arendt points out that many of the stateless were freer in this condition than they had been under the power of despots. Instead, they lost something even more valuable—their voice and recognition. Stateless people could affect politics neither in the states where they had been born nor in the ones in which they found sanctuary. In Arendt's formulation, "Once they had left their homeland they remained homeless, once they had left their state they became stateless; once they had been deprived of their human rights they were rightless, the scum of the earth."[6] They had become superfluous.

According to Arendt, the presence of stateless people also had an ominous effect on the states that harbored them. These states could not deport these stateless people because no other state would have them. Nor was naturalization a solution because nation-states did not want new citizens from other nations and the refugees themselves were loath to join a new state due to their own con-

3. Arendt, *Origins of Totalitarianism,* 274.
4. Ibid.
5. Ibid., 288.
6. Ibid., 267.

tinued loyalties toward the nations (if not the states) they had left behind. Unable to handle the stateless within a legal framework, the state handed responsibility for managing them over to the police. For "the first time the police in Western Europe had received authority to act on its own, to rule directly over people; in one sphere of public life it was no longer an instrument to carry out and enforce the law, but had become a ruling authority independent of government and ministries."[7] Once the stateless were placed under police jurisdiction, there arose the "temptation to deprive all citizens of legal status and rule them with an omnipotent police."[8] Ironically, according to Arendt, it was the very helplessness of states before the problem of statelessness that led them to succumb to totalitarianism.

The labors of the early Weimar Republic to cope with the refugee problem provide ambivalent evidence on which to evaluate Arendt's three arguments: (1) her teleology of the triumph of the nation over the law, (2) her verdict on the rightlessness of stateless people, and (3) her claim that statelessness drove interwar states toward totalitarian. Arendt's contention that the state had become the servant of the nation echoes that of the *völkisch* nationalists, who claimed that the defeat of Germany and the weakness of the Weimar Republic were proof that the nation was more constant than the fickle and impotent state.[9] Nationalism was an extraordinarily popular and widespread discourse in the Weimar Republic, well beyond the precincts of the *völkisch* right. But instead of 1919 marking the subservience of the rule of law to the ideology of nationalism, it would be fairer to say that in 1919 (1) nationalist discourse became the primary language in which the rights and mutual obligations of the state and its citizens were conceptualized and (2) the *Volk* became both the object and subject of politics across the political spectrum, from the right-wing ideologues (who used the supposed betrayal of the *Volk* by the state as a bludgeon to denigrate the republic) to the revolutionary councils (who called for radical democratic participation in political decisions).[10] Indeed, for the parties that accepted the republic, the arrival of democracy on German soil was a vindication of the nineteenth-century equation of constitutional rights with national sovereignty, not its demise.

The very flexibility of nationalism meant that it was more an instrument of political infighting than a triumphant discourse to which the law was rendered subservient. The 1920 naturalization guidelines (see chap. 7) made national belonging the prerequisite for German state citizenship, but ethnic and cultural criteria ex-

7. Ibid., 285.
8. Ibid., 287.
9. See F. F. "Zukunft und Ziele des Auslandsdeutschtums," 164.
10. Carl Caldwell, "The Citizen and the Republic in Germany, 1918–1935," in *Citizenship and Nationality in Twentieth Century Germany,* ed. Geoff Eley and Jan Palmowski (Palo Alto: Stanford University Press, 2007), 45–50.

isted alongside one another and the guidelines were interpreted quite differently in conservative Bavaria than in socialist Saxony. On a whole, however, the naturalization policy of the Weimar Republic provided an easier path to citizenship for Jews and others from Eastern Europe than had the policies of the Kaiserreich. Nationalism was used as both an impetus to demand that Polish Germans be provided for by the German state and a justification for turning them away. In the latter case, the Foreign Office argued that the need of the German state to maintain a claim to Polish territory trumped the suffering of individual Germans, at once the culmination and the rejection of *völkisch* logic (chap. 4).

Aside from the internal contradictions of nationalism itself, the complex interplay of anti-Bolshevism and nationalism also belie the contention that nationalism triumphed entirely after 1919. At times, anti-Bolshevism and nationalism could act in concert. Anti-Bolshevik Germans easily appropriated both anti-Semitic and anti-Slavic stereotypes, and the notion of "Judeo-Bolshevism" became yet another weapon in the arsenal of postwar anti-Semites. But anti-Bolshevism also served to open new avenues for the tolerance of those who were of a different nationality but on the same end of the ideological spectrum. Thus, DNVP delegates to the Reichstag used the defense of German national prerogatives as a reason that the German state needed to provide protection for the anti-Bolshevik Russian POWs being menaced by their Soviet compatriots in the POW camps (chap. 6). The relative tolerance that Russian émigrés enjoyed during the early years of the republic was in part due to the sympathy they enjoyed as victims of Bolshevik tyranny (chap. 8).

The relationship between the nation and the state was thrown into question by the 1914–1922 crisis of sovereignty, but this period did not provide any firm answers about what that relationship should be. This confusion was fueled by the Manichean nature of nationalist discourse itself. Nationalist rhetoric simultaneously papered over the practical and ideological disputes about the meaning and constitution of the nation and provided a potent moral charge to these disagreements, fostering polarization and working against moderation and tolerance.[11] Both the defenders of Polish German immigrants and the opponents of Eastern European Jewish immigrants claimed to speak on behalf of the nation, charging their opponents with moral bankruptcy. When the German state proved itself manifestly unwilling or unable to take such measures as deporting all foreigners or colonizing Eastern Europe, this was seen as a betrayal. The ideology of humanitarianism often went hand in hand with a regretful admittance of impotence (see chaps. 5 and 8). Even the defenders of asylum admitted that Germany was tolerant of immigrants only because it had to be, thus ceding the

11. Sven Oliver Müller, "Die umstrittene Gemeinschaft. Nationalismus als Konfliktphänomen in Deutschland," in *Politische Kollektive: Die Konstruktion nationaler, rassistischer und ethnischer Gemeinschaften*, ed. Ulrike Jureit, 124–45 (Münster: Oldenbourg, 2001); Föllmer, "Problem."

moral high ground of ideological purity to the nationalists, who rejected such realism.

The second part of Arendt's argument concerns the rightlessness of stateless persons. The experience of refugees in Weimar Germany largely confirms this judgment. Defenders of the immigrant Russians and *Ostjuden* argued that they deserved asylum as victims of persecution. Thus, ironically, the very weakness of the refugees gave them a claim to state leniency. These claims could be persuasive; for example, tolerance of the Russians was convincing across much of the political spectrum. But the experience of the Russian émigrés also demonstrated that tolerance had limits—the presence of the Russians would be sanctioned only as long as they knew their place in terms of *Gastrecht*. In the aftermath of the V. D. Nabokov assassination, when it became clear that Russian monarchist violence could spill outside the borders of the Russian community, even supporters of the Russian émigrés stated that their patience was conditional on the willingness of the Russians to avoid German politics or even German space. In the case of the Eastern European Jews, the socialists failed to convince others to provide asylum because they did not argue that such asylum would not negatively impact the already suffering German people. Again, tolerance was dependent on weakness, and the supporters of the *Ostjuden* stressed that the immigrants who were granted asylum would have as little impact as possible. The very arguments used by the advocates for asylum are a paradoxical demonstration of the truth of Arendt's claim.

Finally, Arendt claims that states, unable to use legal measures to manage this population, granted this authority to the police and thus started down the slippery slope that led to fascism.[12] But this indictment of Weimar Germany as a nascent totalitarian state ignores the fact that there was a qualitative difference between the policies enacted during the Weimar Republic and those enacted by the Nazis. To a degree, we could argue this difference was due to a lack of resources. In January 1919, the Prussian Interior Ministry issued an order designed to seal the border to all who could not prove that they were German, but a combination of insufficient border guards and corruption foiled these efforts. A year and a half later, the National Commission for Civilian Internees and Refugees floated a plan to track all foreigners on German soil by registering them at their local police station and then compiling these cards in a national database; here, too, insufficient resources defeated the plan.

But Weimar Germany failed to become a totalitarian state not merely because of a lack of money or workers. Arendt's argument about the totalitarian potential of the interwar states rests on an assumption that states during the interwar period were simultaneously weak (motivated by a sense of frustration at their inability to control stateless people by legal means) and strong (capable of

---

12. Arendt, *Origins of Totalitarianism*, 283–85.

mobilizing the police to perform this task in their stead). Although frustration was undoubtedly present in Weimar Germany, the bitter political divisions and lack of ideological coherence belie the ability of the police or anyone else to gain enough control to rise to the level of fascism.

As James Sheehan argues, state sovereignty can best be understood as a problem in which the "complex, uneven and unfinished aspects of state making" are never commensurate with the theory of the state as an autonomous agent.[13] According to Bob Jessop, states should be envisioned as a collection of institutions in which assorted groups compete to advance their interests. Even functioning states are "emergent, tendential phenomena," engaged in a continual struggle to impose an image of coherence on diverse state actors and institutions.[14] Of course, each state privileges certain forces, ideologies, and actors over others. Even in the relatively open political climate of Weimar Germany, the communist argument that the persecution of *Ostjuden* was akin to the suffering of Jesus was a political nonstarter. But the fact that certain forces are privileged does not mean that their will is directly expressed through the state. Instead, the appearance of unity, or the "state effect," is the "contingent and provisional [outcome] of struggles to realize more or less specific 'state projects.'"[15]

These theories of the state as a contingent product of struggle are useful for understanding the competing pressures in the Weimar Republic. The actions of the Foreign Office reflected the ambivalence of the republic. The plan for the support of ethnic Germans in Poland was an attempt to balance the competing demands of assisting suffering Germans and of preserving a German claim to Polish territory. And even though this plan and the negotiation of the Treaty of Rapallo demonstrated its commitment to reclaiming German territory in the east, the Foreign Office also consistently reminded extremists that international opinion demanded that the republic refrain from severe measures such as the mass deportation or internment of the *Ostjuden*.

Competing imperatives were important not only for the design of policy but also for its implementation. It was not that the Weimar Republic did not have the resources to control its frontiers or the foreigners who crossed them, it was that neither the national nor the provincial governments chose to allocate their resources in this way. The national Interior Ministry repeatedly called for the strengthening of border defenses, but its limited release of resources to achieve this end demonstrates that it judged other priorities equally or more worthy of support. As Robert Lipinski, the Saxon interior minister, drolly observed with regard to plans for the implementation of a national system of foreigner regis-

13. Sheehan, "Problem of Sovereignty," 2.

14. Bob Jessop, *State Theory: Putting the Capitalist State in Its Place* (University Park: Pennsylvania State University Press, 1990), 9.

15. Ibid.

tration, it was unclear whether the goal of registering foreigners was proportional to the resources it would require. This plan was never enacted.

Furthermore, contrary to Arendt's claim that police involvement in the management of immigration was a step toward totalitarianism, this role of the police did not necessarily contribute to the growing power of the central government or the magnetic force of nationalist ideology. For example, the local police controlled the deportation of foreigners in Prussia without the oversight of the Interior Ministry. This appears to confirm Arendt's suspicions about the police running amok; however, due to the lack of Interior Ministry control, such deportations were often a result of purely local considerations and not, as Arendt would have us believe, national imperatives. Furthermore, they were ineffective because undesirable immigrants could just leave one locale for another. As a result, the police and the state were working at cross purposes.

These theories of competing imperatives also help to put political fragmentation into perspective. After all, competition for power among state institutions is a facet of even the most totalitarian states. As Jane Caplan observes of Nazi Germany, "one of the most striking paradoxes of the National Socialist political system . . . is the tension between, on the one hand, the immense concentration of power it embodied and the ideological unity it espoused and, on the other, the fragmentation of its structures and processes in practice."[16] What caused problems for the state in Weimar Germany was not the existence of fragmentation but, rather, the failure to achieve a fiction of coherence (in Jessop's terms, a "state effect") that could conceal the disagreements among the various political parties or branches of the national government. The fractured hegemonies of the Weimar Republic were themselves the products of the 1914–1922 crisis of sovereignty. This demographic and political crisis produced the problem of statelessness and enhanced the appeal of extremist solutions. But it also meant that Weimar Germany failed to achieve the sort of ideological coherence that would enable us to label it a totalitarian state. As previously discussed, nationalism, which in earlier times had provided such coherence, contributed now to conflict because it lent a moral charge to accusations against one's political enemies. Thus, even after the national Interior Ministry released its 1920 guidelines for the naturalization of foreigners, the *Länder* continued to fight bitterly about the criteria that should be used. When Severing and Heine argued that *Ostjuden* deserved asylum, they were accused of selling out the German nation. The heated terms of these disputes—the accusations of betrayal and the warnings about the demise of Germany—make clear that such arguments threatened the ideological coherence of the republic as a whole. The virulence of nationalist rhetoric in the 1920s may have enhanced the appeal of extreme solutions in the following decade, but it was not itself fascist.

---

16. Jane Caplan, "National Socialism and the State," in *Reevaluating the Third Reich*, ed. Tom Childers and Jane Caplan (New York: Holmes & Meier, 1993), 103.

Moreover, the compromises pursued by the national and Prussian governments should not be viewed simply as evidence that the republic was ineffective and doomed. They were moderate by design and not merely by default. In particular, the interior ministries of Prussia and the Reich saw no contradiction between stopping illegal immigration and refraining from the large-scale deportation or internment of those foreigners who were already on German soil. The dogged persistence of Heine and Severing in upholding a policy of asylum for Eastern European Jews reflected their unwillingness to abandon humanitarianism to the iron law of nationalist consistency. The national Interior Ministry may not have agreed with this policy, but neither did it pursue extreme measures to oppose it. This purposeful moderation flies in the face of Arendt's determinism, in which the crisis of statelessness after 1914 led inevitably to the ceding of political control to the police and ultimately to the horrors of the death camps. Furthermore, even as their opponents on the right hammered Weimar officials for failing to seal the border or for coddling those who had crossed it illegally, these accusations were not, alone, fatal to the republic. The mere existence of statelessness was not enough to bring about fascism.

So, if the outbreak of war in 1914 or the treaties signed in 1919 did not lead inevitably to the horrors of Nazism, its roots must be sought elsewhere. Here we must return to the fantasies of expansion or escape that were also present during World War I and early Weimar Germany. These fantasies reveal two things about the extreme ends of the political spectrum that are less obvious when we concentrate solely on the German response to immigration after 1918: the degree of utopianism and the desire for expansion or escape. Of course, a sense of unreality was not entirely absent from German policy toward foreigners. Schemes for a national registry of foreigners were hardly more realistic in 1920 than the idea that Germans could found a workers' colony in southern Russia. However, the appeal of utopianism is particularly striking when we examine the German dreams of annexation during the war and the fantasies of escape after its unhappy conclusion. Wartime planners believed that German military success presented the opportunity to demographically remake Poland and the Baltic territories, creating space for German agricultural settlements that would revitalize the Reich and bring far-flung *Auslandsdeutsche* into a closer connection with the land of their ancestry. An oft-repeated theme in the writings of the Freikorps soldiers who sought adventure or settlement in the Baltics was that the signing of the Treaty of Versailles meant that Germans needed to seek their fortune outside the treacherous German state. For the members of Ansiedlung Ost, the Russian Revolution served to open a new space for German socialists to find work and happiness. The word *utopia* literally means "no place" and in that sense, not even the Freikorps or Ansiedlung Ost were truly utopian—each had ideas about where they wanted to go. It would be more accurate to say that, in each case, they believed that historical events rendered previous political frontiers irrelevant.

Rather than providing a fixed horizon for the practice of nationalist ideology and state practice, which it had done more or less successfully prior to 1914, the border in Weimar Germany became a symbol of political impotence and ideological incoherence. The impossible border was made so by the simultaneous German longing for transnational movement across the border and for securing the border against the incursions of unwanted migrants. During 1914–1922, shifting physical boundaries and revolutionary turmoil combined with fantasies and fears about yet more radical changes. In addition, the nation-state triumphed as a principle of political organization at Versailles at the same time that it was challenged by both the realities of ethnic mixing and the transnational ideology of Bolshevism. Finally, the failure of the Weimar Republic to either expand its frontiers or achieve impermeable borders added yet another dimension of frustration to this already fraught situation.

For the most part, the socialists and members of other moderate parties respected the inviolability of the border. They wished to seal the border against both migrants and ideologies from the east. Furthermore, aside from the revanchist longing for the territory lost to Poland in the Treaty of Versailles that was *de rigueur* during this period, fantasies of territorial expansion or escape found few adherents among political moderates. In this sense, it was the center of the political spectrum that demonstrated the greatest continuity with the Wilhelmine conception of state sovereignty that viewed state, nation, and territory as coterminous. Yet they governed in a world in which fixed borders and homogenous and sedentary populations were a visibly unattainable *idée fixe*. Even those Germans who supported the republic could not help but notice certain inconsistencies among the three different populations representing state, nation, and territory: the German citizens (those who claimed to belong to the state), the ethnic Germans (those who claimed German nationality or ethnicity), and the heterogeneous population that actually lived within German territory. Migrants —be they German refugees from Poland, *Ostjuden,* or Russian émigrés—were symbols of the non-identity of the three groups and, thus, became a barometer for the success (or, all too often, the failure) of the republican nation-state. The political extremes on the right and the left privileged the loyalties of race or class above any conception of sovereignty that equated state, nation, and territory; as such, they achieved an ideological coherence that constantly slipped from the grasp of political moderates.

Whereas the *Regierungsparteien* reluctantly agreed to the frontiers mandated by the Treaty of Versailles, the political extremes paired ideological inflexibility with a highly charged ambivalence toward the German eastern frontier. The populist left-wing movement Ansiedlung Ost envisioned settling in Soviet

Russia, and the Sparticists and, later, communists encouraged Russian POWs and interned Red Army soldiers to join them in fomenting revolution in Germany. Nevertheless, when confronted with the specter of monarchist Russian assassins, the communists did not hesitate to decry the German tolerance of immigration. The ambivalence of the right toward the German frontiers was even more striking. The right-wing parties sometimes acted according to nationalist motives and at other times according to the international solidarity of anti-Bolshevism. DNVP delegates to the Reichstag howled about the indignities perpetrated by the *Ostjuden* who had crossed into Germany and, in the same breath, called for Germany to protect the anti-Bolshevik Russians on German soil. Freikorps members and leaders saw no contradiction between settling in Latvia, or even procuring Latvian citizenship to protect their German identity.

For those on both ends of the political spectrum, the German eastern border stood at the crossroads of utopian longings and resentment about the impossibility of their fulfillment. It is perhaps not surprising that those who rejected the republic also rejected its borders, but it is here on Germany's impossible border—not in the halls of state—that the continuities between the 1914–1922 crisis and the Nazis can be found.

The crisis of 1914–1922 did not alone cause the Weimar Republic to fail. The rise of the Nazis depended on a host of political, social, and economic considerations well beyond the scope of this book. Nevertheless, I suggest that the Nazi racial state was an heir to the crisis of sovereignty explored here. Indeed, the very prominence of propaganda references to the "Days of August" in 1914, the "stab in the back" in 1918, and the supposed perfidy of the Weimar state in selling out the German nation by accepting the terms of the Treaty of Versailles in 1919 bear witness to the hold that this period had in the 1930s. The war and immediate postwar period witnessed a radicalization of the nationalist right. World War I awakened many Germans to the potential for eastern expansion, and the loss of the war seemed to validate pan-German claims that the state was a fragile basis on which to ground national identity. In addition, in a dangerous cycle, fears about the burdens of large-scale immigration were projected on to the Eastern European Jews, and anti-Semitic stereotypes increased this sense of danger posed by immigrants. When the Weimar state proved itself manifestly unwilling or unable to take such measures as deporting all foreigners or colonizing Eastern Europe, these failures were taken as betrayals. The sense of impotence when faced with limitations posed by reality did not have a dampening effect on ambition; quite to the contrary, frustration functioned as a productive force inspiring ever greater levels of utopian imaginings and an ever greater sense of resentment at their failures.

Nazism was one consequence of the intense ambivalence of the right toward German territorial frontiers and this cycle of utopianism, frustration, and resentment. Building on imperial fantasies, Germany was no longer defined in terms of its physical borders but as the epicenter of a movement to support and enrich all Germans. The solution to the impossible border was to disregard existing state borders altogether. As Heinrich Himmler later said, "Blood is our border."[17] Nazi ideas about race offered in theory, if not in reality, clearer boundaries and easier criteria for determining who belonged and who did not than did the complex conglomeration of ideas about race and culture used by Weimar officials. Racial ideology was a means of limiting the kinds of people welcome on German soil, and at the same time, it provided a justification for territorial expansion.[18] It is important to stress, however, that, although Nazism reflects the triumph of nationalism, the desire for expansion, and the intolerance of foreigners that increased during and after World War I, it was also a departure from the moderation and hesitation that also characterized this earlier period. The crisis of the war and postwar period found its end—but not its only necessary conclusion—in the horrors of Nazism.

Finally, the very complexity of attitudes and policies regarding migration during the Weimar period is also an important precedent for the ongoing German struggle with its status as an *Einwanderungsland*. It took until 2000 for Johannes Rau, then the German president, to publicly recognize that Germany is and has always been a land of immigration. Just as migration stood at the center of arguments about the meanings of the nation and the state during and after World War I, so, too, asylum seekers, guestworkers, and other migrants stand at the center of contemporary disputes about German national identity. It would be false to say that the debates of the early twenty-first century are the same as those of the early twentieth. Nonetheless, as a reunified Germany gropes toward an understanding of itself and its place in the world, the failure of its Weimar progenitor to arrive at any but terrible answers to its impossible border is a lesson in the need to learn to live with the paradoxes posed by mobile people in a world of territorial states.

17. Heinrich Himmler quoted in Conze, "'Unverheilte Brandwunden,'" 34.

18. The literature on the Nazi war in the east is voluminous; see particularly Rolf-Dieter Müller, *Hitlers Ostkrieg und die deutsche Siedlungspolitik* (Fischer: Hamburg, 1995); Mark Mazower, *Hitler's Empire: How the Nazis Ruled Europe* (New York: Penguin, 2008); Christian Gerlach, *Kalkulierte Morde: Die deutsche Wirtschafts- und Vernichtungspolitik in Weissrussland 1941–1944* (Hamburg: Hamburger Edition, 1999); Wendy Lower, *Nazi Empire Building and the Holocaust in Ukraine* (Chapel Hill: University of North Carolina Press, 2005); Omer Bartov, *The Eastern War, 1941–1945: German Troops and the Barbarization of Warfare*, 2nd ed. (New York: Palgrave, 2001); Dieter Pohl, *Die Herrschaft der Wehrmacht: Deutsche Militärbesatzung und einheimische Bevölkerung in der Sowjetunion 1941–1944* (Munich: Oldenbourg, 2008); Christian Hartmann, ed., *Der deutsche Krieg im Osten, 1941–1944* (Munich: Oldenbourg, 2009); Götz Aly and Susanne Heim, *Vordenker der Vernichtung: Auschwitz und die deutschen Pläne für eine neue europäische Ordnung* (Hamburg: Fischer, 1991).

Appendix

Map 1. German Gains in the Treaty of Brest-Litovsk, March 1918

Map 2. Prospective German Settlements in the Former Russian Empire

Map 3. German Territorial Losses after World War I

Bibliography

PRIMARY SOURCES

Archives

Politisches Archiv des Auswärtigen Amts (PAAA)
Bayerisches Hauptstaatsarchiv (BayHStA)

MA (Ministerium des Äusseren)
MInn (Ministerium des Innern)
Generalstaatskommissar

Bundesarchiv—Lichterfelde & Koblenz (BArch)

R 43 I (Reichskanzlei)
R 57 (Deutsches Auslands Institut)
R 901 (Auswärtiges Amt)
R 1501 (Reichsministerium des Innern)
R 1507 (Reichskommissar für die Überwachung der öffentlichen Ordnung)
R 3001 (Reichsjustizministerium)
R 8012 (Baltenverband)
R 8025 (Baltische Landeswehr)
R 8039 (Schlageter Gedächtnis Museum)
R 8048 (Alldeutscher Verband)

Friedrich Ebert Stiftung (FES)

NL Carl Severing

Geheimes Staatsarchiv Preussische Kulturbesitz (GStA PK)

Rep. 77 (Ministerium des Innern)
I (Einbürgerungsanträge)
Ost-West-Abteilung
Rep. 84a (Justizministerium)
Rep. 89 (Geheimes Zivilkabinett)
Rep. 191 (Ministerium für Volkswohlfahrt)

Landesarchiv Berlin (LAB)

A Pr.Br.Rep. 30 (Polizeipräsidium Berlin)
A Rep. 358 (Generalstaatsanwaltschaft bei dem Landgericht Berlin)
A Rep. 406 (Polizeidirektion Schöneberg)

Sächsisches Hauptstaatsarchiv (SächsHStA)

Ministerium des Innern

Published Primary Sources

Anonymous. *Was erwartet den deutschen Arbeiter in Sowjetrußland?* Berlin: W. Wegner, n.d [probably 1920].

Balla, Erich. *Landsknechte wurden wir . . . : Abenteuer aus dem Baltikum.* Berlin: Wilhelm Kolk, 1932.

Batalin, R. G., and Gerhard Lindau. *Petersburg am Wittenbergplatz: Roman.* Detmold: Meyer, 1931.

Bischoff, Josef. *Die letzte Front: Geschichte der Eisernen Division im Baltikum 1919.* Berlin: Schützen-Verlag, 1936.

Blücher, Wipert von. *Deutschlands Weg nach Rapallo: Erinnerungen eines Mannes aus dem Zweiten Gliede.* Wiesbaden: Lines, 1951.

Brandis, Cordt von. *Baltikumer: Schicksal eines Freikorps.* Berlin: Kolk, 1939.

Broedrich-Kurmahlen, Silvio. *Das neue Ostland.* Charlottenburg: Ostlandverlag, 1915.

Cartarius, Ulrich, ed. *Deutschland im Ersten Weltkrieg: Texte und Dokumente 1914–1918.* Munich: Deutsche Taschenbuch-Verlag, 1982.

Class, Heinrich. *Zum deutschen Kriegsziel.* Munich: J. F. Lehmanns, 1917.

Dittmann, Wilhelm. *Erinnerungen.* Frankfurt am Main: Campus, 1995.

Döblin, Alfred. "Russisches Theater und Reinhardt, 20.12.1921." In *Ein Kerl muß eine Meinung haben: Berichte und Kritiken 1921–1924.* Olten: Walter, 1976.

Ehrenburg, Ilja. "Zwei Jahre lebte ich hier in Angst und Hoffnung." In *Berliner Begegnungen: Ausländische Künstler in Berlin, 1918–1933, Aufsätze, Bilder, Dokumente,* edited by Klaus Kändler, 43–50. Berlin: Dietz, 1987.

Engelhardt, Eugen von. *Der Ritt nach Riga: Aus den Kämpfen der Baltischen Landeswehr gegen die Rote Armee 1918–1920.* Berlin: Volk und Reich, 1938.

F. F. "Zukunft und Ziele des Auslandsdeutschtums." *Deutschvölkisches Jahrbuch 1920,* edited by Georg Fritz, 163–70. Weimar: Alexander Duncker, 1920.

Fähnrich, Paul. *Kolomna: Erlebnisse von 76 Rückwanderern der Interessengemeinschaft der Auswandererorganisationen nach Sowjetrussland.* Berlin: Germania, 1921.

Fischer, Hans. *Nach Sibirien mit hunderttausend Deutschen: Vier Monate russische Kriegsgefangenschaft.* Berlin: Ullstein, 1915.

Franke, A. *Die Wahrheit über Russland: Die Auswanderung nach Sowjet-Russland und das Diktat der dritten Internationale, Mitteilungen der deutschen U.S.P.-Moskau Delegierten und anderer Zeugen*. Berlin: Birn, 1920.

Friedrich, Hans. *Die Flucht aus Sibirien*. Reutlingen: Ensslin & Laiblin, 1916.

Gengler, Ludwig F. *Rudolf Berthold: Sieger in 44 Luftschlägen im Bruderkampfe für Deutschlands Freiheit*. Berlin: Schliessen-Verlag, 1934.

Gerstmayer, Hermann. *Baltikumkämpfer!* Berlin: Beltz, 1934.

Geymann, Alexander. *Dem Reiche der Knute entflohen: Dem Flüchtling nacherzählt*. Berlin: Scherl, 1917.

Goldschmidt, Alfons. *Moskau 1920: Tagebuchblätter*. Berlin: Rowohlt, 1920.

Goltz, Rüdiger von der. *Als politischer General im Osten, 1918 und 1919*. Leipzig: Koehler, 1936.

——. *Ernste Gedanken zum 10. Geburtstage der deutschen Republik 9.11.1928*. Berlin: Brunnen Verlag-Winckler, 1928.

Göpel, Kurt. "Die Flüchtlingsbewegung aus den Infolge des Versailler Vertrages Abgetretenen Gebieten Posens und Westpreußens und ihre Bedeutung für die deutsche Volkswirtschaft." PhD dissertation, University of Giessen, 1924.

Grimm, Bruno. *Klassenkampf und Arbeiterschaft: Von einem nach Rußland ausgewanderten und wieder zurückgekehrten Arbeiter*. Berlin: Germania, 1920.

Grimm, Bruno, and E. Weber. *Russlandfahrt 1920*. Berlin: Germania, 1921.

Gumprich, Hugo. *Delegationsbericht über die Verhandlungen mit Sowjet-Russland von H. Gumprich: Referat zur ausserordentlichen Mitgliederversammlung und zum Delegiertentag am 31. August 1919 im Volkshaus zu Leipzig*. Leipzig: Verein Ansiedlung Ost, 1919.

Hartmann, Georg Heinrich. "Erinnerungen aus den Kämpfen der Baltischen Landeswehr." In *Der Kampf um das Reich,* edited by Ernst Jünger, 116–45. Essen: Kamp, 1931.

Höss, Rudolf. *Death Dealer: The Memoirs of the SS Kommandant at Auschwitz*. Translated by Andrew Pollinger. New York: Da Capo, 1996.

Jonck, George. *Meine Verschickung nach Sibirien, Erinnerungen und Erlebnisse eines rigaschen Buchhändlers*. Munich: J. F. Lehmann, 1916.

Jünger, Ernst. *Der Kampf um das Reich*. Essen: Kamp, 1931.

Kändler, Klaus, ed. *Berliner Begegnungen: Ausländische Künstler in Berlin, 1918–1933: Aufsätze, Bilder, Dokumente*. Berlin: Dietz, 1987.

Kett, August. *Erlebnisse aus dem Jahre meiner Gefangenschaft in Russland, erzählt von A. Kett*. Regensburg: Friedrich Pustet, 1916.

Köhrer, Erich. *Das wahre Gesicht des Bolschewismus: Tatsachen-Berichte-Bilder aus den baltischen Provinzen November 1918–Februar 1919*. Berlin: Verlag für Sozialwissenschaft, n.d. [1919?].

Majokowski, Wladimir. "Das Heutige Berlin" (1923). In *Berliner Begegnungen: Ausländische Künstler in Berlin, 1918–1933, Aufsätze, Bilder, Dokumente,* edited by Klaus Kändler, 32–34. Berlin: Dietz, 1987.

Marx, Karl. *The Marx-Engels Reader*. 2nd ed. Edited by Robert C. Tucker. New York: W. W. Norton, 1978.

Medem, Walter Eberhard von. *Stürmer von Riga: Die Geschichte eines Freikorps*. Leipzig: Franz Schneider, 1935.

Meinecke, Friedrich. *Ausgewählter Briefwechsel*. Edited by Ludwig Dehio. Stuttgart: Koehler, 1962.

Nabokov, Vladimir. *The Gift: A Novel*. New York: Putnam, 1979.

——. *Speak, Memory: A Memoir*. New York: Grosset & Dunlap, 1960.

Nord, Franz. "Der Krieg im Baltikum." In *Der Kampf um das Reich*, edited by Ernst Jünger, 63–97. Essen: Kamp, 1929.

Noske, Gustav. *Von Kiel bis Kapp: Zur Geschichte der deutschen Revolution*. Berlin: Verlag für Politik und Wirtschaft, 1920.

Oertzen, Friedrich Wilhelm von. *Die deutschen Freikorps 1918–1923*. Munich: Bruckmann, 1936.

Osbahr, H. F. *Menschenhandel: Russische Erfahrungen Hamburger Arbeiter die auf Veranlassung des Ansiedlung-Vereins Ost/Sitz Hamburg nach Russland zur Arbeit auswanderten*. Hamburg: n.p., 1920.

Paquet, Alfons. *Der deutsche Krieg: Politische Flugschriften*, vol. 23: *Nach Osten!* Stuttgart: Deutsche Verlags-Anstalt, 1915.

Rauschning, Hermann. *Die Entdeutschung Westpreussens und Posens*. Berlin: R. Hobbing, 1930.

Rimscha, Hans von. *Russland jenseits der Grenzen 1921–1926: Ein Beitrag zur russischen Nachkriegsgeschichte*. Jena: Frommann, 1927.

Rohrscheidt, Walter von. *Unsere Baltikum-Kämpfer: Die Ereignisse im Baltikum 1918 und 1919*. Braunschweig: Albert Limbach, 1938.

Rosenberg, Arthur. *Die Entstehung der deutschen Republik 1871–1918*. Berlin: Rowohlt, 1928.

Salomon, Ernst von, ed. *Das Buch vom deutschen Freikorpskämpfer*. Berlin: Wilhelm Limpert-Verlag, 1938.

——. *Fragebogen*. Hamburg: Rowohlt, 1951.

——. *Die Geächteten*. Gütersloh: Bertelsmann, 1930.

——. "Sturm auf Riga." In *Der Kampf um das Reich*, edited by Ernst Jünger, 98–111. Essen: Kamp, 1931.

Schiemann, Paul. *Die Asiatisierung Europas: Gedanken über Klassenkampf und Demokratie*. Berlin: Kommissions Verlag, Alexander Grübel, 1919.

Schmidt, Axel. *Der deutsche Krieg: Politische Flugschriften*, vol. 7: *Die russische Sphinx*. Stuttgart & Berlin: Deutsche Verlags-Anstalt, 1914.

Schmidt-Pauli, Edgar von. *Geschichte der Freikorps 1918–1924*. Stuttgart: Lutz, 1936.

Schülter, Joseph. *Der Bolschewismus und seine Gefahr für Deutschland!: Vortrag gehalten am 13.4.1919 im Windhorst-Bunde, Bonn*. Bonn: Kommissions, Rhenania, 1919.

Stavenhagen, Kurt. *Die eigene Scholle in der Baltenmark: Neue Existenzmöglichkeiten für Landwirte, Offiziere, Techniker, Ingenieure, usw*. Stuttgart: Greiner & Pfeiffer, 1919.

Weber, Hermann. *Der Gründungsparteitag der KPD: Protokoll und Materialien*. Frankfurt am Main: Europäische Verlagsanstalt, 1969.

Zobel, Johannes. *Schüler freiwillig in Grenzschutz und Freikorps*. Berlin: Grundel, 1932.

Zuckmeyer, Carl. *A Part of Myself*. Translated by Richard Winston and Clara Winston. New York: Harcourt Brace Jovanovich, 1970.

SECONDARY SOURCES

Ablovatski, Eliza. "Cleansing the Read Nest: Counter-Revoution in Budapest and Munich." PhD dissertation, Columbia University, 2004.

Aly, Götz, and Susanne Heim. *Vordenker der Vernichtung: Auschwitz und die deutsche Pläne für eine neue europäische Ordnung*. Hamburg: Fischer, 1991.

Anderson, James. "Nationalist Ideology and Territory." In *Nationalism, Self-Determination and Political Geography*, edited by Ron J. Johnston, David B. Knight, and Eleonore Kofman, 18–40. London: Croom Helm, 1988.

Arendt, Hannah. *The Origins of Totalitarianism*. New York: Harcourt Brace, 1973.

Aschheim, Steven. *Brothers and Strangers: Eastern European Jews in German and German Jewish Consciousness, 1800–1923*. Madison: University of Wisconsin Press, 1982.

Bade, Klaus. "'Amt der verlorenen Worte': Das Reichswanderungsamt 1918–1924." *Zeitschrift für Kulturaustausch* 39, no. 3 (1989): 312–21.

——, ed. *Deutsche im Ausland. Fremde in Deutschland: Migration in Geschichte und Gegenwart*. Munich: Beck, 1992.

——. *Europa in Bewegung: Migration vom späten 18. Jahrhundert bis zur Gegenwart*. Munich: Beck, 2000.

Balibar, Etienne. "Fichte and the Internal Border: On *Addresses to the German Nation*." In *Masses, Classes, Ideas: Studies on Politics and Philosophy before and after Marx*, 61–84. New York: Routledge, 1994.

Bartelson, Jens. *A Genealogy of Sovereignty*. New York: Cambridge University Press, 1995.

Barth, Boris. *Dolchstoßlegenden und politische Desintegration: Das Trauma der deutschen Niederlage im Ersten Weltkrieg 1914–1933*. Düsseldorf: Droste, 2003.

Bartov, Omer. *The Eastern War, 1941–1945: German Troops and the Barbarization of Warfare*. 2nd ed. New York: Palgrave, 2001.

Bauer, Johannes. *Die Russische Kolonie in München 1900–1945: Deutsch-russische Beziehungen im 20. Jahrhundert*. Wiesbaden: Harrassowitz, 1998.

Baumgart, Winfried, and Konrad Repgen. *Brest-Litovsk*. Göttingen: Vandenhoeck and Ruprecht, 1969.

Baur, Johannes. "Zwischen 'Roten' und 'Weissen'—Russische Kriegsgefangene in Deutschland nach 1918." In *Russische Emigration in Deutschland 1918 bis 1941*, edited by Karl Schlögel, 93–108. Berlin: Akademie, 1995.

Becker, Jean-Jacques. *The Great War and the French People*. Translated by Arnold Pomerans. Dover, N.H.: Berg, 1985.

Bender, Thomas, ed. *Rethinking America in a Global Age*. Berkeley: University of California Press, 2002.

Bessel, Richard. *Germany after the First World War*. Oxford: Clarendon Press, 1993.

Blanke, Richard. *Orphans of Versailles*. Lexington: University Press of Kentucky, 1993.

——. *Prussian Poland in the German Empire (1871–1900)*. New York: Columbia University Press, 1981.

Bosl, Karl. *Bayern im Umbruch: Die Revolution von 1918, ihre Voraussetzungen, ihr Verlauf und ihre Folgen*. Munich: Oldenbourg, 1969.

Brandes, Detlef. "Die Deutschen in Russland und der Sowjetunion." In *Deutsche im Ausland—Fremde in Deutschland: Migration in Geschichte und Gegenwart*, edited by Klaus J. Bade, 85–134. Munich: Beck, 1992.

Brechtefeld, Jörg. *Mitteleuropa and German Politics: 1848 to the Present*. New York: St. Martin's Press, 1996.

Broszat, Martin. *Zweihundert Jahre deutsche Polenpolitik*. Frankfurt: Suhrkamp, 1972.

Brubaker, Rogers. *Citizenship and Nationhood in France and Germany*. Cambridge, Mass.: Harvard University Press, 1992.

Bruendel, Steffan. *Volksgemeinschaft oder Volksstaat: Die "Ideen von 1914" und die Neuordnung Deutschlands im Ersten Weltkrieg*. Berlin: Akademie Verlag, 2003.

Burleigh, Michael. *Germany Turns Eastward: A Study of Ostforschung in the Third Reich*. Cambridge, UK: Cambridge University Press, 1988.

Caldwell, Carl. "The Citizen and the Republic in Germany, 1918–1935." In *Citizenship and Nationality in Twentieth Century Germany*, edited by Geoff Eley and Jan Palmowski, 40–56. Palo Alto: Stanford University Press, 2007.

Campbell, Bruce. "The Freikorps as Model and Myth in German Political Life, 1918–1935." Unpublished paper presented at German Studies Association Annual Meeting, New Orleans, LA, September 18–21, 2003.

Campbell, Joan. *Joy in Work, German Work: The National Debate, 1800–1945*. Princeton: Princeton University Press, 1989.

Canning, Kathleen. "Class vs. Citizenship: Keywords in German Gender History." *Central European History* 37, no. 2 (2004): 225–44.

Caplan, Jane. "National Socialism and the State." In *Reevaluating the Third Reich*, edited by Tom Childers and Jane Caplan, 98–114. New York: Holmes & Meier, 1993.

Carsten, Francis L. *Revolution in Central Europe, 1918–1919*. Aldershot, UK: Wildwood House, 1988.

Chickering, Roger. *We Men Who Feel Most German: A Cultural Study of the Pan-German League, 1886–1914*. Boston: Allen & Unwin, 1984.

Childers, Tom, and Jane Caplan, eds. *Reevaluating the Third Reich*. New York: Holmes & Meier, 1993.

Clark, Bruce. *Twice a Stranger: The Mass Expulsions That Forged Modern Greece and Turkey*. Cambridge, Mass.: Harvard University Press, 2006.

Cobban, Alfred. *The Nation State and National Self-Determination*. New York: Thomas Chrowell, 1969.

Cohen, Deborah. *The War Come Home: Disabled Veterans in Britain and Germany, 1914–1939*. Berkeley: University of California Press, 2001.

Conrad, Sebastian. *Globalisierung und Nation im Deutschen Kaiserreich*. Munich: Beck, 2006.

Conrad, Sebastian, and Jürgen Osterhammel, eds. *Das Kaiserreich transnational: Deutschland in der Welt, 1871–1914*. Göttingen: Vandenhoeck und Ruprecht, 2004.

Conze, Vanessa. "'Unverheilte Brandwunden in der Außenhaut des Volkskörpers': Der deutsche Grenz-Diskurs der Zwischenkriegszeit (1919–1939)." In *Ordnung in der Krise: Zur politischen Kulturgeschichte Deutschlands 1900–1933*, edited by Wolfgang Hardtwig, 21–48. Munich: Oldenbourg, 2007.

Cooper, Rudolf. *The Failure of a Revolution: Germany in 1918–1919*. New York: Cambridge University Press, 1955.

Crew, David. *Germans on Welfare: From Weimar to Hitler*. New York: Oxford University Press, 1998.

Daniel, Ute. *The War from Within: German Working-Class Women in the First World War*. Translated by Margaret Ries. New York: Berg, 1997.

Diest, Wilhelm. *Militär und Innenpolitik im Weltkrieg, 1914–1918*. Düsseldorf: Droste, 1970.

Dodenhoeft, Bettina. *"Laßt mich nach Rußland heim": Russische Emigranten in Deutschland von 1918 bis 1945*. Frankfurt am Main: Lang, 1993.

Doenninghaus, Victor. *Revolution, Reform und Krieg: Die Deutschen an der Wolga im ausgehenden Zarenreich*. Essen: Klartext, 2002.

Domansky, Elizabeth. "Militarization and Reproduction in World War I Germany." In *Society, Culture, and the State in Germany, 1870–1930,* edited by Geoff Eley, 427–64. Ann Arbor: University of Michigan Press, 1996.

Eghigian, Greg. "The Politics of Victimization: Social Pensioners and the German Social State in the Inflation of 1914–1924." *Central European History* 26, no. 4 (1993): 375–403.

Eley, Geoff. *Forging Democracy: The History of the Left in Europe, 1850–2000*. Oxford: Oxford University Press, 2002.

———. "Remapping the Nation: War, Revolutionary Upheaval and State Formation in Eastern Europe, 1914–1923." In *Ukrainian-Jewish Relations in Historical Perspective*, edited by Howard Aster and Peter J. Potichnyi, 205–46. Edmonton: Canadian Institute of Ukrainian Studies Press, 1983.

Eliasberg, George. *Der Ruhrkrieg von 1920*. Bonn-Bad Godesberg: Neue Gesellschaft, 1974.

Englander, David. "Military Intelligence and the Defense of the Realm: The Surveillance of Soldiers and Civilians in Britain during the First World War." *Bulletin of the Society for the Study of Labor History* 52 (1987): 24–32.

Ezergailis, Andrew, and Gert Pistohlkors, eds. *The Russian Baltic Provinces between the 1905/1917 Revolutions*. Cologne: Böhlau, 1982.

Fahrmeir, Andreas. *Citizens and Aliens: Foreigners and the Law in Britain and the German States, 1789–1870*. New York: Berghahn Books, 2000.

Feldman, Gerald. *The Great Disorder: Politics, Economics and German Society in the German Inflation, 1914–1924*. New York: Oxford University Press, 1993.

Fink, Carole. *Defending the Rights of Others*. New York: Cambridge University Press, 2004.

Fischer, Fritz. *War of Illusions: German Policies from 1911 to 1914*. Translated by Marion Jackson. New York: W. W. Norton, 1975.

Fischer, Lars. *The Socialist Response to Antisemitism in Imperial Germany*. Cambridge, UK: Cambridge University Press, 2007.

Flechtheim, Ossip Kurt, and Sigrid Koch-Baumgarten. *Die KPD in der Weimarer Republik*. Hamburg: Junius, 1986.

Fleischhauer, Ingeborg, Benjamin Pinkus, and Edith Frankel. *The Soviet Germans: Past and Present*. London: Hurst & Co., 1986.

Föllmer, Moritz. "The Problem of National Solidarity in Interwar Germany." *German History* 23, no. 2 (2005): 202–31.

Föllmer, Moritz, and Rüdiger Graf, eds. *Die "Krise" der Weimarer Republik: Zur Kritik eines Deutungsmusters*. Frankfurt: Campus, 2005.

Fritzsche, Peter. "Did Weimar Fail?" *Journal of Modern History* 68, no. 3 (1996): 629–56.

———. *Germans into Nazis*. Cambridge, Mass.: Harvard University Press, 1998.

Gatrell, Peter. *A Whole Empire Walking: Refugees in Russia during World War I*. Bloomington: Indiana University Press, 1999.

Geiss, Immanuel. *Der polnische Grenzstreifen 1914–1918: Ein Beitrag zur deutschen Kriegszielpolitik im Ersten Weltkrieg*. Lübeck: Matthiesen Verlag, 1960.

Gerlach, Christian. *Kalkulierte Morde: Die deutsche Wirtschafts- und Vernichtungspolitik in Weissrussland 1941–1944*. Hamburg: Hamburger Edition, 1999.

Geyer, Michael. "Insurrectionary Warfare: The German Debate about a Levée en Masse in October 1918." *Journal of Modern History* 73 (September 2001): 459–527.

Goodwin, Barbara, and Keith Taylor. *The Politics of Utopia*. New York: St. Martin's Press, 1982.

Gosewinkel, Dieter. *Einbürgern und Ausschließen: Die Nationalisierung der Staatsangehörigkeit vom Deutschen Bund bis zur Bundesrepublik Deutschland*. Göttingen: Vandenhoeck & Ruprecht, 2001.

Gottmann, Jean. *The Significance of Territory*. Charlottesville: Virginia University Press, 1973.

Guratzsch, Dankwart. *Macht durch Organisation: Die Grundlegung des Hugenbergschen Presseimperiums*. Düsseldorf: Bertelsmann Universitätsverlag, 1974.

Habedank, Heinz. *Geschichte der revolutionären Berliner Arbeiterbewegung: Von den Anfängen bis zur Gegenwart, Vol. 2: Von 1917 bis 1945*. Berlin: Dietz, 1987.

Haffner, Sebastian. *Failure of a Revolution: Germany 1918–1919*. Chicago: Banner Press, 1986.

Hagen, William. *Germans, Poles & Jews: The Nationality Conflict in the Prussian East, 1772–1914*. Chicago: Chicago University Press, 1980.

Hagenlücke, Heinz. *Deutsche Vaterlandspartei: Die nationale Rechte am Ende des Kaiserreiches*. Düsseldorf: Droste, 1997.

Hajdu, Tibor. "Socialist Revolution in Central Europe, 1917–1921." In *Revolution in History*, edited by Roy Porter and Mikulas Teich, 101–20. New York: Cambridge University Press, 1986.

Hardtwig, Wolfgang, ed. *Ordnung in der Krise: Zur politischen Kulturgeschichte Deutschlands, 1900–1933*. Munich: Oldenbourg, 2007.

Hartmann, Christian, ed. *Der deutsche Krieg im Osten, 1941–1944*. Munich: Oldenbourg, 2009.

Hausen, Karin. "The German Nation's Obligations to the Heroes' Widows of World War I." In *Behind the Lines: Gender and the Two World Wars*, edited by Margaret Hignonet, Jane Jenson, Sonya Michel, and Margaret Weitz, 126–40. New Haven: Yale University Press, 1987.

Hauser, Oswald. "Polen und Dänen im Deutschen Reich." In *Reichsgründung 1870/71: Tatsachen, Kontroversen, Interpretationen*, edited by Theodor Schneider and Ernst Deuerlein, 291–318. Stuttgart: Seewald, 1970.

Heid, Ludger. *Maloche—nicht Mildtätigkeit: Ostjüdische Arbeiter in Deutschland 1914–1923*. Hildesheim: Georg Olms, 1995.

Herb, Guntram. *Under the Map of Germany: Nationalism and Propaganda 1918–1945*. London: Routledge, 1997.

Herbert, Ulrich. "'Generation der Sachlichkeit': Die völkische Studentenbewegung der frühen zwanziger Jahre in Deutschland." In *Zivilisation und Barbarei*, edited by Frank Bajohr, 114–44. Hamburg: Christians, 1991.

——. *Geschichte der Ausländerbeschäftigung in Deutschland, 1880 bis 1980: Saisonarbeiter, Zwangsarbeiter, Gastarbeiter*. Berlin: Dietz, 1986.

Hiden, John. *The Baltic States and Weimar Ostpolitik*. New York: Cambridge University Press, 1987.

———. "The Weimar Republic and the Problem of the Auslandsdeutsche." *Journal of Contemporary History* 12 (1977): 273–89.

Hillmayr, Heinrich. *Roter und Weißer Terror in Bayern nach 1918*. Munich: Nusser Verlag, 1974.

Hinsley, Frances Harry. *Sovereignty*. 2nd ed. New York: Cambridge University Press, 1986.

Hinz, Uta. "'Die Deutschen Barbaren' sind doch die 'Besseren Menschen': Kriegsgefangenschaft und gefangene 'Feinde' in der Darstellung der deutschen Publizistik 1914–1918." In *In der Hand des Feindes: Kriegsgefangenschaft von der Antike bis zum Zweiten Weltkrieg*, edited by Rüdiger Overmans, 339–61. Cologne: Böhlau, 1999.

———. *Gefangen im Grossen Krieg: Kriegsgefangenschaft in Deutschland, 1914–1921*. Essen: Klartext, 2006.

Hoerder, Dirk, and Jörg Nagler, eds. *People in Transit: German Migrants in Comparative Perspective, 1820–1930*. New York: Cambridge University Press, 1995.

Holquist, Peter. *Making War, Forging Revolution: Russia's Continuum of Crisis, 1914–1921*. Cambridge, Mass.: Harvard University Press, 2002.

Hosking, Geoffrey. *A History of the Soviet Union*. London: Fontana, 1990.

Jászi, Oszkár. *Revolution and Counter-Revolution in Hungary*. New York: H. Fertig, 1969.

Jessop, Bob. *State Theory: Putting the Capitalist State in Its Place*. University Park: Pennsylvania State University Press, 1990.

Johnson, Sam. "'Communism in Russia Only Exists on Paper': Czechoslovakia and the Russian Refugee Crisis, 1919–1924." *Contemporary European History* 16, no. 3 (2007): 371–94.

Johnston, Robert. *New Mecca, New Babylon: Paris and the Russian Exiles, 1920–1945*. Kingston, Canada: McGill-Queen's University Press, 1988.

Kellogg, Michael. *The Russian Roots of Nazism: White Émigrés and the Making of National Socialism, 1917–1945*. Cambridge, UK: Cambridge University Press, 2005.

Kershaw, Ian. *Weimar: Why Did German Democracy Fail?* New York: St. Martin's Press, 1990.

King, Jeremy. *Budweisers into Czechs and Germans: A Local History of Bohemian Politics, 1848–1948*. Princeton: Princeton University Press, 2002.

Koenen, Gerd. "Der deutsche Russland-Komplex: Zur Ambivalenz deutscher Ostorientierung in der Weltkriegsphase." In *Traumland Osten: Deutsche Bilder vom östlichen Europa im 20. Jahrhundert*, edited by Gregor Thum, 16–46. Göttingen: Vandenhoeck & Ruprecht, 2006.

———. *Der Russland-Komplex: Die Deutschen und der Osten*. Munich: Beck, 2005.

———. "Vom Geist der russischen Revolution: Die ersten Augenzeugen und Interpreten der Umwälzungen im Zarenreich." In *Deutschland und die russische Revolution 1917–1924*, edited by Gerd Koenen and Lev Kopelev, 49–98. Munich: Fink, 1998.

Kolakowski, Leszak. *Main Currents of Marxism*. Vol. 1. Translated by Paul S. Falla. Oxford: Clarendon Press, 1978.

Kopelew, Lew. "Am Vorabend des grossen Krieges." In *Russen und Russland aus deutscher Sicht. 19./20. Jahrhundert: Von der Bismarckzeit bis zum Ersten Weltkrieg*, edited by Mechthild Keller, 11–107. Munich: Wilhelm Fink, 2000.

———. "Zunächst war Waffenbrüderschaft." In *Russen und Russland aus deutscher Sicht*.

19 Jahrhundert: Von der Jahrhundertwende bis zur Reichsgründung (1800–1871), edited by Mechthild Keller, 11–80. Munich: Wilhelm Fink, 1992.

Kopelew, Lew, and Gerd Koenen, eds. *Deutschland und die Russische Revolution, 1917–1924*. Munich: Fink, 1998.

Kopp, Kristin. "Contesting Borders: German Colonial Discourse and the Polish Eastern Territories." PhD dissertation, University of California, Berkeley, 2001.

Krause, Hartfrid. *USPD: Zur Geschichte der Unabhängigen Sozialdemokratischen Partei Deutschlands*. Frankfurt am Main: Europäische Verlangsanstalt, 1975.

Krekeler, Norbert. *Revisionsanspruch und Geheime Ostpolitik der Weimarer Republik: Die Subventionierung der deutschen Minderheit in Polen*. Stuttgart: Deutsche Verlagsanstalt, 1973.

Kulischer, Eugene. *Europe on the Move: War and Population Changes, 1917–1941*. New York: Columbia University Press, 1948.

Kumar, Krishnan. *Utopia and Anti-Utopia in Modern Times*. New York: Blackwell, 1987.

Kvistad, Gregg O. *The Rise and Demise of German Statism: Loyalty and Political Membership*. New York: Berghahn, 1999.

Lang, Markus. *Grundkonzeption und Entwicklung des deutschen Staatsangehörigkeitsrechts*. Frankfurt am Main: Verlag für Standesamtswesen, 1990.

Leuschen-Spiegel, Rosemarie. *Sozialdemokratie und Antisemitismus im Deutschen Kaiserreich*. Göttingen: Vandenhoeck & Ruprecht, 1978.

Levitas, Ruth. *Concept of Utopia*. Syracuse: Syracuse University Press, 1990.

Lih, Lars. *Bread and Authority in Russia, 1914–1921*. Berkeley: University of California Press, 1990.

Linke, Horst. *Deutsch-sowjetische Beziehungen bis Rapallo*. Cologne: Wissenschaft und Politik, 1970.

Liulevicius, Vejas. *War Land on the Eastern Front: Culture, National Identity and German Occupation in World War I*. New York: Cambridge University Press, 2000.

Long, James W. *From Privileged to Dispossessed: The Volga Germans, 1860–1917*. Lincoln: University of Nebraska Press, 1988.

——. "The Volga Germans and the Famine of 1921." *Russian Review* 51, no. 4 (1992): 510–25.

Lower, Wendy. *Nazi Empire Building and the Holocaust in Ukraine*. Chapel Hill: University of North Carolina Press, 2005.

Lucas, Erhard. *Märzrevolution 1920*. 3 vols. Frankfurt am Main: Roter Stern, 1970–1978.

Macartney, Carlile A. *National States and National Minorities*. New York: Russell and Russell, 1968.

Macmillan, Margaret. *Paris 1919: Six Months That Changed the World*. New York: Random House, 2003.

Mahnke, Julia. *Auswanderungsvereine mit Ziel Ukraine und Sowjet-Russland in der Weimarer Republik*. Munich: Ost-Europa Institut, 1997.

Mai, Joachim. *Die preussisch-deutsche Polenpolitik, 1885/87: Eine Studie zur Herausbildung des Imperialismus in Deutschland*. Berlin: Rütten & Loening, 1962.

Maier, Charles. "Consigning the Twentieth Century to History: Alternative Narratives for the Modern Era." *American Historical Review* 105, no. 3 (2000): 807–31.

Mallmann, Klaus-Michael, and Wilfried Loth. *Kommunisten in der Weimarer Republik: Sozialgeschichte einer revolutionären Bewegung*. Darmstadt: Wissenschaftliche Buchgesellschaft, 1996.

Marrus, Michael. *The Unwanted: European Refugees in the Twentieth Century.* New York: Oxford University Press, 1986.

Mauersberger, Volker. *Rudolf Pechel und die 'Deutsche Rundschau': Eine Studie zur konservativ-revolutionären Publizistik in der Weimarer Republik (1918–1933).* Bremen: Schünemann Universitätsverlag, 1971.

Maurer, Trude. *Ostjuden in Deutschland, 1918–1933.* Hamburg: Hans Christian, 1986.

Mayer, Arno J. *Wilson vs. Lenin: Political Origins of the New Diplomacy, 1918–1918.* New Haven: Yale University Press, 1959.

Mazower, Mark. *Hitler's Empire: How the Nazis Ruled Europe.* New York: Penguin, 2008.

Merz, Kai-Uwe. *Schreckbild: Deutschland und der Bolschewismus, 1917–1921.* Berlin: Propyläen, 1995.

Meyer, Henry Cord. *Drang nach Osten: Fortunes of a Slogan-Concept in German-Slavic Relations, 1849–1990.* New York: Peter Lang, 1996.

——. "Paul Rohrbach and His Osteuropa." *Russian Review* 2 (1942–1943): 60–69.

Mitchell, Allan. *Revolution in Bavaria, 1918–1919: The Eisner Regime and the Soviet Republic.* Princeton: Princeton University Press, 1965.

Mitchell, Timothy. "The Limits of the State: Beyond Statist Approaches and Their Critics." *American Political Science Review* 85, no. 1 (1991): 77–96.

Moch, Leslie Page. *Moving Europeans: Migration in Western Europe since 1650.* Bloomington: Indiana University Press, 1992.

Mócsy, István. *The Effects of World War I: The Uprooted, Hungarian Refugees and Their Impact on Hungary's Domestic Politics, 1918–1921.* New York: Brooklyn College Press, 1984.

Morgan, David W. *The Socialist Left and the German Revolution: A History of the German Independent Social Democratic Party, 1917–1922.* Ithaca: Cornell University Press, 1975.

Müller, Rolf-Dieter. *Hitlers Ostkrieg und die deutsche Siedlungspolitik.* Hamburg: Fischer, 1995.

Müller, Sven Oliver. "Die umstrittene Gemeinschaft: Nationalismus als Konfliktphänomen in Deutschland." In *Politische Kollektive: Die Konstruktion nationaler, rassistischer und ethnischer Gemeinschaften,* edited by Ulrike Jureit, 124–45. Münster: Westfälisches Dampfboot, 2001.

Münz, Rainer, and Rainer Ohlinger. "Auslandsdeutsche." In *Deutsche Erinnerungsorte,* edited by Hagen Schulze and Etienne François, 370–88. Munich: Beck, 2001.

Murphy, David Thomas. *The Heroic Earth: Geopolitical Thought in Weimar Germany, 1918–1933.* Kent, Ohio: Kent State University Press, 1997.

Naranch, Bradley. "Beyond the Fatherland: Colonial Visions, Overseas Expansion, and German Nationalism, 1848–1885." PhD dissertation, University of North Carolina, Chapel Hill, 2006.

Niewyk, Donald L. *The Jews in Weimar Germany.* Baton Rouge: Louisiana State University Press, 1980.

Nolan, Mary. *Visions of Modernity: American Business and the Modernization of Germany.* New York: Oxford University Press, 1994.

Oertzen, Peter von. *Betriebsräte in der Novemberrevolution.* Düsseldorf: Droste, 1963.

Oeter, Stefan. "Die Entwicklung des Kriegsgefangenenrechts: Die Sichtweise eines Völkerrechtlers." In *In der Hand des Feindes: Kriegsgefangenschaft von der Antike bis zum Zweiten Weltkrieg,* edited by Rüdiger Overmans, 41–59. Cologne: Böhlau, 1999.

Oltmer, Jochen. "Flucht, Vertreibung und Asyl im 19. und 20. Jahrhundert." In *Migration in der europäischen Geschichte seit dem späten Mittelalter,* edited by Klaus Bade, 107–34. Osnabrück: IMIS Beiträge, 2002.

———. *Migration und Politik in der Weimarer Republik.* Göttingen: Vandenhoeck & Ruprecht, 2005.

———. " 'The Unspoilt Nature of German Ethnicity': Immigration and Integration of 'Ethnic Germans' in Wilhelmine and Weimar Germany." *Nationalities Papers* 34, no. 4 (2006): 429–46.

———. "Zwangsmigration und Zwangsarbeit: Ausländische Arbeitskräfte und bäuerliche Ökonomie im Ersten Weltkrieg." *Tel-Aviver Jahrbuch für Deutsche Geschichte* 27 (1998): 135–68.

Ong, Aihwa. "Cultural Citizenship as Subject Making: Immigrants Negotiate Racial and Cultural Boundaries in the United States." In *Race, Identity and Citizenship: A Reader,* edited by Rodolfo D. Torres, Louis F. Míron, and Jonathan Xavier Inda, 156–78. Oxford: Oxford University Press, 1999.

Osterhammel, Jürgen, and Niels P. Petersson. *Globalization: A Short History.* Translated by Donna Geyer. Princeton: Princeton University Press, 2003.

Paddock, Troy. "Still Stuck at Sevastopol: The Depiction of Russia during the Russo-Japanese War and the Beginning of the First World War in the German Press." *German History* 16, no. 3 (1998): 358–77.

Panayi, Panikos. *The Enemy in Our Midst: Germans in Britain during the First World War.* Oxford: Berg, 1991.

———. *Ethnic Minorities in Nineteenth and Twentieth Century Germany: Jews, Gypsies, Poles, Turks and Others.* New York: Longman, 2000.

———, ed. *Minorities in Wartime.* Oxford: Berg, 1993.

Pastor, Peter. *Hungary between Wilson and Lenin: The Hungarian Revolution of 1918–1919 and the Big Three.* New York: Columbia University Press, 1976.

Pearson, Raymond. *National Minorities in Eastern Europe, 1848–1945.* London: Macmillan, 1983.

Péteri, György. *Effects of World War I: War Communism in Hungary.* New York: Columbia University Press, 1984.

Peters, Michael. *Der Alldeutsche Verband am Vorabend des Ersten Weltkrieges (1908–1914): Ein Beitrag zur Geschichte des völkischen Nationalismus im spätwilhelminischen Deutschland.* Frankfurt am Main: Lang, 1992.

Peukert, Detlev. *The Weimar Republic.* New York: Hill and Wang, 1993.

Pohl, Dieter. *Die Herrschaft der Wehrmacht: Deutsche Militärbesatzung und einheimische Bevölkerung in der Sowjetunion 1941–1944.* Munich: Oldenbourg, 2008.

Pommerin, Rainer. "Die Ausweisung von Ostjuden aus Bayern 1923—ein Beitrag zum Krisenjahr der Weimarer Republik." *Vierteljahrshefte für Zeitgeschichte* 34 (1986): 311–40.

Pulzer, Peter. *Jews and the German State.* Detroit: Wayne State University Press, 2003.

Raeff, Marc. *Russia Abroad: A Cultural History of the Russian Emigration, 1919–1939.* New York: Oxford University Press, 1990.

Reichardt, Sven. *Faschistische Kampfbünde.* Cologne: Böhlau, 2002.

Reinecke, Christiane. "Riskante Wanderungen: Illegale Migration im britischen und deutschen Migrationsregime der 1920er Jahre." *Geschichte und Gesellschaft* 35 (2009): 64–97.

Rosenberg, Clifford. *Policing Paris: The Origins of Modern Immigration Control between the Wars*. Ithaca: Cornell University Press, 2006.

Rosenfeld, Günter. *Sowjetrussland und Deutschland, 1917–1921*. Berlin: Akademie, 1995.

Roshwald, Aviel. *Ethnic Nationalism and the Fall of Empires: Central Europe, Russia and the Middle East, 1914–1923*. London: Routledge, 2001.

Rudin, Harry R. *Armistice 1918*. Hamden, Conn.: Archon Books, 1967.

Rürup, Reinhard. *Probleme der Revolution in Deutschland 1918/1919*. Wiesbaden: Steiner, 1968.

Sanborn, Joshua. "Unsettling the Empire: Violent Migrations and Social Disaster during World War I." *Journal of Modern History* 77, no. 2 (2005): 290–325.

Sassen, Saskia. *Migranten, Siedler, Flüchtlinge: Von der Massenwanderung zur Festung Europa*. Frankfurt am Main: Fischer, 2000.

Sauer, Bernhard. "Die Baltikumer." Arbeitspapier des Instituts für Internationale Politik und Regionale Studien 7. Freie Universität-Berlin, 1995.

Schade, Franz. *Kurt Eisner und die bayerische Sozialdemokratie*. Hannover: Verlag für Literatur und Zeitgeschehen, 1961.

Schattkowsky, Ralph. *Deutschland und Polen von 1918/19 bis 1925: Deutsch-polnische Beziehungen zwischen Versailles und Locarno*. Frankfurt am Main: Peter Lang, 1994.

Schirmer, Dietmar. "Closing the Nation: Nationalism and Statism in Nineteenth and Twentieth Century Germany." In *The Shifting Foundations of Modern Nation States*, edited by Sima Godfrey and Frank Unger, 35–58. Toronto: University of Toronto Press, 2004.

Schlögel, Karl. *Berlin–Ostbahnhof Europas: Russen und Deutsche in ihrem Jahrhundert*. Berlin: Siedler, 1998.

——, ed. *Der grosse Exodus: Die russische Emigration und ihre Zentren 1917 bis 1941*. Munich: Beck, 1994.

——, ed. *Russische Emigration in Deutschland 1918 bis 1941*. Berlin: Akademie, 1995.

Scholte, Jan. *Globalization: A Critical Introduction*. New York: Palgrave, 2000.

Schönwalder, Karen. "Invited but Unwanted?: Migrants from the East in Germany, 1890–1990." In *The German Lands and Eastern Europe: Essays on the History of Their Social, Cultural and Political Relations*, edited by Roger Bartlett and Karen Schönwalder, 198–216. New York: St. Martin's Press, 1999.

Schultz, Hans-Dietrich. "Deutschlands 'natürliche' Grenzen." In *Deutschlands Grenzen in der Geschichte*, edited by Alexander Demandt, 32–93. Munich: Beck, 1991.

Schulze, Hagen. *Freikorps und Republik, 1918–1920*. Boppard am Rhein: H. Boldt, 1969.

——. "Der Oststaatplan 1919." *Vierteljahreshefte für Zeitgeschichte* 18, no. 2 (1970): 123–63.

Schulze, Hagen, and Etienne Francois, eds. *Deutsche Erinnerungsorte*. Munich: Beck, 2001.

Schumacher, Rainer. "Die preussischen Ostprovinzen und die Politik des deutschen Reiches, 1918–1919: Die Geschichte der östlichen Gebietsverluste Deutschlands im politischen Spannungsfeld zwischen Nationalstaatsprinzip und Machtanspruch." PhD dissertation, University of Cologne, 1985.

Schumann, Dirk. *Politische Gewalt in der Weimarer Republik 1918–1933: Kampf um die Strasse und Furcht vor dem Bürgerkrieg*. Essen: Klartext, 2001.

Seton-Watson, Hugh. *Nations and States*. London: Methuen, 1982.

Sheehan, James. "The Problem of Sovereignty in European History." *American Historical Review* 111, no. 1 (2006): 1–15.

Simpson, John Hope. *The Refugee Problem: Report of a Survey*. New York: Oxford University Press, 1939.

Skran, Claudena. *Refugees in Inter-war Europe: The Emergence of a Regime*. Oxford: Oxford University Press, 1995.

Sládek, Zdeněk. "Prag: Das 'russische Oxford.'" In *Der grosse Exodus: Die russische Emigration und ihre Zentren 1917 bis 1941*, edited by Karl Schlögel, 218–33. Munich: Beck, 1994.

Smith, Anthony D., and Colin Williams. "The National Construction of Social Space." *Progress in Human Geography* 7, no. 4 (1983): 502–18.

Smith, Paul. "The Kiss of France: The Republic and the Alsatians during the First World War." In *Minorities in Wartime*, edited by Panikos Panayi, 27–49. Oxford: Berg, 1993.

Snyder, Timothy. *The Reconstruction of Nations: Poland, Ukraine, Lithuania, Belarus, 19569–1999*. New Haven: Yale University Press, 2003.

Stone, Norman. *The Eastern Front 1914–1917*. London: Hodder and Stoughton, 1975.

Sullivan, Charles L. "The 1919 German Campaign in the Baltics: The Final Phase." In *The Baltic States in Peace and War, 1917–1945*, edited by Vytas Stanley Vardys and Romuald J. Misiunas, 31–42. University Park: Pennsylvania State University Press, 1978.

Tarle, Galina Jakovlena. *Druz'ja strany sovetov: Ucastie zarubeznyh trudjascihsja v vosstanovlenzii narodnogo hozjajstya SSSR v 1920–1925 gg.* Moscow: Nauka, 1968.

Ther, Phillip. "Beyond the Nation: The Relational Basis of a Comparative History of Germany and Europe." *Central European History* 31, no. 1 (2003): 45–73.

Theweleit, Klaus. *Male Fantasies*. Translated by Stephen Conway, Erica Carter, and Chris Turner. Forward by Barbara Ehrenreich. Minneapolis: University of Minnesota Press, 1987.

Thum, Gregor. "Mythische Landschaften: Das Bild vom deutschen Osten und die Zäsuren des 20. Jahrhunderts." In *Traumland Osten: Deutsche Bilder vom östlichen Europa im 20. Jahrhundert,* edited by Gregor Thum, 181–212. Göttingen: Vandenhoeck & Ruprecht, 2006.

——, ed. *Traumland Osten: Deutsche Bilder vom östlichen Europa im 20. Jahrhundert.* Göttingen: Vandenhoeck & Ruprecht, 2006.

Todd, Lisa. "Sexual Treason: State Surveillance of Immorality and Infidelity in World War I Germany." PhD dissertation. University of Toronto, 2005.

Torpey, John. *The Invention of the Passport: Surveillance, Citizenship and the State.* Cambridge, UK: Cambridge University Press, 2000.

Trevisiol, Oliver. *Die Einbürgerungspraxis im deutschen Reich, 1871–1945*. Göttingen: Vandenhoeck & Ruprecht, 2006.

Vatlin, Aleksandr. "The Testing-Ground of World Revolution: Germany in the 1920s." In *International Communism and the Communist International 1919–43,* edited by Tim Rees and Andrew Thorpe, 117–26. Manchester, UK: Manchester University Press, 1998.

Verhey, Jeffrey. *The Spirit of 1914: Militarism, Myth and Mobilization in Germany.* Cambridge, UK: Cambridge University Press, 2000.

Völgyes, Ivan. *Hungary in Revolution, 1918–1919: Nine Essays*. Lincoln: University of Nebraska Press, 1971.

Volkmann, Hans Erich. *Die deutsche Baltikumpolitik zwischen Brest-Litovsk und Compiègne: Ein Beitrag zur "Kriegszieldiskussion."* Cologne: Böhlau, 1970.

——. *Die russische Emigration in Deutschland, 1919–1929.* Würzburg: Holzner, 1966.

Vourkoutiotis, Vasily. *Making Common Cause: German-Soviet Relations, 1919–1922.* New York: Palgrave Macmillan, 2007.

Waite, Robert G. L. *Vanguard of Nazism: The Free Corps Movement in Postwar Germany, 1918–1923.* Cambridge, Mass.: Harvard University Press, 1952.

Walter, Dirk. *Antisemitische Kriminalität und Gewalt: Judenfeindschaft in der Weimarer Republik.* Bonn: Dietz, 1999.

Weeks, Theodor. *Nation and State in Late Imperial Russia: Nationalism and Russification on the Western Frontier, 1863–1914.* DeKalb: Northern Illinois University Press, 1996.

Wegner, Michael, ed. *Rußland und Europa.* Leipzig: Rosa Luxemburg, 1995.

Wehler, Hans-Ulrich. "Polenpolitik im deutschen Kaiserreich." In *Krisenherde des Kaiserreichs 1871–1918: Studien zur deutschen Sozial- und Verfassungsgeschichte,* 184–203. Göttingen: Vandenhoeck & Ruprecht, 1972.

Weidenfeller, Gerhard. *VDA: Verein für das Deutschtum im Ausland. Allgemeiner Deutscher Schulverein (1881–1918): Ein Beitrag zur Geschichte des Nationalismus und Imperialismus im Kaiserreich.* Bern: Peter Lang, 1976.

Weindling, Paul. *Epidemics and Genocide in Eastern Europe, 1890–1945.* Oxford: Oxford University Press, 2000.

Weiss, Claudia. "Russian Political Parties in Exile." *Kritika* 5, no. 1 (2004): 219–32.

Weiss, Yfatt. "Homeland as Shelter or as Refuge?: Repatriation in the Jewish Context." *Tel Aviver Jahrbuch für deutsche Geschichte* 27 (1988): 195–219.

Weitz, Eric. *Creating German Communism, 1890–1990: From Popular Protests to Socialist State.* Princeton: Princeton University Press, 1997.

Welch, David. *Germany, Propaganda and Total War, 1914–1918: The Sins of Omission.* New Brunswick: Rutgers University Press, 2000.

Wertheimer, Jack. *Unwelcome Strangers: East European Jews in Imperial Germany.* New York: Oxford University Press, 1987.

Wette, Wolfgang. "Rußlandbilder der Deutschen im 20. Jahrhundert: Kristallisationspunkte, Haupt- und Nebenlinien." In *Rußland und Europa,* edited by Michael Wegner, 169–79. Leipzig: Rosa Luxemburg, 1995.

Whalen, Robert. *Bitter Wounds: German Victims of the Great War, 1919–1939.* Ithaca: Cornell University Press, 1984.

Wheeler-Bennett, John. *Brest-Litovsk, the Forgotten Peace, March 1918.* New York: W. W. Norton, 1971.

Williams, Robert. *Culture in Exile: Russian Émigrés in Germany, 1881–1941.* Ithaca: Cornell University Press, 1972.

Wilms, Johannes. *Die deutsche Krankheit: Eine kurze Geschichte der Gegenwart.* Munich: Carl Hanser Verlag, 2001.

Winkler, Heinrich August. "Revolution by Consensus?: Germany 1918–1919." In *The Problem of Revolution in Germany, 1789–1989,* edited by Reinhard Rürup, 93–108. New York: Berg, 2000.

Wippermann, Wolfgang. "Das Blutrecht der Blutnation: Zur Ideologie- und Politikgeschichte des Ius Sanguinis in Deutschland." In *Blut oder Boden: Doppelpass, Staatsbürgerrecht und Nationsverständnis,* edited by Andreas Dietl, Jochen Baumann, and Wolfgang Wippermann, 10–48. Berlin: Elefanten Press, 1999.

———. *Die Deutschen und der Osten: Feindbild und Traumland.* Darmstadt: Primus, 2007.

Wurzer, Georg. "Das Schicksal der deutschen Kriegsgefangenen in Russland im Ersten Weltkrieg: Der Erlebnisbericht Edwin Erich Dwingers." In *In der Hand des Feindes: Kriegsgefangenschaft von der Antike bis zum Zweiten Weltkrieg,* edited by Rüdiger Overmans, 363–84. Cologne: Böhlau Verlag, 1999.

Zahra, Tara. *Kidnapped Souls: National Indifference and the Battle for Children in the Bohemian Lands, 1900–1948.* Ithaca: Cornell University Press, 2008.

Zelt, Johannes. "Kriegsgefangene in Deutschland: Neue Forschungsergebnisse zur Geschichte der russischen Sektion der KPD." *Zeitschrift für Geschichtswissenschaft* 15, no. 4 (1967): 621–38.

Zolberg, Aristide. *A Nation by Design: Immigration Policy in the Fashioning of America.* Cambridge, Mass.: Harvard University Press, 2006.

Index